THE GERMAN FOREST

Nature, Identity, and the Contestation of a National Symbol, 1871–1914

GERMAN AND EUROPEAN STUDIES

General Editor: Rebecca Wittmann

JEFFREY K. WILSON

The German Forest

Nature, Identity, and the Contestation of a National Symbol, 1871–1914

UNIVERSITY OF TORONTO PRESS
Toronto Buffalo London

ISBN 978-1-4426-4099-3

Printed on acid-free, 100% post-consumer recycled paper with
vegetable-based inks.

German and European Studies

Library and Archives Canada Cataloguing in Publication

Wilson, Jeffrey K., 1970–
The German forest : nature, identity, and the contestation of a national
symbol, 1871–1914 / Jeffrey K. Wilson.

Includes bibliographical references and index.
ISBN 978-1-4426-4099-3

1. Forests and forestry – Germany – History.   2. Forests and forestry –
Political aspects – Germany – History.   3. Forest management – Germany –
History.   4. Landscape protection – Germany – History.   5. National
characteristics, German.   I. Title.

SD195.W54 2012   333.750943   C2012-900878-8

University of Toronto Press acknowledges the financial assistance
to its publishing program of the Canada Council for the Arts
and the Ontario Arts Council.

Canada Council **Conseil des Arts**
for the Arts **du Canada**

ONTARIO ARTS COUNCIL
CONSEIL DES ARTS DE L'ONTARIO

University of Toronto Press acknowledges the financial support of the
Government of Canada through the Canada Book Fund
for its publishing activities.

Contents

Maps, Figures, and Tables   vii

Acknowledgements   ix

Abbreviations   xiii

Introduction   3

1 National Landscape and National Memory   16

2 Contested Forests: Ideal Values and Real Estate   49

3 Environmental Activism in the *Kaiserreich*:
Berlin and the Grunewald   86

4 Reforestation as Reform: Pomerelia and the Tuchel Heath   132

5 Meaningful Woods: Sylvan Metaphors and Arboreal Symbols   175

Conclusion   215

Notes   227

Works Cited   285

Index   313

Maps, Figures, and Tables

Maps

3.1 Berlin and Its environs, 1894   89
3.2 Carstenn's plan for the Grunewald, 1872   99
3.3 State plans for the Grunewald, 1907   105
3.4 Greater Berlin, 1920   123
4.1 East and West Prussia, 1890   134
4.2 The Tuchel Heath, 1908   135

Figures

3.1 The Hubertusjagd in the Grunewald under
Friedrich Wilhelm IV, 1857   91
3.2 Arrival of Kaiser Wilhelm I for the Hubertusjagd, 1887   92
3.3 Spectators at the Hubertusjagd, 1891   94
3.4 'From the Hubertusjagd in the Grunewald:
Uninvited Guests as Retinue,' 1899   95
3.5 'Pod[bielski] the Forest Destroyer,' 1904   106
3.6 'Fellow Citizens! Help Us Protect Our Forests!' Berlin Forest
Protection Association poster, 1907   107
4.1 Cases of forest theft in the Woziwoda Forest District, 1875   146
4.2 Illegal grazing, 1878   150
4.3 Criminal statistics, Ciss forest district, 1880–1915   151
4.4 Penal labour in Königsbruch forest district, 1878–1913   152
4.5 Poacher, 1878   154
4.6 Forest fire, 1878   155
4.7 'An old woman carrying wood in the Tuchel Heath,' 1908   170

4.8 'Forester with an owl. (Underneath lies a shot goshawk),'
1908   170
4.9 'Chief forester's residence at Taubenfließ,' 1908   171
4.10 'Also a house in the Tuchel Heath,' 1908   171
5.1 'The German Oak. Gift of Honor for His Majesty the German
Kaiser,' 1871   204
5.2 Cover of This Is the German Fatherland, 1896   206
5.3 Heilbronn postcard, 1910   211

Tables

1.1 Numbers of postcards sent from national sites, 1893–8   30
4.1 Forest fires in the Tuchel Heath, 1860–89   157

Acknowledgments

This book had its origins as my University of Michigan PhD dissertation, and therefore I owe a significant debt of gratitude to my mentors – Geoff Eley, Brian Porter, and Kathleen Canning – without whose inspiration and guidance I would not have been able to begin this project. Also especially important at Michigan were my fellow graduate students, particularly Andy Donson, among many others too numerous to list. Their friendship, interest, and support have been helpful throughout. And naturally, the fantastic collections of the Hatcher and Buhr libraries made it possible for me to even conceive of this project in the first place.

A variety of institutions helped fund my research in its early stages. I participated in an archive tour and palaeography program sponsored by the German Historical Institute (Washington DC) in the summer of 1995 that not only provided me with the skills necessary for archival research (particularly the deciphering of nineteenth-century German handwriting!), but also introduced me to several young scholars of German history whose aid and friendship have been important for the completion of this book, especially Andy Evans and Marline Otte.

I conducted the bulk of the research for this project between the fall of 1996 and the spring of 1998, thanks to the generous support of the Fulbright Foundation and the Berlin Program for Advanced German and European Studies. Besides providing funding, the Berlin Program ran a fantastic seminar for its fellows, exposing us to many facets of that fascinating city, as well as providing a forum for us to share our work. I'm also grateful to the program for introducing me to Elizabeth Drummond, Alon Confino, Patricia Stokes, and Wolfgang Kaschuba, among many others. In Berlin, the camaraderie of Andy Evans and Andy Donson at the Stabi – especially our lunches in the lobby, escaping the smoke of the cafeteria – was invaluable for both my mental and physical health from the outset. Also deserving thanks are the staffs of the institutions where I conducted my research in Germany and Poland: both the eastern and western houses of the Staatsbibliothek Berlin, the Zentrum für Berlin-Studien, the Friedrich Meinecke Institut and the Universitätsbibliothek of the Freie Universität Berlin, the Geheimes Staatsarchiv Preußischer Kulturbesitz, both the eastern and western branches of the Landesarchiv Berlin, the Brandenburgisches Landeshauptarchiv in Potsdam, the Bundesarchiv Koblenz, the Archiwum państwowe w Bydgoszczy, and the Archiwum państwowe w Gdańsku. Various forms of funding at the University of Michigan allowed me to develop my research into a coherent dissertation.

After completion of my dissertation in 2002, I began my career at the University of New Orleans. There the aid and friendship of my colleagues, particularly Warren Billings, Günter Bischof, Jim Mokhiber, and Andrew Goss – along with Marline Otte at Tulane University – proved essential for the transformation of my dissertation into a book manuscript. This support was all the more necessary in the dark days after Hurricane Katrina, which interrupted our careers and wrecked our beloved city. I left New Orleans in 2009 for a position at California State University, Sacramento, where my colleagues have been equally generous. I'm grateful to both universities for their aid in publishing my book; UNO granted me a June Scholar Award in 2008 that helped me prepare my manuscript for publication, and CSU Sacramento awarded me a UEI Faculty Development Grant to subvent publication costs. During this period of revision, the libraries of the University of New Orleans, Tulane University, and California State University, Sacramento were extremely helpful.

My participation in conferences has been influential in shaping this manuscript. The Young Scholars' Forum at the German Historical Institute in 2004 brought me together with others interested in German environmental history, including Scott Moranda and Charles Clossman. The German Studies Association, which I've attended fairly regularly since the late 1990s, has provided me with useful feedback from several scholars, including Lynn Nyhart, Vejas Liulevicius, Janet Ward, Celia Applegate, David Blackbourn, Tom Lekan, Bradley Naranch, John Alexander Williams, and Timothy Guinnane.

It was at the GSA in 2005, while I was still in evacuation six weeks after Hurricane Katrina (and which I was only able to attend thanks to the financial support of the German Studies Association), that Jim Retallack, then head of the University of Toronto Press series in German and

European Studies, approached me about publishing my work. I'm glad he did; I'm also happy to have worked with Jennifer Jenkins, his successor at the series, as well as Richard Ratzlaff, Doug Richmond, Ian MacKenzie, and the two anonymous readers who responded to my manuscript, all of whom have helped me complete the transformation of this project into a book.

Above all, I'd like to thank my companion on this journey, Ellen Willow. Her love and support have been critical to my completion of this work. I know she's made many sacrifices over the years, and it's to her that I dedicate this book.

Jeffrey K. Wilson
Sacramento, March 2011

Abbreviations

German Term	Abbreviation	English Translation
Oberbürgermeister	OB	Lord Mayor
Regierungspräsident	RP	District governor
Oberpräsident	OP	Governor
Regierungsbezirk	RB	Administrative district
Stadtverordneten Versammlung	SVV	City Assembly
Abgeordnetenhaus	AH	House of Deputies
Herrenhaus	HH	House of Lords
Zweckverband	ZV	Communal Association
Forstmeister	FM	Forester
Oberförster	OF	Chief forester
Oberforstmeister	OFM	Provincial forester
Oberlandforstmesiter	OLFM	Department of Forestry Chief

THE GERMAN FOREST

Nature, Identity, and the Contestation
of a National Symbol, 1871–1914

Introduction

The 'German Forest'

Wilhelm Heinrich Riehl, the pioneer of German ethnography, insisted in 1852, 'We must preserve the forests, not simply so that the oven is not cold in winter, but also in order that the pulse of German folk life continues to beat warmly and cheerfully, *in order that Germany remains German.*'[1] Over the course of the nineteenth century, an entity known as the 'German forest' arose out of Central Europe's sylvan diversity. Despite great differences among the blankets of firs on the slopes of the Alps, the copses of beech trees on the cliffs above the Baltic, the mixed deciduous woodlands along the banks of the Rhine, and the piny monocultures of eastern Prussia, many authors subsumed all of these biomes under the label of the 'German forest.' But what purpose did this rather artificial concept have? What was it supposed to mean? Why did so many authors find it necessary to invent this category? For Riehl and all those writing on 'German forest,' the woods contained the German national essence. This book investigates the connections between nature and nation in late-nineteenth-century Germany, shedding light on the contested national meanings invested in the forest, and in turn, exploring the influence of this sylvan discourse on social relations, political conflicts, and German national identity during the period of the German Empire, or *Kaiserreich*, from 1871 to 1914.

Interest in the 'German forest' as a source of national identity dates back as far as the Reformation, when Protestant German scholars encountered Tacitus's *Germania*. For them, Tacitus's description of the Teutonic noble savages waging war against a decadent and declining Rome mirrored their own situation. Emerging from the woods, identified as the source of their strength and freedom, they beat back a corrupt empire that sought to subjugate them. In the late eighteenth century – deriving inspiration from the patriotic philosopher Johann Gottfried Herder – the poet Friedrich Gottlieb Klopstock drew symbols from this ancient past to articulate what he regarded as the essence of the German national character, in reaction to the universalizing tendencies of the French Enlightenment. He chose the oak as the emblem of Germanic resolve and independence, and inspired the creation of the Göttingen Grove League (1772) by poets in an early revolt against French neo-classicism. This mood of defiance only grew with Napoleon's occupation of the German states at the beginning of the nineteenth century. The memory of the ancient Battle of the Teutoburg Forest, in which the Germanic hero Arminius (Hermann) ambushed and defeated three Roman legions in the woods, resonated with German nationalists. Heinrich von Kleist, moved by the patriotic spirit of the times, called for a national uprising against French occupation in his thinly veiled play *Hermann's Battle*, recalling Arminius's victory. The celebrated painter Caspar David Friedrich likewise mobilized the forest against the French invaders, depicting a French *chasseur* lost in the woods. Inspired by romanticism, the nationalist Ernst Moritz Arndt called in 1815 for the resurrection of 'the old Germanic groves' because 'the German person must nowhere lack trees,' and believed such forests could serve as a defensive barrier against the Germans' enemies, particularly the French.[2] Riehl, as Arndt's student, inherited his passion for the forest and sought to protect it, along with German society, from the depredations of capitalism, perceived as a foreign invader ravaging the German countryside.

While the discourse about the 'German forest' had its roots in the romantic nationalism of the early nineteenth century, the concept blossomed around 1900. Riehl's work found little reception during the confident economic boom years of the 1850s and 1860s; the rapid pace of industrialization, and the dramatic transformation of the German lands into a nation state, led to widespread confidence among educated elites. However, the economic crash of 1873 and the emergence of a mass socialist movement created some doubt about the current order for bourgeois Germans. During the last quarter of the nineteenth century, some on the right and the left began to fear social revolution, eroding tradition, intellectual disorientation, and national degeneration. Authors sought solutions to Germany's pressing problems – whether real or imagined – everywhere. Some turned to the forest for their answers.

The period between 1880 and 1914 witnessed a proliferation of popular works – written by foresters and botanists, geographers and historians, lawyers and politicians, poets and painters, nature preservationists and urban reformers – invoking the 'German forest' in their text and in their titles. These works generally agreed on a common set of ideas, comprising the sylvan discourse. First, Germans shared a common reverence for the woods, rooted in their barbarian past. Second, this special relationship with the forest had been preserved in Germany until at least the late eighteenth century, despite the encroachment of feudal rights on once commonly held woodlands. Third, forests came under pressure with the arrival of capitalism, as many unscrupulous landowners (including perhaps the state) transformed their stands of timber into profits. Fourth, the loss of woodlands carried costs for the nation, whether environmental (greater erosion and flooding), medical (less clean air and declining opportunities for healthy recreation, especially for the urban populace), social (fewer sources of income and resources for peasants), economic (dwindling sources of wood at a time of rampant worldwide consumption), cultural (less opportunity for artistic inspiration and scientific investigation), or political (waning attachment to the region [*Heimat*] and the nation). Fifth, Southern European cultures had already decimated their forest in ancient times and declined as a result; it might only be a matter of time before Western Europeans – and further in the future, the Americans and the Russians – would suffer a similar fate. Sixth, Germany's continued success relied on defending the forest against the threat posed by unbridled capitalism. The notion of the 'German forest,' and its importance for the nation, achieved near universal assent; it was open enough to encompass a broad range of political and economic attitudes, yet specific enough to be meaningful.

Yet precisely because the 'German forest' was such a widely disseminated symbol of Germandom, a broad range of groups attempted to mobilize it for their own ends. Although inspired by the traditionalist Riehl, these actors sought some kind of accommodation with modernity, using the forest in a variety of ways to adapt to an industrializing and urbanizing society. Landowners, hunters, timber producers, peasant-rights activists, hikers, charitable organizations, and state officials all deployed the term 'German forest' for widely divergent purposes, illustrating the ways nationalist and proto-environmentalist language could be used for material aims. Thus, perhaps more interesting than the fact that Germans invested their landscape with national meaning are the ways in which this symbol – intended to unite the nation – became an object of bitter contention in the *Kaiserreich*.

While Germans thought of their relationship with nature as unique, this was by no means the case. This book should not be understood as an argument that Germany somehow diverged significantly from the rest of the Western world in this regard. Other peoples invested their landscapes with national meaning and saw themselves as products of the native soil. German authors frequently praised their nation for its deep roots in the countryside, but this was hardly unique in Europe. Starting in the eighteenth century, the British in particular invested enormous meaning in their pastoral landscapes, quite at odds with the country's burgeoning industrial development. And while forests, of which there were relatively few left by the nineteenth century, did not stand at the centre of British landscape ideology, for Sweden they did. The Swedes, perhaps influenced by German developments, articulated a forest discourse strikingly similar to Germany's. Even the French, renowned as an urban and urbane nation with rigidly geometric gardens (and denigrated by the Germans for their divorce from nature), engaged in large-scale reforestation and sought out their roots in the native soil. Likewise, the frontiers of the two incipient superpowers, the United States and Russia, played a critical role in the development and identities of those nations.[3]

Historiography

The scholarly literatures on the nation and landscape have identified both as human constructions. Benedict Anderson famously illustrated the ways in which print capitalism allowed readers of a vernacular to imagine themselves as part of a national community.[4] While the character of this process of imagination has been disputed – the debate centring on when these identities arose and how subservient they were to the state[5] – a variety of actors mobilized the concept of the nation during the modern era, defining and redefining the contours of the national community. For example, nationalists have created myths about their homelands, disseminating national memories to legitimate the national movement and its demands (often for territory).[6] Anthony Smith argues landscapes play an important part in the imagination of the nation. He notes that communities have often encoded their landscapes with ethnic 'meaning,' uniting the fate of a homeland with its residents.[7] These constructed national pasts and landscapes, frequently intertwined, comprise a central element of national identities.

At the same time, historians of landscape have shown how the countryside is constructed not just physically, but also ideologically. As the Swedish ethnographer Orvar Löfgren notes, 'All nature is a cultural landscape; even when it has not been physically shaped by the exertions of cultivators or land developers, it is filtered through our consciousness.'[8] Powerful interests shape the land, not just for their economic benefit or personal pleasure, but also to inscribe ideologies on the environment. Chandra Mukerji's book on the gardens of Versailles demonstrates wonderfully the ways in which Louis XIV's landscape architects, influenced by new ideologies about the state, produced palace gardens that expressed the might of French absolutism. Employing techniques borrowed from the construction of fortifications, they sought to impose on the land emblems of the monarch's control of nature.[9] At about the same time, English aristocrats sought to articulate ideas about their own power – vis-à-vis the king and the rising middle class – by substantially altering the grounds of their estates. They chose to create an illusion of a free and bucolic countryside, from whence they had arisen, screening out evidence of peasant labour and oppression.[10] Thus various actors invested the land with political meaning. When the ideologies of nation and landscape – two forms of legitimizing claims to power – combined in the nineteenth century, they produced a powerful new form of nationalism prepared for the age of mass politics. And as these examples suggest, the process of imagining landscapes freighted with symbolism was hardly unique to Germany.

German scholars of the nineteenth century grew increasingly aware of the importance of this ideological combination (although they were by no means alone in this recognition). While liberal nationalists felt a strong connection to the German nation state erected in 1871, millions of other German citizens – particularists loyal to regional identities, conservatives repelled by the liberal aspects of the new regime, Catholics alienated by Protestant dominance in a Prusso-centric Germany, and the multitudes without much formal education and indifferent to national politics, not to mention nationally minded members of ethnic minorities concerned with their inclusion in the German nation state – felt no special attachment, if not outright hostility, to this recent political invention.[11] Moreover, Otto von Bismarck, a conservative stalwart and the new imperial chancellor, was only a reluctant convert to the national idea and remained fiercely loyal to his native Prussia; he saw no particular need to cultivate a national identity once he had extended Prussian power. Without much support from above or below, liberal nationalists felt the urgency of constructing a national identity that would sustain the new nation state. Landscape, providing the nation with territorial and historical rootedness, would help enormously in this process.

The landscape could serve as a venue, along with museums, monuments, parades, and festivals, to experience the nation. Indeed, as the British cultural geographer Stephen Daniels maintains, 'To imagine a nation is to envision its geography,' thus creating a 'portrait of the nation.'[12] Bourgeois German travellers, stimulated by an interest in their local *Heimat*, took to the land to gain a more intimate knowledge of their nation. Whether as avid hikers, casual tourists, leisurely strollers (*Spaziergänger*), or armchair consumers of postcards and picture books, over the course of the nineteenth century the middle classes ventured into the countryside to discover the national essence they believed resided there. In small towns and quiet woods, they discovered what to them appeared to be a timeless terrain, and they invested it with elements of national memory.[13] Every locality could claim some connection to the pantheon of German history, linking the local scenery and memories with the national story.

Endowing the countryside with national memories constituted more than a dreamy romanticism or a flight from modernity. By consuming images of this newly imagined national geography, and by venturing out into it, the middle classes claimed the landscape for themselves, mapping out a new image of the nation.[14] Guidebooks and maps gave them new access to the land, and rather than remaining confined by the tangle of feudal boundaries dividing Germany, hikers and tourists crossed them both physically and mentally, imagining a nation united.[15] Increasingly, bourgeois nature enthusiasts articulated claims to both public and private land, demanding access to the national patrimony of healthy forests and beautiful scenery. This entailed mobilizing public protest and even trespassing. As historian Celia Applegate puts it, 'Tourism and romanticism combined to make the out-of-doors into a public space, equally infused with local patriotism and national pride.'[16] The German countryside, as a new site of leisure, helped create a new middle-class public and at the same time became increasingly political.

Until recently, those assessing this German relationship with nature, and with the forest in particular, have cast it in a harshly negative light. George Mosse, in his exploration of the ideas and culture of German nationalism, firmly linked discourses around landscape to radical ethnic, or *völkisch*, nationalism. *Völkisch* thinkers, he demonstrated, imagined the German landscape as a site of rootedness, joining the soil and its

tillers in a mystical, timeless unity. As such, the land supposedly inspired an emotional and irrational sense of national identity – in contrast to Western Europe's moderate civic nationalism – thus creating an
intellectual *Sonderweg* (or special path) leading to the rise of National
Socialism.[17] Fritz Stern also contrasted the rationality of the West with
Germany's fatal irrationalism, as expressed in 'racial thought, Germanic
Christianity, and Volkish nature mysticism.'[18] While Mosse and Stern described an important aspect of radical nationalist thought, which provided a clear foreshadowing of the Nazis' blood and soil ideology, they
nevertheless presented only one part of the story. Radical nationalists by
no means dominated interest in nature.

Over the course of the 1970s and 1980s, scholars appropriated this
model of an intellectual 'special path,' condemning the Germans' passion for the landscape as anti-modern, anti-democratic, manipulative,
feudal, unenvironmentally conscious, and claiming the popular affinity
for nature necessarily helped to produce fascism. 'Forest history is,' the
foreword to a collection of essays on the topic states, 'a history of German self-understanding, a *Sonderweg* on which a late nation seeks an identity.'[19] According to this interpretation, a passion for the woods was part
of the German bourgeoisie's rejection of modernity, the fatal flaw that
doomed Europe. Over the course of the nineteenth century, this argument goes, the woods became 'the reactionary counter-symbol to modern industrial class society.'[20] Radical nationalists opposed to Germany's
modernization took up Wilhelm Heinrich Riehl's critiques of capitalism
and demands for forest preservation.[21] Interest in nature was promoted
by an insecure bourgeoisie that had 'abandoned itself to romantic longings – irrational daydreams without any real foundation, arising from
latent anxiety and fed by an apparent crisis into which Wilhelmine Germany had fallen.'[22] Serious efforts at preserving nature came too late
in Germany, and nature enthusiasts' goals were made 'questionable'
by their national motives. One historian even insists that wood tariffs,
selfishly imposed by Germans who apparently could not recognize the
value of free trade, contributed to the First World War.[23] As a result of all
this irrationality, another account concludes, 'for a good two-hundred
years, German nationalism and the romanticization of nature have been
disastrously interwoven, and above all the French suffered (in 1870/71,
1914, and 1940) from the aggressive sense of mission that we Germans
acquired in the forest, so to speak.'[24] Apparently, the 'German forest' has
much to answer for. Although the theory of Germany's alleged *Sonderweg*
came under intense criticism in the 1980s and 1990s – to the point of

being largely abandoned by social historians today – among historians of culture and ideas, the concept retains some currency.[25]

Some scholars have begun to draw distinctions. Condemning the 'bourgeois' understanding of nature, Ulrich Linse – along with Gert Gröning, Joachim Wolschke-Bulmahn, and William T. Markham – seek to salvage the German Social Democrats' rational and unpatriotic embrace of the woods.[26] Yet these authors homogenize the views of radical nationalists with those of all middle-class Germans, leaving Mosse's *Sonderweg* largely intact. Simon Schama distinguishes between a rational and an irrational approach to the forest, contrasting the advanced techniques of German forestry with the primitivism of Germany's radical nationalists.[27] But Schama's account likewise makes little room for anyone other than oft-despised foresters on one hand, and right-wing cranks on the other.

Implicit in all of these arguments is the assumption of a German *Sonderweg* to modernity that culminated in the disaster of Nazism. They posit a deviant, distinctly un-Western relationship with nature. At the centre of this landscape perversion is the Germans' infusion of their countryside with national meaning. But as the 1990s boom in landscape studies on Britain and North America has shown, investing the landscape with national significance was a Western norm, not an aberration.[28] One of the reasons for this persistent misunderstanding of the Germans' relationship with their environment has been the scholarship's emphasis on the history of ideas. By concentrating on the views of certain personalities (and in turn implying their widespread acceptance), many historians have ignored local experience and social practice. As the British cultural geographer W.T.J. Mitchell insists, we should consider landscape an 'instrument of cultural power' and concern ourselves with 'not just what landscape "is" or "means" but what it does, how it works as a cultural practice.'[29] Raymond Williams made much the same point in *The Country and the City*: 'It is possible and useful to trace the internal histories of landscape painting, and landscape writing, landscape gardening and landscape architecture, but in any final analysis we must relate these histories to the common history of a land and its society.'[30] By turning our attention away from the pronouncements of a few highly placed individuals, and towards the sentiments and activities of those at the local level, a different image of the land comes into focus.

Fortunately, a few historians have begun to take up this challenge. In the 1990s, scholars of the *Heimat* movement – which sought to preserve the landscapes, architecture, and folkways of Germany's many regions

– have significantly revised our image of those interested in landscape preservation, transforming our understanding of the groups involved from bastions of reaction into relatively liberal organizations.[31] John Williams insists that older scholarship has relied too heavily on the history of ideas approach – drawing from a narrow range of sources associated with particular prominent individuals – and has eschewed cross-cultural comparisons. This tendency has produced, according to Williams, a misleading impression of Germans as irrationally preoccupied with nature, and of the German environmental movement as led by equally irrational *völkisch* thinkers. He therefore explores attitudes towards nature among a variety of locally based organizations.[32] Investigating environmental attitudes in imperial Germany's *Heimat* movement, William Rollins reasons that while nature enthusiasts seemed irrationally engaged in an aesthetic critique of industrialism and capitalism – at the expense of a critical engagement with the more corrosive effects of pollution, for example – they inspired an 'aesthetic environmentalism' that invested Germans' emotions in their landscape, thus laying the foundation for the public's currently strong concern with environmental issues.[33] Thomas Lekan draws significant distinctions between the German conservationists in the Rhineland, who pursued their own agenda from the late nineteenth century on, and the Nazi state, with which these groups came into conflict after an initial honeymoon.[34] The straight road from conservationism to Nazism has been made significantly more crooked.

The recent trend in literature on the *Kaiserreich* in general has been to highlight the ambivalence of modernity. Rather than believing a deficit of modernity lead to fascism, scholars have concentrated their attention on the ways that the embrace of modernity contributed to the catastrophes of the twentieth century. Detlev Peukert pioneered this approach in the 1990s, which has subsequently produced valuable research.[35] The works of Kevin Repp and Thomas Rohkrämer on the ambivalent potential of social reform stand out in this regard.[36] The 'German forest' was itself a modern invention, a product of the era of nation states. This was true both as a mental construct and as a material reality. Although many liked to envision the woods as an ancient space and imagined trees as relics of the past, many also recognized that Germany's forests were orderly, managed spaces – a far cry from the mythical primeval forest (*Urwald*) of the Teutons. And as any modern invention, the 'German forest' had both its positive and negative characteristics. James Scott uses German forestry as the prototypical example of the 'high modernist' approach to the environment; the emphasis on highly managed fast-growing pine monocultures delivered steady supplies of timber for expanding German markets, yet at the same time inaugurated environmental damage and social displacement that continue to this day.[37] David Blackbourn makes a similar point in his book on water management in Germany; human interventions in the environment lead to varying degrees of costs and benefits, both for the environment and for society.[38] While this is true on the environmental and social levels, it applies on the cultural level as well. The widespread invocation of the 'German forest' led in many different directions; on one hand, it helped stimulate a genuine early concern with environmental issues, and on the other, helped foster racist notions of the national community. Indeed, many different groups mobilized the concept for disparate aims, leading to competing claims on this national symbol.

Chapter Outline

This book begins by laying out the national discourses surrounding the woods, and then descends to the local level to explore their resonance. The first two chapters consider the broader meanings of the woods in the national context. Chapter 1 explores the symbolic resonance of the forest. An examination of a variety of published sources, ranging from forestry handbooks and geography texts to popular middle-class magazines and hiking-club journals illustrates that the 'German forest' played a dual symbolic role, representing the nation's geographical and historical unity. Germans not only read about these symbols, but also developed practices around them. Tens of thousands of hikers, as well as countless casual tourists, took to the forests on holidays and Sundays to immerse themselves in nature. Guidebooks, tourist maps, postcards, guided hikes, and club meetings with slide shows, not to mention the proliferation of publications, all attempted to interpret the meanings of the forest for the active and armchair tourist alike. These sources led to the various sites of memory, be they aged trees or constructed monuments, scattered throughout the woods. Wandering through the forest (either physically or imaginatively) thus brought the national landscape together with the national memory in an activity that supposedly encompassed the entire German people. Thus, the idea of exploring the 'German forest' helped to transform the abstract and artificial concept of nation into a tangible and 'natural' experience.

Yet this idealized image of the woods as a marker of national unity should not blind us to the very real conflicts that engulfed the forest –

the theme of chapter 2. Timber formed an important part of the German industrial economy, and as such, significant private and public interests drove the increasing rationalization of woodland. From 1878 to 1880, the Prussian legislature, the *Landtag*, discussed instituting legal measures to restrict public access to timberlands to facilitate rational forest management, as well as private hunting. Liberals, Catholics, and others mobilized stiff resistance to the desires of landlords. Over the course of the *Kaiserreich*, debates continued to rage about the people's access to public and private woodlands. The nationalists and social reformers drew on discourses about the 'German forest,' claiming the woods were 'national property' and insisting on the public's right to them. In particular, they worried that revolution would ensue, should the state limit public access. Ironically, conservative landowners sought to modernize property laws, while urban liberals, peasant advocates, and *völkisch* nationalists insisted on maintaining tradition.

To juxtapose these broader discussions of the forest with local conflicts and practices, the following two chapters investigate two case studies: the Grunewald outside of Berlin, and the Tuchel Heath on Germany's eastern frontier. I chose these two sites in particular because they tend not to conform to what one normally imagines under the rubric of the 'German forest.' Studies of the *Heimat* movement, critical to understanding the German relationship with nature, have tended to focus either on the movement at the national level or on largely rural regions in western Germany.[39] Therefore, a study of woods on the margins of a metropolis and in the Polish-German borderlands would add new dimensions to our understanding of the construction of German national identity.

The Grunewald local study (chapter 3) reveals just how well the forest discourse fit with the progressive and modernizing tendencies of the greatest German metropolis, in stark contrast with the radical-right, *völkisch* image so often conveyed by the literature. Left liberals led the campaign to save the Grunewald for Berlin's citizens, preventing the state from selling off its high-valued forests around the city to real estate developers.[40] Progressive newspapers, politicians, and a dizzying array of voluntary associations mobilized the public against the government, circulating petitions and holding several meetings in which a broad range of public associations took part. Their arguments highlighted the need of the people, especially those without resources to travel, for access to healthy recreation. The scale and vehemence of the protests led the Prussian cabinet to offer the Grunewald to Berlin at greatly reduced prices out of fear of social unrest and an erosion of state authority. The liberal champions of public access to nature succeeded in securing the Grunewald for Berliners.

Of course, there will be those who claim that left-liberal Berlin is the exception that proves the rule. Therefore, the next case study examines the Tuchel Heath – a forest much farther to the east, in a landscape dominated by conservative agrarians and characterized by ethnic strife between Germans and Poles. Here one might expect to find the forest linked to a strident and reactionary German nationalism at odds with the Berliners' campaign for greater public access to the woods. Yet here again we learn the forest was not a romanticized symbol of reaction against modernity. Instead, we discover the state using the 'German forest' itself – in the context of the nationality struggle – as an agent of modernity.

Over the course of the late nineteenth century, Prussian state forest policy became increasingly concerned with the ethnic struggle in the German east – the focus of chapter 4. Starting in 1893, Prussia began a program of reforestation specifically in its eastern provinces, rapidly expanding the size of state forests in the region. Developing domestic timber reserves, improving local agriculture, and cultivating the eastern economy formed the core of public arguments for reforestation, but ethnic motives came subtly to the fore. Reforestation would help increase the direct influence of Prussian authority (and hence Germanization) in this ethnically contested territory via two avenues: (1) the ownership of large swaths of land, much of which had Slavic majorities, and (2) the employment of a large number of local Slavs. These two factors allowed the Prussian state to directly discipline both the wild landscape and its unruly populace. Overwhelmingly throughout this process, those advocating reforestation expressed no interest in an aestheticized or romantic image of the woods. For them, the ethnic struggle was about modernization, and they deployed the 'German forest' as a rationalized and productive space, in contrast to the wild and unregulated forests left behind by centuries of archaic Polish 'mismanagement.' The campaign to reforest the Tuchel Heath cannot be understood as the invocation of a romanticized symbol of reaction against modernity. Instead, we discover the state using the 'German forest' itself – in the context of the nationality struggle – as an agent of modernity.

Chapter 5 addresses the role of racism in forest discourse. Contrary to the dominant view, racism did not permeate the woods in the nineteenth century. Liberal biologists projected onto the forest their visions for a harmonious and productive society, while liberals and conservatives clashed over the symbolism of the oak and the linden as the national tree. Only with the onset of the twentieth century, a narrow range of authors, primarily scientists, utilized the 'German forest' as a racial metaphor. Quite in contrast to the cosy cultural landscapes imagined by nature preservationists and *Heimat* activists, these scientists articulated a racialized vision of the woods, in which struggle, not pleasure, reigned supreme. It is thus in scientific discourses, stressing their modernity, that one can best identify the origins of National Socialism in the *Kaiserreich*, and not in the more widespread historical and aesthetic understandings of the landscape. This sylvan discourse thus illustrates the uncomfortable ways in which tradition and progress, liberalism and conservatism, science and history, collided with one another, creating an ambivalent modernity.

Although my study ends roughly with the First World War, the influence of the 'German forest' persists through the present. Of course, as I have suggested, many older studies of the German relationship with nature have ended with the Third Reich, seeing in it the culmination of an aberrant, atavistic tradition that collapsed under the weight of its own contradictions. Yet if one moves from a narrow focus on the National Socialist era, extending the view beyond the horizon of 1945, one quickly recognizes that versions of the sylvan discourse remain deeply embedded in German society. Like the Nazis, today's Greens – and a much broader pro-environmental consensus – link the fate of the nation and the forest together, although in significantly different ways. One only need think of the forest death (*Waldsterben*) crisis of the 1980s to recognize how closely Germans continue to identify with their wooded landscapes. While some polemicists have sought to discredit environmentalism by rooting it in Nazism, it would be more productive to think about both the blood-and-soil rhetoric and the anxiety over acid rain as two (very distinct) branches of the same tree. Both have drawn on the widespread sense, taking root in the nineteenth century, that capitalism threatens nature, especially forests, and that Germans would find a unique and superior way of managing that threat. For the Nazis, however, this idea was largely ancillary to their anti-capitalism and racism, whereas for the Greens, concern for the environment stands at the heart of their movement, alongside a dedication to pacifism and human rights. Nonetheless, both ideologies have their roots in nineteenth-century discourses about the 'German forest,' indicating just how ambivalent modernity can be.

chapter one

National Landscape and National Memory

Introduction

When Bismarck welded together a united Germany in 1871, the new nation state lacked a cohesive national identity and continued to lack one for some time. This was perhaps clearest at the symbolic level. Although Bismarck has a reputation for manipulating nationalist liberals into supporting the new empire, he clearly avoided cultivating symbols of German national identity. Following unification, he delayed Berlin's architectural and monumental transformation into the national capital, forestalling the construction of a central emblem of Germany's newly centralized national identity, the imperial parliament (*Reichstag*). Both Bismarck and Wilhelm I satisfied themselves with Berlin as it stood, preferring to imagine the new nation state as a princely confederation headed by Prussia. Neither the imperial nor the state governments built monuments to national unification in the 1870s and 1880s; the initiative and funding for the gargantuan Hermann (1875) and Niederwald (1883) Monuments celebrating the nation came overwhelmingly from the bourgeoisie, not the state. Indeed, Bismarck pointedly avoided the dedication of the Niederwald Monument. Meanwhile, although army recruits were required to swear an oath to Wilhelm I, these oaths differed according to faith and from state to state. Likewise, German Protestants were never unified into a national church. Not until Wilhelm II took the throne and deposed Bismarck did the German state seriously set about cultivating a German national identity. Wilhelm attempted to redress the absence of state symbols by investing in monuments and state pageants, in both Berlin and the provinces. Starting in the 1890s, school curricula became decidedly more nationalist, and in 1892, the German Empire finally adopted its first national flag.

But even Wilhelm II's grandiose vision of the nation remained fragmentary and incomplete. For instance, the German state never officially decided on a national anthem. The Prussian monarchical tune 'Hail to You in Victor's Laurels' (*Heil Dir im Siegerkranz*) continued to serve at many state functions, while some preferred the anti-French 'The Watch on the Rhine' (*Die Wacht am Rhein*). Only starting in the 1890s did the strains of the *Deutschlandlied* ('*Deutschland über Alles*') informally fill the role of a national anthem. Furthermore, Germany lacked an effective national holiday. As Alon Confino illustrates, attempts to institute Sedan Day (2 September, commemorating the French defeat in 1870) as a national celebration failed, at least among most citizens of Württemberg. The inculcation of official nationalism through the schools remained ineffectual among large segments of the school-age population, who were often taught in classes of sixty pupils or more in primary school. Moreover, by 1914 a vast number of Germans, if not a majority, belonged to organizations (as among the Catholics and the Social Democrats) sceptical of the official pomp and bluster. The divisions between Germans were too deep to be overcome by the occasional royal birthday or military brass band. The traditional symbols of statehood seemed to have been embraced quite late and to little effect.

This failure of a German national identity to coalesce around state symbols arose from the serious divisions plaguing German culture and society. Since the Middle Ages, increasingly powerful regional states wore down the central authority of the Holy Roman emperors, preventing the formation of meaningful national political institutions and instead promoting provincial loyalties that lasted into the nineteenth century. Since the Reformation, serious antagonism between German Protestants and Catholics (roughly evenly split) continued to rend Central Europe, and these divisions were only aggravated by the new state's campaign against Catholic influence in public life in the 1870s (the *Kulturkampf*). Economic tensions emerged in the nineteenth century as some regions rapidly industrialized (the Rhine, Ruhr, Saxony, and Upper Silesia) and others stagnated (most of eastern Prussia and southern Germany). Advancing industrialization led to the rise of significant social cleavages, especially between the working classes and the rest of society, and these social distinctions carried over into the political arena, laying the foundations for Europe's largest socialist party, the Social Democratic

Party of Germany (SPD). Despite formal national unification, the nation
appeared anything but unified.

Adherents of the *Sonderweg* have argued that the state, along with allied conservative elites, whipped up nationalism to paper over differences between some segments of the population and stigmatize others
regarded as disloyal. But rather than simply being a tool of the state,
the forest discourse – and by extension, German nationalism in general
– arose from civil society, and that public discourse about the 'German
forest' was shaped by private individuals and associations, and not primarily by the state and its agents. Moreover, rather than being an instrument of top-down manipulation, the concept of the 'German forest'
could be mobilized by a wide range of groups for divergent ends, as will
become clear in subsequent chapters.

The language of nation first took firm root among members of the
educated bourgeoisie (*Bildungsbürgertum*) in the early nineteenth century, and they intervened to create attractive national myths and symbols
to overcome the German lands' profound divisions both before and
after the creation of the German nation state. Among these, the 'German forest' took on significant importance, becoming a critical element
in the definition of the new German nation in the *Kaiserreich*. Bourgeois professionals and experts in several fields identified forests as an
important locus, if not the only one, for the formation of the German
national character. Foresters, ethnographers, geographers, historians,
archaeologists, linguists, and botanists all contributed to the construction of the Germans as a 'woodland nation' (*Waldvolk*). These professionals regarded themselves as the guardians of the nation's patrimony,
both natural and cultural, and the heralds of progress and modernity.
They regarded it as their mission to cultivate a new, national identity
among the majority of German citizens only dimly aware of it. They
sought to supersede the traditional bases of political loyalty – the royal
houses and established churches of the individual German states – with
the new nationalism. Their ideas were echoed widely throughout society, finding resonance in the popular press, in schools, and among hiking enthusiasts. And while several of these professionals were employed
by the state, the impetus for their activities emanated not from high
government officials, but from the realm of civil society. Private citizens
and all manner of voluntary organizations – botanical societies, hiking
clubs, and the *Heimat* movement, for instance – developed and propa-
gated this new image of the nation. For the most part, they were successful, inculcating the notion of deep connections between the German

people and their landscape. Yet at the same time, the political meaning of this connection, often assumed to be uniformly conservative, was in fact highly contested.

The woods served as a flexible, malleable symbol, transcending Germany's myriad divisions to encompass the entire nation. For bourgeois Germans, the forest functioned as a green band that tied the nation's land and its heritage together. Transcending the constructed political, social, and cultural boundaries, the 'German forest' united a landscape and a history splintered by internecine struggles. Moreover, the idea of the 'German forest' helped to transform the abstract and artificial concept of nation into a tangible and natural experience. Hiking through the woods and visiting sylvan monuments aided patriotic Germans in connecting with the nexus of national geography and history. The 'German forest' served as a metaphor for the nation itself, linked together across both time and space. Woodlands rested like a symbolic green blanket over the entire landscape, physically uniting the nation. Thus many considered it important for the nation to explore this landscape through hiking. The hike into the woods was not an aimless excursion, however. The wanderer sought out particular sites, frequently connected with the national history. Monuments, both 'natural' and constructed, filled the sylvan landscape, evoking images from an epic past, when heroic Teutons defended a morally upright Germany from the wanton excesses of Rome. Thus, as a geographical marker, a space for hikers to actively explore the nation, and a site of historical memory, the 'German forest' provided the bourgeoisie with a new symbol with which to imagine the nation.

Imagining the 'German Forest'

In many ways, it is not surprising that the Germans sought the essence of their nation among the trees. Forests comprised a little over a quarter of the German landscape in the late nineteenth century, a figure that continued to grow slightly throughout the period. These woodlands, moreover, were spread fairly evenly throughout the country (excepting the relatively barren North Sea coast), generally comprising between 20 and 30 per cent of the countryside. The forest was an easily recognizable element in almost all regional landscapes, leading one forester to note in 1907, 'He who is asked what gives the German landscape its character will usually name the forest, [which] is hardly ever missing from any region.' This sylvan blanket covered Germany's diverse landscapes of mountains, hills, flat lands and river valleys.[1] The distinguished anthropologist and geographer Friedrich Ratzel described the German landscape in 1909 as 'more uniform than that of any other western or central European country.' For him, Germany was a 'land of forests and pastures, of green landscapes from one end to the other ... The beech forests that are reflected in the Baltic Sea are the same as those that shade the ravines of the middle Isar Valley. Just as Westphalian or Lower Rhenish farms stand under oaks, so too do those of Upper Bavaria. All of the characteristic forest trees are common throughout Germany; only in remotest East Prussia is the beech not present.' Ratzel contrasted this image of a Germany united by forests with both the Austrian Empire and France, where the green hues of Bohemia and Normandy contrasted sharply with the white shades of Dalmatia and Provence. For Ratzel, these geographical 'facts' were 'furthermore not without political implication. While physical and geographical unity does not create political unity, it can promote and solidify it.'[2] This sylvan omnipresence helped secure the forest's place as a logical and natural symbol of a generalized, unified, and truly national landscape in a country otherwise divided by political, social, and cultural boundaries. Woodlands thus aided in the definition of a German national landscape by presenting it as a cohesive whole.

Johannes Trojan, the liberal editor of the satirical *Kladderadatsch* and a nature enthusiast, further identified Germany's terrain with its forests, demarking its boundaries with trees. In his 1911 *Our German Forests*, he presented a series of ninety-five photographs of trees and forests taken throughout Germany. Organized in no apparent order, they represented the diversity of German sylvan life. Yet beyond simply illustrating the many varieties of German woodland settings through their juxtaposition, the sequence of the pictures revealed an additional message; tellingly, Trojan accompanied the first photograph with a quote from the poet Eichendorff: 'The forest wants to speak.' But what did the forest have to say? Consider the geographical distribution of the first four photographs depicted: an Alpine woodland in the Allgäu (south), a beech forest on the Mecklenburg coast (north), a woodland stream in the Viersener Bruch (west), and snow-laden firs in the Riesengebirge (east). Was it simply a coincidence that Trojan's German forest resembled the nation as imagined in Germany's unofficial anthem, the *Deutschlandlied*? From the Maas in the west to the Memel in the east, from the Etsch (Adige) in the south to the Belt in the north, Trojan seems to have replaced Germany's symbolic riparian boundaries with arboreal border posts. Moreover, these trees did not simply mark out the four cardinal directions; they also stood at the very edges of the *Kaiserreich*. In the south, the Allgäuer Alps divided Germany from Austria; in the north, the beeches could advance no farther than the Baltic coast; in the west, the Viersener Bruch lay barely ten miles from the Dutch border and the Maas itself; and in the east, the Riesengebirge divided Silesia from Bohemia and formed the backbone of Germany's Silesian wedge between Austria-Hungary and Russia.[3] Trojan's trees thus marked off the nation's boundaries.

In addition to defining Germany as a forested land, many authors were equally adamant about what Germany was not. As Trojan seemed to suggest, if the forests united the Fatherland, they also differentiated it from the rest of Europe. While most acknowledged that Germany was not the most heavily forested country on the continent, many asserted that its woodlands nonetheless distinguished their country. One forester noted that despite Germany's significantly lower number of wooded hectares per capita than the European average (0.25ha versus 0.79ha), it was a relatively well-forested country (at 25 per cent of its area) when compared with its western and southern neighbours.[4] And while Russia, Sweden, Norway, and Austria-Hungary had larger forest reserves than Germany, Germans felt that the survival of so much forest in their much more densely populated, intensively cultivated, and highly industrialized land was an indication of their special affinity for the woods. Ratzel considered it 'indicative of our loyal cultivation of the forest' that they continued to thrive in Germany's oldest areas of settlement.[5]

This sylvan environment helped nationally minded Germans define themselves as lovers of the forests, in contrast to their neighbours. In 1871, one forest historian contrasted the Germans' sylvicultural passion with the attitudes of other peoples towards the woods, concluding, 'None of this is evident in the national character of the Romance or Slavic peoples, as a comparison of the forestation of the lands occupied by these peoples with our own dear *Heimat* proves.'[6] German authors revelled in their nation's supposedly unparalleled love of its native forests, as in this 1900 article from a botanical journal: 'No other people has internalized the loving sense for the forests to the same extent as the Germans, and nowhere are there such wonderful plantations of trees and well-maintained forests as in Germany.' By way of contrast, this same author observed that France, England, and Italy had no 'wonderful forests,' for lack of rational forestry regulations and downright 'ignorance.'[7] Love for the woods seemed an essentially German characteristic.

Indeed, when German nature-enthusiasts looked abroad, they saw

devastated landscapes. In the west, the Romance peoples seemed downright hostile to nature. One observer singled out the Italians as having a
particular 'antagonistic attitude' (*Widerwille*) against trees. Horrified, he
reported that Rome's municipal government razed a number of beautiful arbours (mistakenly convinced of their insalubrity) without complaint
from the otherwise boisterous Italian press. In general, such commentators described the Italian landscape as desolate and infertile.[8] France suffered from the disastrous privatization of state forests during the French
Revolution, when over 3 million hectares were sold off and promptly cut
down in what one forester called an 'insane deluge of speculation.' As a
result, German scientists concurred, the French government was spending an annual 100 million Francs on timber imports and another 150
million for the reforestation of the Alps, not to mention the ecological
injury to the land.[9] According to an instructor at Prussia's prestigious
Eberswalde Forestry Academy, France's '*laisser faire, laisse passer*' attitude
toward the economy, including the privatization of state woodlands, led
to the rapid decline of its forests.[10]

   While the French had recently taken measures to ameliorate the
situation, Russia and the United States seemed completely insensitive
to the environmental damage they wrought on their frontiers. German
foresters characterized the enormous Russian timberlands as still ruled
by 'mismanagement' (*Unwirtschaft*) and a 'system of plunder without
compare.' Despite attempts at management, Russia lost an estimated 4
per cent of its vast woodlands between 1888 and 1911. Moreover, much
of the deforestation took place in the heavily populated areas of the
west and south, threatening to destroy the forests in those regions entirely. The Smolensk district suffered some of the highest losses, with 38
per cent razed during this period, resulting in serious environmental
damage. Forest fires set by disgruntled peasants in the 1905 Revolution
further contributed to this decline.[11] And while the lack of forest management in Russia distressed many German sylviculturalists, the United
States' onslaught against its untamed wilderness provoked outrage. In
the 1880s, one commentator observed that American civilization was
razing forests 'in truly demonic haste,' and wondered how long this 'cultural struggle' (*Kulturkampf*) against the woods would last. In 1899 a distinguished professor of forestry identified American forestry practices as
nothing more than an 'intensive economy of plunder.' Ten years later,
a radical nationalist author condemned the 'vandalism of the American
rapid-civilization' for massacring the continent's forests and laying waste
to ancient woodlands for the construction of countless wooden houses.[12]

The bounty of trees in the North American and Siberian wilderness had apparently accustomed their inhabitants to plunder.

Of the major powers, only the British had avoided the devastating effects of deforestation, according to German experts, because of their oceanic climate and easy access to Scandinavian timber reserves. Yet the German forestry establishment proudly reported that the British relied on it to train foresters for service in the colonies (especially India).[13] Outside of Germany, it seemed, there was little consciousness for the careful stewardship of nature.

Of course, Germans did not have a solely harmonious relationship with nature, despite the effusions of romantic poetry and the smug self-satisfaction of the forestry establishment. Not all of Germany was well forested, and this was mostly the result of human action. As the German lands' population expanded in the eighteenth and nineteenth centuries, and as proto-industrialization increased demand for raw materials and fuel in the form of wood and charcoal, Germany's forests came under significant pressure. Between 1700 and 1900, according to one conservationist, Germany's forests declined dramatically from 40.0 per cent of the landscape to 25.5 per cent. Just in the fifty years before 1872, Prussia had lost about 14 per cent of its forests. Most of the land had been turned over to cultivation, but something on the order of 7,500 square kilometres had degenerated to sandy wastes.[14] In some regions, authors complained deforestation had achieved Mediterranean proportions. Upland areas associated with proto-industry seemed worst affected, such as the Eifel, Erzgebirge, Thüringerwald, and Rhön, along with the Prussian east, resulting in the impoverishment of these regions, as well as environmental problems associated with deforestation: erosion, flooding, and lower soil fertility.[15] The desire to ameliorate agricultural conditions, along with fears of wood shortage, whether real or imagined, prompted governments to act.[16]

Already in the late eighteenth century, the fear of dwindling wood supplies led some German states to establish schools of forestry. Income from forests already comprised a significant portion of state budgets (an eighth of Prussian and a quarter of Bavarian revenues in the early nineteenth century), and there was an incentive – both in terms of promoting economic development and generating revenue – in organizing timber production along rational lines. Yet the rationality that emerged was a strictly economic one; while the state benefited, the costs were displaced onto the environment (and the public, as chapter 2 explains). New forests were planted to replace the old, but these forests were quite

different. Rather than the mixed forests of the past, often filled with deciduous trees of various ages, the new forests were geometric and monotonous. To ease oversight and harvesting, trees were planted in rows, and
all undergrowth was stripped away. In place of the oaks and beeches and
other deciduous trees that had predominated in western and central
Germany, foresters planted monocultures of fast-growing pines and firs.
The planting and harvesting of these plots would be staggered over the
years, so as to provide a constant supply of trees reaching maturity. Thus,
this new, standardized forest consisted of several large blocks, each comprising rows of trees of the same species and age – and precious little else.
Several species of wildlife found these forests inhospitable and declined.
Moreover, these uniform monocultures created long-term problems for
the forests themselves. The absence of a wide range of animals undermined the soil-building process, leaving trees undernourished over time.
Such weakened trees could then more easily fall prey to diseases and
parasites, which could spread uninhibited through the densely packed
monoculture. In the twentieth century, acid rain would also plague these
highly managed forests, leading to the forest death (*Waldsterben*) crisis
of the 1980s.[17] Far from being universally cheerful places, some of Germany's forests already began to suffer from the intensified production
regime in the late nineteenth century. Nonetheless, Germans continued
to celebrate their forestry and their forests as unparalleled anywhere.

Hiking to Find the Nation

With the identification of Germany as a forested land, and the Germans
as a forest-loving people, it was no surprise that in 1873, shortly after
the foundation of a German nation state, a congress of botanists and
gardeners in Munich demanded the creation of a wooded *Volkspark* that
would spread its tendrils out across Germany. These nature enthusiasts
desired that a hiker could – in terms evoking the *Deutschlandlied* – 'wander from the Belt to the Etsch, from the North Sea to the Adriatic, in the
shade of the forest.'[18] In 1885, the Silesian noble Heinrich von Salisch,
heavily influenced by Riehl's writings on the woods, similarly proposed
the proliferation of public forests for the rambler's delight throughout
Germany: '*I wish to be able to see at least one [forest], even if it is only on the
horizon, and that it would be possible for the hiker in any place to walk there
and back in a day in order to take a forest excursion.*' He recommended that
every five-square-mile section of the nation should at least have its own
quarter-square-mile patch of woodland (5 per cent of the landscape),

in addition to the roughly 25 per cent of Germany already covered by forests.[19] While neither of these proposals overcame the enormous obstacles blocking their implementation, their idealized vision of the nation as an integral whole, whose diverse parts were held together by a network of forest paths, did prove resilient. In addition to revealing the important function of the forest as a bond uniting the various German landscapes, these ideas also suggested that the purported uniformity of Germany's landscape and its difference from the rest of Europe could not by itself, as Ratzel indicated, inculcate a greater national unity; indeed, the 'German forest' required German hikers to unite the nation in their footsteps. By exploring the woods and walking the land, middle-class Germans found a concrete emblem of their national identity that they could experience first-hand. And they could further enact national unity through the very act of joining with their fellow Germans in this exploration. Hiking, like tourism, could promote a collective identity.[20]

Starting early in the nineteenth century, the study of the landscape and its inhabitants through walking excursions became a preferred way to gain an appreciation for the nation. Moreover, hiking through one's home district, and eventually farther afield, fulfilled the bourgeois requirements for healthy and edifying recreation. The early-nineteenth-century bourgeois took to the countryside on foot, spurning the aristocratic conveyances of the horse or carriage for a more 'democratic' form of transportation and ignoring the 'artificial' feudal boundaries to consider the landscape as a whole. In the countryside, he hoped to discover, according to Wolfgang Kaschuba, 'old roots in history and new vigour in nature.' Such explorations of the countryside resulted in a new fascination with the *Volk* and its culture as a product of nature.[21]

This new interest in the countryside prompted several scholars to explore it. Inspired by Johann Gottfried Herder's interest in folk cultures, urbanites alienated from the countryside sought to recover authenticity from the landscape and its people.[22] The Napoleonic occupation of the German lands stimulated a nationalist backlash among some of the educated elite, who increasingly sought to fashion a new Germany in contrast to France. Prominent among them were the renowned philologists Jakob and Wilhelm Grimm, who believed they could recover German antiquity through the folklore of the forest. Under the influence of their mentor Friedrich Karl von Savigny, the founder of the historical school of jurisprudence in Germany, they believed that a nation's laws emerged from its ancient customs, rather than being derived from universal (French) principles. By understanding these customs and their language, one could decipher the spirit of the laws and learn a great deal about the character of the nation. The Grimms investigated the folklore surrounding the forest, believing it to be a reservoir of national memory. One study of the Grimms indicates that they 'conceived of forests as symbolic preserves of the popular and oral traditions they set out to recover through their sustained philological work.' Their 1813 publication of a journal called *Old German Forests* 'explicitly linked German forests to the genesis and continuity of authentic German culture,' something deep and profound when contrasted with the alleged superficiality of the French.[23] During this same period, Friedrich Ludwig Jahn, a prominent early-nineteenth-century nationalist and founder of the gymnastics movement, sought to bring his bourgeois brethren outdoors to strengthen their bodies for the defence of the nation. In 1810, Jahn advocated 'patriotic hiking' to discover the Fatherland.[24] Thus, already in the early nineteenth century, nationalists had begun to regard the landscape as full of national memories, and advocated hiking to discover them.

In the 1850s, the prominent ethnographer Wilhelm Heinrich Riehl – inspired by the nationalism of the Napoleonic era and in particular the liberal Ernst Moritz Arndt – stressed the importance of foot travel for the discovery of the national culture. In the opening line of his *Travelogue* (*Wanderbuch*) he insisted, 'The researcher of folk life must above all travel. This is obvious. I mean travelling on foot, however, and for many this is not obvious.' In the era of increasing rail transportation, one could be conveyed from one end of Germany to the other without having significant contact with the intervening landscapes or populace at all. The *Wanderer*, on the other hand, had the opportunity to both observe and interact with regional landscapes and their people. Hence, Riehl argued that for those who wanted to understand the German nation in all its colourful variety and complexity, it was necessary to travel slowly along the roads that the majority of the people used. Only in this way could the wandering researcher become integrated into the folk life of the German nation; therefore, Riehl claimed, 'Every thorough excursion [*Wanderung*] is at least a partial process of becoming a citizen [*Einbürgerung*].'[25] In close touch with the countryside, the cosmopolitan bourgeois *Wanderer* could become reintegrated into the *Volk* and the nation, and at the same time claim to represent them.

Perhaps surprisingly, Riehl's purpose was conservative: shaken by the violence of the Revolutions of 1848, he abandoned his liberal convictions to become a supporter of the monarchical reaction. The peasants and artisans rose up, he argued, because they had been alienated from their traditional lifestyles by the encroachment of capitalism. Capitalism's corrosive effects – in the form of the expanding power of the market (aided by the extension of the railways), and the rationalization of property relations (implemented by landlords seeking to expropriate the remnants of communal use rights) – had undermined their ability to make a decent living, turning them into rootless savages attacking all symbols of authority. It came as no surprise, he commented, that the peasants had turned against the forests that local landlords had seized from them, burning them to the ground. Riehl therefore called for restrictions on capitalism and the defence of pastoral Germany in order to avoid future unrest. Travel through the countryside, as part of Riehl's ethnographic research, could provide the state with the information necessary to adjust its policies to local conditions, thus avoiding the universalizing and levelling tendencies of capitalism that had so disrupted traditional life.[26] So, although *Wandern* could liberate the individual from social constraints, as a research tool it could also provide the state with the means to better regulate communities. In both cases, however, hiking reinforced the link between the bourgeois observer and nature, between the urban individual and a national landscape.

Yet *Wandern* had by no means become a solely conservative tool. Riehl's critiques of modernity cut across bourgeois and noble economic interests alike, with his hostility to railways and the noble usurpation of peasant use-rights. His advocating the expanding power of the state, through anthropological investigation and tailoring policies to local conditions, was far from a simple-minded reactionary stance. Indeed, this former liberal hoped to create a new kind of state, one that would better cater to the needs of its citizens (as he defined them) than either bourgeois capitalism or Junker paternalism had done. In later years, radical nationalists and agrarian reformers would take up Riehl's mantle, hostile to industrial modernity *and* noble dominance in the countryside (see chapter 2). Their reaction to modernity, like Riehl's, demonstrated a profound ambivalence about the changing nature of their society.

The right was not alone in thinking about the countryside. Liberals, too, sought to instrumentalize the outdoors for their own purposes. Emil Adolf Roßmäßler, another veteran of the 1848 Revolution, wanted to use hiking to strengthen the individual, not the state. In May 1849, following Prussian intervention against the nascent German National As-sembly, this Saxon left-liberal politician and scientist fled Frankfurt with the rump parliament. As he 'botanized' his way through the Schwarzwald en route to Stuttgart, he realized the need for popular scientific education.[27] During the period of repression that followed the revolution, when political education and 'enlightenment' were banned, Roßmäßler championed popular education (*Volksbildung*), especially in the natural sciences, as an essential part of the 'struggle against reaction.'[28] A scientific education, he felt, would be the most effective means of creating resistance to the authoritarian state. In a subtly worded statement, Roßmäßler complained, 'Our *Volk* suffers greatly from insufficiently developed senses. It often goes with half-closed eyes through the surrounding nature.' The task of popular education (*Volkserziehung*), he noted, was to open the people's eyes through excursions to the countryside, bringing a 'whole new world' into focus.[29] Knowing Roßmäßler's politics, this 'new world' likely included more than the realm of flora and fauna (see chapter 5).

Hiking continued to have political implications into the late nineteenth century. Following an 1872 parody of bourgeois hiking appearing in a prominent Viennese newspaper, the journal *Der Tourist* defended the practice, claiming that those ridiculing it simply feared change: 'Not without reason did Kaiser Franz fear the railroads, and the rulers of that time saw in its spirit the changes it would initiate; unholy England, where everyone thinks, speaks and writes for himself, without everything being officially arranged, set a bad example.' Likewise, *Wandern* – as an opportunity for people to break the constraints of their local communities – threatened to unleash the powers of individual liberation. Much like Roßmäßler's conception of a liberal *Volksbildung*, *Der Tourist* emphasized that hiking 'is a means of education and enlightenment.'[30]

This emphasis on liberal 'education and enlightenment' took precedence over the physical act of hiking. As the advocates of hiking indicated, ramblers should above all learn something from their experience outdoors. And frequently that lesson taught greater love for the nation. The goals one hiking association dedicated to the 'Saxon Switzerland,' a popular tourist area south of Dresden, reflected this pedagogical predilection; according to one member, the group desired 'to open to science and tourism this beautiful corner of the world, and to protect and promote its natural beauties and its *Volkstum*. This can be accomplished only through an exact and thorough knowledge of the land and people, and this cannot be achieved by racing by in a steam engine or in other means of conveyance, but rather by a contemplative rambling over hill and valley, from the town to the simple hut of the naïve resident.'[31]

The youth hiking association known as *Wandervogel* defined similar goals in its 1904 charter: 'to promote hiking among the German youth, to awaken a sense for natural beauty, and to provide the youth with the opportunity to get to know the land and people of the German *Heimat* from personal experience.'[32] The hiking enthusiast E.W. Trojan argued that hiking 'should awaken a love of the earth, love of the soil, of the land and of the *Heimat. For only out of it does the nation gain its invincible strength.*'[33] And shortly before the First World War one hiking author still maintained that 'the discovery of Germany is – although even both poles are no longer "blank areas" on the map of the world – still a task for the future for the vast majority of hikers. We do not know our Fatherland.'[34] Hiking thus was a means to learn about the nation.

During the *Kaiserreich*, hiking became an increasingly popular activity. By the 1870s, hiking had lost its purely upper-middle-class (*bildungsbürgerlich*) character, with wider and wider portions of the population taking part. Hiking clubs (*Touristenvereine*) sprang up across Germany through the 1870s and 1880s, with thirty-two being founded from 1876 to 1884 with perhaps as many as 40,000 members. By 1883, the newly founded Union of German Hiking Associations claimed over 10,000 members among its constituent groups.[35] Even the state succumbed to the hiking mania; in 1882, the Prussian minister of education enjoined the kingdom's schools to encourage hiking among their pupils. Hiking became so popular that in 1883 one teacher regarded 'Wanderlust' as essentially German.[36] In 1893, the popular Thuringian Forest Association (*Thüringerwald Verein*) alone had over forty-three chapters and 4,000 members, and by 1906 those figures stood at over one hundred and 10,000 respectively.[37] Furthermore, this phenomenon was by no means limited to bourgeois men. Increasingly, workers and youth formed their own hiking organizations at the turn of the century. The socialist Friends of Nature (*Naturfreunde*) hiking club, spreading to Germany after its 1895 formation in Vienna, boasted 30,000 members by 1914.[38] About the same time, the bourgeois youth hiking association, the *Wandervogel,* claimed a circulation of 25,000 for their journal.[39] Women also participated in the growth of hiking, albeit in small numbers.[40] These figures do not tell us about the numbers of people who actually hiked, but they do let us know that large numbers of Germans found the idea attractive enough to at least join a hiking club or subscribe to a journal.

Where were all these hikers headed? Most ventured into nearby woodlands, the most affordable option for vacationers and day trippers with limited resources. Local hiking clubs organized excursions into the forest with well-planned itineraries, including visits to noteworthy and picturesque sites, lectures by an expert in a particular field, and stops

TABLE 1.1   Numbers of postcards sent from national sites, 1893–1898.

Site	1893	1896	1898
Niederwald Monument	139,000	128,000	216,000
Kyffhäuser Monument	14,000	148,000	168,000
Die Bastei	51,000	77,000	154,000
Wartburg Castle	64,000	117,000	146,000
Brocken	80,000	119,000	144,000
Schneekoppe	n/a	n/a	139,000
Rudelsburg Castle	n/a	n/a	57,000
Heidelberg Castle	n/a	n/a	45,000

Source: 'Verschiedenes,' *Mittheilungen des Touristen-Klub für die Mark Brandenburg* 8 (1899): 87.

for refreshments. Individual hikers could choose their own routes from a range of hiking guides. Many visited monuments in the forest, such as the ubiquitous Bismarck Towers or the enormous national monuments that sprang up in the countryside during the *Kaiserreich*, such as the famous Hermann Monument in the Teutoburger Wald, commemorating an ancient Germanic tribe's victory over the Romans.[41] The growing popularity of such sites was manifest in an 1899 survey of hiking destinations. Within a matter of five years, many sites saw a doubling and even tripling of the numbers of postcards sent from them (see table 1.1).

While these statistics neither directly tell us that the numbers of visitors to these sites increased nor give us any indication that all or even most of the visitors hiked to the site, they do indicate the broadening consumption and dissemination of these outdoor national/historical symbols.

This list of sites, while by no means exhaustive, suggests the kinds of places hikers visited. Of the eight locations listed, two were national monuments, three were castles, and three were geological features. Most of them, however, resonated with national appeal. Clearly, the national monuments invoked national history and tied it to the landscape. The Niederwald Monument, commemorating the Franco-Prussian War and German national unity, stood above the Rhine at Rüdesheim, an already well-touristed area. The Kyffhäuser Monument, erected by veterans of the Wars of Unification, stood atop the mountain in which the legendary

Kaiser Barbarossa supposedly continued to slumber, awaiting Germany's hour of need. The castles on the list also represented momentous events in the national history. Primary among them, the Wartburg Castle attracted large numbers of visitors because of its association with Martin Luther. Luther translated the New Testament into German there, thus the castle represented an important point both in the development of the German language (through standardization) and the history of Protestantism (seen through a particularly national lens). Another Thuringian fortress, the partially ruined Rudelsburg Castle, likewise reminded visitors of the destruction of the Thirty Years' War. At the same time, it evoked the romance of medieval Germany, with its thirteenth-century core being restored in the nineteenth century. The ruins of the Heidelberg Castle, a fine example of German Renaissance architecture, evoked national memories of wars against France. Even the mountains on the list had some national significance. The Harz Mountains' highest peak, the Brocken, stood out as the site of the legendary *Walpurgisnacht*, or witches' sabbath, immortalized in Goethe's *Faust*. The Schneekoppe, the highest point in Silesia's Riesengebirge (and indeed in all of Germany north of the Alps), near the source of the Elbe, attracted attention for its wild ruggedness (much like the Bastei in the 'Saxon Switzerland' south of Dresden). The border between Silesia and Bohemia (or Germany and Austria) ran over its summit, demarcating the limits of the German nation state.

Almost all of these sites embedded national memories within a wooded landscape. One might argue that in the case of the national monuments, their sylvan setting was purely incidental, a function of their being placed in the heavily wooded German landscape; yet the forest played a significant role in the visitors' experience of them. Charlotte Tacke observes in her study of the Hermann Monument that its setting in 'explicitly national nature' was an important aspect, as 'it represented the national, German history as a union of monument, nature and landscape, as a timeless continuity of the Teutonic and German nations.' Moreover, the association with the landscape helped to naturalize the nation: 'Nature, although it was tied to a process of birth, growth and decay, conveyed in its entirety the image of permanence and stability that was directly carried over to the history of the "German *Volk*."' A description of the project from 1842 explicitly linked the Hermann Monument's sylvan setting to the nation: 'For centuries the Teutonic woods have continued to blossom, similarly immortal is the Teutonic *Volk*! Just as storms crash here upon these mighty cliffs, so too the storms of time break on the German *Volk!*'[42] The wooded landscape surrounding the Hermann Monument was therefore a national landscape, itself resonant with meaning.

The Niederwald and Kyffhäuser Monuments were likewise embedded in a national nature. Set in the woods above the Rhine, the Niederwald Monument also incorporated nature into its composition. A call for donations to the project noted that the site combined the advantages of local industry and progress with the 'refreshing breeze of the German world of nature and legend arising from the roar of the forest and the river.' The jury selecting the design praised their first choice for its placement in the 'atmospheric environment of the woods.'[43] With regard to the Kyffhäuser Monument, George Mosse noted that its planners intended it 'to be a part of a terrain on which the masses could gather, surrounded by a Germanic wood, to perform acts of national worship.'[44] Like the Hermann Monument, then, both the Niederwald and Kyffhäuser Monuments were placed in the woods and conceived as part of a national landscape.

Yet the forest was not simply a suitable space in which to erect monuments, for the trees themselves could become living monuments to the past. Just as the state identified castles and churches as historical monuments worthy of protection, the prominent Prussian nature-conservationist Hugo Conwentz argued, so too should old trees and other venerable elements of the German landscape. Conwentz labelled his efforts *Naturdenkmalpflege* (care of natural monuments), suggesting that not only nature, but also the memories inhabiting it, deserved protection.[45] Frequently such monuments of nature would be included on the hiking itinerary.

A *Naturdenkmal* – a term coined by Alexander von Humboldt in the early nineteenth century – referred to just about any natural feature that local nature enthusiasts considered worthy of the name. Geologic formations such as cliffs, moraines, and erratic boulders counted, as did rare species of flora and fauna. Particular trees were also identified as natural monuments, either for their paucity, their unique forms, their age, or their historical or ethnological significance. A vast literature arose around the propagation of *Naturdenkmäler*. Numerous articles and books, including regional *Baumbücher* (tree books) and tourist guides, flourished at the turn of the century, leading the interested rambler through forests studded with many noteworthy botanical specimens.

Indeed, the explosion of *Baumbücher* illustrated the popularization of trees as tourist destinations. Originally, foresters undertook such studies as a means of cataloguing state property. Starting in 1850, an official Württemberg forestry journal included a regular section on 'Remarkable Trees,' and in 1858 the forester Heinrich Burkhardt created an inventory of all the remarkable trees in the Hanoverian state forests. It was not until later in the century, with the growth of tourist associations, that the broader public began to cultivate arboreal interests. Periodicals dedicated to hikers published a number of articles regarding noteworthy trees.[46] But perhaps the leading organ to promote trees as tourist destinations was the *Gartenlaube*.

Starting in 1883, the aptly named *Die Gartenlaube* (the arbour) – a family magazine devoted to raising national consciousness and one of the most widely read German publications, with a readership potentially exceeding two million in the 1880s[47] – initiated a series of articles highlighting 'Germany's Remarkable Trees' (*Deutschlands merkwürdige Bäume*). The series – coinciding with the booming interest in hiking – presented its readers with trees it regarded as noteworthy elements of the national heritage. The succession of fifty-three short articles, included in its aptly titled 'Leaves and Blossoms' section of brief news items, ran from 1883 to 1905 with great success. As the *Gartenlaube*'s editors attested in 1901, 'From the many letters over the course of the years we have been able to ascertain that there has always been a lively interest in Germany's remarkable trees among our readers.'[48]

Although the *Gartenlaube*'s series was illustrated with photos (some of them on the cover of the magazine), it is clear that these trees were not only meant to be admired from afar. Many of those featured stood in popular tourist areas, such as the spa towns of Bad Homburg, Pyrmont, and Oeynhausen, as well as the Erzgebirge, the Harz, and along the Rhine, where they could be easily reached by the vacationing public. Indeed, virtually all the 'remarkable trees' were found in localities accessible by train. Moreover, the *Gartenlaube*'s photos frequently portrayed bourgeois tourists admiring the tree, or perhaps the tree in a domesticated setting, such as near a village church, along a path, or surrounded by benches, further underscoring accessibility. Several articles gave instructions on reaching the trees, and some mentioned local initiatives to maintain the sites and make them more accessible. Authors recommended hikes to the 'Wendelinus Oak' and the old linden at Grimmenthal from Bamberg and Meiningen respectively.[49] At Remilly in Lorraine, a local hiking club planned a path to the 'Crazy Beech Trees,' while near the spa town of Homburg another club shored up the sagging branches of the 'Crinkly Tree' with iron rods.[50] Sometimes the articles referred to other nearby attractions, such as the seven Stone Age tombs near the 'Giant Juniper Tree' at Clossow in Brandenburg, or the ruins of the Schaumburg from which the 'Schmorsdorfer Linden' grew.[51] Some authors made little attempt to hide their goal of promoting local tourism. The author of an article on the 'Priory Linden' at Dahl sought to promote tourist interest in the Sauerland, praising the local beauties and recommending a guidebook.[52] Thus the contributors to the *Gartenlaube* attempted to fit their local 'remarkable trees' into a network of tourist sites and encouraged their readers to visit them.

While to the modern reader an individual tree, such as the ones mentioned above, seems hardly likely to attract the attention of tourists, there were indeed many who ventured out into the forests to see them. One author commented on the 'droves' who came in 'pilgrimage' to see the 'Royal Oak' at Peisterwitz in Silesia, and others noted that countless tourists had carved their initials into the linden near Eckersdorf in East Prussia and the 'Ducal Bush' near Koblenz, demonstrating 'how many people make the pilgrimage to delight in this wonder of nature.'[53] These claims of frequent visits were not necessarily the self-aggrandizing fantasies of local tourism promoters 'advertising' their regions in the *Gartenlaube*. Publishers increasingly included references to such notable trees in their tourist guides, one observer reported.[54] Furthermore, a natural science journal complained that 'remarkable trees' had become a staple of tourist literature, enjoying 'a particular place in the Baedeker ... "one has to have seen them."' It recommended two alternatives, both of which were likewise situated in tourist areas.[55] Thus these 'remarkable trees' were promoted as natural tourist destinations. With all of this human activity around these sites, it is hard to imagine that anyone could regard them simply as atavistic icons. Embedded in a web of local tourist attractions and surrounded by benches, fences, and other intrusions of modernity, these natural monuments stood integrated into the world of the present.

Around 1900, with mounting interest in natural monuments, the weight of publishing activity concerning them shifted from periodicals to books. The oldest *Baumbuch*, according to one expert on the subject, was published in 1896 in Switzerland, a land well attuned to the tourist potential of natural sites. The wonderfully illustrated (and expensive) *Tree Album of Switzerland* was intended to 'raise the people's sense for the country's beauty.' An expanded and much cheaper version of the book appeared in 1908, better equipped to address the mass audience. In Germany, a number of tourist guides included in their pages guides to remarkable trees, while local pamphlets led their readers through the countryside and made arboreal *Naturdenkmäler* more accessible to the public (if only in its imagination).[56]

Natural science associations throughout Prussia also sought to attract the public's attention with *Baumbücher*. The natural science associations in the provinces of East Prussia, Poznania, Westphalia, and Schleswig-Holstein, along with the Brandenburg Botanical Association and the Zoological-Botanical Section of the Silesian Society for Patriotic Culture, took on the role of cataloguing remarkable trees.[57] In the introduction to his 1900 catalogue of East Prussian *Naturdenkmäler*, the state geologist and natural science association leader Alfred Jentzsch insisted that the catalogue would provide a guide to forests where schoolchildren and patriotic history buffs could hike and discover the '*Heimat* of our ancestors.'[58] Fritz Pfuhl, museum director and member of Posen's natural science association, actively gathered information on natural monuments in the region and published a *Baumbuch* for the province in 1904. He further desired to make the information even more available, through the publication of maps and guides, as well as a yearly report. Moreover, Pfuhl mobilized local youth to explore the countryside, under the guidance of their teachers, to seek out, photograph, and report on *Naturdenkmal* candidates.[59] Thus natural science associations not only brought natural monuments to the attention of the public, but they engaged the public in their identification and preservation.

As publishers and associations highlighted the monuments of the German countryside for the public, the German states again initiated arboreal inventories, although this time with a somewhat different purpose. Hugo Conwentz's 1900 *Forest-Botanical Notebook*, a catalogue of remarkable trees in the province of West Prussia, served as the model for a whole series of similar Prussian provincial efforts. While these books followed the older pattern of merely listing trees without regard to their historical or ethnological significance, these listings were intended as much for the general public as for the forester. As Conwentz noted in his introduction, he compiled his inventory so that 'our *Volk*' would not lose access to these 'wonderful witnesses of the past.'[60] Furthermore, in contrast with earlier efforts, the project was not directed by a forester (like Burkhardt), but rather a museum director, and it was not the Prussian Ministry of Agriculture that had commissioned the work in the first place, but rather the Ministry of Culture. Thus even the state began to feel that trees were worthy objects of the tourist's gaze.[61]

This tourism – which inspired bourgeois hikers all over Germany to identify noteworthy sites, name and catalogue them, and eventually propagate them in the form of postcards, maps, tourist guides, and picture books – was a middle-class appropriation of the national landscape. Through the creation and consumption of these sites and their representations, members of the German bourgeoisie had an opportunity to claim the national landscape for themselves.[62] Not only were they redefining the countryside and giving it a national inflection, as had the early-nineteenth-century hikers that Wolfgang Kaschuba describes, but they also infused that landscape with a new national history. In contrast to the conservative forms of national memory, which emphasized the descent of kings and martial glory, this new history celebrated the land and its people, much as Reihl's work had done.[63] The natural monuments, and the memories they contained, offered 'an alternative idea of nation,' as William Rollins puts it, 'a collective which was defined by its common history and its social solidarity, and not just by its rulers or its economic power.'[64] Late-nineteenth-century bourgeois authors projected the nation's history onto nature, seeing in the trees tangible ties between past, present, and future. Rather than being an atavistic effort, this emphasis on Germans' roots in nature was meant to overcome the destabilizing effects of modernity.

Discovering Memories in the Woods

As we have seen, Germans filled their forests with historical markers and natural objects dedicated to historical memory. These memorials were not placed in the forest by chance; frequently, the meaning of these symbols heavily relied on the historical ambience of the woods. As Charlotte Tacke has argued, the landscape provided a 'direct connection between the present and the past of the German nation.'[65] But what past in particular did the bourgeois interpreters of the landscape identify as worthy of memory? What historical memories did they value in their landscape? How did they bend pre-existing memories to suit their national message? An examination of the *Gartenlaube*'s *merkwürdige Bäume* series suggests many middle-class Germans viewed the forest as a conduit to an explicitly national past, where Germans stood united, despite their history of internecine struggles. The series depicted trees dedicated to the national unification of 1871, to Protestantism's challenge to the papacy (ignoring the divisions it unleashed among Germans), and to ancient Teutonic pagans united in their worship of nature. Other authors echoed these themes, using the trees and forests to link the national past, present, and future into a temporal whole, parallel to the woods' geographical uni-fication of the nation. Indeed, the scholarly discipline of forest history arose in part to explore this critical element of the national history. At the same time, however, while many Germans demonstrated enthusiasm for the 'German forest' as a historical setting, they also realized it was not the woods of their ancestors. It symbolized an ancient past that most recognized as quite distinct from the present.

The *Gartenlaube*'s *merkwürdige Bäume* series valued aged trees as 'living witnesses of the past.' A tree's evocative power lay in the idea that it had lived far longer than any person in a particular place. According to one essayist, 'It is a feeling of part reverence, part melancholy, which moves us when we look at that which has survived the centuries intact. What was once built and planted by industrious hands – house and tree and forest – still stands, although the trace of those who had put it there has long been scattered.' When we look at a building, or an oak or a linden, the writer continued, we 'look back through time ... and we think about the series of generations who before us, in joy and misery, cultivated and protected and quickly sank away.'[66] Trees could transcend the in-dividual and link one to past and future generations. They could even transcend the buildings erected in stone, as did the old linden at the ruined fortress of Schaumburg: 'Out of the thousand-year past of the old castle, only a turret and, in half-height, the massive block of the castle precincts ... remain as mute witnesses. Living, however, the old linden loyally keeps watch outside the castle gates!'[67] Yet another article echoed these sentiments, noting that while we normally consider stone and iron as lasting materials, 'stronger than these dead things is the driving force in living nature, and it is not rare that the expanding roots of an old tree break an opposing rock, or that the obstacle which stands in the way is pushed aside.'[68] Thus the *Gartenlaube* endorsed ancient trees as suitable monuments to reflect on the past.

If stately old trees provided an opportunity to contemplate former times in general, they also became sites to memorialize a specifically national history. In the spa town of Pyrmont, the mighty linden on the castle wall evoked for Robert Geißler a host of former visitors: 'Many generations had rested under the leafy canopy: armoured knights and their ladies and the company of their servants, peasants and soldiers from the time of the Thirty Years' War, then learned men with their wigs, powdered and made-up ladies, Friedrich the Great and his follow-ers, Goethe, and virtually all the great men and women of modern Ger-many, in addition many guests from foreign lands.' A pageant of German history passed through Geißler's imagination, colourfully evoking the triumphs and tragedies of the nation's past. Unlike buildings, monuments, and other human constructions, trees did not bear the architectural imprint of a particular era and therefore were symbols flexible enough to represent all historical periods. While a gothic church immediately calls to mind the Middle Ages, Geißler could imagine anyone from a medieval knight to himself or to generations still unborn standing under the linden: 'By all appearances the ancient linden tree will long flourish, and new generations will look back on today as a pale prehistory.'[69]

The linden at Bordesholm in Holstein, near which the founders of both the Russian and Oldenburg dynasties were buried, also recalled the passing of many generations: 'Still each summer the scent of your blossoms delights a generation whose ancestors breathed your exquisite fragrance centuries ago.' This linden also served as a national monument. A wooden plaque posted on the tree proclaimed,

> Much has your immense dome seen, rapturous linden,
> You have watched the joys and sorrows of many generations;
> But you have never seen anything greater than the Holstein Uprising,
> Germany's tribes [*Stämme*] united, reborn into an empire![70]

Holstein's revolt against Denmark, according to the plaque, helped graft together the German *Stämme* (*Stamm* denoting both tribe and stem) into one national tree. By placing the plaque on the linden, its creator transformed this tree from a local ancestral memorial into a monument of national unity. Thus the Bordesholm linden became a means of connecting generations of Holsteiners to the present, and all these generations to the new German nation state. Such trees helped readers and visitors place themselves in a unbroken lineage of local ancestors and a broader national community. This case in particular illustrates how *Gartenlaube* authors worked to, in Rudy Koshar's words, 'create a new layer for the memory landscape, the goal of which was to channel and transform earlier pasts' to form new, national memories.[71]

The 1883 article on the Luther Elm near Worms, published in conjunction with the Luther celebrations of that year, similarly united Germany's past with its national present. The anonymous writer A.B. asserted, 'Worms is a plot of German earth, where in one view the signs and milestones of millennia hover in the mist of the unmeasured distances of mythical time.' In this German landscape lost in time, A.B.

encountered the Luther Elm, which 'like no other called to mind the image of the holy world-tree of Edda [an icon of pagan tree-worship].'[72] Luther, according to one version of the story, stopped under this elm, on his way to his famous interrogation at Worms, and preached to the local peasants. This alone evoked the rapturous line from A.B.: 'Luther under the village elm preaching to the Rhenish peasant – an essentially German [*urdeutsches*], poetic moment.' In another rendition, Luther halted under the elm to speak to a local landlord. When asked about his experience at Worms, Luther looked back to the city and replied, 'If it's the work of men, it will crumble on its own; if it's of God, then it will last.' Luther's statement here referred both to his teachings and to the tree: 'As this sapling will grow into a tree, they [Luther's opponents] will not stifle my teachings.'[73] A.B. went on to explain, 'The Luther Elm stood as a symbol, a holy tree as it were, the tree-of-fate of Protestantism. Struck by lightning, damaged by weather, even its mighty trunk became hollow and rotten over the course of centuries. Nevertheless, its foliage burgeoned annually in spring, and as late as 1870 it waived enthusiastically to the columns headed for France; and as victory after victory was announced, it no longer felt it could hold out. On the eve of the capitulation of Metz (26 October 1870), a storm broke the crown of the tree from its trunk. The *Volk* stood shocked ... Broken, dead, branchless, stripped and completely hollow stood only the low stump.[74]' Although the Luther Elm snapped during the Franco-Prussian War – as if fearing for defeat – the author assured his audience that it survived; indeed, 'new life swells in this venerable emblem of Protestantism.'[75] Out of the tempest that engulfed the splintered old German tree, a vibrant new *Protestant* German sapling emerged, presaging the dawn of the *Kulturkampf*, imperial Germany's campaign to subordinate the Catholic Church. The trunk of the Luther Elm, in A.B.'s imagination, linked Germany's ancient pagan roots with the Protestant Reformation and the eventual blossoming of the German Empire. Each, it seemed, embodied the German essence.

While some of the trees the *Gartenlaube* highlighted were associated with the period of national unification, most of them referred to a much more distant past. For the *Gartenlaube*'s authors, these remarkable trees most often evoked early medieval Germany, when Teutonic tribes still roamed the primeval forests and pious missionaries expanded the reach of Christianity. Essays occasionally made references to other periods – the Reformation, the Thirty Years' War, the era of Friedrich the Great, the Napoleonic Wars, and national unification – but at their root, the *Gartenlaube*'s trees told stories about antiquity. Authors frequently

mentioned pagan tree-worshiping rituals and the Christian appropria-
tions of them. Remarkable trees such as the four lindens at Grotenhof
in Westphalia were identified as sites of ancient sacrifices.[76] This nature-
religion lived on in the Christian appropriation of the tree cult, and it
was not uncommon for founders of churches and monasteries to plant
holy linden trees in front of their houses of worship, or build next to
existing pagan holy lindens.[77] Thus the original nature-loving character
of the ancient Germans supposedly survived – albeit perhaps only in the
backwoods – into the nineteenth century. During the 1850s, many inva-
lids still made a pilgrimage to the Cripple Oak near Völkshagen in Mecklenburg in order to climb through the tree's yonic aperture, created by
the fusing of two branches.[78] The persistence of this pagan rebirthing
ritual, meant to rid the body of disease, illustrated for the *Gartenlaube*'s
readers the German people's continued intimate contact with nature.
Hence, the *merkwürdige Bäume* series reiterated the links between the
nature-loving ancient German and his modern-day counterpart.[79]

The *Gartenlaube*'s contributors were not alone in considering trees
a temporal link between past, present, and future generations of Germans. The respected Prussian forester and parliamentarian August
Bernhardt proposed that, unlike the grain in the field, trees in the forests
linked one to the future as well as to the past. While the farmer harvests
only what he has planted, Bernhardt explained, the forester reaps what
others have sown, and plants with a mind towards coming generations:
'The rustling of the broad crowns speaks to us of what came before us,
and what will remain after us. The forest raises our consciousness high
above the narrow boundaries of our own existence, and its longevity
through the centuries reminds us that our lives are but only a span of
time.'[80] As a metaphor for the nation, the forest linked the past and the
future and placed individuals in a continuum greater than themselves.
It demanded respect and gratitude for the achievements of those past,
and care and cultivation for those to come; thus the forest as national
monument was as much a commemoration of the past as a reminder of
posterity.

Repeatedly, authors and scholars insisted that the 'German forest'
transported them to the ancient past. While the Greeks and Italians had
their classical ruins to remind themselves of their antiquity, they noted,
the Germans laid claim to the 'holy groves' of their ancestors. When
the poet and author of *Our German Forests*, Johannes Trojan, looked
at the forest, he saw trees 'that as saplings could have belonged to the
ancient forests and the period of German paganism.'[81] Another author

argued that 'the forest was the temple and the parliament of the Germanic tribes, in which most of their religious and state life took place,' and as such should be protected like built monuments.[82] One nature-protection advocate regarded Oldenburg's Hasbruch Forest as 'a monument from old Teutonic times, and it tells us more about the life of our ancestors than ruined walls.'[83] Another author advocating the preservation of natural monuments observed, 'The forest was the setting of our ancient history, the forest is the setting of our native legends, and even the last descendants of these legends, our fairy tales, take place largely in the forest.'[84] When Germans entered the forest, they were supposedly transported to the ancient past.

German scholars had long looked to the woods as a monument to the national past; Tacitus's description of *Germania* as a wild sylvan utopia full of noble barbarians provided the starting point for many histories of the German people. Even the name *Germania* supposedly referred to their association with the forests. One author explained that the term came from the Latin *Girimana*, which meant 'people of the wooded mountains.'[85] In another version, a geographer proposed instead that the word was derived from a German term for 'forest-dwellers,' coming from the Lithuanian *gérme*, meaning 'thick forest.' This made sense, since he imaged ancient Germany as a 'raw, rough land covered with forests and trees.' He also demonstrated other connections between Sanskrit words for forests and forests-dwellers and *Germania*.[86] Archaeology further reinforced the relationship between the ancient past and the woods, for it was in those areas away from modern human settlement and agriculture in which one could still find remnants of ancient burial mounds, fortifications, altars, and artefacts. Indeed, many early-nineteenth-century foresters were themselves amateur archaeologists, documenting their discoveries in their districts.[87]

The history of the forest was so important that an entire discipline of *Forstgeschichte* developed to study it. As one historian explained, 'The history of the forests is especially closely linked with the history of the German people; in fact, a history of the German tribes is totally incomplete and incomprehensive without a history of the German forest.'[88] Such forest history was inspired by the cultural history and folklore of the Grimms, who in their journal *Old German Forests* attempted to analyse German culture in order discover its 'natural' unity.[89] Moreover, historians did not simply use the forests as a colourful backdrop to describe the sagas of ancient Germany; rather they often cast the woodlands in the role of the creator of the German nation.

Until the turn of the century, many scholars accepted Tacitus's account of ancient Germany as a sylvan sea, blanketed by a dense forest in which the Romans only fearfully tread. A cultural history of the Germans from 1887 described the scene: 'There we see an immense forest, out of whose monotonous gloomy surface mountains loom like forested islands.' Germans lived in isolated settlements within this landscape.[90] Accordingly, these tribes living among the huge trees of the primeval forest had become a *Waldvolk* through centuries of interaction with their environment. Drawing on theories of environmental determinism developed by Herder, forest historians identified Germany's sylvan landscape as the crucial element in creating the German national character. In his 1871 *History of the German Forests to the Close of the Middle Ages*, the forest historian C.H. Edmund von Berg argued, 'Man is dependent in his entire development on the surroundings in which he is raised and lives; the violent force of nature manifests itself to the largest extent in the particularities of the national character, in manner, lifestyles, and economic activity of the peoples.' With ancient Germany purportedly covered by a virtually unbroken canopy of foliage, it is not surprising that Berg concluded that 'the forest played a significant leading role' in the formation of the German national character.[91] By returning to the forest, then, a hiker would find not only the stage on which the ancient national drama had unfolded, but in some sense also the playwright who had written the script.

One did not need to subscribe to crude environmental determinism to accept the important influence the forest had on the economic, social, and cultural development of the German people, however. Berg outlined the development of German society in relation to the forest. The woods provided the game and fruit for the ancient Germanic nomads, who then evolved into semi-nomadic herdsmen who settled in the forests in winter, where they produced goods. This allowed for the growth of trade and a rise of public life. As agriculture improved, more Germans became settled farmers, further drawing on the forest for resources during winter. With increasing economic development, Germans increasingly relied on timber for construction and manufacturing, and this in turn led to a system of forestry to provide for the high demand, as well as a unique thousand-year tradition of state protection of the forests.[92]

Another historical account of Germany's woodlands stressed the myriad ways in which the forest 'helped to create the German character.' Instead of a mystical relationship, the forest influenced such concrete details as the forms of agriculture, commerce, and architecture in the

German lands, not to mention the development of industry well into the nineteenth century (before the introduction of iron and coal). Thus the 'history of the forest therefore stands as a significant part of German cultural and economic history.'[93]

Those documenting German forest history also emphasized that this intimate relationship with the woods resulted in a particular German love for the forests. As the founder of the *Heimatschutz* movement, musicologist Ernst Rudorff, expressed it in 1880, 'In the inner and deep feelings for nature lay the true roots of the German essence. What captivated our forefathers in Wodan's holy oak forests, what we hear in the sagas of the Middle Ages ... comes forth in a new, unexpected fullness in the lyricism of Goethe or Eichendorff; it is always the same basic tone, the same deep pull of the soul to the wonderful and unfathomable mysteries of nature, that speaks in these expressions of the national spirit.'[94] This love of the forest supposedly differentiated Germans from other peoples, for as another author put it, 'not every people loves its trees as do the Germans.'[95]

The decline of several ancient peoples served as both a warning to the Germans to protect their forests, and as confirmation of the German's inherent love of nature and wise use of natural resources. Many parts of the Mediterranean and the Levant, stripped of forests in ancient times, were cited by German nature writers as warnings against the abuse of woodlands. Alexander von Humboldt explored this issue in his 1826 *Views of Nature* (followed by Riehl in his 1854 *Land and People*), arguing that modern Italians were 'drained and dried out' because the Romans had deforested their peninsula.[96] Such critiques persisted through the turn of the century. Authors postulated that the lost civilizations of Persia, Babylonia, Syria, Palestine, Asia Minor, and North Africa, now surrounded by deserts, had to have fallen victim to the results of deforestation. Similarly, they observed that the current agricultural production of Greece, Sicily, and Spain amounted to only half of ancient harvests in those regions.[97] Thus German foresters and nature preservationists were well aware of the importance of woodlands for agriculture, and credited the fertility of German farms to the continued presence of forests.

Despite the constant emphasis on the forest as a witness to the ancient past, few Germans were fooled into thinking that the 'German forest' was a primeval wood (*Urwald*) removed from civilization. The author of a series of articles in 1871 on 'Forests and Forest Trees' began enthusiastically by describing the forest as a 'mysterious, in places even unexplored land in otherwise well-known parts of the world,' home to wild animals and far from civilization. Yet throughout the series, he did not describe any such forests, and indeed in the final article he depicted Germany's woods quite in contrast with his original image. Instead of an uncharted territory, he described a bucolic landscape full of 'villages hidden in fruit trees' and 'estates and castles looking out from behind mighty oaks, lindens, or elms.' Moreover, in this scene the hiker beheld a 'beautiful landscape that speaks of a rich culture, with mighty mountains wreathed in forests.' All of this led him to exclaim, 'Here reigns peace, joy, and culture!' Moreover, this depiction of a rustic valley not only emphasized its cultivated nature – much in contrast to the opening picture of the forest – this kind of landscape depended on human intervention. If one removed culture, the author remarked, this beautiful landscape would decline into a wild 'struggle' between competing forms of vegetation. As the author concluded, looking at this lovely scene one would have to 'praise that culture that with wisdom reigned in the various plant forms' untamed drive to dominate.'[98] Thus the series concluded not with a celebration of wilderness, but a validation of human intervention in nature.

Beyond praising human shaping of the landscape, many authors recognized that the 'German forest' was almost universally a product of this intervention. Very few scholars were blinded by the idea that there remained primeval forests untouched by human culture. The celebrated novelist Theodor Fontane, famous for his depictions of the Brandenburg countryside, noted frankly in 1861 that 'our landscape long ago stopped being a simple product of nature.'[99] After the turn of the century, the popular botanist Raoul Heinrich Francé went even further, arguing that 'the German soil has been almost totally stripped of its original plant cover … our flora has been artificially reigned in, altered, partly plundered [and] partly expanded.'[100] The original *Urwald*, in Francé's opinion, was an unpleasant place permeated with death and decay that had nothing to do with the 'well-known expectations of size and beauty.'[101] Referring to his expeditions into what he believed to be a small remnant this once ominous forest, Francé noted, 'He who has not seen this wilderness does not know how "unnatural" our beloved German forest really is.'[102] Many others agreed with Francé's assessment, remarking that such *Urwälder* had 'long since vanished' from most of Europe.[103] Friedrich Ratzel concluded that whereas once the forest had been a dangerous place, it had been converted over the centuries into an important element of the cultural landscape. Just as Germans loved the Rhine as much for its cultural value – the towns, churches, and castles along its banks – as for its natural beauty, he observed, 'We also love the German forest because it is embedded in culture and is, even in its depths, shrouded in history.'[104] Thus most scholars acknowledged that there were no *Urwälder* left in Germany, and that the 'German forest' was constructed. Rather than serving as the original venue of the ancient German past, then, the 'German forest' stood as a symbol for that past.

While the broad agreement that there remained no primeval German forests might be surprising, there were even many who disputed the idea that the forests had ever covered the majority of Germany in the first place. Through the 1870s, Tacitus's view of an ancient Germany covered by dense primeval forests filled with brave Teutonic warriors prevailed. Starting in the 1880s, however, scholars began to express their doubts about such claims. Certainly impressive forests covered parts of Germany, historian August Sach argued, but the Romans, unaccustomed to the landscape, surely exaggerated their depictions.[105] The forestry professor Adam Schwappach agreed, noting that while woodlands did cover more of Germany in ancient times than in his own day, they could not have dominated the entire landscape.[106] In 1901, the geographer Robert Gradmann published an article challenging the view that the ancient Teutons had lived in the woods, in harmony with nature. Animated by Friedrich Ratzel's findings that forest-dwellers were supposedly always less developed than their neighbours, Gradmann insisted that the Germanic tribes were not the 'half-wild' barbarians of legend, drinking beer, wearing bearskins, hunting, and raiding the civilized lands.[107] Such a view was 'completely false,' he contended, and this erroneous belief needed to 'be corrected with decided emphasis.' He offered instead an image of the ancient Germans as an agricultural people, settled on open land before the arrival of the Romans. The large German population, which the Romans reported pouring out of the forests, had to have been supported by settled agriculture, Gradmann noted. Using archaeological and palaeontological evidence, he then argued that the primeval forest would have been too difficult for a people with Stone Age technology to clear, and therefore concluded that there must have been significant areas of open land when the ancient Germans migrated to the region. He estimated that only about half of Germany had been forested in ancient times.[108] Gradmann's view was quickly accepted; as one expert on ancient Germany reported observed, the Germans could not have flourished in a heavily wooded landscape, for 'the *Urwald* is the enemy, not the friend, of man.'[109] Thus the image of an ancient Germany shrouded by thick forests encountered increasing scepticism. Woodland romanticism had its place, of course, but needed to yield before science.[110]

Public Reception of the 'German Forest'

Determining what the majority of Germans thought about the woods is
a difficult project. It is safe to say that middle-class reading material was
suffused with the forest mythos; books and articles extolling the virtues of
the 'German forest' appeared with increasing frequency in the decades
before the First World War. German and foreign commentators on German culture alike recognized the enormous importance of the forest in
the German imagination; one travel guide to Germany devoted 16 per
cent of its length to a chapter on '*Der deutsche Wald*,' and another noted,
'The sentiment connected with the forest in Germany is a dominant feature of the country, and no wonder, for the forest has played a great part
in the history of Germany.'[111] And this discourse appeared to have an
effect, being repeated, as we shall see, in parliamentary discussions and
press debates over concrete policy issues. The nobility, too, held forests
close to their hearts. After analysing scores of noble memoirs, Wolfram
Theilemann has identified hunting (and the forests in which it took
place) as crucial to aristocratic identity. Moreover, he claims there was a
'close identification – in the broadest sense' between the nobility and the
forest, both of which were symbols of age, persistence, and distance from
the workaday world.[112] Yet evidence for other social groups is much more
scanty. We can infer from agricultural advice literature, as well as analyses
of peasant practices, that their own immediate well-being trumped any
romantic notions.[113] Of course, some industrial workers began organizing hiking clubs at the turn of the century, but this provides little idea of
what exactly they sought to gain from their woodland excursions.

Fortunately, there is one source that sheds some light onto workers'
attitudes towards the woods. In 1912 the sociologist Adolf Levenstein,
himself of working-class origin, published a study of working-class attitudes that included a section on the forest. Levenstein asked his participants – miners, textile workers, and metalworkers – if they spent time in
the woods, and if so, what they thought about there. He then included
dozens of these unedited responses in his book.[114] The answers reveal,
however tentatively, that the majority of workers appeared to have little
interest in the forest. They did not answer the question, complained they
had no time or energy to enjoy the woods, or gave perfunctory answers.
Those providing substantive responses were split roughly evenly between
those who adopted (at least for the purposes of the survey) a fairly bourgeois conception of an idealized forest and those for whom the forest
was either demoralizing or aggravating.

Apparently reflecting the larger bourgeois discourse, several workers associated the woods with health, peace, beauty, and faith, with some even citing romantic poetry as an inspiration. At the same time, a significant number of respondents expressed personal despair and frustration, social criticism and anticlericalism, laden with widely varying degrees of Marxist theory.[115] It is interesting to note, however, that even those workers who espoused idealistic notions of the forest never associated it with nationalism. Indeed, the term 'German forest' never came up among their answers. None of them appeared to conceive of their local woods as part of a larger national geography or history. The spatial and temporal bonds of the German nation, which seemed so clear to bourgeois authors, were apparently invisible to the workers; they either failed to understand its national resonance or rejected it unanimously. The '*German* forest' meant nothing to industrial workers.

Conclusion

The 'German forest' provided bourgeois Germany with a national landscape and a national memory. Middle-class Germans could imagine their nation state as unified by a broad band of forests reaching from one end of the country to the other. These woods provided the opportunity for the hiker to wander out into the countryside and 'discover' the nation. What that hiker should have found under the shade of ancient trees, above all else, were powerful historical memories, which linked all generations of the nation into a single unity, stretching back into the mists of time. Thus the 'German forest' provided a site in which patriotic Germans could imagine themselves in any era of the national history, embedded in a national landscape. Above all, however, the woods pointed to the memories of the Teutonic past (rivalling the glories of the Romans), where the Germans acquired their character as *Waldvolk*. Yet we should be careful not to be carried away by their romanticization of the woods. Most authors came to acknowledge that modern Germany's arbours were not the 'holy groves' of their imagined ancestors. They understood the forest instead as a symbol – one that they hoped would overcome the cleavages fragmenting German society.

While this sylvan discourse painted a wonderful image of German unity, the story of the woods was no fairy tale. Germany remained a fragmented land in many respects, with a widening chasm between the working class and the rest of society reflected in their divergent understanding of the woods. Moreover, while bourgeois nationalists may have rhapsodized about the majesty of the 'German forest,' they also understood it as a real place. And that real place repeatedly intruded into this enchanted wood, leading to a protracted battle between the friends of the forest and its owners.

chapter two

Contested Forests:
Ideal Values and Real Estate

Introduction

In the second half of the nineteenth century, tens of thousands of middle-class hikers tromped off into the woods, where they imagined themselves in a national landscape resonant with historical memories. Yet they were far from the only forest users. The gulf between the nature enthusiast's 'German forest' and the landlord's stand of timber was profound. Property rights divided these two understandings of the sylvan landscape, with ideal values standing opposed to real estate. The 'German forest' could not be owned; many of Germany's forests, however, were owned by a stubborn class of rural elites who increasingly surrounded their land with legal sanctions, and this conflict led to repeated and protracted battles over the public's rights to the woods.

Over the course of the late nineteenth century, two basic attitudes towards the forest evolved. On one hand, Wilhelm Heinrich Riehl and his intellectual offspring demanded the preservation of public access to the 'German forest' (especially the traditional peasant use-rights then being phased out) in order to forestall social decay and revolution. On the other, great landlords sought to close their woodlands to the public in order to protect their property and promote its rational management according to the latest methods. These views clashed in the late 1870s, as the Prussian Junkers – arch-conservative noble landlords – began to regain their political footing, during the debates over what became the 1880 Field and Forest Law (*Feld- und Forstpolizeigesetz*). East Elbian estate owners strengthened the limitations on the public's use of private forests, but not without arousing strong opposition from liberals, Catholics, and even some conservatives.

Social reformers, agrarian activists, and nationalists all feared that the separation of Germans from their beloved forest would spark a rebellion in the long term, if not in the near future. Each group advanced a particular argument against a restrictive definition of sylvan property. Social reform advocates sympathized with urbanites, worrying that without an occasional respite in the woods, they would either decline in efficiency or lash out against urban squalor and industrial oppression. Agrarian reformers worried about the erosion of rural society, stressing the necessity of peasant access to the woods for the prevention of impoverishment and the flight from the land (*Landflucht*). Nationalists, largely embracing the arguments of both camps, insisted that Germans without connection to the forest would lose their sense of national solidarity and turn to socialism. Thus it is no surprise that, from the 1880s onward, those concerned with public access to the woods declared Germany's forests 'national property,' open for all to use.

Understanding the relationship between sylvan ideals and the timber trade not only contextualizes the national and political meanings of the 'German forest,' but also clarifies the role of nationalism in the *Kaiserreich*. In the *Sonderweg* interpretation of German history, nationalism served as a 'false ideology' manipulated by aristocratic elites to maintain their control over a populace increasingly drawn into mass politics. Nationalism, so the argument goes, channelled popular discontent away from the ruling Prussian Junkers – who sought to maintain the status quo – and towards external threats (England, France, Russia, and the United States) and unpatriotic scapegoats (Social Democrats, national minorities, Catholics, and Jews). By keeping such suspicions and hostilities alive, the Junkers and their allies manipulated nationalist sentiment and prevented real social change.

As Geoff Eley and others have demonstrated, the relationship between nationalist organizations and German elites cannot be described as manipulative.[1] Indeed, the nationalists showed little subservience to their supposed Junker masters. The late-nineteenth-century debates over access to the forest illustrate this point clearly. Nationalist sentiment turned against large landowners, denouncing their selfish self-interest and warning that their policies would destabilize the nation. Rather than acting as the Junkers' puppets, agrarian reformers and *Heimat* activists – two groups often regarded as subservient to elite interests – turned against their putative patrons to question absolute property.[2] These nationalists thus set their own agenda, protecting the sacred 'German forest' from debasement and refusing to be cowed by conservative opposition.

The forest debates also fail to conform to the *Sonderweg*'s model of modernity. According to this interpretation, East Elbian landowners, along with their nationalist and agrarian allies, stubbornly resisted social, economic, cultural, and political change. The middle classes, manipulated from above and browbeaten into submission, failed to challenge them and instead gravitated to the elite's feudal values. In the case of the conflict over woodland access, however, the roles are far more confusing. Supposedly 'reactionary' landlords insisted on a modernization of property law, seeking to rationalize timber production at the expense of feudal peasant rights. Conservative agrarian reformers, envisioning a future Germany of small farmers, challenged the Junkers in this regard, insisting that peasant farmers needed access to the fruits of the forest to thrive. While their vision was rural, it cannot be regarded as simply backward-looking. At the same time, urban social reformers endorsed public access to the woods for entirely different reasons. Rather than attempting to preserve rural society, they wanted to create a more contented and efficient working class in an effort to overcome the flaws of industrial capitalism. As they saw it, nature could serve as grease to keep industrial Germany humming. Their vision was undoubtedly modern. *Heimat* activists and radical nationalists, appropriating the arguments of both social and agrarian reformers, attempted to effect social change in the face of Junker resistance, claiming that the 'German forest' was the nation's patrimony, and that without it, Germany would be ruined. Both envisioned a revitalized nation state that would be fit to meet the modern challenges of the twentieth century, and neither prostrated themselves before the interests of landlords. All parties to the debate over the woods believed they were on the side of modernity: Junkers *modernizing* property rights, agrarian reformers *modernizing* peasants into sustainable small-farmers, social reformers *modernizing* the living conditions of urban workers, and *Heimat* activists and radical nationalists *modernizing* the concept of the nation state and national identity in their own unique ways. And yet all of them defended traditional institutions and legal concepts in their struggle to modernize: on one hand, the Junkers insisting on their right to usurp traditional community rights, as they had gradually since the dawn of feudalism, accruing ever more power for themselves, and on the other, reformers and nationalists of all types asserting ancient rights to the woods that were not compatible with modern Roman law. Thus this struggle over the woods undermines the neat dichotomy of modern/anti-modern so common in the historiography, producing a far more nuanced picture of nationalism in the *Kaiserreich*.

Sylvan Freedom

Freedom plays a central role in nationalist ideologies. Nationalists often strive to achieve freedom of the nation from foreign influence, be it military occupation, diplomatic pressure, political interference, economic penetration, or cultural domination (or, in the case of powerful nation states, freedom to engage in some or all of these activities against others). Achieving liberation from outside sources of oppression or opposition would bring about social harmony for members of the nation – or so nationalists believed. At the same time, nationalists generally also believed, at least in the nineteenth century, that national liberation also meant personal liberation. It therefore should not be surprising that the concept of the 'German forest,' an important part of German national identity, was imbued with a sense of personal freedom.

Throughout the late nineteenth and early twentieth centuries, several authors drew comparisons between the forest and the sea. This repeated linkage of the sylvan and maritime realms was by no means coincidental; indeed, it highlighted a fundamental quality that many Germans felt distinguished the forest from the rest of the landscape. In short, the woods, like the seas, were free. In their ideal form, both connoted the unfettered power of nature outside the laws of society. In particular, both offered the opportunity to observe nature, and thus contemplate God; both had salutary effects on mental and physical health; both allowed an escape from law and social conformity, as among high-seas pirates and woodland brigands; and finally, neither could be owned, affording access to everyone seeking to enjoy their stimulating atmospheres and harvest their fruits.[3]

Wilhelm Heinrich Riehl, a critical figure in the development of the sylvan discourse, drew a fundamental comparison between the forest and the sea. He argued that both were powerful forms of nature that exerted a huge influence on the character of individuals and nations. These geographical features maintained a nation's vigour; thus, 'just as the sea keeps a coastal people fresh in its original state [*rohe Ursprünglichkeit*], the forest has the same effect on continental peoples.' Moreover, Riehl averred, catastrophe threatened those nations that ignored this principle, for 'a people must die out if it can no longer fall back on refuges in the woods, in order to gain in them the renewed energy of the natural, raw national character [*Volkstum*]. A nation without significant forests is to be regarded the same as a nation without a coastline.'[4] These great natural features, the sea and the forest, ensured the youth of a people by maintaining its ties to nature.

Nature, in Riehl's conception, led one to contemplate God. Thus he noted that 'poetry has also called the free forest and the free sea the holy forest and the holy sea, and nowhere does the sanctity of undisturbed nature affect us, as where the forest descends to the sea. Where the breaking of waves and the rustling of leaves come together as a hymn … is the truly holy forest.'[5] Beyond identifying both forest and seas as sacred spaces, Riehl's statement also indicated he imagined them as free. He even went so far as to compare the free men of the sea (pirates) with the free men of the forest (wood thieves and poachers).[6] For Riehl, both oceans and woodlands provided crucial avenues for escape from a society increasingly constrained by middle-class social norms.

While both the sea and the forest were free, only the woods allowed the majority the opportunity to escape the strictures of everyday life. 'The forest alone allows us civilized people [*Culturmenschen*] to dream of personal freedom undisturbed by police supervision,' Riehl averred. 'One can still at least walk wherever one pleases without being bound to the paved military road. Indeed, a sober man can still run, jump, and climb to his heart's content without being considered a fool by old Aunt Decency.'[7] In western Europe, however, where commerce and revolution had destroyed the woodlands, such sylvan freedom was impossible:

> Politically freer neighbouring lands, where objectionable fences have brought the unrestrained desire for wandering to an end, do not know this freedom any more. How does the policelessness of his streets help the North American urbanite if he cannot walk around free in a nearby forest, because the horrible fences there block his way more despotically than a whole regiment of policemen. How do liberal laws help the English, since they have only enclosed parks and hardly any open forests? The pressure of manners in England and North America is intolerable for a German man. Since the English no longer treasure the open forest, it comes as no surprise that one should bring in addition to the entrance fee, which one pays for visits to the theatre and concerts, a black tailcoat and a white collar. Germany has a greater future of social freedom than England, because Germany has saved its open forests. One could eradicate forests in Germany, but to close it off would call forth a revolution. From this German sylvan freedom, which stands out so strangely from our otherwise modern condition, pours forth a deep influence on the customs and character of all classes [*Volksschichten*].[8]

For Riehl, sylvan liberty prevented revolution because it was available to

all Germans. Free access to the holy forest thus stood as a cornerstone
of German social conditions, he believed, assuring smooth passage into
modernity.[9] Here again the comparison with the sea was instructive. Just
as the oceans could not be divided into exclusive, private plots, so too the
woods. In principle, then, central to the definition of the ideal German
forest was freedom of access and freedom from restrictive notions of
property. This idealized forest stood in direct contrast to the real forest,
which landowners sought to transform into a piece of real estate like any
other. This tension between the ideal and the real set out the parameters
of the increasingly contentious struggle for the woods.

Timber Profits

All this romantic talk about the woods should not blind us to the
economic role of the forest.[10] Indeed, it is hardly imaginable that late-
nineteenth-century Germany would be covered with as much forest as
it was, had there not been an economic incentive for its maintenance.
Roughly a quarter of German territory was wooded, producing about
fifty million cubic metres of wood annually and contributing a gross income of 430 million (and a net income of 200 million) marks to the
national economy in the 1890s. Prussian state forests, which generated 15 per cent of the nation's gross forestry income, alone employed
150,000 seasonal workers for a total of twelve million labour days.[11] With
one estimate of the German gross domestic product standing at 23.5 billion marks in 1895, the timber industry constituted about 2 per cent of
the entire national income.[12]

Beyond the income from raw timber, wood processing added to the
value of Germany's sylvan production. In the 1890s, woodworking industries employed some 600,000 carpenters, joiners, coopers, turners,
wainwrights, and workers in other trades, generating a further 500 million marks (or roughly 2 per cent of the gross national product) for
the German economy. Beyond those fashioning lumber into a variety of
products, other artisinal trades depended on wooden tools and imple-
ments. Shoemakers, artists, smiths, weavers, butchers, tanners, tailors,
and glassblowers, for example, all required wooden instruments to carry
out their crafts. Furthermore, tanners required resins drawn from wood
for their trade.[13]

Although the artisanal market for wooden tools gradually eroded during the nineteenth century, the industrial demand for timber more than
made up for the shortfall. While we might consider the nineteenth cen-

tury's economy increasingly founded on coal, iron, and steel, wood also played an important role in industry. The German railways required one million cubic metres of wooden railroad ties annually for repair and new construction, while at the turn of the century extending and maintaining electricity and telephone lines required large numbers of wooden poles. Mines consumed four million cubic metres of wood annually; one Zwickau mine alone purchased a quarter of a million marks of wood in one year, requiring delivery by 4,500 railroad flatcars. Ships, harbours, and river installations all required a great deal of wood, not to mention wood for the building trades. The paper industry, crucial to the expanding spheres of the mass media, education, and modern packaging, clearly depended on the forest. In 1912, one million cubic metres of wood shavings fed 600 pulp mills, 525 paper mills, and 406 cardboard factories throughout Germany, with half of the production concentrated in Saxony.[14] Overall, woodworking and paper manufacturing steadily occupied roughly 11 per cent of Germany's industrial workforce between 1871 and 1913, and comprised between 8 and 9 per cent of the total value of all manufacturing and construction output over that same period. Indeed, the Prussian state forests counted among the largest German employers.[15] Far from being an outmoded economic sector, timber, paper, and other wood products formed a vital and significant part of the modern German economy.

With wood a valuable commodity, foresters developed new techniques to increase production. Fear of a wood shortage (*Holznot*) in the late eighteenth century prompted cameralist states to find ways of maximizing production.[16] Foresters imposed new mathematical models on the woods, transforming the forest into statistical data that could be manipulated for greatest output. Their methods transformed the forest from an ecosystem into an abstract natural resource, 'imposing on disorderly nature the neatly arranged constructs of science.' With a greater knowledge of which trees provided the greatest amount of timber in the shortest amount of time under specific conditions, forestry experts began to reshape the woods. Fast-growing pines, some of them non-native species, proved most efficient, and large swaths of territory were given over to their production. Moreover, foresters eliminated all 'unproductive' plant life (and with it, many sylvan animals) and planted trees in grids for easier surveillance. For the forester, a new aesthetic arose that took 'geometric perfection as the outward sign of a well-managed forest.'[17] These changes allowed for the deskilling of sylvan labourers through the standardization of cutting procedures. It also required the exclusion of the peasantry, who in many places still maintained feudal use-rights (*Servituten*) to the woods, for 'unauthorized disturbances – whether by fire or by local populations – were seen as implicit threats to management routines.'[18] This new method of production, pioneered in Germany and emulated across the globe, required new legal standards regulating wooded property. The Field and Forest Law of 1880 attempted to address the needs of the state and landowners alike.

Sylvan Law

Landowners had long worked to eliminate peasant rights to the forest. Particularly in the western German lands, peasant communities had use-rights that emanated from ancient tradition. Peasants carved new farmland from the woods, grazed their animals there, and collected forest fruits and fodder for their livestock. Wood also figured prominently in the rural economy, being the source of building materials, chemicals (potash, tannins, resins, and turpentine), as well as, most importantly, fuel. Already with the dawn of feudalism in Germany, however, nobles began to appropriate the woods for themselves, restricting ancient communal use of the forests to codified use-rights. These use-rights gradually eroded over the centuries, as landlords placed ever greater limitations on peasant economic independence. This process culminated in the early nineteenth century, with the Stein-Hardenberg reforms liberalizing property law, eliminating several state-imposed restrictions on private forest management in an effort to transform wooded land into the absolute property of their owners. Forester Wilhelm Pfeil spearheaded efforts to dissolve use-rights on state and private lands through cash payments to peasants and communities.[19] At the same time, the state also moved to enhance the rights of property owners by criminalizing the removal of wood from the forests (now wood theft), often a product of peasants continuing to engage in traditional practices. Whereas Prussia's law code of 1794 (*Allgemeines Landrecht*) did not identify taking wood from others' property as a crime – given that 'popular opinion' held 'that the felling and transporting of uncut timber does not constitute theft' – by the 1820s the state's attitude had begun to change. In 1821 Prussia criminalized wood theft, and rigorous enforcement began in the 1830s, to landowners' satisfaction.[20]

This growing collaboration of the state and landlords only exacerbated the social tensions of the 1840s, exploding into violence in 1848, when long-simmering rural resentments unleashed violence on the woods.

Peasants, growing progressively angrier over the landowners' increasingly capitalistic attitude towards property, lashed out. They cut the nobles' timber, poached the lords' game, and torched the state's property.[21] Riehl observed that the forests always bore the brunt of rural uprisings, for 'the rebelling rural proletariat can build no barricades and tear down no royal castles; but it destroys instead of these the noble woods ... We saw in 1848 how [the rebels] obliterated – rather than plundered – the forest; one cut the forest down and intentionally left the timber to rot, or one burned it down, in order to force further concessions with every further acre burned.'[22]

This violent rural upheaval disturbed Riehl, whom the revolution had transformed from a liberal into a conservative supporter of the peasantry, and he therefore sought to shore up its crumbling foundation. In his *Land and People* – published in the early 1850s and based on his personal exploration of the countryside – Riehl identified the stabilizing elements of rural life in the hopes that state policy would reinforce them. In particular, Riehl believed communal uses of the forest were critical to forestalling peasant revolt. He correctly recognized the corrosive influence of the capitalist economy, with its principle of absolute property rights, as a major peasant grievance. Traditional communal rights to the woods remained intact in many parts of Germany, particularly in the west, and peasants violently protested their gradual dissolution in favour of the landlords. As Riehl put it, 'In German public opinion, the forest stands as the only great property that has not yet been entirely divided up. In contrast to fields, pastures, and gardens, everyone has a certain right to the forest, and it persists only in that he can walk around in it as he likes.' Indeed, the forest remained as the one part of the landscape that was still used communally, much as it had been for centuries. These communal rights Riehl regarded as 'the root of true German social conditions.' And these social conditions would, he hoped, preserve Germany from social upheaval, for 'a people that maintains open, communal forests beside fields enclosed in private possession not only has a present, but also a future.' Lands without such forests (in particular, England and France), Riehl asserted, would eventually decline, while heavily forested lands like Russia would prosper.[23]

Despite Riehl's dire warnings, both the state and private landowners sought to further strengthen the absolute nature of property rights. Over the course of the nineteenth century, the state bought up peasant use-rights to disencumber the land and had largely completed the task by the 1870s, with local rights to collect wood virtually eliminated throughout the country, and grazing rights remaining intact only in scattered upland areas. In the 1870s, forest experts demanded new legislation to counter the continuing popular notion that the woods were common property. A Bavarian forester complained of the prevailing 'folk consciousness' that determined wood theft could be no crime, as trees grew freely. This position was reinforced in law, he felt, as 'this popular belief has more or less been confirmed by nearly all the legislation so far.'[24] The Prussian forester Richard Hess likewise complained of the continuing popular belief in communal sylvan rights: 'Unfortunately such sylvan crimes are always considered in popular opinion as less punishable than other violations. "Wood and misfortune always grow," or the ingenuous pun "*Holt's* [get it]" (for *Holz* [wood]), or the Anglo-Saxon phrase "the axe is an alarm, not a thief," or the expression "the axe calls the forester," and similar characteristic folk sayings illustrate the ways in which the common man soothes his conscience with regard to his forest crimes.' Such crimes, Hess believed, were only encouraged by the continuing existence of legitimate *Servituten* to the woods, blurring as they did the boundaries of property rights. He recommended their abolition, along with stronger police measures, to put an end to these popular abuses.[25] But while collecting timber and grazing livestock in others' forests had largely been prohibited, one stubborn principle remained: the public's right to walk through the woods and, at least in practice, to collect mushrooms, berries, and other fruits of the forest.

The 1880 Field and Forest Law

Walking through the woods was the cornerstone of the forest ideology. How could Germans be expected to survive as a nation if they did not have recourse to the forests, Riehl would ask. This became an important sticking point in the debates over the 1880 Field and Forest Law, first submitted to the Prussian legislature, the *Landtag*, for approval in 1878. This coincided with a revival of conservative political fortunes arising from the economic crisis of the mid-1870s, during which timber prices fell alongside those for grain.[26] The Prussian state, as a major timber producer, quickly joined landlords in their demands for wood tariffs. Battle lines hardened between right and left. The House of Deputies (*Abgeordnetenhaus*) subjected the Field and Forest Law bill to serious scrutiny. The bill had originally been conceived to include more stringent punishment of wood theft, a principle that received little opposition. When Ministry of Agriculture officials early on recognized the storm brewing

over other provisions of the bill, which strengthened landowners' property rights, they extracted the portion governing wood theft and issued
it as a separate bill. The Forest Theft Law (*Forstdiebstahlgesetz*) passed in
1878 without significant contest, but it would be two more years before
the House of Deputies would approve Field and Forest Law.[27] It voted to
send the bill to committee in 1878, with no action taken before the end
of the session. Introduced again in 1879, the bill was repeatedly returned
to committee after contentious bouts in the lower house. In all, it went
through five drafts.

The major bone of contention in the Prussian parliamentary debate
was the provision permitting landowners to refuse anyone entry to their
wooded property – a major challenge to the sylvan freedom praised by
Riehl and his successors. This position found support largely among
East Elbian landlords in the house, leading a conservative insurgency
against liberal dominance. By contrast, those vocally supporting the public's right to the forest were drawn from a broader political, regional,
and professional spectrum. Ironically, it was a prominent forester and
moderate conservative, August Bernhardt, who set the tone for the opposition to the new regulations. Insisting on at least limited public access
to the woods, he intoned, 'The *Volk* must have certain inalienable and
eternal rights to the forest … that no law and no force of this earth can
withdraw from it.'[28] Liberals and many Catholics agreed with Bernhardt,
elaborating their own themes.

Liberals focused on what they regarded as the legal arbitrariness of the
bill, which they regarded as emblematic of Prussian authoritarianism.
Starting from the surprising position (for liberals) that 'it is a general
human right [*Menschenrecht*] to enjoy the surface of the earth,' urban
liberals from across Prussia complained landowners wanted to use the
law to harass 'the harmless stroller' who plucked a couple of flowers or
gathered a few berries.[29] Liberals seemed to agree, despite their general
belief in the sanctity of private property, that the public had a right of access to the woods, and any attempt to block it would violate a higher law.

This arbitrariness, many observed, stemmed from the selfishness of
large landowners. Although some of them supported the bill, Centre
delegates in particular regarded it as the creature of Prussia's great landholders and sought to remind them of their moral obligations. While
they recognized the need 'to protect landed and wooded property from
crime,' they complained the bill was based on the premise that 'the landowner does not have to worry about anyone,' and arose 'primarily out
of concern for game, fields, and forests.' Centre Party leaders reminded

estate owners 'that they should use their property in a Christian manner' and held out the hope that a solution based on 'practical, working Christianity' would take into account the needs of the poor.[30] Political Catholicism thus expressed qualms about the bill on moral grounds, although those on the right of the party ultimately chose to support it.

The centre and liberal parties advanced the notion that the bill was not only arbitrary and selfish, but also completely unfounded in German legal tradition and unsuited to property customs in many parts of the country. Indeed, one Centre delegate complained the bill stood 'in direct contradiction with the German *Volk*'s understanding of justice.' Landlords who insisted otherwise were subverting one of the foundations of rural life.[31] Westerners in particular resented the bill, for they perceived it as an effort by East Elbian Junkers to impose their own stark vision of rural landownership on the rest of Prussia. They contrasted the general western German 'popular freedom [*Volksfreiheit*]' with the more severe feudal regime imposed by medieval conquest east of the Elbe.[32] Representatives from heavily forested Hessia-Nassau, where the state owned over half of all forests, particularly resented the draft law, and dissent among Hessians even spread to the Conservative Party. One Hessian Conservative worried the bill's restrictions would cut off impoverished villages in his district from important sources of sustenance, such as collecting deadwood, grazing their livestock in the woods, and picking berries and mushrooms.[33]

This concern for (and about) the poor was echoed loudly by representatives of urban districts. Primarily urban liberals worried about the law's impact on workers should nearby woodlands be closed to them. With over half of all Germans living in largely squalid urban areas or working under deplorable industrial conditions, urban liberals argued, the forest played a vital role in public health and staunching working-class alienation.[34] For these liberals, woodlands offered a positive public space for the kind of rational recreation – active family life, abstinence from alcohol, healthy physical activity, and the potential for an education in aesthetics and the natural sciences – which liberals so desperately thought the working classes needed.

Besides its services to the poor, the liberal Alexander Meyer also stressed the importance of access to the forest for popular patriotism. German literature depended on it: 'Destroy the books that start with the assumption that one has a right to be free in the forest, and you eliminate our German national literature,' Meyer claimed. This literature had inspired his generation of liberal nationalists to agitate for a united

Germany, he argued, and 'without the impetuous patriotic pressure of the *Volk* there is no success for statesmen, and without our poets there would be no impetuous patriotic pressure that would have led to our successes. You put the axe to our national life if you prevent our poets to draw artistic inspiration from the forest.'[35] Thus national unification, far from simply being Bismarck's personal project, depended on a popular national movement inspired by the national memories resident in nature, Meyer insisted. Without access to the woods, he warned, enthusiasm for the nation would whither.

Vocal support for the proposed law came almost exclusively from Conservatives, most of whom were aristocratic East Elbian landowners, confirming the opposition's prejudices. Junkers particularly sought to combat the opposition's notion that reserved some exceptional legal status for the forests. Again and again, aristocratic estate owners proclaimed a liberal 'freedom of property,' deriding the notion that a stand of trees somehow changed the legal status of the ground they grew on. Moreover, they asserted, although the public believed it had a right to the woods, in point of fact, it did not.[36] For the Conservatives, property was property, pure and simple.

A few Conservative voices, significantly not those of landowners, tried to assuage public concerns over access with assurances that landlords would not prosecute the innocent.[37] Most, however, were hostile to any excursions on their property. One source of grievance was 'the flood of workers' associations,' whose members' 'ignorance, inattentiveness, and boisterousness' led to significant damage.[38] Another was the criminal, who might appear innocent, but was merely scoping out his prospects for a night-time raid.[39] Allowing public access to the forest, most landowning Conservatives implied, was merely an invitation to steal.

Besides the fear of theft, forest owners worried about the disruption of their hunting. Preserving game on their land often seemed a critical concern. Indeed, for many 'the profit from the forest consists mainly in exercising the noble art of hunting.' One Conservative landowner worried outsiders could come onto his land and drive the game elsewhere to be shot; another noted that the noisy and boisterous public disrupted this sport, venturing into the woods during the deer mating season, disturbing the reproduction cycle.[40] For many Conservatives, forests were almost worthless if they could not be sealed off from public intrusion.

The battle over the 1880 Prussian Field and Forest Law was not simply an affair of mushrooms and berries, timber and game. It was a battle over an important symbol. In the 1870s, liberals still laid claim to the

national idea, struggling to overcome the particularism of landed elites
and stitch a nation together, and the forest was an important symbolic
site for that work. But at the same time, the woods played an important
role for the nobility as well. Of course, timber was a source of income for
Prussia's landed elite. Interference with the strict routines of scientifically trained foresters threatened to undermine yields, many landowners
feared. However, profitability is only part of the story. For the majority
of landowners, wood was not a substantial source of income. Owners
of holdings under 800 hectares struggled to break even. Far more important for the Junkers were the social and symbolic functions of the
woods. Bismarck famously made much of sylvan myth; after his dismissal
in 1890, he held court at his Sachsenwald estate outside of Hamburg, en-
tertaining visitors as a country squire. Publicly styling himself as a 'wood
fool' (*Holznarr*) and sentimental steward of the forest, he reportedly had
difficulty turning a profit on his wooded estates because of his reluctance to cut old trees.[41] Other nobles similarly professed a deep affinity
for the woods. Like many bourgeois, nobles embraced the forest as a
retreat from the hectic life of urban modernity. Both groups enjoyed
the fresh air and physical exertion of the outdoors as healthy recreation.
But unlike much of the middle class, nobles experienced the forests not
through hiking, but through hunting. And hunting played a key role
in forging the social identity of Prussia's rural elites. The exhilaration
of the hunt, with its rites of passage, tests of skill, and elements of danger, evoked great passion among its adherents. Repeated victories over
nature reassured nobles of their status and appears to have functioned
as compensation for their loss of influence in the dynamic urban world.
Furthermore, hunts on noble estates, by invitation only, established
exclusive social networks, reinforced family relations, and provided a
venue for cultivating a collective identity.[42] With the hunt so central to
the identity of rural elites, bourgeois demands for access to the woods
appeared quite radical. To insist on the right of all Germans to the forest
was to challenge elite control over this symbolic space.

Despite vociferous opposition from many liberals and Catholics, the
bill passed to become the 1880 Field and Forest Law. But the law seemed
to satisfy no one. On the eve of its passage, Bismarck complained that
wooded property remained less protected from the public than other
kinds of property, and expressed concern for the potential damage done
to the 'terrifically important interests of landowners.'[43] Naturally, left
liberals used their opposition to the law, which they claimed 'brought
old, long-forgotten restrictions back to life and added new ones,' as a

campaign issue to attract rural votes.[44] At the same time, forest owners claimed to be frustrated by the lack of teeth in the new law. Landlords could order interlopers off their wooded property, but there was no punishment unless they resisted; even repeat offenders could not be charged with a crime. Those seeking to pick berries, mushrooms, or herbs needed to have a permit, but the lack of one did not result in any penalty.[45] The law did standardize the right of landowners to close their property to outsiders, but it does not seem that many took this opportunity; in the decades following the bill's passage, landowners continued to complain of a popular disrespect for their private property.

The Wood Tariff Debates

Although the discourse of the 'German forest' prevented conservatives from attaining everything they had hoped for in 1880 Field and Forest Law, they found it useful in at least one other context. When the Reichstag considered raising the tariff on lumber in 1883, conservatives mobilized the language of the 'German forest' to their own advantage. Remarkably, they did not appear to resort to this discourse when tariffs were first introduced in 1879, when government sources spoke of 'the preservation of German forest stocks [*Waldbestandes*].'[46] But by 1883, government press coverage of the debate frequently invoked the term and sought to turn the tables on the liberal opposition. For example, in March the official *Provinzial-Correspondenz* cited a speech by a senior forestry official that identified tariffs as critical for 'the preservation of the German forest.' The paper then turned to describe all the positive economic, environmental, and social benefits of the forest that the opponents of the 1880 Field and Forest Law had cited, including the collection of berries, which Prussian conservatives had worked so hard to restrict.[47] Liberal opponents again characterized this law as only 'for the benefit of the large landowner.'[48] When in May the new tariff was defeated, the *Provinzial-Correspondenz* fretted over 'the preservation of the German forest.' The declining value of wood, the paper claimed, meant maintaining forests would become unprofitable. 'With this decision,' it continued, 'the demise of the German forest has been announced and the way has been opened for immeasurable national damage.'[49]

Conservatives were not satisfied to abandon things as they stood. Again in 1885, the government introduced lumber tariff legislation in the Reichstag, and again the rhetoric of the German forest was deployed to sway at least elite opinion, this time more floridly than before.

Whereas the official press had relied primarily on economic arguments in defence of the woods in 1883, two years later it was willing to adopt more romantic and nationalist language to get its point across. An article entitled 'Protect the German Forest' in the official *Neueste Mittheilungen* opened with the line 'the German forest has become dear to the heart of the German *Volk*,' and argued that it was a 'national duty' to protect it. While identifying the economic benefits of raising the tariff, the article claimed the measure would save 'the forest for the German *Volk*.' Indeed, new tariffs would preserve existing woodlands and promote the planting of new ones, 'so that in the interest of the German nation the German forest is preserved as an inheritance from our ancestors and a bequest to later generations.'[50] This overheated rhetoric may have had an effect; the Reichstag agreed to raise the tariff in May 1885.[51] Although this did not stanch the ever-increasing flow of foreign wood into Germany, Conservatives showed they could muster the forest discourse for their own cause as well.

Social Reformers

While Conservatives called for new lumber tariffs to protect the German forest, advocates of urban social reform continued to call for public access to the woods, even as the debates of the 1870s faded from public memory. Although a growing segment of the urban middle class had access to nature through suburbanization and holiday excursions, many authors contended, the working class remained out of touch with the world outside the city. The workers, trapped in musty rental barracks (*Mietskasernen*) and noisy factories, needed a temporary reprieve from their living and working conditions in order to 'refresh' themselves in nature. Already in 1869, the forester and parliamentarian August Bernhardt recommended that workers be offered the opportunity 'to go on a walk on Sunday with wife and child out in the fresh nature of the forest, from which he surely will return home healthier and better, more satisfied and happier to work than from the bar [*Branntweinkneipe*], which would otherwise have been the goal of his Sunday outing.' Bernhardt noted that the industrial cities of Elberfeld, Barmen, and Wuppertal, along with private individuals, were working to expand public forests for working-class recreation. He cheerfully greeted the news that thousands of workers and their families had been spending their Sundays in the woods, praising 'the morally improving influence of walks rich in the pure pleasures of fresh nature,' which apparently already had an influence on the region.[52] He thus optimistically imagined that the woods could forestall working-class alienation.

Although years of spreading urbanization, industrialization, and socialist party membership may have undermined this kind of optimism, several bourgeois authors clung to the belief that forests could address these challenges. In 1887, the liberal social reformer Karl Viktor Böhmert bemoaned the physical and social decay of Germany's cities. While medieval peasants once fled oppression in the countryside to breathe 'free city air,' now the children of farmers seeking their fortune encountered only 'poverty and misery, sin and shame.' The only way to counteract these odious influences, he proposed, was not simply providing urban access to forests, but resettling workers in the wooded areas within commuting distance of factories. In addition to producing longer-living and calmer workers, this rural lifestyle would also ensure they were 'more satisfied' with their lot (that is, less revolutionary).[53] Nature, in such formulations, formed a bulwark against revolution, soothing agitated nerves and removing some of the immediate sources of discontent.

The fear of revolution came through strongly in an article by forestry professor Lorenz Wappes, 'On the Aesthetic Meaning of the Forest,' from the same year. 'The forest is in a position, through its inscrutable mechanisms, to contribute to the solution of the great cultural problems of our time,' he asserted. Wappes observed that the Germans were losing touch with nature as peasants migrated to the cities to find factory jobs. This alienation from nature, he contended, threatened to tear apart the German social fabric. Echoing Bernhardt, Wappes argued that walking through the forest was healthier and less expensive than visits to the local tavern, noting it 'diminishes drunken excesses' and 'promotes family life, which is not possible in the bar.' Moreover, it reduced social radicalism. Wappes compared the industrial labourer with his woodland counterpart, 'who because of heavy forest labour lives under much more miserable conditions than any factory worker,' yet did not participate in strikes or other unrest. Taking a page from Reihl, Wappes favourably contrasted German lumberjacks with the labourers of 'the forestless lands of England and Belgium,' which 'have long been hotbeds of such agitation.' Thus forests apparently contributed not only to worker efficiency, but also to the 'contentedness' of the labourer. Without access to forests, he postulated, one had to fear the society 'dissolving into its elements,' that is, class warfare. Wappes thus urgently called for 'the facilitation of healthy outdoor recreation, especially in the forest, and the direction of the thoughts [of the worker] as well as the little man –

whose mind would otherwise remain solely on work – to the beauty and sublimity of nature.'[54] The woods offered everyone the opportunity to experience natural splendour, whose 'meaning, and thus also its effect – at least to a limited degree – is also accessible to the uneducated, and … its powerful influence works even when it is unintended and unsuspected.' Workers, who could not appreciate high art, Wappes contended, could certainly recognize the loveliness of a group of trees. And given Germany's abundance of forests, 'visiting [the woods] is unlimited and free, so that everyone, even those of little means, can take advantage of its benefits.'[55] More than cultural institutions, then, forests could provide cultural, spiritual, and moral elevation for those of little education and few resources.

Besides alleviating social tensions, authors starting in the 1880s also drew attention to the health benefits of the forests. Many regarded woodlands as a source of healthy air, in contrast with the polluted atmosphere of the city. An 1889 article in the popular *Gartenlaube* insisted that those who spend the winter months in the musty confines of the city required 'a few weeks of the pleasant summertime in God's free nature in order to escape the oppressive, dusty, and disease-bearing city air and to refresh and strengthen [themselves] in the fresh forest, meadow, and mountain air.' The author approvingly remarked on the growing numbers of urbanites – including impoverished children dispatched by charities – seeking a healthy environment during their holidays, stressing that 'the summer vacation must offer above all pure air, healthy soil, and positive levels of vegetation.'[56] Many regarded forest air as particularly clean; since the early nineteenth century, scientists had demonstrated that forests infused the air with more oxygen and filtered out 'damaging gasses, smoke, dust, [and] bacteria cells.'[57] Another author cited studies of cholera epidemics in India that indicated villages surrounded by forests were less susceptible to the disease.[58] Thus forests offered an antidote to some of the environmental problems posed by increasing urbanization.

While some researchers remained sceptical of the magnificently salubrious effects of forest air, none denied nature's positive psychological impact on the urbanite. Forestry professor Adam Schwappach, who criticized what he regarded as an unbridled enthusiasm for the health effects of forest air, did endorse the woods as an antidote to urban stress. 'The nerve-shattering unrest of the cities in connection with the rapidly increasing intensity of work makes a periodical break an absolute necessity,' he claimed, 'and where better to find this than in the majestic peace of the forest, which in this regard can only be compared to the

endless ocean!' Wooded areas, because of their aesthetic value, soothed
the rattled nerves of modern men, Schwappach asserted. So while he
acknowledged that 'the German preference for the forest ... has led
to many equally well-intentioned and beautiful-sounding effusions and
contentions that do not stand up under a cool assessment,' Schwappach
conceded that the forest 'has an extremely beneficial and highly important social function in the whole development of our modern life.'[59]
Healthy air therefore did not stand alone as a reason for public access
to the woods.

Echoing Schwappach, many reformers insisted on the positive social
effects of the woods. In contrast to agrarian romantics, these authors embraced the forest as a suitable retreat from the rigours of city life, but not
the negation of it. Nature, and the forest in particular, provided a temporary refuge from urban stress (or 'nervousness,' as it was often called),
conveying restorative powers to those engaged in the ongoing struggles
of the professional world.[60] In this conception, the forest played an important role in the modern economy, returning the bourgeoisie, and
eventually also the working classes, to work refreshed and reinvigorated.
Already in 1871, one article described the woods as a 'nerve-strength-
ening institution of natural healing' for the urban denizen.[61] But it was
not until after the turn of the century, and the burgeoning of cities and
new technologies that accompanied it, that interest in the forest as a
respite from urban stress blossomed. Urban parks, one nature enthusiast noted in 1900, were an 'emergency measure' to soothe the nerves
of a population long alienated from the countryside.[62] A 1905 forestry
handbook proclaimed that the woods became increasingly important as
'the nervous and material life of individuals and peoples are all the more
shaped by the struggle for economic existence.'[63] A government official
contended in 1907 that forests were increasingly popular because they
counteracted the rising levels of urban stress: 'The upheaval and exhaus-
tion of life in the metropolis demands rest and relaxation in the outdoors. It is especially the forest – which raises the heart and spirit above
common everydayness, over the cares and worries of life – that allows us
to return to our professional duties armed with new vigour. Its physical
influence, as well as the psychic impressions it offers, regenerates blood
and nerves.'[64] The prominent Social Democrat and former editor of the
socialist *Vorwärts*, Heinrich Ströbel, likewise insisted that forests required
preservation, especially near cities, because 'the recreational needs of a
large part of the population will always increase the more our modern
economic system creates an industrial population and the more the rush

and intensity of the earning one's daily bread, the modern economic life, the modern lifestyle, strains the nerves.' As citizens of a modern industrial state, Ströbel argued, Germans required relief in nature. The expansion of cities demanded 'that sufficient sites for recuperation for the industrial population be preserved in the form of our forests.'[65] Thus for several authors, forests served as an important element in modern industrial society, ensuring the ability of urbanites of all classes to function efficiently on the job.

As in the discussion of nervousness, after the turn of the century authors stressed the importance of the woods for healing all of society. Rather than simply being a blanket that could suffocate the flames of revolution, the forest was now conceived as a tent in which all classes could congregate to overcome social tensions in their shared appreciation of nature. Already in the early nineteenth century, bourgeois strollers understood the woods as a place where the classes mixed.[66] This fact seemed to take on renewed social importance in the decade preceding the First World War, as some reformers sought to combat the growing rifts between classes with social reconciliation. A 1905 article from a Berlin hiking journal extolled the virtues of woodland excursions, opening the eyes of hikers to the lives of others: 'One is freed from the false impressions.... The contact with people of all classes and estates creates better means of communication.'[67] In a society increasingly fragmented by class, the forest at least seemed one common interest upon which everyone (except perhaps the landlords) could agree.

The problems of urban alienation and social fragmentation also concerned Konrad Guenther, an ornithologist at the University of Freiburg and nature enthusiast. Like Wappes and others, he believed in the power of the forest to ameliorate social tensions. Yet Guenther pushed Wappes's argument even further, arguing woodland strolls could bring about social reconciliation and human solidarity. Guenther felt city life and its diversions exacerbated class tensions: 'The pleasures of the city are for the most part accessible only to the well-to-do, and the [social] contrasts stand out most crassly there,' he observed. As a moderating alternative, of course, Guenther proposed a turn to nature, which offered free access to all, while culture depended on social distinctions and exclusion: cultivating a taste for art or music required too much money, while an interest in poetry or history demanded too much time. The people, Guenther stated, needed some other source of inspiration, something that stressed human ideals but did not 'raise the distinctions between rich and poor before the eyes.' Nature, whether considered from the scientific or aesthetic angle, seemed to offer a significant alternative, apparently devoid of social distinction. A walk in the woods required no fee, so 'here there is no distinction between high and low, rich and poor. Nature is the mother of all people in the same way.' Thus, he concluded, 'only before nature are we human.'[68]

Although none of these authors directly addressed the debates surrounding the 1880 Field and Forest Law, they illustrated that many of the arguments made during those debates continued to be relevant; indeed, they were taking on greater importance with the advancing alienation of urbanites from nature. Perhaps one reason for the public silence concerning the law itself was its fundamental ambivalence and ambiguity. Without a clear-cut success for either conception of property, the law was apparently quickly forgotten. Further evidence came in 1906, when the press debated access to the forest. Although the majority of legal scholars regarded the matter as clearly settled, newspapers throughout Prussia espoused widely conflicting interpretations of the law.

Forest Law in the Newspapers

Although the 1880 Field and Forest Law had received little public discussion during the generation after its passage, the debate erupted with renewed force in the summer of 1906, when newspapers throughout Prussia focused their attention on the issue. National and local papers took legal and political stands, asserting conflicting interpretations. As in the parliamentary debates of the late 1870s, left liberals supported public access while Conservatives opposed it. National Liberals, however, reflecting their drift to the right, were now divided over the issue. The 1906 newspaper skirmish also witnessed the introduction of new voices to the debate. Radical nationalists and agrarian reformers increasingly demanded public access to the woods, splitting the right between those who defended landowners' property rights and those who stressed the rights of the nation.

The *Magdeburger Zeitung,* a National Liberal paper, touched off the dispute by publishing an article insisting, 'Neither the *Fiskus* nor other forest owners have the right to close forest paths.' Across town, the rival *Magdeburger Generalanzeiger* responded by stressing that trespassers in forests with posted warnings were liable to fines or imprisonment according to the 1880 Field and Forest Law. Local papers in other Prussian cities quickly took up the debate: in deepest East Prussia, Gumbinnen's Conservative *Preußisch-Littauische Zeitung* derided the *Magdeburger Zeitung* for its conclusions. Within days, the debate spread to the national press, with conservative papers in particular leading the charge against the public's right to the woods. The Free Conservative *Die Post* questioned the *Magdeburger Zeitung*'s judgment, while the Conservative *Hamburger Nachrichten* ridiculed the Magdeburg newspaper for positing a 'co-ownership of real estate by the public ... that does not legally exist.' Citing these conservative papers' critiques, the illustrated hunting journal *Wild und Hund* likewise supported the prerogatives of landowners, reaffirming their right to prosecute trespassers and accusing the Magdeburg paper of inciting the public to trespass. After all, *Wild und Hund* warned, those disregarding No Trespassing signs placed themselves at risk of injury or death in a hunting accident, for which the landowner legally could (and should) not be held accountable. Echoing the magnanimous gentry of 1880, it intoned, 'The liberality of the great forest owners towards the public has always been so great that one can only be thankful for it.' *Die Post* and the *Schlesische Zeitung* subsequently published similar articles, underlining the conservatives' commitment to this stance, and they were soon joined by two local National Liberal papers, the *Liegnitzer Tageblatt* and Wiesbaden's *Rheinische Courier*, which entered the debate in the last week of July, defending the rights of property owners.[69]

Following the conservative press campaign against the *Magdeburger Zeitung*, other liberal papers came to its defence. Towards the end of July, the National Liberal *Dortmunder Zeitung* published a bitter complaint from a woman who was fined three marks (and threatened with a day in prison) for guiding forty 'ailing patients in need of recreation' through a private forest and collecting about fifteen berries. A few days later, the left-liberal *Königsberger Hartungsche Zeitung* argued that neither the state nor private parties had the right to close forest paths, and that harmless hikers could legally wander where they liked in the woods. Defending the local tourist trade, the National Liberal *Hannoverscher Courier* reported the rising number of complaints from hikers about the 'systematically conducted and unjust closure of forest paths, in certain cases even whole forests, particularly in the Harz, to public traffic.' The *Courier* concluded such bans were illegal. The pre-eminent left-liberal *Berliner Tageblatt* weighed in by mid-August, reproducing an article from the hunting journal *Hubertus*, which reported that neither the police nor private landowners could legally ban the public from the woods. Less unequivocal was the left-liberal *Breslauer Zeitung*, which warned against what it regarded as some of the fallacies in the *Magdeburger Zeitung*'s argument. Yet at the same time, the Breslau paper bemoaned the closing of many local forests to the public: 'In Silesia, the public is kept in check by No Trespassing signs, as if all the people seeking light and air in God's beautiful nature behaved like wild animals, going out into the forest to do nothing other than perpetrate mischief and damage.'[70] Liberals continued to assert public access to the woods over the prerogatives of landowners.

Interestingly, two right-wing papers also supported public access to the woods. The *Deutsche Tageszeitung*, organ of the Agrarian League (*Bund der Landwirte*), reported the growing number of public complaints about forest closures around Berlin. Surprisingly, the *Tageszeitung* sympathized with the Berliners, arguing that harmless hikers could enter any Prussian forest and that neither the state nor private landowners had the right to close the woods to trespassers. Friedrich Lange's radical nationalist *Deutsche Zeitung* published a gloomy commentary by a judge who grumbled, 'We see that the forest and its inhabitants are surrounded, as if by a wall, by an abundance of legal sanctions, and this without the possibility of objection to individual regulations.'[71] Interestingly, the right-wing critique of the 1880 regulations was not perceptibly different from the liberal one. How did agrarian reformers and radical nationalists come to embrace the public's right to the woods?

Agrarian Reformers

Agrarian reformers came from a variety of political backgrounds, but they agreed on the necessity of shoring up the peasantry in the face of competition from abroad and the spectre of socialism at home. This often meant an attack on the dominance of conservative aristocratic landlords in the countryside. From the 1870s onward, figures as diverse as Lujo Brentano, Georg Friedrich Knapp, Friedrich Naumann, and Max Weber on the left, and Johannes Miquel, Max Sering, Adolph Wagner, and Alfred Hugenberg on the right engaged in wide-ranging discussions of how best to shore up rural Germany, often under the umbrella of the Association for Social Policy (*Verein für Sozialpolitik*). Rather than being simple tools of elite landowners, as those on the right of this group often have been portrayed in the *Sonderweg* scholarship, these agrarian reformers proposed wholesale land reform, particularly in the Prussian east, to create a class of independent farmers that would serve as a political bulwark (whether liberal or conservative) against the growing socialism of Germany's industrial working class.[72] Wagner in particular advocated the nationalization of all Germany's forests, stripping private owners of control over this vital environmental and economic resource.[73] Such plans necessitated the dismantling of landed estates, and naturally Prussia's Junkers resisted such proposals as stubbornly as they defended their woods. Beyond land reform, agrarian activists on both left and right proposed other measures to ameliorate the plight of the rural poor, central among them being the effort to secure peasant access to the forests.

The importance of the forest for rural life led agrarian reformers to criticize large landowners and the state for their attempts to exclude the people from it. Primary among them was Heinrich Sohnrey, a disciple of Riehl and a former teacher from a peasant background. The discovery in 1890 that Germany's rural population had declined in number since national unification alarmed him, and he sought to reform farming conditions in order to combat the dissolution of rural life and the rise of working-class radicalism. For agrarian reformers like Sohnrey, preserving the peasantry in a rapidly modernizing economy meant preserving peasant use-rights. They worried that peasants without access to the forest would become impoverished, driven into the cities, where they would become fodder for the Socialists. Therefore, Sohnrey and his supporters challenged the trend towards a more restrictive interpretation of property legislation and proposed instead measures that would alleviate rural poverty.

In 1893, a year of agrarian political insurgency, Sohnrey launched his Committee for the Cultivation of Rural Welfare and *Heimat* (*Ausschuß für ländliche Wohlfahrts- und Heimatpflege*) – along with his journal *Das Land* – at an early meeting of the right-wing agricultural interest group, the Agrarian League (whose paper in 1906 would endorse public access to the woods).[74] He hoped the rural middle classes, in particular teachers, pastors, landholders, and agricultural officials, could effect a program of rural reform, making peasant farming more economically viable. This social group indeed dominated his organization (after 1900 renamed the German Association for the Cultivation of Rural Welfare and *Heimat*), making up half the membership in 1905.[75] The main body of Sohnrey's organization grew by leaps and bounds, rising from 926 members in 1905 to 8,821 by 1913, along with another 15,287 organized in local branches. Mounting concern over Social Democratic penetration of the countryside around 1909 moved the small-town middle class to address rural poverty; Sohnrey's association therefore sponsored the creation of a Christian trade union for agricultural labourers.[76] He also played an important role in the foundation of the national League for *Heimat* Protection (*Bund Heimatschutz*), an umbrella organization

uniting diverse local efforts.[77] Along with the advancing size of his movement, Sohnrey commanded a series of periodicals addressing a broad
range of rural concerns, from inner colonization and rural pastoral
care to the development of agricultural industries and the promotion
of greater educational opportunities for rural youth.[78] With all of these
activities, Sohnrey stood at the nexus of the agrarian reform movement.

Forests played an imperative part in the reforms Sohnrey hoped to
enact. In the guides to agricultural policy he published after the turn of
the century, Sohnrey repeatedly stressed the importance of the woods
for the peasant economy. Farmers depended on the forest for fuel, building materials, and supplements to their diets, he declared, echoing the
Junkers' opponents from the debate over the 1880 Field and Forest Law.
For the individual peasant, or for rural communities, planting a grove
of trees could serve as a kind of 'compulsory piggy bank,' into which
they could invest their time and energy, and which could yield needed
income in times·of agricultural crisis. And such small copses scattered
through the countryside could improve local agriculture by reducing
winds and improving soil moisture. Moreover, they could also provide
work during the winter, a time when many peasants had less to do since
abandoning hand threshing. Winter labour in the woods afforded hard-
pressed farmers with an additional source of income, obviating the need
for seasonal factory work in the cities. Women and children could also
join in the effort, collecting fallen wood (*Leseholz*) for fuel, as well as
mushrooms and berries for home consumption or sale. Sohnrey appreciated their contribution to the peasant economy, noting that the roughly
four million cubic metres of *Leseholz* (valued at 8,000,000 marks) collected in Germany each year probably satisfied the fuel needs of 40,000 families. The Province of Hanover, he observed, estimated the annual berry
harvest at 435,000 marks, while village of Frammersbach in the Spessart
alone earned 3–4,000 marks from its harvest.[79] Forests therefore offered
several means of sustaining and stabilizing the rural economy, if only
peasants could maintain their access to them.

Sohnrey's journal illustrated the problems plaguing rural communities, including limits on forest use-rights. Writing in *Das Land*, Pastor Adolf Korell – a left-liberal associate of the leading social reformer
Friedrich Naumann – reported in 1902 that the Grand Duchy of Hessia
was gradually stripping his village of Königstädten (near Mainz) of its
traditional forest rights, threatening to 'proletarianize' its inhabitants.[80]
Roughly one thousand villagers, mostly peasants and artisans (but also
including some factory workers) lived in what Korell regarded as 'a quiet

farming village with a pleasing social character,' that is, almost all lived in their own house and owned a plot of land, and few migrated to or from the community. The basis for this stability, he felt, 'is our right to the forest,' citing the many ways the woods were 'closely intertwined' with village life. But the community owned only a small part of these woods; the rest belonged to the Hessian state. Traditionally villagers could collect firewood 'as needed' on certain days in certain seasons and could cut down trees for a small fee. Furthermore, villagers' livestock were permitted to graze in two-thirds of the forest during the summer. But state authorities now demanded a fee for collecting wood and reduced the area open to livestock, proposing ultimately to end these practices altogether. While some argued that the forest actually belonged to the village and not the state, Korell dismissed this argument as 'irrelevant.' The local damage caused by the loss of traditional rights, he averred, trumped the state's rights as landowner, regardless of how 'social democratic' this proposition sounded. 'We don't want to be "proletarianized"' Korell insisted. 'Rather, we want to remain people with a feeling for the *Heimat* and a firm hold on payments in kind.'[81] Agrarian reformers thus attempted to defend rural customs against the foresters' rationalization of the landscape by claiming their abolition would result in a serious disruption of traditional peasant life.

Yet the agrarian reformers were swimming against the tide. Over at least the last century, changes to property rights had in many places eliminated or restricted peasant access to the woods. In the Middle Ages, Sohnrey noted, common use-rights to the forest stood as an 'especially characteristic feature of German property law.' But nobles had usurped those rights, moving from an equal member of the sylvan community to an outright owner. Many of those communal forests that had survived into the nineteenth century suffered from the Enclosure Act (*Gemeinheitsteilungs-Ordnung*) of 1821, he complained. Hence, Sohnrey maintained, 'here too the little man must again carry the burden of suffering.' The right to collect deadwood remained, but the state soon moved to abolish this right as well. In many places, landowners now profited from the rising cost of wood, charging peasants for a commodity they once gathered for free. Such exploitation unleashed a 'war over the woods,' most recently enacted by peasants in the Oberpfalz during their bloody standoff with the Bavarian army at Fuchsmühl in 1894. Even with the evidence of damage to peasant communities, the states continued to back landowners' prerogatives. When a senior Agrarian League functionary called on Prussia to devote funds to the establishment of more communal forests in 1900, the minister of agriculture tellingly evaded the request by aver-ring, 'Above all, the devastation of the forest by the intrusion on private property rights must also be prevented.'[82] Landlords and the Ministry of Agriculture, in Sohnrey's understanding, stood together in defence of absolute property at the expense of peasant welfare.

This defence of liberal property rights came under attack by Franz Hoermann, who published a work on deforestation at the instigation of Sohnrey's association. In it, he bemoaned the loss of Germany's for-ests, particularly those in private hands, further accusing conservative deputies of being 'unconsciously infected' with 'liberal economic ideas,' leading them to assert absolute property rights for the 'greater private exploitation' of the woods. Indeed, he argued – reflecting the irony of the discourse that emerged in the 1880 Field and Forest Law debates – that the '"Manchesterite" left' (the free-trade left liberals) had become a greater friend of the forest than the so-called '"conservative" right.' Al-though he conceded that very large estates generally did manage forests properly for the long term, the most secure forests were to be found in state and communal hands. Although agrarian reformers, like the con-servative economist Adolph Wagner, had called for the nationalization of forests for their protection and long-term security, Hoermann pre-ferred municipal or cooperative ownership of forests instead.[83] Only in this way, he felt, could the devastation of private forests be stopped and rural life secured. Far from being agents of agricultural elites, Sohnrey and his movement represented the rural middle class in their efforts to shore up life in the countryside, challenging landlord interests.

While agrarians stressed forests' meaning for rural communities, this argument could not prevail alone. In an industrializing society, where urban concerns began to outweigh rural ones, where liberals generally scorned the reinstitution of feudal rights, and where the Junker elite often defined rural interests, agrarian reformist demands for a restora-tion of peasant use-rights fell on many deaf ears. Rhetoric of 'national property,' originally inspired by nationalists but eventually appropriated by a politically disparate forces opposed to the Junkers, became another important strategy.

National Property

Alongside agrarian reformism emerged another discourse challenging Junker domination of the landscape – likewise inspired by Riehl – this time from an aesthetic and nationalist perspective. Already present from the 1870s, language describing the woods as national property began to gain wider currency around the turn of the century. Nationalists of various stripes revived the notion that the public had a fundamental right to the woods, but in contrast to the agrarian reformers, who emphasized the economic importance of forests for local communities, they stressed the nation's need for contact with nature. Beyond simply extolling the virtue of hikes through the woods, however, they challenged state and private efforts to close some land to the public, claiming forests to be national property co-owned by the public. This challenge to landowners' authority, like that posed by agrarian reformism, fit neatly neither on the left nor right. Instead, it emanated from a critique of capitalism, along with the liberals and conservatives who embraced it.

As the debate over the 1880 law illustrated, the notion that Germany's forests were 'common property' was widespread. Forest historians, at least since the middle of the century, had documented the ancient Germanic custom of communal forest use. Communal forests in this sense had almost completely disappeared, as conservative landowners liked to remind the public, but this precedent fed the hopes of many nature enthusiasts and peasants, who continued to insist on their rights to the woods. Growing scientific evidence underscoring the forest's role in the environment added to this perception of the woods as common property.[84] Matthias Jakob Schleiden, a biologist and liberal, penned a call for forest protection in 1870 that condemned Roman law, the nobility's historic monopoly on hunting, and monarchical greed in seizing the common property of the people, arguing, 'All the drawbacks that deforestation causes for the state, its inhabitants, and their well-being, are rooted in the quality of forests as private property.' He called instead for its nationalization for the common good.[85] In an 1872 book arguing for sylvan conservation, a Bavarian forester listed the many agricultural, climatic, and health benefits of the woods, concluding, 'The forest is therefore the common property [Gemeingut] of all in the best sense of the word, and it has an immeasurable value for everyone. It is the most important factor in the entire balance of nature and mankind.'[86] In 1877, an Austrian geographer issued an early environmental appeal entitled 'Protect the Forest' in a popular science journal. He chided the state for not taking tough measures to protect forests from rampant exploitation, and insisted that 'the entire Volk ... maintain as holy the forest as an inalienable property of the country [Gut des Landes], a possession to whose natural use all generations have an equal right.'[87] The Prussian nature-protection advocate Hugo Conwentz repeated these words verbatim in his own appeal in 1883.[88] A rhetoric was beginning to emerge even before the passage of the 1880 Field and Forest Law that cast forests, regardless of their legal owners, as the common property of the public.

After the passage of the Field and Forest Law, those seeking to protect Germany's woodlands took a more strident tone. Over the course of the next few decades, the chorus of opposition to the nearly absolute right of landowners to dispose of their forests as they wished grew louder. A number of factors came together to encourage this trend. As in the *Landtag* debates, agrarian reformers and romantics worried about peasant impoverishment as a result of the bill, while advocates for the urban poor worried selfish landowners would deny desperate workers fresh air. In addition to these voices, *Heimat* enthusiasts added new aesthetic concerns. For this constituency, dismay at the corrosive effects of Germany's burgeoning commercial and industrial economy to the landscape dovetailed with agrarian reformers' arguments. Ernst Rudorff in particular saw the 1880 legislation as part of the larger tendency towards the commodification of German society, which destroyed the aesthetic and moral character of the landscape, undermined social solidarity, and tore Germany from its national roots in nature.

Although historians have failed to note it, the *Heimat* protection movement in Germany owed its beginnings in part to the debates over the 1880 Field and Forest Law. Ernst Rudorff, a musicologist and the founder of the prominent League for *Heimat* Protection (*Bund Heimatschutz*), first publicly proposed his ideas for a general protection of Germany's cultural landscape in 1878, as the debates got underway.[89] He again issued an appeal in an 1880 article entitled 'On the Relationship of Modern Life to Nature,' making explicit reference to the struggle in the *Landtag* over the proposed regulations. Above all, Rudorff – like Sohnrey, a disciple of Riehl – rejected the capitalist transformation of landscape into little more than a source of profits and denounced the growing wave of nature tourism sweeping Germany, which he perceived was animated not by a desire to commune with nature, but by the lust to consume it. At the same time, Rudorff decried the accompanying rationalization of the countryside. Farmers and foresters, eager to capitalize on new methods, razed hedges and copses, straightened streams, and expunged unwanted plants and creatures to create monotonous monocultures, destroying the traditional varied landscape in a search for profits.[90] Simultaneously, they cleared away the traditional social relations, dismissing the shepherd in favour of wire fences and terminating peasant use-rights to the woods in favour of lump-sum payments.

This instrumental relationship with nature, Rudorff worried, would soon be enshrined in law; as he understood it, the Field and Forest Bill aimed to prevent the poor from picking berries and mushrooms in the forest and limit Germans' freedom to walk in the woods. While not wanting to undermine landowners' control over their property, Rudorff protested the *Landtag*'s efforts, lamenting, 'The ideal co-ownership [*Mitbesitz*] of God's earth – which belongs to all by virtue of their humanity, and which finds its most beautiful expression in the freedom to enter the forest – will be abolished by those legal paragraphs, and this is a kick in the heart of the German *Volk*.' By asserting a popular spiritual co-ownership of the German countryside, Rudorff hoped to use national sentiments to overcome the individual's absolute property rights. In this case, he insisted on public access: 'I want to have the right, in the world and above all in my *Heimat*, to place my foot and to breathe in the living air and joy where my heart desires, and I want to neither damage nor disturb my neighbour's pleasure in his property.' Rudorff feared a countryside inaccessible to the German people, especially the German workers, cutting them off from the healthy pleasures that would create a self-conscious *Volk* and forestall revolution. He therefore chided the Prussian *Landtag*'s Conservatives for failing to understand the revolution in law they were perpetrating, and suggested that their actions – a boon to the recently banned Social Democrats, he believed – would provoke a social revolution in turn.[91] Like Riehl and Sohnrey, Rudorff wanted to save Germany from the ravages of capitalism but found the Conservative leadership of the country too beholden to the capitalist system to do the job.

In a speech in 1892 – just a year before Sohnrey founded his Committee for the Cultivation of Rural Welfare and *Heimat* – Rudorff again denounced the advancing commercialization and rationalization of the countryside, chastising tourist and agricultural interests alike for seeking to maximize profits at the expense of ruining rural charm and stability. The commodification of the landscape, he warned, was an 'extremely dangerous game' with serious social consequences. Rudorff regarded the dissolution of forest use-rights as 'such a radical attack on the entire historical development of rural relations' that he felt it 'loosens the roots of social and ethical life.' Landowners, he complained, were consumed with increasing their crop yields, all the while ignoring the social impact of their efforts. For Rudorff, however, 'the socio-political point of view is undoubtedly the more important!'[92] He charged such disregard for rural tradition with 'more and more ruin[ing] and finally destroy[ing] the holy property of the entirety of the people.'[93] Rudorff's strategy here, as a decade before, was to invoke the public's right to the landscape, identifying it as an idealized national property to which all Germans had some claim. As a member of the cultural elite, Rudorff understood his task as safeguarding the national patrimony from unscrupulous exploitation.

Heinrich von Salisch, a Silesian nobleman and another adherent of Riehl, regarded his project in a similar way. He developed the field of 'forest aesthetics,' considering it the duty of forest owners and managers to create greater sylvan beauty for public enjoyment. While directly referring to neither the 1880 regulations nor Rudorff, Salisch's contribution fit neatly into this context. In his 1885 book *Forest Aesthetics*, Salisch stated in language reminiscent of Rudorff's 1880 article that 'not everyone can own a forest, but the wonderful thing about the enjoyment of beauty is that one who surrenders oneself to this pleasure and shares the joy with the owner feels in a certain way to be a co-owner [*Mitbesitzer*].' Thus Salisch wanted to promote among the public the sense that they had a right to enjoy the woods. Elaborating further, he quoted Field Marshall Helmuth von Moltke: 'For he who enjoys, owns, and can an owner do more?' Encouraging enjoyment of the landscape promoted a feeling of common ownership of the forests, Salisch contended, and thus a common identity. 'As every Silesian speaks of the beauties of "our" Riesengebirge,' he noted, 'so the German considers himself as a co-owner [*Miteigentümer*] of the German forest.'[94] Aesthetically pleasing woodlands could thus promote a relationship with nature, and through it, the nation.

Neither Rudorff nor Salisch had much luck in attracting widespread attention to their campaigns to preserve and cultivate rural beauty before the turn of the century. Likewise, their belief in the public's 'co-ownership' of the landscape, the foundation of their aesthetic reforms, failed to garner much attention. Although their demands for public access to the woods likely resonated with those constituencies that had fought for the same in the late 1870s, their desire to place the aesthetics of the woods over its use-value prompted many to pause. In an age of increasing economic rationalization, few could accept the challenge Rudorff posed to the expansion of fields at the expense of hedgerows, or Salisch's demand that beauty be considered an element of commercial forestry. Therefore, both had difficulty in achieving institutional respect for their proclamation of the public's right to the national landscape.

The fortunes of both authors – and the idea of a national right to the woods – gradually gained wider currency around the turn of the

century, resonating with wider economic and social concerns. Starting
in the 1890s, Germans began fretting over their rising dependence on
lumber imports. Fears of dwindling timber reserves and rising wood consumption worldwide, in addition to agrarian and nationalist arguments
for greater economic autarky, prompted some to call for an outright
nationalization of Germany's forests.[95] An 1894 article in an illustrated
geography magazine stressed the need for state ownership of all forests,
in order that they could be managed in the public's interest.[96] In this
formulation, the public's right to the woods dovetailed with national
economic considerations, despite the Junkers' claims to the contrary.
Moreover, fears of working-class alienation began to escalate in the 1890s
as the Social Democratic Party underwent a significant period of expansion, and many middle-class Germans hoped forests might help inspire
workers' patriotism.

The League for *Heimat* Protection, founded by Rudorff in 1904, arose
out of these fears. Quickly spreading throughout the country, with tens
of thousands of members and countless local branches, it sought to protect local landscapes as part of a larger project of cultivating a more vigorous German national identity. Not surprisingly, then, the *Heimatschutz*
movement argued that there were significant values rooted in the soil
that were far more important than an individual landowner's prerogatives. Echoing Salisch's comments connecting a sense of ownership with
patriotism, for example, headmaster Hermann Bieder argued for the
importance of public rights to the woods in Brandenburg's provincial
Heimat protection journal in 1909. 'The love of the *Heimat* is bound to
the possession of the soil,' he contended. 'It is therefore necessary that
among the increasing population the feeling of common ownership of
the forest be cultivated as the root of *Heimat* feeling and the love of the
Fatherland.'[97] In Bieder's formulation, part of *Heimat* protection consisted of stimulating in the public a sense of entitlement to the landscape,
and through it, membership in the nation.

Salisch also saw a rising interest in his work after the turn of the
century, which in turn spurred a subtle escalation of the discourse. In
1902, after seventeen years of relative neglect, his *Forstästhetik* was republished for a growing audience; indeed, Ernst Rudorff, who obviously
demonstrated a deep interest in the issue of landscape aesthetics, learned
of Salisch's work only in 1903.[98] During this period, the foresters' associations of the heavily wooded Grand Duchies of Hessia and Baden endorsed
his views.[99] Moreover, the Hessian state attempted to institute Salisch's
recommendations in its extensive woodlands, adding *Forest Aesthetics*

to its foresters' curriculum, and issuing an edict stressing the importance of cultivating sylvan beauty.[100] The regulation might have meant that little changed in practice, for it is likely foresters and aesthetes had different standards of beauty. Yet at the same time, Hessia did concede that aesthetics, by whatever standard, did have a role to play in state forests. Moreover, this concession implied that the public had a right to use the state forests for recreation. This triumph led Salisch to radicalize his rhetoric. Instead of insisting on co-ownership, at a national meeting of foresters in 1905 he now spoke of the forest 'as national property [*Volksgut*], and everyone has a right to its spiritual use.'[101] Likewise, Hans Thoma, a painter and *Heimat* activist, in his campaign to convince the Badenese state to follow Hessia's lead, insisted the forest was a 'national property' (*Nationalgut*), there for public enjoyment.[102] Salisch and his allies were beginning to gain concessions from political authorities, and as they did so, their rhetoric took on a more explicitly nationalist tone.

Characteristic of this new stridency was a 1910 speech – later issued as a pamphlet – given by the conservative historic preservationist and *Gymnasium* teacher Richard Haupt to vacationers on the North Sea isle of Sylt. According to ancient Germanic custom, he insisted, forests 'are property of the entire nation.' The creation of the 1880 regulations – based on Roman, not Germanic, law – established 'a system of clear injustice' at the behest of landowners. This system arose, Haupt described, out of the rural conditions of the east, where landlords treated the peasantry, both Slav and German, as a conquered people and subjected them to 'this un-German development, this condition of servitude.' Through the 1880 legislation, the Junkers had succeeded in imposing their absolute understanding of sylvan property on the rest of the nation. Leavening his anti-Junker tirade with anti-Semitism, he provocatively postulated that the same legal concept would allow the Rothschilds to buy up all of Germany and expel the Germans. Haupt asserted that 'many landowners' essentially were doing the same thing by blockading their forests, for 'they rob the members of our nation of their *Heimat*.'[103] Not only were landlords treating the rest of the population unjustly, Haupt contended, but they were also sowing the seeds of revolution wherever they denied the people access to the woods by stripping them of their 'national character [*völkischen Eigenart*], indeed [their] patriotic outlook.' Therefore he called on the *Heimatschutz* movement to convince the state to protect the 'all the forests standing in the Fatherland,' whether they occupied public or private property. Only in this way would the public be assured of the access to nature so important for the maintenance of the national character.[104] As a result of the meeting, the local Tourism Association organized an Association for *Heimat* Protection.[105]

Haupt's speech brought together several elements of the national property discourse in a more pointed form. Heavily laden with nationalist formulations, it nonetheless challenged Prussian and Junker domination of Germany and called upon the ancient past for a more appropriate legal model for organizing property relations. Like Riehl, Sohnrey, and Rudorff, Haupt rejected the capitalist intrusion on the landscape, and the profit-driven changes it brought about. This is not surprising, given his conservatism. Neither was his anti-Semitism. Yet at the same time, like the agrarian reformers, he denounced the Junkers for their self-interest. Not only the peasantry had to suffer under their yoke, but everyone, as their policies threatened to cut Germans off from their source of their national identity. He placed his hopes in the *Heimat* movement to save the woods from their masters.

The national property rhetoric was by no means limited to *Heimat* activists and advocates of sylvan aesthetics. Urban reformers, Socialists, and Catholics also invoked the public's right to the woods. In 1907, an article in the social reform journal *Volkswohl* insisted, 'Even the metropolitan resident possesses a right to the forest and to the land, which is unshakable and that he may not be barred from, as to air and sunshine. His right is natural and is necessary for the people's health, and therefore the common good.'[106] In 1911, the former editor of the Socialist daily *Vorwärts*, Heinrich Ströbel, announced in the Prussian House of Deputies, 'The forests are surely one of the most significant elements of our national property.' Ströbel demanded that forests near urban centres be made accessible to the public.[107] The following year, the Catholic *Kölnische Volkszeitung* called on landowners to preserve public access, for 'the consciousness of a certain natural right to the forest also resides in the modern person of culture; especially the German connects the term "forest" with the image of the outdoors.'[108] Thus the rhetoric of national property, cultivated among *Heimat* enthusiasts, was appropriated by other groups in their attack on absolute property rights to the forest.

Trespassing in the Woods

The concept of national property was not merely rhetorical, for it inspired some to action. Starting in 1909, middle-class members of the Berlin's Union of Brandenburg Hiking Associations challenged the authority of local landowners to close their property to hikers.[109] In an article entitled 'Allures of Brandenburg Estate Owners,' the group's leader, Georg Eugen Kitzler, criticized the 'strange and arrogant behaviour' of local landlords, 'who imagine themselves as little monarchs, and who are asserting their ownership rights to wretched parks and some wooded land in a merciless way against the public.' He felt that 'their behaviour stands in the starkest contrast with the modern sense of justice,' complaining they lacked civility, 'which has apparently passed over Brandenburg's backwoods without a trace.' Those estate owners who denied the public access needed to be reminded, Kitzler averred, 'that the forest has been the common property [*Gemeingut*] of the Germans since the mists of prehistory, that the forest stood as the greatest and most sacred national treasure, and this remains so today, long after the property seizures of the last remaining common wooded lands by our Brandenburg Quitzows, Köckeritzes, and Itzenplitzes were completed.... It must be stressed that even today the people's sense of justice has difficulty understanding that it should have no right to the forest, which grows because of natural forces rather than the will of the owner.'[110] Kitzler's strident attack on noble landowners not only identified the erosion of peasant communal rights to the woods as 'property seizures,' it also named some still-prominent aristocratic families as culprits.

The abuses of great estate owners did not include simply denying the public access to the forest, but consisted of violence as well. Citing a report in the apolitical *Berliner Lokal-Anzeiger*, Kitzler protested 'the bad treatment of quiet, harmless strollers by overeager foresters or the landowner himself.' According to the *Lokal-Anzeiger*, a nasty landowner accosted an innocent mother on a country road outside of Königs-Wüsterhausen, southeast of Berlin. While the woman stopped to feed her baby, the gun-toting proprietor emerged from the woods complaining that her dog had strayed into his forest. Livid, he shot the dog on the spot, despite the mother's cries and pleas.[111] Such cruelty only demonstrated the landlords' unreasonable and unjust stance towards the public.

Forest owners' disrespect for the public had infiltrated the state forest administration as well. The Prussian authorities had decided to close a path running along Griebnitz Lake, southwest of Berlin. For Kitzler, this incident 'must demonstrate clearly to every friend of nature how the *Forstfiskus* disregards the feelings and the needs of the public, how little attention they pay to the common good, how much the people's ancient and indisputable right to the forest has been ever more diminished.' In response, Kitzler argued that the path could not be closed. He exclaimed, 'The state forest is free! Everyone can enter it; the *Forstfiskus* has no right to forbid walking in the forest and on forest paths!' He recalled promises made by Minister of Agriculture Lucius in the debates over the 1880 regulations to keep state-owned forests open to the public, and insisted that 'the right of the *Volk* to enter the forest in order to enjoy nature is inalienable.'[112] There could be no clearer articulation of the 'national property' concept.

Kitzler's attacks on private and public forest owners led others in his group to make similar objections. In 1911, an anonymous author complained that an estate owner named Spickermann had blocked access to the Rangsdorf Lake. The chairmen of the 'Societas' Hiking Club wrote asking Spickermann for permission, but he denied their request. As a result, the author insisted that the public had 'a right to the forest.'[113] A few weeks later another anonymous author indicated that he and two friends had decided to trespass on Spickermann's property. He indicated the venture was 'worth it' for the wonderful view, implicitly encouraging others to follow in his footsteps.[114] Kitzler's invective against public and private landowners alike probably inspired these (and likely other) trespassers to their defiant acts, illustrating the power of the 'national property' concept.

Conclusion

Over the course of the *Kaiserreich*, numerous voices opposed the Junkers' attempts to exclude the public from the woods. In the 1870s, liberals and Catholics argued that such limitations were arbitrary and harmful to the public good. Social reformers followed their lead, concerned the lack of healthy recreation for the working class would either destroy it or society as a whole. Agrarian reformers, on the other hand, fretted that the peasantry would be destroyed if it lacked access to the forest. Nationalists feared Germans would lose their identity without the ability to return to the woods. Landowners thus faced a wide array of opposition from both the left and the right, as well as those hard to place on the political spectrum.

This campaign against landowners suggests imperial German politics, with its diverse cast of actors, was not as deferent to this elite's demands as some historians suggest. Junkers found resistance to their plans not only among dissident liberals and Catholics, but also among fellow Conservatives and even the nationalist and agrarian interests supposedly under their control. Far from serving the landowners' agenda, *Heimat* enthusiasts and agrarian reformers asserted their own interpretations of the national good and spoke out accordingly.

Just as this conflict fails to conform to the *Sonderweg* understanding of nationalism in this period, applying the *Sonderweg* model of modernity to this case also proves difficult. The Junkers, rather than seeking to maintain some kind of pre-modern stasis, aggressively pressed for the modernization of property laws to accompany their rationalization of timber production. Agrarian reformers thus rallied to defend the peasantry against the destabilization of the countryside at the hands of the large landowners. At the same time, liberals found themselves struggling against the standardization of legal principles and defending feudal rights. These political divisions thus complicate the picture of nationalism and agrarian politics in the *Kaiserreich*.

chapter three

Environmental Activism in the *Kaiserreich*: Berlin and the Grunewald

Introduction

A profound tension developed over the course of the late nineteenth century over the 'German forest.' On one hand, popular depictions of the woods portrayed them as a crucial element of the national geography and history, uniting Germans in their love of nature. On the other, Germans fought contentious battles over just who had the right to walk on wooded property. The national struggle over the woods pitted competing social and economic interests against one another, revealing a far more varied and complex picture of the German passion for nature than the current literature often suggests. But how did these tensions play out at the local level? In the case of the Grunewald, a large forest on the western outskirts of Berlin, the battle lines were drawn between the Prussian state, which sought to capitalize on land values and Berlin, and a wide array of public interest groups, which wanted to preserve the Grunewald and other forests for public recreation.

Berlin witnessed a long-running struggle between the state and the metropolis over the future of the region's forests, especially the Grunewald. Between 1902 and 1915, as the city and its environs grew from roughly 2.7 to 3.7 million inhabitants, the state sought to capitalize on the climbing value of its properties near the capital. A broad range of Berliners responded to this threat with a campaign to save the surrounding forests. Contrary to those who – based on selective readings of elites like Riehl, Rudorff, and Salisch – might consider German discourses about nature in this period to be fundamentally mired in a reactionary outlook, the case of the Grunewald demonstrates how municipal left liberals (and to a lesser extent reformist socialists) actively sought to use nature to address the problems of the city in a rational and progressive way.[1] By contrast, conservatives and radical nationalists, with whom an interest in nature has most often been associated, found their ranks rent by this issue.

Not only do the debates over the fate of the Grunewald demonstrate the ability of liberals to harness interest in the woods to their own ends, but they also reveal the strength and vitality of urban liberalism. Although contemporary observers hailed imperial Germany's city governments as models of municipal order, historians have long regarded them as the realm of apolitical local elites (*Honoratioren*) retreating from national politics. Jan Palmowski, on the other hand, has called for a greater recognition of the politicization of urban administration. With vigorous challenges coming from mass political parties at the end of the nineteenth century, liberal city administrators, while invoking the essentially political rhetoric of 'apoliticality,' engaged increasingly in political activities.[2] In Berlin, the socialists posed by far the greatest threat to liberal dominance, almost entirely replacing liberals in the city's delegation to the Reichstag by the turn of the century. Left-liberal municipal authorities, conscious of the burgeoning strength of the socialist movement, sought to boost their credentials by dedicating themselves to social reform and public health.[3] Such liberal reformers saw themselves engaged in a civilizing mission among the urban working classes, seeking to influence their lives in the workplace, at home, and in public.[4]

The forest provided a key element in this campaign. Berlin's left-liberal establishment – which ran the city government (maintaining more than a two-thirds majority of the City Assembly down to the First World War), dominated the metropolitan press and led the city's associational life – sought to secure greater working-class access to nature, hoping to relieve the strains of urban life and improve public health. They argued the forest provided a healthy alternative to the teeming capital's musty taverns (*Kneipen*) and cramped tenements (*Mietskasernen*), allowing workers to fill their lungs with fresh air, exercise their bodies, and find more edifying forms of recreation. Providing these elements, liberals implied, would help integrate the working class into the nation, turning them away from socialism and transforming them into patriotic citizens.[5] When the state refused to guarantee the preservation of woodlands around Berlin, the liberal city fathers took it upon themselves to secure the forests for their constituents. As Palmowski noted in his study of Frankfurt am Main, the state's failure to deal more aggressively with social problems in the 1890s led municipalities – strongholds of liberalism – to intervene.[6] Thus, the Berlin city government engaged itself heavily in providing social and health services, developing a municipal infrastructure of welfare agencies, orphanages, elementary schools, hospitals, sewers, and clean drinking water.[7] The Grunewald and other woodlands surrounding Berlin, which the city attempted to buy in 1892–3 and again in 1906–15, represented another aspect of this municipal effort to address the social and public health needs of its citizens.

The campaign to preserve the woods also demonstrates the depth and strength of environmental action in this period. One study of German environmental politics bemoans the failures of early-twentieth-century activists, complaining of their anti-modernism, conservatism, timidity, lack of vision, and inability to form broad coalitions. Dismissing the follies of the past, it concluded, 'From subjects have arisen active citizens.'[8] While Berliners fighting for the preservation of the Grunewald may not have utilized the confrontational techniques of today's environmental activists, their efforts were far from romantic, diffident, or fragmented. Along with Berlin's political leaders, the city's press and associational life rallied to save the woods, pressuring the government not to sell state forests for real estate development. This broad and sustained mobilization of public opinion, from about 1904 to 1914, put great pressure on the Prussian state to accede to their demands. By the First World War, the forest administration had abandoned its plan to profit marvellously from its extensive wooded properties around Berlin and instead transferred the forests to Berlin at a small fraction of their real estate value. While some participants at the time felt the affair had been a defeat for the municipality – subsequently colouring historical accounts of the events – Berlin's purchase of the greenbelt signalled a triumph for urban interests over rural ones.[9] Although significant institutional barriers, primarily the Prussian three-class voting system, impeded the progress of Berliners' demands, the state was not impervious to public pressure.[10] The liberal establishment's efforts to preserve the Grunewald and other woodlands extended beyond the anaemic efforts described by some historians; rather, the campaign to save the Grunewald presaged contemporary environmental efforts.[11]

The Public Appropriation of the Grunewald

The Grunewald, a largely coniferous forest, stood on the sandy soil between the western boundary of Charlottenburg, a suburb to the west of Berlin, and the broad stretch of the River Havel (see map 3.1).

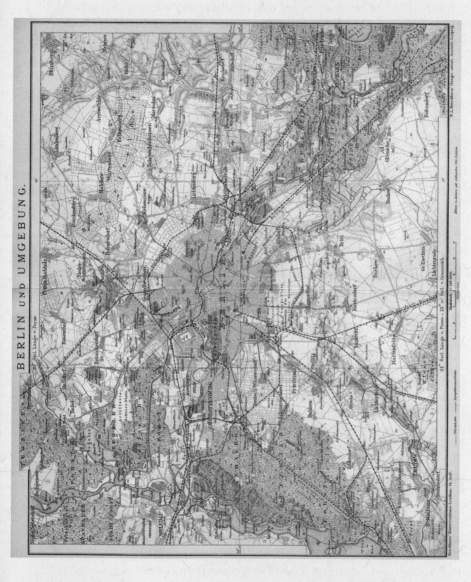

Map 3.1 'Berlin and Its Environs,' 1894. The Grunewald appears west-southwest of Berlin as the 'Spandower Grunewald Forst.' From 'Berlin und Umgebung,' *Brockhaus' Konversations-Lexikon (Leipzig: F.A. Brockhaus, 1894)*, 2:812a.

Prussian princes had hunted there since at least 1543, and it remained a royal hunting ground down to 1903, when Kaiser Wilhelm II withdrew his sport to the more distant woods at Lehnitz (outside of Oranienburg), north of Berlin. Hunting proved an important ritual of the court in the late nineteenth century, and the imperial entourage marked Saint Hubertus Day – honouring the patron saint of the sport, celebrated on 3 November – with a colourful hunt in the Grunewald known as the *Hubertusjagd*. The hunting party would eat breakfast outdoors at the royal Grunewald hunting lodge and then proceed on horseback in pursuit of forty wild boar released into the woods. The so-called *Hauptschwein* was released first, and participants aimed to wound and immobilize it, so as to allow the kaiser the opportunity to dispatch the boar personally with his hunting knife. Wilhelm I continued to participate in the *Hubertusjagd* into the 1870s, despite his advanced age, along with about two hundred members of German high society, mostly aristocrats. After the hunt, members of this elite would return to the royal hunting lodge for an elaborate meal. The whole affair captured the elegance and taste of the imperial court. As a toast from around 1900 put it, 'In the Grunewald grows very much / A root of the German cavalier spirit' (see figures 3.1 and 3.2).[12]

Historians have argued that such court displays were becoming increasingly anachronistic as time wore on. Wolfram G. Theilemann has taken the *Hubertusjagd* as a symbolic invasion of the metropolis by the rural elite, arguing that staging such an elaborate and ceremonial hunt so close to the capital indicated the continuing dominance of Prussia's feudal elite into the twentieth century. As he puts it, 'The countryside came into the city.'[13] Katharine Lerman has shown how the ritual surrounding this court hunt 'served to emphasise social boundaries and assert social exclusivity through the opulence and pageantry of its display.'[14] While this is certainly true on one level, it fails to put this anachronism into its larger context, for the aristocratic elite did not gallop through the woods alone, but were accompanied by thousands of spectators who did not content themselves with being deferent or even passive observers of the court.

Starting in the 1870s, curious city-dwellers marred this noble sport, and the presence of the public became increasingly palpable in images of the *Hubertusjagd*. Official works showed one perspective; an 1857 painting of the hunt under Friedrich Wilhelm IV placed the king (wearing a blue coat) and his entourage at the centre, surrounded by a gathering of well-dressed spectators cheering him on (see figure 3.1). A painting

3.1 The Hubertusjagd in the Grunewald under Friedrich Wilhelm IV, 1857. From Eduard Grawert, *Hubertusjagd im Grunewald unter Friedrich Wilhelm IV*, 1857. Courtesy of the Stiftung Preußische Schlösser und Gärten Berlin-Brandenburg, Potsdam. Photograph by Jörg P. Anders.

from 1887 presented the monarch similarly, yet there were important changes. Rather than taking place in the forest, the scene unfolded securely within the walls of the royal hunting lodge. Moreover, a contingent of armed guards stood ready for the kaiser's inspection (see figure 3.2).

These guards became increasingly necessary for the orderly conduct of the hunt. Popular images by the illustrator Georg Koch provided the perspective of the crowd; large groups of people stood in very close proximity to the riders or got in their way. Less respectably dressed than their counterparts in the official paintings, these crowds were far more dynamic, restlessly awaiting the release of the *Hauptschwein* or attempting to negotiate the course along with the riders, whether on bicycle or even barefoot (see figures 3.3 and 3.4). Even if these commoners were good-natured, they certainly could become a nuisance for hunters unaccustomed to such commotion. Indeed, Koch subtitled his 1899 drawing, 'Uninvited Guests as Retinue.'

There is plenty of evidence to indicate that these 'uninvited guests' were not simply over-enthusiastic bystanders, at least from the perspective of elites. In 1889, the conservative travel writer and hiking enthusiast August Trinius disdainfully referred to the 'dense hordes [of] uninvited old Berliners' that followed the hunting party, complaining that the commoners had transformed the *Hubertusjagd* into a degenerate 'people's festival' (*Volksfest*) after 'the rabble of the capital had beaten the original festival to death.'[15] Prince Heinrich von Schönburg-Waldenburg described the tumult surrounding the *Hubertusjagd* in the 1880s, relating how 'ten thousand Berliners of all calibres' gathered outside the hunting lodge to abuse the participants. While 'especially well-known and popular jockeys were greeted with cheers,' those not so fortunate 'were met with bad jokes.' Indeed, almost every rider had some taunt shouted at him by the crowd; Schönburg-Waldenburg recalled that one could choose either to respond with a clever repartee or, if things got rude, ignore the remarks altogether. Any rider showing signs of anger 'made himself totally ridiculous' in the eyes of the crowd. Schönburg-Waldenburg concluded, 'A kind of free rein was proclaimed for the Berliners.'[16] By 1894, it took forty gendarmes and an army contingent to hold back the crowds. According to a hiking guide to the Grunewald, 'The fault for the expanded closure [of the forest] lies with the mob of Berlin, which in the last few years has been responsible for ever greater ill-mannered disturbances.'[17]

By 1904, however, the disruptive crowds had driven the Kaiser and

3.2 *Arrival of Kaiser Wilhelm I. for the Hubertusjagd*, 1887. From Johann Carl Arnold and Herrmann Schnee, *Ankunft Kaiser Wilhelms I. zur Roten Jagd*, 1887. Courtesy of the Stiftung Preußische Schlösser und Gärten Berlin-Brandenburg, Potsdam. Photograph by Jörg P. Anders.

An der Saubucht.

3.3 Spectators at the *Hubertusjagd*, 1891. From an 1891 Georg Koch illustration, reprinted in Hermann Berdrow, *Der Grunewald* (Berlin: Hermann Eichblatt, 1902), 95.

his entourage from the forest altogether.[18] As Hermann Berdrow, the author of a guide to the Grunewald explained, 'Unfortunately, a certain part of the public has earnestly tried to spoil the visits of the Kaiser and his guests in the Grunewald. These noble souls, who lack the organ to distinguish between a good time and blatant roughness, have finally brought it to a point where the kaiser – who surely would have liked to have maintained the *Volksfest* – gave an order to remove the *Hubertusjagd* to a more distant reserve not easily reached by troublemakers.'[19] Public pressure thus seems to have played a role in the decision to remove hunt-

3.4 'From the *Hubertusjagd* in the Grunewald: Uninvited Guests as Retinue,' 1899. From Georg Koch, 'Von der Hubertus-jagd im Grunewald: Ungebetene Gäste als Gefolge,' *Illustrierte Zeitung* 2941 (9 November 1899): 637.

ing to more rural locales. Instead of the rural elite parading haughtily
through the urban landscape, as Theilemann suggests, the Grunewald's
Hubertusjagd at the turn of the century represented the growing public
claim on an ancient royal hunting ground. Turning Theilemann's formulation on its head, the city had invaded the countryside.

One might argue that, in response to encroachment of the urban infrastructure on the Grunewald in the 1890s, the kaiser had been gradually losing interest in hunting there anyway. However, Wilhelm II appears
to have paid a great deal of attention to the Grunewald through the
turn of the century. He ordered foresters to replace the dominant pines
with more deciduous trees starting in 1895, with the long-term goal of
increasing the amount and variety of game. And as Wilhelm anticipated
spending more time there, he initiated significant renovations to the
Jagdschloß Grunewald, beginning in 1897. Plans included building
a new road and barriers arcing around the hunting lodge as a means
to cut it off from easy public access. One project even commenced as
late as 1903, coming to completion only in 1908, years after the kaiser
had abandoned hunting in the Grunewald.[20] This seems to suggest that
rather than being an inevitable outcome of urban expansion, Wilhelm
II's withdrawal from the Grunewald came as the result of outside pressure. In the end, Berlin's expanding urban population managed to seize
the forest for itself. The celebration had also given many Berliners their
first taste of the Grunewald, as one local journal reminisced.[21] The forest
thus worked its way into the public consciousness, and Berliners began
to appropriate it for their own recreation.

Already by the 1890s, Sundays in the Grunewald teemed with human
activity. A 1902 account of a day in the woods illustrated the wide range
of diversions: boatloads of urbanites disembarked at the Schildhorn
landing on the banks of the Havel, encountering an amateur orchestra
playing the popular tune '*Im Grunewald, im Grunewald ist Holzauktion!*'
Hundreds of excursionists had already arrived there, by foot, bicycle,
charabanc, or other vehicles. The crowds soon dispersed to enjoy a glass
of beer or a cup of coffee at one of the several restaurants and beer gardens, or moved off into the shady woods for a picnic. Following refreshments, Berliners of all classes participated in games and races of various
kinds, as well as tree climbing, butterfly hunting, and stealing cakes from
the picnic baskets of other visitors. Many also swam or paddled around
in rowboats. Later, flautists took up a position by a monument and per-
formed '*Wer hat Dich, Du schöner Wald.*' As evening approached, restau-
rant bands struck up popular dance tunes as the girls demonstrated the

latest steps.[22] A *Gartenlaube* illustration of an outing to the Grunewald from 1899 included many of these familiar elements arranged under the pines: a singing club, a picnic, games, beer-drinkers around a keg, a couple reclining on the grass, someone relaxing in a hammock, and wagons waiting for the end of the day.[23] Berliners had discovered the Grunewald and through these activities shaped it in their own image.

Developers' Plans for the Grunewald

Interest in the Grunewald stemmed not only from its recreational value for elites and commoners alike; as Berlin expanded with the mid-century economic upswing, and particularly after it became the national capital, some began to eye these woods and the surrounding territory as valuable real estate. The Hamburg developer Johann Anton Wilhelm von Carstenn – known among Berliners as the 'Napoleon of real estate speculators' – anticipated the enormous profits locked away in the wooded waterfront property and began lobbying Prussian authorities repeatedly between 1866 and 1892 for rights to transform the Grunewald into an elegant suburb.[24] Perhaps his most telling proposal came in the fall of 1872, when Carstenn proposed in letters to Bismarck and the kaiser that they create a 'New Berlin.' The Berlin of 1872 stood singularly ill-suited for the task of being the capital of the powerful new nation state, Carstenn asserted, and the wild land speculation and municipal laissez-fairism of the economic boom years after national unification led him to complain about the lack of a master plan.[25] In particular, he raised the spectre of revolution as justification for his project.

While Carstenn dreamed of creating a German rival to the former imperial city of Paris, he also feared that Berlin's rapid growth would provide the conditions for its own version of the Paris Commune. Without intervention by planners, Carstenn foresaw 'Berlin soon crowded by a circle of working-class suburbs.' This possibility appeared all the more dangerous in light of growing antagonism between capital and labour.[26] The unplanned growth of Berlin worsened the living conditions of the workers. Pollution on the streets and in the air and water, not to mention poor sanitation, led to rising death rates and a falling number of capable draftees. Rising rents compounded these abominable living conditions, and finding a solution to these problems, Carstenn argued, was nearing the impossible. He warned that such conditions not only raised labour costs, but also placed the city in danger. And unlike the 'undisciplined, raw, fanatical hordes' of French proletarians, these German workers

were 'a mighty mass trained in arms, easily organized and capable of
united action!' A Berlin surrounded by armies of disciplined German
workers (there were already 30,000 metal workers in Berlin, they noted)
meant that in times of crisis 'all conflicts must be dealt with in the heart
of the city! A localization of a movement of social rebellion seems under present circumstances almost impossible.'[27] Berlin required rebuild-
ing not only to glorify the regime, but also to contain the revolutionary
threat, Carstenn maintained.

This 'New Berlin' would incorporate the towns of Charlottenburg and
Potsdam, with a string of luxurious suburbs in and around the Grunewald
uniting them (see map 3.2).[28] With the wealthy concentrated in the west,
the centre of the city would be dominated by magnificent state edifices.[29]
Despite his professed concern for the working class, Carstenn provided
few specifics about his plans for the eastern part of the city, where he
proposed to essentially quarantine labour. He acknowledged the duty
of the class of 'capital and luxury' to provide healthy accommodations
for their employees, and recommended that their homes be removed
further from the factories, and that cheap and efficient rail links improve workers' access to them.[30] Furthermore, he emphasized that the
withdrawal of the wealthy from the centre of the city would mean a sink-
ing of the high rents that stimulated unrest among the workers.[31] In addition to pacifying the workers, evacuating the wealthy to the Grunewald
facilitated their defence in case of civil unrest. Carstenn emphasized the
'*moral* and *practical* meaning' of isolating the working class, stressing the
need 'to provide the volcanic material a *given* bed, otherwise the over-
flowing lava might easily and mercilessly destroy everything around it!
– Should such social eruptions break into the city, not only would the
elegant parts of town stand *miles* away from *those* parts of the city which
we know from experience contain the elements of all social movements,
but the *Spree* and the [Landwehr] *canal* would also lie between these two
so unfortunately heterogeneous poles of society.' Carstenn explained
that the plan would cost the state little. By selling desirable plots of the
Grunewald along the banks of the Havel and the lakes for development,
the state could generate more than enough money to finance the infrastructure for the new luxury suburbs. Private developers, like Carstenn,
would do the rest.[32]

Despite his anticipation of the rise of Berlin's 'villa-colonies' to the
west and southwest of the city, Carstenn did not presage the importance
that hundreds of thousands of Berliners would come to place on the
Grunewald. Ironically, the government recognized the fundamental flaws

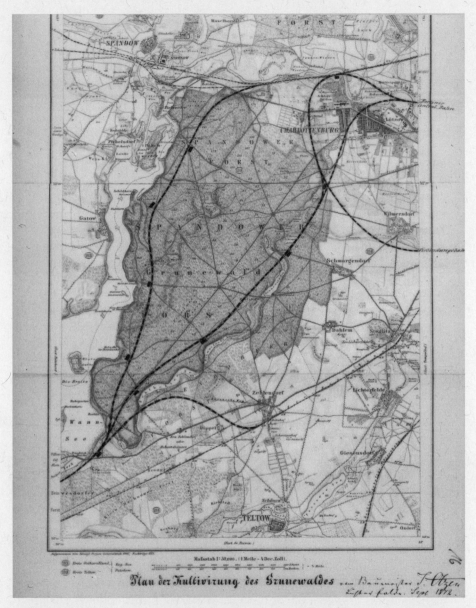

Map 3.2 Carstenn's plan for the Grunewald, 1872. From 'Plan der Kultivierung des Grunewaldes,' GStAPK, I HA Rep.89, Nr.31820. Courtesy of the Geheimes Staatsarchiv Preußischer Kulturbesitz, Berlin-Dahlem.

of the Carstenn plan. The Prussian ministers of trade and finance outlined their reservations in a letter solicited by the kaiser. Above all, they
objected that any attempt to profit from the sale of the Grunewald would
be illegal, as all state forests were held as collateral for the Prussian state
debt. Moreover, they expressed concern over the public health impact
of the project. While Carstenn claimed that developing the Grunewald
would improve the health of Berliners, the ministers doubted it would
achieve that goal. Precisely because the region's prevailing winds came
from the west, they noted, 'the expansion of Berlin increases the sanitary
importance of a source of air improved by trees.' They concluded 'that
while it would be permissible, out of the 18,700 *Morgen* [4,775 hectares]
of the Grunewald, to withdraw from cultivation a few areas suitable for
villas, it would be injurious to the salubrity of Berlin if, in its entirety
or even only large parts, this forest were given over to development.'[33]
The ministers thus argued against the plan and recommended instead
that the Grunewald be turned into a public park.[34] Prussian officials
thus blocked private development and tacitly acknowledged the public's
claim to the royal hunting ground in the early 1870s.

The state did not always maintain this clear vision of the public good.
Indeed, Prussian officials admired Carstenn's capitalist spirit and sought
to emulate him in their own real estate dealings, citing him explicitly
as inspiration. They exhibited no qualms in the sale of the Castle Park
in Steglitz, a potentially important recreation area, to developers a few
years later. As the largest single landholder in Berlin's environs, the Prussian *Fiskus* (the financial arm of the state) demonstrated a keen desire
to develop Berlin's suburbs. Furthermore, it displayed great acumen in
handling its landholdings. Rather than unloading all its property in the
speculative boom of the early 1870s (the *Gründerjahre*), the state slowly
offered its property for sale, keeping prices high. Moreover, it held onto
its land during recessions (such as after 1873, the end of the *Gründerjahre*), seeking the most favourable conditions for sale.[35] But perhaps the
most significant obstacle to the development of the Grunewald, as the
ministers noted, was the fact that proceeds from such a sale could not
flow into ministerial budgets, but had to be applied to state debt. This,
however, would change in 1901.

Carstenn was not the only person to regard the Grunewald as a solution for the revolutionary tendencies of the working class in the early
1870s. The Countess Adelheid Dohna-Poninski also made a proposal but
approached the problem in an entirely different manner. Criticizing the
escalating misery of Berlin's workers, increasingly housed in deplorably

cramped 'rental barracks' (*Mietskasernen*), she called for greater worker access to the forests around the city. In 1874, Dohna-Poninski issued a pamphlet proposing to limit the expansion of the city and to preserve green spaces for public use. Fearing that Bismarck's political repression of working-class dissent would provoke revolution, she insisted 'that the right of every inhabitant to reach open space within a half hour from home not be injured.' This required parks within two kilometres of any point in the city, including a great 'green ring of the metropolis,' where 'the entire population, with all of its classes,' could come together to enjoy all manner of 'recreational sites in the outdoors, including kitchen gardens, suited to their various natural needs.'[36] In order to strengthen her argument with patriotic appeal, Dohna-Poninski chose to publish her work under the pseudonym Arminius, the Latin name for the Germanic hero of the Battle of the Teutoberger Forest, then being commemorated in the nearly completed Hermann Monument (*Hermannsdenkmal*). Here she invoked not just the forest, but specifically the *German* forest, as a solution to the dual and pressing problems of industrialization and urbanization. Her argument for public access to the woods presaged those of social reformers in decades to come.

Municipal Plans for the Grunewald

While the Prussian state refused to sanction Carstenn's division of Berlin into two cities – one for rich and the other for poor – it also refused to take Dohna-Poninski's urban reform initiative seriously. In general, it preferred to profit from its land and let private developers work as they wished, leaving the burden of urban planning to them.[37] By the 1890s, Berlin found itself surrounded by a welter of suburbs, without any central plan for utilities, traffic, and other urban amenities. The constricting ring of development around the capital compounded Berlin's own internal urban planning problems. The City of Berlin had been growing rapidly since the 1860s with little central planning, leading to a densely packed urban core with few recreational possibilities. Whereas James Hobrecht, Berlin's chief urban planner in the early 1860s, had laid out large city blocks where he anticipated low-density housing surrounded by private gardens, by the end of the century these lots had been developed to the fullest extent, rising five stories high and preserving no green space around them. Some buildings attained enormous sizes, extending back from the street around a series of small courtyards. Such patterns of construction made Berlin one of the densest cities in Europe, suffering from all the attendant public-health consequences.[38] This haphazard development, chalked up to the laissez-faire policies pursued by the communal administration during this period, prompted Berliners in the 1890s to propose regulations on metropolitan growth and plan major new parks.[39] Inspired by the example of Vienna, which in 1892 initiated a competition for a greenbelt around the city, municipal architect Theodor Köhn published a book advocating the annexation of the suburbs and the forests around Berlin. While Berlin historian Felix Escher claims municipal authorities at the end of the century ignored plans like Köhn's, communal officials did indeed attempt to secure forests for the city.[40] The blame for the failure of Berlin to acquire the Grunewald lay with the state, not the city.

In late 1892, during the negotiations over suburban annexation, Berlin's communal authorities offered to buy the Grunewald from the state.[41] This offer was the culmination of public and private discussions over the course of the previous year.[42] Carstenn, not losing the opportunity to involve himself in the future of this vast piece of real estate, again lobbied politicians at all levels.[43] Yet Prussian officials demonstrated no interest in a deal, indicating that 'there is no intention of alienating the Grunewald, either as a whole or in part.'[44] A similar municipal proposal from early 1893 was apparently ignored.[45] The state frustrated Berlin's efforts to purchase the Grunewald in the 1890s, and municipal authorities remembered the episode bitterly.

State Plans for the Grunewald

The Grunewald's growing popularity among the public, and the increasing danger of its development, had motivated the City of Berlin to attempt to buy it in 1892. The state's rejection of the capital's offer raised some doubts about the future of the forest. By the 1890s, already 200 hectares of timber had been cut down over the previous twenty years, leading composer Otto Teich to pen the popular ditty 'The Wood Auction' about the Grunewald in 1890.[46] While Teich put a light-hearted spin on these developments, others intervened more critically. Conservatives in the House of Lords of the Prussian *Landtag* intervened in 1897, in an attempt to preserve the Grunewald as a 'primeval forest' (*Urwald*), managed according to aesthetic, not fiscal, principles, and their proposal found support in the conservative press.[47] Yet the state objected to the House of Lords' intervention, feeling it impinged on the state's right to dispose of its property as it wished. One government official suggested that, rather than create a state park, the House of Lords satisfy itself with assurances from the king that the Grunewald would be 'effectively culti-vated in the interest of the public' with 'special attention to the preserva-tion of old groves,'[48] and in the end, the House of Lords accepted this concession.[49] Apparently, although it announced it would consider 'aes-thetic concerns' in the cultivation of the Grunewald, and agreed to plant more deciduous trees in place of pines at scenic spots – which accorded with the kaiser's desires anyway – the Prussian state regarded even these modest demands by the House of Lords to be an encroachment of its property rights.[50] Fear of eroding control motivated the state to resist nature-protection legislation, as it had impelled conservative landown-ers to defend their woods against the public in the 1880 Field and Forest Law. By the turn of the century, municipal and parliamentary efforts to secure the Grunewald for the public faltered, and the forest remained protected only by vague assurances from Prussian cabinet officials.

　　Pressure to preserve the Grunewald for the public, whether emanat-ing from the Prussian *Landtag*, the City of Berlin, or the unruly crowds attending the *Hubertusjagd*, prompted Kaiser Wilhelm II to play the role of Berlin's benefactor. Indeed, he liked to style himself as the people's emperor, and in January 1902 Wilhelm announced that he would con-vert the Grunewald, his royal hunting preserve, into a 'people's park' (*Volkspark*), and the Berlin press largely greeted the kaiser's decision with enthusiasm. Liberal papers praised the proposed lawns, playgrounds, and sports facilities that would facilitate public recreation and provide the 'light and air' so lacking in the city. This new project seemed to ad-dress Countess Dohna-Poninski's complaints from the 1870s. Taking a more nationalist tack, one conservative paper imagined the Grunewald would become a jewel in the crown of Germany's imperial capital, mak-ing the parks of other cities look like 'dwarves' in comparison.[51] Yet other conservative papers were more reluctant. As details of the plans – drawn up by Hermann Geitner, the director of Berlin's main urban park, the Tiergarten – began to circulate, conservative papers rejected Geit-ner's idea of a highly cultivated park filled with opportunities of public recreation, and instead harkened back to rhetoric about preserving a 'primeval forest.'[52] A liberal paper, the *Volks-Zeitung*, echoed some of this concern about the loss of sylvan tranquillity and beauty in the new *Volks-park* but expressed more distrust of the government. In particular, it sus-pected that the state sought to use the *Volkspark* as a cover for land sales to subsidize its growing investments in the Prussian east.[53] Certainly, the government had provided no explicit reassurance that the Grunewald would be maintained in its entirety, and while many in the press waxed enthusiastic about the kaiser's plans, at least the *Volks-Zeitung* began to suspect there was more than met the eye.

The *Volks-Zeitung*'s suspicion was justified. Indeed, until 1901 the *Fiskus* had been required by law (since 1820) to use all income from the sale of woodlands to repay state debts.[54] With that restriction out of the way, the ministry secretly hoped to generate enormous funds not subject to the oversight of the *Landtag* for land acquisitions in the Prussian east, as the *Volks-Zeitung* intuited.[55] In late 1904, in conjunction with the *Volks-park* project, the Ministry of Agriculture requested permission from the kaiser to sell over five hundred hectares of the northern Grunewald for the development of a fifty-metre-wide boulevard (the Heerstrasse) and a luxury residential district, as well a smaller parcel of land around the Schlachtensee station on the southeastern end of the forest (for an overview of the proposed development, see map 3.3). The remaining 3,725 hectares of land would provide 'significantly more [territory] than could ever be claimed in anticipation of a *Volkspark*,' observed the minister of agriculture, Victor von Podbielski.[56] Although initially reluctant, the kaiser eventually permitted these sales to go forward, ignoring the brewing public discontent over the plans.[57]

The Press Campaign to Save the Grunewald

As early as January 1903, while Prussian officials plotted to dismember the Grunewald, rumours of their plans began to circulate in the capital's press.[58] But it was not until the autumn of 1904 that the rumours intensified and the liberal press responded with indignation. Characteristically, it was the progressive *Volks-Zeitung* – the first to suspect government dishonesty – that led the charge.[59] Amid growing public fears for the Grunewald, the satirical journal *Kladderadatsch* – edited by the future author of *Our German Forests*, Johannes Trojan – published a cartoon of an imaginary monument to Agriculture Minister Podbielski erected by grateful Berlin developers (figure 3.5). Entitled 'Pod the Forest Destroyer,' the cartoon depicted a statue of an axe-wielding Podbielski surrounded by tree stumps and set against a featureless horizon, with the caption, 'If two thousand acres of the Grunewald are really to be "made available for building," this is how thankful Berlin property speculators want to memorialize the minister of agriculture.'[60] The criticism could not have been more pointed.

By November, Berlin's liberal press had reached a fever pitch, de-

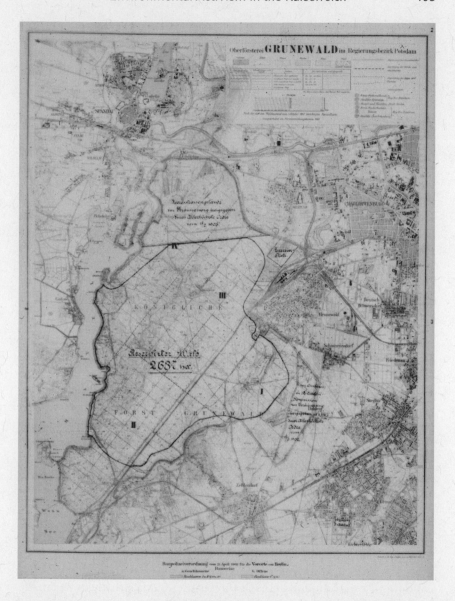

Map 3.3 State plans for the Grunewald, 1907. From Arnim to the kaiser, 4 July 1907, in GStAPK, I HA Rep.89, Nr.31820, b.235–8. Courtesy of the Geheimes Staatsarchiv Preußischer Kulturbesitz, Berlin-Dahlem.

Pod der Waldverwüster

Wenn wirklich zweitausend Morgen des Grunewaldes „der Bebauung erschlossen" werden, so wollen die dankbaren Berliner Grundstückspeculanten
dem Herrn Landwirthschaftsminister dort ein Denkmal setzen.

3.5 'Pod[bielski] the Forest Destroyer,' 1904. From Stutz, 'Pod der Waldverwüster,' *Kladderadatsch* 57 (9 October 1904): 164.

nouncing the government's plans for 'forest slaughter' as inimical to
the common good. Aroused by the campaign in the press, a wide range
of Berlin associations began to mobilize. A Berlin homeopathy association called a public meeting at the Viktoria Brewery to draw attention
to the problem. Drawing on the sylvan discourse, the organizers of the
meeting cited the growing population density of Berlin, the danger of
epidemics, the role of forests in providing cities with fresh air, the lack of
playgrounds for schoolchildren, and the ongoing '*mutilation of the beauty*
of their local Brandenburg *Heimat*' by speculative forces, and stated they
'rise in protest against the planned partial parcelling of the Grunewald,'
demanding the city and the *Landtag* fight for the public's 'threatened
rights.'[61] Berliners – or at least those assembled at the Viktoria Brewery
– regarded the Grunewald as theirs and were prepared to fight for it.

At the same time, the *Volks-Zeitung* joined with another prominent progressive paper, the *Berliner Tageblatt*, to formally address the government
on the issue. On 13 November 1904, the day following the protest meeting at the Viktoria Brewery, the editors-in-chief of the two papers handed

3.6 'Fellow Citizens! Help Us Protect Our Forests!' Berlin Forest Protection Association poster, 1907. From Lucian Bernhard, 'Mitbürger, helft uns unsere Wälder erhalten!' 1907. Courtesy of the Münchner Stadtmuseum, Munich.

over of a petition with 30,000 signatures protesting the development of the Grunewald to Minister of Agriculture Podbielski. In a meeting lasting over an hour, according to newspaper reports, Podbielski assured them that the Grunewald would not become a fairground (*Wurstelprater*) as the press feared, and that the large portion of the forest south of the proposed military road, over four thousand hectares, would be protected from development. The minister asserted the Department of Forestry 'gets no pleasure from cutting down trees.' But this was not all. Podbielski also indicated that the *Fiskus* could not be expected to maintain urban parks and cited several cases where cities had purchased woodlands from the *Fiskus* for recreational purposes. Apparently the editors protested, observing that the state owed Berlin special consideration, as it alone generated a sixth of the Prussian tax revenue. This prompted Podbielski to respond that such a wealthy city should therefore have enough money to buy the Grunewald.[62]

Needless to say, the liberal papers were unhappy with the response to their petition. The *Volks-Zeitung* and the *Berliner Tageblatt* doubted the government's promises to preserve the Grunewald and concluded that since the state seemed motivated primarily by cash, Berlin would probably have to purchase the forest.[63] An article running in both papers expressed Berliners' outrage by paraphrasing Podbielski's comments as 'Either you must bleed a lot, or one fine day we will raze the two thousand *Morgen* [510 hectares].' Calling on Berlin and its suburbs, the article argued for the need to organize, so that they could take action to preserve the forests the next time Podbielski offered an either/or deal.[64] The liberal press thus sought to mobilize Prussian citizens to protest government policy.

In this clash with the state, left liberals styled themselves as champions of not just Berliners in general, but also specifically Berlin's working class. As the autumn press campaign against government land deals began, the *Volks-Zeitung* complained that development plans would hurt Charlottenburg's working-class neighbourhoods.[65] In the wake of the *Berliner Tageblatt*'s official petition, the newspaper proudly published a grateful letter from 'a number of unionized Berlin workers' thanking the editors for their 'manly and energetic intervention for the preservation of the Grunewald.' The letter testified, 'You spoke to us Berlin workers from the heart, because in the end we alone are the victims, as the propertied classes can substitute summer holidays and longer excursions.' They echoed the recurrent discourse on the importance of the Grunewald for the health of Berlin, but more intriguing was their animus against the Social Democrats. The preservation of the Grunewald was not just about health, rather:

> For us workers this matter also has another side; we regret, namely, that '*Vorwärts*,' [the socialist daily] which always describes itself as a 'Berlin peoples' paper' and as the only patented workers' paper, has not lifted a finger in the matter. Here, where it matters, other than pointing to the usual phrases about practical socialism, both the paper as well as the party have failed. Mass assemblies, called by the Social Democrats, would probably not have failed to impress, and had it been about a tax proposal, military or navy spending, then, man, it would have been different. But for such trivialities as the peoples' welfare [*Volkswohl*], our 'workers' leaders' can't be bothered. They should not forget this, because we've finally had enough of letting ourselves be fed with these high-sounding, hackneyed expressions and the failure to see anything positive out of dreary criticism. We want to rub the cries from the 'isolated reactionary mass' outside of Social Democracy in the faces of our 'leaders' again as a lie and show them that if Berlin workers only depended on them, then they would really be deserted.[66]

The preservation of the Grunewald, a liberal reader of the *Berliner Tageblatt* might surmise, functioned therefore not only as a public health measure, but also as a means to reach out to the workers.

Appealing to the working class held great importance for Berlin left liberals at the turn of the century, for their monopoly on political power in municipal politics and the city's delegations to the *Landtag* and the Reichstag was being seriously eroded by socialist candidates. Already in 1883 – despite the official ban on the party and the income-based, three-class voting system – Social Democrats entered Berlin's City Assembly, and by 1914, they held 44 of the 142 seats in that body. In 1893, shortly after the party had been legalized, it controlled five of Berlin's six seats in the democratically elected Reichstag, and when the Social Democrats finally entered the Prussian House of Deputies (*Abgeordnetenhaus*) in 1908 – in spite of the discriminatory three-class voting system – they captured six of Berlin's twenty-one seats.[67] Thus, in making their case to government and the public, left-liberal newspapers and politicians must have had the socialist threat in mind. It seems likely, therefore, that they predicated their repeated emphasis on the importance of forests for the working classes on political considerations, and not simply on goodwill.[68] As time progressed, and the strength of Berlin's Social Democratic Party increased, the working-class motif to the debates only grew.

As the level of tension rose between Berliners and the Prussian state, and as left liberals attempted to appropriate the issue for themselves, rightward-leaning newspapers that had criticized official pronouncements in the past now downplayed the confrontation. In the wake of the 13 November meeting, the nationalist *Tägliche Rundschau* – which had articulated largely the same critical stance as the *Volks-Zeitung* – now concluded rather anaemically that the only question that remained was how much Berlin would have to pay to secure the Grunewald for itself.[69] The Free Conservative *Berliner Neueste Nachrichten*, another early critic of the state's Grunewald policy, similarly demurred, providing only a simple account of the meeting.[70] With the progressive newspapers aggressively taking control of the story by actively participating in it, protecting the Grunewald became a largely left-liberal issue.

While the progressive newspapers' indignation over the proposed sales caused some on the right to drop the issue, it called forth invective from more traditional conservatives. The archconservative *Kreuzzeitung* stepped forward to defend Podbielski from attacks in the liberal press, expressing frustration with the Berliners and the *Berliner Tageblatt*: 'According to the logic of the "B.T.," the state has to do everything for the rich municipalities, and as good as nothing for the poor ones.' While the public might have demonstrated its attachment to the Grunewald, the *Kreuzzeitung* noted this was no reason for the state to simply give it away as a gift. Instead, the paper recommended a parental approach: the state should treat the capital as a child that needs to learn responsibility and should demand a price for the forest.[71] Thus the struggle for the Grunewald pitted Berlin's left-liberal champions against the Prussian administration and its agrarian allies in something of a retread of the Field and Forest Law debates of the 1870s. As the press campaign yielded few concessions, the debate leapt from the headlines into the Prussian parliament.

The Parliamentary Campaign to Save the Grunewald

With the government's hostile stance towards Berliners and their efforts to save the Grunewald from development, political forces at the state level organized to block the Ministry of Agriculture's agenda. Between 1905 and 1909, the conflict played out on the floor of the Prussian *Landtag*. Left liberals rallied to the cause of forest protection, denouncing state policy as selfish and short-sighted, as it ignored public health to the detriment of Berliners and Germany as a whole. Echoes of the 1880

Field and Forest Law debates reverberated through the chamber; urban liberals demanded public access to and preservation of state forests, while the state insisted on its right to dispose of its property as it pleased. Yet this time, like the 1906 newspaper debate over property rights, some on the right began to express discomfort with the government's hard line, suggesting that the Grunewald was more than just another piece of urban real estate. This resistance placed the minister of agriculture in a difficult position, requiring him to navigate a course between acknowledging the state's responsibility to the public (and in particular the kaiser's promise of a *Volkspark*) on the one hand, and the administration's desire to realize significant funds from its land around Berlin for reinvestment in the Prussian east on the other. While opponents of state policy could not restrain the Ministry of Agriculture through parliamentary mechanisms, they did shape the debate, putting the government on the defensive and eventually forcing the administration to negotiate a settlement. Pressure from below forced concessions.

In January 1905, following the wave of protest the previous autumn, Minister of Agriculture Podbielski stood before the Prussian House of Deputies and defended himself against vigorous accusations of sponsoring secret development deals in the Grunewald, announcing, 'I have always been an enemy of land speculation.' He then went on the offensive, claiming that Berlin was responsible for its own problems. If only the great cities would spread out their development, he argued, there would be sufficient room for private gardens 'in which children and women could take in the fresh air.' He contended there would be no need to create parks out of state property had the city controlled its expansion.[72] Of course, this logic suited the Ministry of Agriculture well, for if upscale, low-density villa colonies and garden cities sprawled their way into the countryside, the ministry – as the largest single landholder in the Berlin area – would profit fabulously.

Placing the capital's problems of urban growth squarely on Berlin's shoulders became a favoured government strategy. When the issue came up in the 1907 forestry budget debate, Department of Forestry Chief Hermann Wesener argued that Berlin, not the state, bore the responsibility for the welfare of its inhabitants. While Berliners had long accused the *Forstfiskus* of 'hacking down forests around Berlin,' he observed, 'one should note that other cities have done significantly more for the creation of city parks.' Wesener insisted (falsely) the capital refused to enter negotiations with the state, threatening the health and welfare of its own residents. Indeed, not only did Berlin endanger its inhabitants by failing to buy woodlands as other cities had, municipal authorities actually cut down forests while demanding them from the state, Wesener contended, citing the loss of hundreds of hectares of woodlands on municipal property at Buch and Birkholz. Contrasting Berlin's negligence with the state's responsibility, Wesener noted proceeds from limited sales of state forests around Berlin contributed to the 'great task of culture [*Landeskulturaufgabe*], the purchase and afforestation of wastelands in the west as well as the east of the monarchy.' Each hectare sold around the capital, he claimed, meant a thousand reforested in the Eifel or eastern Prussia.[73] Thus, while Berlin chose to squander its forests, the state chose to multiply its holdings a thousand-fold. Such fiscal and environmental irresponsibility, the state forestry chief implied, meant the capital should pay for its sins and buy the Grunewald outright.

Ultimately, the argument came down to finances. Wesener was convinced Berlin could afford the Grunewald. He portrayed the capital as a spoiled and ungrateful child, demanding gifts from its parent. Had it not been for the state and its investments, Wesener scornfully contended, 'Berlin might today still be a fishing village.' Instead, the imperial capital had grown rich and thus could well afford to buy the forest.[74] Yet a fundamental question remained: what would happen to the Grunewald if Berlin would not (or could not) pay the *Fiskus*'s price? Podbielski and Wesener's silence on this issue echoed ominously through the chamber.

This silence led some left liberals to move beyond the call for the preservation of the Grunewald by the state, insisting instead on its purchase by the city. Only in this way, they felt, could Berlin guarantee the forest's integrity. Following Podbielski's defiant speech in January 1905, the left-liberal representative and member of Berlin's City Assembly Robert Kreitling argued that Berlin should indeed buy the Grunewald, for fear that leaving it in state hands exposed the forest to unnecessary risk. He was concerned like the others, however, that the prices demanded by the *Fiskus* for other properties in the past indicated that the cost of the Grunewald would be high, probably equivalent to prices offered private developers. The government's hard bargaining in previous cases thus led Kreitling to characterize Podbielski not as an axe-wielding backwoodsman, but as 'a very good businessman.'[75]

While many other left liberals rejected Kreitling's call to purchase the Grunewald, they characterized Podbielski and Wesener as real estate speculators, much as the press had since 1904. The senior left-liberal deputy Otto Fischbeck, a member of Berlin's City Assembly, complained in the House of Deputies in 1907, 'In the newspapers we hear all kinds

of rumours that the state has begun to use *parts of the Grunewald for speculative purposes*.' Should Berlin have to buy the forest at such prices, he
stressed, the extra tax required would accelerate the flight of the wealthy
to the suburbs, leaving the poor to pay the tab.[76] The following year, the
implacable leader of the left liberals in *Landtag*'s House of Lords, Georg
Bender, likewise paraphrased Wesener as saying, 'Either I cut down the
forest, or you pay me building-site prices for it!'[77] Such characterizations
threatened to undermine the state's claim to represent the common
good.

　　In addition to painting the Ministry of Agriculture as overly materi-
alistic, left-liberal Berliners defined the issue as one of public welfare
(*Volkswohlfahrt*), public health (*Volksgesundheit*), and 'moral education'
(*Volkserziehung*), along the lines of previous debates. For the left liberals, the *Volk* stood at the centre of the Grunewald debate, and the state
was neglecting it. Moreover, they argued, the *Fiskus* was undermining
the very foundation of patriotism, the local *Heimat*. Ridiculing reforestation efforts and the portrayal of the project as a *Landeskulturaufgabe*,
Müller insisted, 'No, the "exchange" of Grunewald for distant wastelands
would not be a cultural task [*Kulturwerk*] of the first order. Instead it is
my firm belief that it would be as injurious to culture [*Kulturwidrig*] and
as unpatriotic as any plan imaginable.'[78] Left liberals thus claimed that
sacrificing the interests of the capital for those of the borderlands would
alienate Berlin's working classes. The National Liberals, although then
in Chancellor Bülow's ruling coalition, joined the left liberals in their
stand against the administration.[79]

　　While the City of Berlin would normally find few supporters among
the East Elbian elites who dominated the party, Conservative politicians
from suburban Berlin began to express concern over government policy. Berlin's Conservative sympathizers appeared receptive to the capital's public health arguments but understood them in their own way. In
particular, they feared that the poor condition of urban children would
hinder their induction into the army and ultimately weaken Germany's
military. With no space to play, a generation of urban youth was growing
up that was, according to Friedrich Hammer, 'no longer suited to the
physical tasks of able-bodied soldiers in the army.' The suburban Conservative deputy carefully distinguished his position from that of the liberals, however, arguing that the forest did not belong to Berlin, and never
demanding explicitly that the state preserve the Grunewald.[80] Similarly
calling on the interests of national health, Berlin's Conservative Voters'
Association petitioned the Ministry of Agriculture twice that year, calling

on it to save the forests around Berlin.[81] This position was also adopted
by other conservatives from beyond the capital, who came to the conclusion that Berlin should buy the Grunewald at a reasonable price.[82]
Perhaps the most striking element of the Conservatives' position was the
fact that none of them – not even a *Junker* – spoke unequivocally in favour of the government. Wesener alone had to defend the Agriculture
Ministry's policies before an increasingly critical chamber.

As time went on, and the government dug in its heels, conservatives
began to work more closely with liberals in challenging state policy. Although conservatives, along with the Catholic Centre Party, had managed
to defeat a bill sponsored by the liberal parties attempting to protect the
entirety of the Grunewald in 1909, they now seemed prepared to cooperate with liberals in protecting the loveliest part of the Grunewald – the
banks of the Havel. The Conservative Hans von Brandstein proposed
a bill to this effect that same year, and although it attracted opposition
from aristocratic landowners within his own party – as well as the more
conservative wing of the Centre Party – he built a coalition with the liberals.[83] A number of conservatives now agreed to directly block at least
some of the Ministry of Agriculture's speculative land sales. With liberals
and conservatives united in support, the Brandstein bill passed.[84] But
the law protected only the Grunewald's Havel waterfront, leaving the
majority of the forest exposed to continuing government contrivances.

The Popular Campaign to Save the Grunewald

While suburban conservatives became increasingly critical of government policy, reflecting the interests of their constituents, the broader
metropolitan public mobilized to campaign for the protection of the
Grunewald. As far back as the autumn of 1904, tens of thousands of Berliners had petitioned the government to save the woods. But with media
and legislative efforts to reign in the regime stalling, a wide range of Berliners turned to more vocal forms of protest. Berlin's lively network of
public associations, encompassing everything from landowners' societies
to hiking clubs, rallied together to stymie government plans. They drew
on the familiar forest discourse, arguing that greater access to the forest would help address the problems of unregulated urban expansion,
declining public health, rising social unrest, and deteriorating national
sentiment.

Through 1907 and 1908, Berlin's myriad public associations – the
fabric of German civil society – began to use their influence to lobby

the government. Surprisingly, several targeted the stodgy Prussian House of Lords, known as a bastion of conservatism. An April 1907 petition from the United Communal Associations of Zehlendorf, a southwestern Berlin suburb near the Grunewald, called on the government to preserve the entirety of the forest.[85] A second set of petitions originated from a January 1908 meeting dubbed the Forest Protection Conference (*Waldschutztag*), convened by the Berlin Forest Protection Association to strategize the defence of the Grunewald.[86] High-profile dignitaries studded the attendance list, including Walter Leistikow, the celebrated secessionist painter, Arthur von Gwinner, the director of the Deutsche Bank, Baron Octavio von Zedlitz und Neukirch, the leader of the Free Conservative Party with close ties to industrial interests, and Prince Heinrich zu Schönaich-Carolath, a wealthy reformist aristocrat with ties to industry who left the Free Conservatives to join the National Liberals. This collection of prominent personages championing Berliners' right to the woods reflected the modernizing wing of imperial Germany's elites, not reactionaries waxing romantic over the beauties of the Grunewald. Moreover, this assemblage illustrated the broad alliance of political interests mobilizing to defend the woods; the radical nationalist Pan-German League's Admiral Eduard von Knorr sat in the meeting alongside the left-liberal Bernhard Schnackenburg, soon to be elected Lord Mayor of Altona.

Joining these distinguished social and political figures were a number of scientists and academics, three of whom addressed the assembly on key topics. The director of the University of Berlin's Hygiene Institute (and successor of the famous Robert Koch), Professor Max Rubner, spoke on the climatic and hygienic importance of the Grunewald; state geologist Dr Hans Potonié focused on its botanical and zoological significance; and the teacher Dr Henting reported on the recent tree felling and real estate development in the woods.[87] Following the speeches, this dignified assembly drafted a petition calling on the *Fiskus* to limit its sale of forests near cities and asked that any such sales be brought to the attention of the *Landtag*. Twenty-six groups, ranging from the German Entomological Society and the Botanical Association of the Province of Brandenburg to Berlin's elite *Heimat* group, Brandenburgia, submitted the petition separately to the *Landtag*'s House of Lords, of which Schönaich-Carolath was a member.[88]

Surprisingly, their message of protest received a hearing in the House of Lords. Although sniping from the House of Deputies was to be expected, the compliant House of Lords likely startled *Fiskus* officials with its intervention in their affairs. Despite government opposition, the House of Lords' Agriculture Commission unanimously endorsed the petitions' recommendations and forwarded them to the plenary session.[89] The full house agreed with the commission and in turn resolved that the government should limit its sales and inform the *Landtag* of them.[90] Although the bill had no teeth, it indicated the seriousness with which the unelected House of Lords regarded the growing popular discontent. After all, the body could have simply ignored the petitions with impunity. Now, however, even this overwhelmingly conservative body began to impinge on state plans. In an official statement to the House of Lords, the government agreed to avoid the sale or exchange of land in the Grunewald 'insofar as this can be reconciled with the purposes of the state.'[91] Again, the *Fiskus* responded to public pressure with vague guarantees, which only further mobilized the public.

While the first Forest Protection Conference appears to have achieved little, it paved the way for the far more popular second *Waldschutztag* the following year. There, Berliners of many different stripes, and from far more modest social backgrounds, expressed their demands for access to the forest. Thirty groups representing teachers, housing reform advocates, public health officials, and *Heimat* enthusiasts, among others, expressed their dismay at the continual loss of woodlands in the region and advocated their purchase by the municipalities. In contrast to the first, this second meeting had a much more activist flavour. Now public associations, not scholars and dignitaries, directed the discussion.

On 16 January 1909, medical professor Dr Karl Anton Ewald – the chairman of the Berlin Forest Protection Association – opened the second Forest Protection Conference in the Architects' House on the Wilhelmstrasse, in the heart of Berlin's government district. In attendance was not only a panoply of Berlin associations, but also government and municipal officials. Ewald opened the meeting by describing the changing role of his Forest Protection Association. While it had been founded for 'purely aesthetic reasons' – specifically, to prevent littering in the forests surrounding Berlin – the political situation had moved Ewald's club from combating '*Schmutz*' (filth) in the woods to advocating public '*Schutz*' (protection) of them. The preservation of the forests around Berlin, Ewald argued, furthered the social, cultural, aesthetic, and public health agendas of all the groups participating in the *Waldschutztag.*[92]

Besides the Berlin Forest Protection Association, an additional five groups sponsored the meeting, each representing differing interests in

the conservation of the Grunewald: the League of German Land Reformers under the leadership of the property reform advocate Adolf
Damaschke; the Bureau for Social Policy, a coalition of liberal social reformers, represented by its founder Ernst Francke, a moderate liberal;
the German Garden City Society, a group promoting more affordable
suburban living to counterbalance the increasing density of cities, headed by the moderate socialist Bernhard Kampffmeyer; the Brandenburg
Branch of the League for *Heimat* Protection, led by the left-liberal House
of Deputies representative, nature enthusiast, and school headmaster
Karl Wetekamp; and the Central Commission of Health Insurance Companies of Berlin and Its Suburbs, represented by a Herr Simanowski.[93]
These groups set the agenda for the conference.

The organizers of the meeting illustrated the broad array of interests coalescing around the opposition to state policy. Property reform
advocates, concerned with rising rents and poor housing conditions,
sought to prevent the state from selling its land to real estate speculators, in order to avert a further escalation of land prices throughout the
region. Moreover, they sought to preserve the forest for the use of their
impoverished constituency. Kamppffmeyer's vision of a garden city, with
light and air for all, likewise sought to reform urban housing conditions
and preserve parklands in and around the metropolis. Naturally, insurance companies also had an interest in improving the living conditions
of their clients, promoting better public health. A healthier population
with better access to recreation would also contribute to the goals of
social reform, ameliorating the misery of Berlin's working class and
thus alleviating the social tensions liberal reformers felt fuelled political radicalism. In a similar vein, *Heimat* protection interests believed the
preservation of the Grunewald would not only address the problems
of cramped urban housing, deteriorating public health, and the social
crisis arising from them, but also felt the forest would contribute to
growing local and national patriotism that would inoculate the impoverished against political radicalism.

These motives found their echo and some elaboration in the further
thirty groups participating in the meeting. Twelve groups focused on
social concerns: five stressed urban issues, four were liberal labour
unions, two were social reform associations and the last was a league
of women's groups.[94] Another ten of them addressed themselves to
public health issues: four groups were dedicated to public health generally, three to combating alcoholism, two to athletics, and one to holistic
medicine.[95] These two clusters of associations comprised the majority

of the interest groups at the conference, reflecting the dominance of social and public health concerns at the organizers' level. In addition, a further five groups represented youth and educational interests: three were teachers' associations, one promoted science education, and the last was a youth welfare organization.[96] A final three represented academic interests: the Association for the History of Berlin, the German Botanical Society, and a scientific society promoting the preservation of the Grunewald's moors.[97] While these diverse groups all approached the Grunewald problem from a different angle, the need to maintain workers' access to nature held the conference together. As the representative of the liberal League of German Unions, Herr Goldschmidt, argued, 'The interest of the workers is closely connected with the preservation of woodlands around Berlin,' stressing that this issue would determine the 'national future.'[98] The speakers all agreed on the importance of workers' access to nature as an important means to overcome the problems of urbanization that threatened their health, living standards, morality, and patriotism.

The *Waldschutztag* stressed the importance of the woods for securing the health and loyalty of the working class. A wide range of socially active groups, representing the diversity of Berlin's associational life, came together to champion their cause. As the Berlin Forest Protection Association summarized in its annual report that year, 'The destruction of the woodlands and the excessive herding together of people endangers and damages the public health, leads to a disavowal of all moral connections to the *Heimat*'s soil, and aggravates the job of raising the culture of the urban population above its present level.'[99] The meeting therefore ended with a long petition to the kaiser, asking him to preserve the Grunewald for these reasons. Behind this appeal stood dozens of organizations with local and national memberships, representing a broad and politically active public. Indeed, the influence of the *Waldschutztag* spread well beyond the Architects' House. Not only did it receive newspaper coverage, journals associated with groups participating in the function reported on it, spreading the news throughout Germany. The League of German Land Reformers, the Bureau for Social Policy, and the Brandenburg Branch of the League for *Heimat* Protection all reported extensively on the meeting.[100] The proceedings of the meeting proved such popular reading in municipal reform circles that Karl von Mangoldt's Berlin Central Committee for the Forest and Settlement Question, which had published them, cheerfully reported in 1910 that it would have to issue another edition. The proceeds from the publication contributed towards their publicity campaign.[101] A broad range of public sentiment thus ran counter to government plans, and myriad organizations mobilized to challenge them.

Berlin Intervenes

The rising public discontent over the Ministry of Agriculture's policy towards the Grunewald prompted Berlin and other municipalities to respond. In March 1907, following heated debates in the parliament demonstrating the state's total intransigence, Berlin's city government called a conference of its western suburbs to discuss 'the preservation of the Grunewald as a public recreation area.'[102] Meeting in Berlin's City Hall the following month, the communes – after an address by House of Deputies and City Assembly representative Otto Fischbeck, who had led the fight for the Grunewald in the *Landtag* – agreed unanimously to send an appeal to the kaiser declaring their disquiet with the plans for the disposal of the Grunewald and asking him to stop the ministries' speculation with state land.[103] By entreating the kaiser to intervene, they hoped to circumvent the obstinate Prussian bureaucracy and hold the emperor to his promise of a *Volkspark*.[104]

The kaiser, however, did not seem to feel bound by his promises and yielded to pressure from his Ministry of Agriculture not to provide Berlin with further assurances. Indeed, correspondence from the summer of 1907 between the kaiser and the minister of agriculture, Bernd von Arnim, clearly indicates that the government envisioned reserving far less than Geitner's 4,000-hectare park. Arnim insisted on the necessity of raising funds from the sale of 'small portions' of 'significant real estate value' from the Grunewald, particularly for 'very great national and social policy tasks, among others in the east of the monarchy.' These 'small portions,' along with the Heerstrasse project, amounted to almost a third of the Grunewald; of the 4,335 hectares comprising the Grunewald State Forest in 1904, Arnim suggested sales reducing it to 3,000 hectares. Subsequently, on the planning map used for the discussions, someone adjusted this figure downward in pencil to 2,637 hectares, almost half its original size! Moreover, these sales would have entailed the loss of the most popular attractions of the Grunewald, including the lovely Havel shoreline from the Pichelswerder to Schildhorn in the north and the Wannsee in the south (see map 3.3). Aware that such plans would arouse public indignation, Arnim recommended that the state continue to make vague references to preserving the 'main part' of the Grunewald.[105] In

August 1907, the ministry – apparently on behalf of the kaiser – tersely
responded to the Berlin authorities 'that it is not the intention of His
Majesty the Kaiser and King to approve the sale of the main part of the
Grunewald for building.'[106] The 500 hectares of the Heerstrasse project
were apparently just the tip of the real estate iceberg.

In September 1907, Berlin's City Assembly took up the matter. Within two weeks of the Ministry of Agriculture's response, municipal authorities submitted a report to the City Assembly on its petition to the
kaiser.[107] While the City Assembly, composed solely of left liberals and
Social Democrats, was united in its demand that the Grunewald be preserved and unanimous in its dissatisfaction with the ministry's curt reply
(many had expected a statement from the kaiser himself), its deputies
were divided over strategy.

The left liberals believed that the Ministry of Agriculture was operating
without the consent or knowledge of the kaiser, and therefore urged a
more confrontational approach, calling on the city to enforce Wilhelm's
promise of a *Volkspark* through new legislation. They hoped to win over
some conservatives in the *Landtag* to their cause. With Wesener's eva-
siveness and hostility, as well as some astronomical estimations of price
(Finance Minister Miquel valued the Grunewald at a billion marks in
1892), negotiations with the state seemed destined to fail. Berlin would
have to force the government to recognize its duties as the protector of
public health.[108]

Despite general rejection of the government's response by left liberals, Berlin's Lord Mayor Max Kirschner – himself a left liberal of high
regard – apparently found it useful to accept the state's promise at face
value. In an interview with the *Berliner Tageblatt*, he noted, 'I believe we
Berliners can be very satisfied with this decision.' Underlining the fact
that the kaiser stood behind the pronouncement, the mayor stressed,
the terse wording could be ignored: 'Rather, the serious intent of the
party dictating this order must be kept in mind.'[109] Unlike his party colleagues in the City Assembly, Kirschner appeared to accept the idea that
the *Fiskus* would sell parts of the Grunewald, and indeed he saw this as
inevitable with the growth of the metropolis.[110] This stance laid the left
liberals open to criticism from Social Democrats in the City Assembly.

The Social Democrat Hermann Weyl, along with the party organ *Vorwärts*, expressed serious disappointment with Kirschner's interview. The
Lord Mayor's position would open the door to further government abuse
and deception, Weyl argued. Deeply distrustful of the government, he
believed authorities could technically keep their word and still decimate

the Grunewald. Weyl felt, however, that the City Assembly was united in its opposition to royal policy and that evidence of this unanimity would be important in confrontation with the state; he therefore withdrew his resolution calling for negotiation.[111] Consequently, the meeting ended with the universal approval of the left-liberal bill calling on the city to demand that Prussia preserve the Grunewald as a public recreation area.[112] The socialists, once content to play an intransigent role, now began to cooperate with the liberals in a common front against the government.

Kirschner's seemingly gullible acceptance of government assurances likely stemmed from his decision to approach the problem of the Grunewald in a new way. Rather than antagonize the patently unreliable Prussian government by making new demands, Kirschner had begun to consider buying the forest outright. Left liberals had long opposed this option, anticipating extortive prices. The Lord Mayor, however, felt negotiations might yield a reasonable price. Kirschner was not the only one on the left who advocated this position. An article in the *Berliner Tageblatt* that year called for the city to purchase not only the Grunewald, but also a broad belt of forests and pastures around the metropolis, making them available for public recreation.[113]

As it happened, Kirschner had already been contemplating action to save not only the Grunewald, but also other large tracts of woodland around his metropolis for some time. In the spring of 1906, inspired by Vienna's purchase of woodlands the previous year, he imagined creating a 'forest and pasture belt' surrounding the capital and asked the city's Parks Department for a map showing the forests in the area suitable for the project.[114] After the parliamentary debates of early 1907 made it clear that the *Fiskus* would not preserve the Grunewald on its own, Kirschner found increasing support for his greenbelt idea among the public and suburban authorities. That same year, the Berlin Architects Association sponsored a competition to develop a master plan for the city, including a greenbelt. Hermann Jansen, one of the architects speaking at the 1909 *Waldschutztag*, won the award for the best submission in early 1910, with a plan that featured extensive woodlands surrounding the city, linked to the metropolis by far-reaching suburban railways.[115] Municipal authorities as well as planning professionals began contemplating a city surrounded by and infused with nature.

In the wake of the contentious 1907 *Landtag* debates, concerned suburbanites turned to Berlin for leadership.[116] Within a week of Wesener's stubborn performance in the House of Deputies, Kirschner – along with the mayors of Charlottenburg and Schöneberg, the largest of the western suburbs – began discussing the possibility of creating a 'communal association [*Zweckverband*]' to purchase and protect the forests around the metropolis.[117] The head of the Department of Forestry himself openly welcomed the possible creation of a communal association, as it would likely ease the sale of the Grunewald to the cities. Over the next two years, municipal officials prepared the groundwork for purchasing the woods. City governments asked the Prussian legislature to create a formal and legal basis for the organization of a communal association, which in turn would have the authority to negotiate with the state over the purchase of forests.[118] They also drafted a 'Memorandum Concerning the Preservation of Woodlands around Berlin,' which proposed that the communes initially buy 10,600 hectares (including 3,000 from the Grunewald) to add to the 9,677 hectares already in municipal hands. Ultimately, they envisioned a belt of forests and parks in and around Berlin in excess of 30,000 hectares.[119] In April 1909, city officials drew up a list of Berlin's western suburbs with their populations, later used to calculate their respective financial contributions to the anticipated purchase of the Grunewald.[120] By that point, before the *Zweckverband* had been formally established, Berlin and its suburbs felt ready to bargain.

As their first act, they hoped to negotiate the purchase of the Grunewald, before proceeding to discussions on other land. These negotiations failed, however, when the Ministry of Agriculture insisted on a price of two marks per square metre and the municipalities refused to pay more than one.[121] The following spring, Berlin reinitiated negotiations for the forest, this time attempting to circumvent the *Fiskus*. Municipal authorities had already garnered support for the project from surrounding counties and the provincial government.[122] On behalf of representatives from the capital and its western suburbs, Mayor Kirschner issued a memorandum concerning the importance of the Grunewald to provincial and Prussian authorities in March 1910.[123] Citing a study identifying Berlin as one of the most crowded cities in Europe, with the metropolitan area hosting a population larger than most Prussian provinces, the communes hoped to bolster their argument that the state had a duty to sell the Grunewald and other forests to the nascent *Zweckverband*, encouraging the passage of the appropriate legislation.[124] Kirschner sent a copy of the memorandum to imperial chancellor and minister-president of Prussia, Theobald von Bethmann-Hollweg, who directed the ministers of agriculture and interior to report on the problem.[125] After reading Berlin's memorandum, Prussian interior minister Friedrich von Moltke 'greeted … with pleasure' the proposal to sell woodlands to

Map 3.4 Greater Berlin, 1920. From Städtische Plankammer, 'Übersichtsplan der Stadt Berlin nach dem Gesetz vom 22. April 1920' (Berlin: J. Straube, 1922). LAB, F Rep.270, Nr. A 3178. Courtesy of the Landesarchiv Berlin.

the capital.[126] Within a few weeks, Minister of Agriculture Arnim indicated to the municipal authorities his willingness to negotiate.[127] By the fall of 1910, officials had drafted detailed demands and offers, and placed their recommendations on a map.[128] Kirschner's strategy of appealing to members of the administration outside the Ministry of Agriculture had achieved some effect.

The State Relents

Over the course of 1911, the Prussian parliament hammered out the details of the Communal Association, uniting Berlin and its suburbs into a legal entity for the purpose of addressing three urban planning issues: local rail transportation, city planning, and the acquisition of green spaces.[129] In his speech opening the 1911 session of the *Landtag*, Wilhelm II endorsed the organization of a *Zweckverband* to purchase a greenbelt around the capital, and in the House of Lords, the Ministry of Agriculture announced itself prepared to negotiate with the nascent Communal Association, although officials characteristically insisted they would pursue the question only 'insofar as it is compatible with state interests.'[130] The *Landtag* debates of 1911 saw remarkably little acrimony, with the Pomeranian Conservative Baron Hans von Maltzahn agreeing with the Berlin Social Democrat Heinrich Ströbel on the importance of forest preservation around the capital.[131] In July, the *Landtag* passed legislation creating the Communal Association of Greater Berlin (*Zweckverband Groß-Berlin*), which formally came into existence on 1 April 1912.[132] Although Werner Hegemann, an urban planner and associate of land reformer Karl von Mangoldt, regarded the form of the *Zweckverband* – which limited the power of Berlin vis-à-vis its suburbs – as a defeat for the metropolis, it did prove successful in countering the power of the administration.[133] And as it soon became apparent, the government came to fear that the failure of the *Zweckverband* could lead to a much worse outcome down the road.

Nevertheless, negotiations did not get off to a good start. In May 1912, the minister of agriculture offered the *Zweckverband* 11,200 hectares for 178.6 million marks on the condition that it be maintained as woodland. The *Fiskus* also claimed the right to buy back some of the land as it pleased.[134] Although far less than the figure of one billion marks estimated by Miquel back in 1892, this demand provoked outrage from the *Berliner Tageblatt*.[135] Sensing growing public irritation, Wilhelm II met with Dr Karl Steiniger, Berlin city treasurer and head of the *Zweckver-*

band, and asked him about his goals. In response, Steiniger lectured the emperor, 'Yesterday I drove for an hour from eastern to western Berlin. Every building I passed had one, two, three, or more courtyards with hinter buildings. Here live Your Majesty's subjects, without light or air, in four to five storeys. What kind of generation does Your Majesty think is growing up here? Can these people gain a love for the dynasty, for the *Heimat,* for the Fatherland? If not, then in my opinion it is Your Majesty's royal duty to change these circumstances.' Ten days later, the kaiser announced to a meeting of Communal Association and government officials that Steiniger had convinced him 'that it is my duty as king of Prussia to have Berlin's living conditions changed.' He therefore instructed his minister of agriculture to develop a new offer.[136] Steiniger, with the weight of the metropolis behind him, had begun to gain some traction on the issue.

One key to the Communal Association's early success, Steiniger believed, was the growing opposition within the government to *Fiskus* demands. He hoped to use this opposition to pressure the Ministry of Agriculture to lower its price. Already in 1908, the House of Lords had requested that the entire Prussian cabinet, not just the profit-driven Ministries of Agriculture and Finance, approve land sales from the Grunewald. The following year, Georg Bender, the leader of the House of Lords' left liberals, asked that the ministers of interior and culture be included in negotiations with the city.[137] Steiniger made much the same request after his meeting with the kaiser, believing other ministries would moderate *Fiskus* demands. Moreover, Steiniger noted, opponents of negotiations in both the municipal and state governments grew stronger by the day, raising the spectre that the negations could collapse.[138] This threat had a powerful effect on the administration.

Government officials worried that the derailment of talks would lead Berlin to annex its suburbs – thus expanding the influence of its left-liberal and socialist leadership – which the state wanted to prevent. As Minister of the Interior Friedrich Wilhelm von Loebell stated in a cabinet meeting, 'The *Zweckverband* was created with the intention of preventing … the formation of a "Greater Berlin" as a single municipality.' Should it fail, 'then the government will no longer be able to resist the demands by the suburbs to be incorporated into Berlin.' Other ministers agreed, with the war minister concluding the *Fiskus* must sacrifice its profits to block the growing influence of the Berlin's socialists.[139] Government officials thus had a powerful impetus to keep the negotiations on track.

Of course, concerns about the political fallout of the Grunewald policy had long dogged the Prussian cabinet. In November 1908, when financing problems stalled construction on the Heerstrasse, Minister of Finance Georg von Rheinbaben opposed requesting funds from the *Landtag*. He feared that in the increasingly acrimonious atmosphere of the House of Deputies – recently exacerbated by the kaiser's inflammatory comments on British foreign policy to the *Daily Telegraph* – the matter would attract criticism that would 'turn against His Majesty and therefore would be very unfortunate, especially now.' Instead, Rheinbaben recommended postponing construction to avoid another showdown in parliament.[140] The administration thus feared that in the Grunewald matter, so intimately connected with the kaiser since his *Volkspark* declaration, a truthful discussion of its means and motives would only damage the emperor's authority.

This concern persisted during the negotiations with the Communal Association. In late 1911, as the *Zweckverband* gradually came into being, Brandenburg's Governor Alfred von Conrad quietly appealed to the Prussian cabinet to stop the ongoing land sales, fearing public anger would scuttle negotiations.[141] Although the ministries of agriculture and finance ignored this advice, other ministries began to express their reservations in cabinet meetings. In a June 1912 cabinet meeting, the *Fiskus* proposed lowering its initial 178 million mark offer to 113 million, but the minister of public works objected that this figure remained far too high.[142] Later that year, the Ministries of Agriculture and Finance actually recommended raising the price, arguing that they could receive far more on the open market.[143] The Ministries of Public Works and the Interior vehemently objected to the inflated sum on political and public health grounds. Representing the Ministry of Public Works, Dr F. Münchgesang maintained that it was 'politically absolutely necessary' that the Fiskus moderate its price and that sale go through 'especially in *consideration* of the fact that the person of His Majesty the King has already been associated with the matter.' Otherwise, he warned, 'the good will of the government would be doubted.' Given the high political stakes, Münchgesang threatened the intervention of the Prussian cabinet in order to prevent the *Fiskus* from derailing the negotiations.[144] Subsequent cabinet meetings echoed these themes. By January 1913, internal and external pressure had forced the *Fiskus* to reduce its offer to 70 million marks for 10,000 hectares. This represented a reduction of the area slated for sale by slightly more than 10 per cent, but the price now stood at less than 40 per cent of the original offer. Certainly, the Ministries of Agriculture and Finance had detached the most valuable land for themselves, but the offer remained a large concession. Yet others in the cabinet still considered this price too high. The Ministries of Culture and the Interior, along with the chancellor, felt the price should be set at 53 million marks (less than 30 per cent of the original offer) out of concern for 'general political considerations,' while the Ministries of Trade, Justice, and Public Works were willing to entertain even lower figures.[145] When negotiations with the *Zweckverband* again stalled in the spring of 1913, several ministries renewed speculation that Berlin aimed to undermine the Communal Association and annex the suburbs.[146] Political concerns thus pushed most cabinet members to place pressure on the Ministries of Agriculture and Finance to moderate their demands, for they clearly feared government intransigence could erode the foundations of the monarchy.

From April 1912 to April 1914, the Communal Association and the government engaged in a cycle of negotiations and mutual recriminations, echoing many of the arguments made over the past decade. While the *Fiskus* first proposed 178 million marks for 11,200 hectares of woodland around Berlin in 1912, the *Zweckverband* decided to offer roughly 30 million for them.[147] Adolf Wermuth, since September 1912 Lord Mayor of Berlin, chose to put extra pressure on the government by threatening to annex the suburbs in January 1913, causing a stir in the press.[148] The Prussian authorities responded by dropping the price to 53 million marks, which the Communal Association rejected, even though the government had made many concessions. Growing concern over the environmental health of the woods, suffering from a falling water table (brought on by increased urban demand for water), led many to argue the *Fiskus*'s proposed sum bore no relation to the condition of the forest.[149] The socialist daily *Vorwärts* even accused the *Fiskus* of deliberately allowing the Charlottenburg Waterworks drain the Grunewald's water table in order to destroy the woods.[150] Another sticking point involved the clause reserving the right of the state to buy back any portion at the sale price over the next three hundred years.[151] *Vorwärts* viewed this stipulation as a cynical plot to have the communes foot the bill for administering the dying forest until the land was 'ripe for building,' when the *Fiskus* could buy back the land at the low sale price and resell it to private entities for a significant profit.[152]

Yet some felt that the deal was reasonable. Bernhard Dernburg, a publicist for the Communal Association (and former head of the Imperial Colonial Office), argued in the *Berliner Tageblatt* that the government's price was not unreasonable. While the *Zweckverband* would be

technically required to pay a projected 2 million marks annually, with
creative accounting and tax loopholes Dernburg claimed that figure
could be brought down to 1.2 million. Moreover, he noted that the price
had come down dramatically from the original 178 million marks offer,
and warned it might not be on the table for long.[153] Meanwhile, voices
on the right complained. The *Deutsche Tageszeitung*, no friend of the capital, claimed the price constituted merely a drop from Berlin's budgetary
bucket.[154] Likewise, the conservative *Hallesche Zeitung* ridiculed Berlin as
a greedy 'village of extravagance,' and complained that the 53 million
was too little.[155] The *Zweckverband* nevertheless remained steadfast in its
resistance to *Fiskus* and conservative pressure.

Several more months of negotiations finally yielded a deal acceptable
to both parties. By April 1914, the *Fiskus* had reduced the price to 50
million for 10,000 hectares (fifty pfennigs per square metre), less than
a third of the rate the government had proposed in 1912 and far below
real estate prices (between 1901 and 1909, the state had been able to
sell parcels of the Grunewald for development at ten to thirty marks
per square metre, which was still below average urban land values).[156]
Furthermore, it made two important concessions. First, the administration agreed to compensate the *Zweckverband* for any expropriated woodlands not in cash, but in other local forests, limiting the *Fiskus*'s ability to
profit from land deals. Second, the *Fiskus* agreed to accept incremental
payment without charging interest, which saved the Communal Association a few million marks.[157] On 2 May 1914, the *Zweckverband* voted
sixty-seven to twenty-eight to approve this new offer, with the opposition coming mainly from the Social Democrats and some left liberals,
who felt the municipalities should not have to buy the forests in the
first place.[158] For the majority, however, there was a sense that they had
saved the Grunewald and its siblings from destruction at the hands of
developers, and would now be able to manage the forests in the interest
of the city's residents.

While several of Berlin's champions expressed their dissatisfaction
with the arrangement, the *Fiskus* also complained, which might be taken
as the best evidence of a fair compromise. The minister of agriculture estimated the government has lost twelve million marks on the deal by sacrificing interest payments. Moreover, inflation would erode the value of
the fixed payments over time, further reducing profits from the deal.[159]
Following the *Zweckverband*'s acceptance of the offer, one provincial
official warned the minister of interior not to take the vote as a sign of
victory. 'The mood in general is not favourable to the forest purchase,'

he noted, describing the intense lobbying efforts to win over the un-decided and the possibility the deal might not go through. He cautioned the administration not to push for more compromises from the Com-munal Association, for fear of derailing the negotiations entirely and creating a 'disgraceful fiasco.'[160] Neither side completely accepted the compromise, but both resigned themselves to its provisions.

In the end, Berlin had negotiated a hard bargain and received a great swath of property at a fairly generous price. Other Prussian cities paid significantly more for their parks and woodlands. In 1880, for example, Cologne bought 120 hectares of antiquated fortifications around the city from the state for conversion into city parks for close to 12 million marks; that worked out to be a fairly expensive 9.8 marks per square me-tre. The Prussian *Fiskus* did sell other future parklands for significantly less: Cologne, Essen, and Charlottenburg bought forests between 1890 and 1910 for between 1.50 and 1.75 marks per square metre, although in 1910 Halle was wrangling with the state over the Döhlauer Heath, for which it wanted at least 7.00 marks per square metre. Vienna, whose for-est and meadow belt became a model for Berlin, bought large tracts of land in 1905 for the equivalent of roughly 1.60 marks per square metre. Of the forest purchases by major Prussian cities, only Düsseldorf man-aged to negotiate a price comparable to Berlin's fifty pfennigs per square metre.[161] It seems unlikely other cities experienced a similar popular outcry over public parks, which in Berlin's case clearly helped to drive down the *Fiskus*'s price.[162] However, leaders from Elberfeld, Halle, and Breslau took a keen interest in the Berlin developments, faced as they were with their own pending forest purchases.

Adolf Wermuth, who assumed office as Lord Mayor of Berlin just five months after the establishment of the *Zweckverband*, found himself as-tonished by how rapidly such a complicated agreement was reached. All sorts of technical questions had to be overcome on both sides, and negotiations were complicated by differences between the city and the suburbs, the Communal Association's director, Dr Steiniger, and the previous Lord Mayor, Kirschner, and of course, between the *Zweckver-band* and Prussian officialdom. Wermuth commented later that his office quickly became overwhelmed with the task of coordinating transpor-tation, city planning, and green spaces with the other municipalities. Symbolically, plans for infrastructure improvements soon hung over the kaiser's portrait as the city executive rolled up his sleeves and got down to business managing a metropolis. The socialists were quickly recon-ciled to his administration, according to Wermuth, as 'many municipal proposals materialized because the Social Democrats were enthusiastically interested in them.'[163] Berlin strode onwards into what many hoped would be a marvellously modern future.

Within four months of the Communal Association's decision to buy the greenbelt, and before it signed the formal agreement, the First World War broke out. The economic disruption that ensued benefited the *Zweckverband*. Prior to the final agreement, signed in March 1915, wartime financial dislocation led Prussian authorities to compromise on the April 1914 offer even further, reducing the initial down payment from five million marks to a mere 500,000.[164] Moreover, the Ministry of Agriculture's concerns about the eroding value of the annual payments proved all the more accurate with rising levels of inflation. In Communal Association Director Steiniger's assessment, his organization paid less than half the agreed fifty million marks.[165] Following the war, with the intransigent Prussian elites removed from office, the Communal Association provided the framework for the creation of a Greater Berlin in 1920, laying its current boundaries (see map 3.4). The Grunewald and the other forests around the new metropolis were included in the city boundaries, and continue to serve the recreational needs of Berliners.

Conclusion

Berliners fought hard for their woods. They infiltrated the Grunewald, symbolically driving the kaiser out by 1904. In the course of the next eleven years, they transformed the Grunewald from a royal hunting ground into a municipally owned public park. They protested the state's plans to profit from the sale of public woodlands, insisting they be preserved for their health and enjoyment. In the press, in parliament, and in their associations, citizens of the metropolis articulated their demands. They believed a belt of forests around their congested city could help solve the pressing urban, medical, social, and political problems of the day. Left liberals, and later socialists, championed the city's cause, calling for the state to justify its policies to the public. Nature could help solve the enormous problems posed by industrialization and urbanization, left-liberal and socialist reformers insisted, and they demanded the state compromise on its goals. When Berlin's leaders realized they could not trust the state to preserve the woods, they turned to buying them. Pressure from the public split conservatives and Prussian officials, forcing the state to relinquish the woods surrounding Berlin at a fraction of their real estate value and frustrating government plans to cash in on its property.

The struggle to protect the Grunewald demonstrates the rational and progressive aspect of the forest discourse. Far from being a preserve of reactionaries and romantics, the campaign to protect the Grunewald represented a serious attempt to deal with the consequences of modernization, not to flee from them. This fight also points up the power of Berlin's liberal municipal administration, along with their allies in the press and the network of associational life, to overcome the self-interested motives of the Prussian state. An active city government assumed responsibility for social reform when reform at the state level stalled, hoping through its efforts to win the working classes to liberalism. Finally, the Grunewald story documents the potential of the public, energized by this strong leadership, to confront the state over social welfare, public health, and environmental protection. By the First World War, Berliners had wrested what they wanted from the state.

chapter four

Reforestation as Reform:
Pomerelia and the Tuchel Heath

Introduction

In the ethnically contested territories of the Prussian east, the concept of the 'German forest' meant something quite distinct from what it did on the outskirts of Berlin. Rather than a refuge from the stresses and strains of urban life, the 'German forest' functioned in the borderland as a marker of order and German civilization in what many Germans regarded as wild and inhospitable terrain. Indeed, foresters and other authors considering the region displayed widespread 'environmental chauvinism,' considering the local populace helpless in the face of extensive deforestation. German foresters would, as self-proclaimed masters of nature, create a healthy, sylvan landscape that would draw the region into the German nation and modernity. Like Berlin, the forests of eastern Prussia also saw a struggle between the local populace and the state. However, in this case, it was the state that mobilized the values of the German forest in its interest, seeking to impose on the local population its own vision of the woods and modernity.

A borderland of particular concern to Prussian officials and German nationalists alike was Pomerelia – roughly the area that would later gain fame as the 'Polish Corridor' – comprising two distinct regions, the Tuchel Heath (Tucheler Heide / Bóry Tucholskie) in the south and Kashubia (Kassubei/Kaszuby) in the north (see maps 4.1 and 4.2). Pomerelia came into Prussian possession with annexations from Poland in 1772, when Friedrich II seized most what would become the provinces of Poznania and West Prussia from the ailing Polish Republic. Some Germans liked to imagine Pomerelia as Prussia's answer to the North American frontier. In the eighteenth century, Prussia's Friedrich II apparently compared

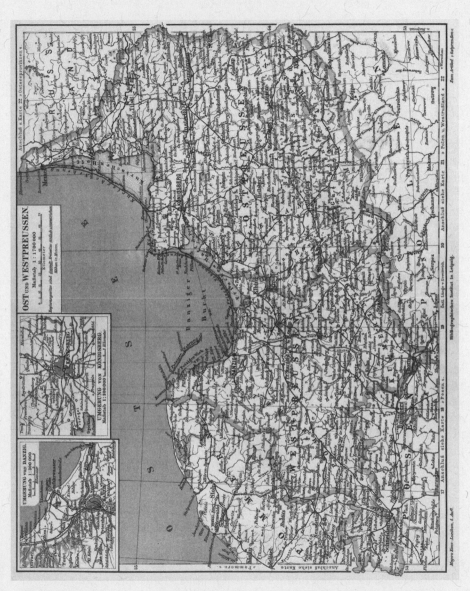

Map 4.1 East and West Prussia, 1890. From 'Ost- und Westpreußen,' in *Meyers Konversationslexikon* (Leipzig: *Verlag des Biblio-graphischen Instituts, 1890*), 12:541a.

it to Canada and 'jokingly named the inhabitants his Iroquois.'[1] Gustav
Freytag immortalized Friedrich's arrival on the frontier, characterizing
the place as 'an abandoned land, without law, without authority; it was a
wasteland.'[2] Certainly, the harsh climate, the sprawling pine forests and
barrens, and the impoverished populace suggested a certain affinity. In
one description of the region from 1879, the author depicted the Slavic
game poacher 'as a red Indian on the warpath.'[3]

The Germans, of course, were the bearers of civilization (or *Kultur*) in
this colonial fantasy. In one description of the Tuchel Heath, the author
described a primitive Slavic population 'interspersed with Germans, who
more and more bring culture here,' and contrasted the piney wastes of
the heath with the 'fertile and well-cultivated land settled by Germans'
just to the west, in which 'we feel ourselves in the German countryside.'[4]
German authors thus identified the introduction of a rational agriculture as one of the primary benefits to the region of Prussian rule.[5] According to an 1881 *Gartenlaube* article entitled 'German Pioneers in the
East,' the German cultural mission involved cutting flourishing agricultural communities out of the wild woodlands.[6] Medieval German monks
in the east spread 'Christianity and civilization' among the heathen
Slavs, and 'with shovels and axes created a secure home for their cultural
work.'[7] Nationalists celebrated the agricultural achievements of German
peasants, who 'won blossoming fields from forests and swamps.'[8] This
orderliness was all the more distinct when one contrasted it with Russian
territory just over the border. One author describing a Vistula cruise was
surprised by the poverty and disorder just beyond the German frontier:
'Yes, here Poland began – the contrast between either side of the border,
which was only an imaginary line drawn on political maps and not created by nature, was astounding. Upstream a tightly organized, clearly
discernable dredged riverbed – downstream a broad plain, traversed not
by a river but a chain of lakes overgrown with marshy woods.'[9] Such wild
forests and swamps were regarded as impediments to culture, deserving
to be swept away by a German colonization that would bring order to the
unkempt landscape and expand productive agriculture.

Lawlessness in the east, and in Pomerelia in particular, contributed
to its reputation as a wild frontier. Shortly after the region's annexation
to Prussia, a 'decent person' could not travel through the heath without an armed escort for fear of robbery or even worse at the hands of
'vagabonds.' In the Napoleonic era, many Poles and Kashubs reportedly
celebrated Prussia's defeat in 1806 with acts of defiance. Two peasants
from Repiczno ambushed and killed Tuchel's chief forester after he con-

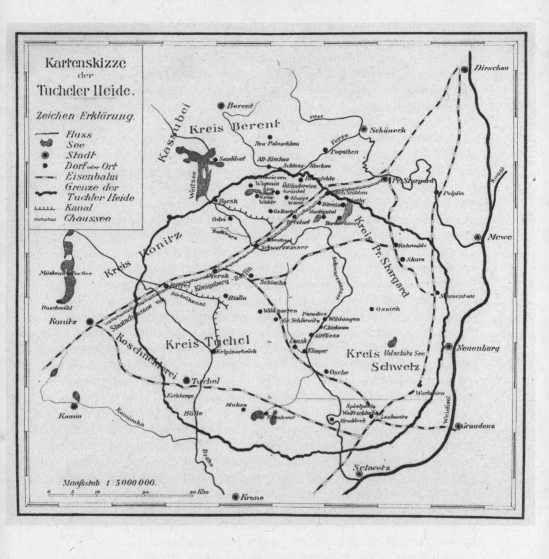

Map 4.2 The Tuchel Heath, 1908. From Johannes Mühlradt, *Die Tucheler Heide in Wort und Bild. Ein Besuch in Grüntal* (Danzig: Kafemann, 1908), 1:37.

fiscated their ploughs in a land dispute (and in 1848, a cross erected in his memory was subsequently vandalized), while others put state property to the torch. When French troops withdrew from Napoleon's disastrous Russian campaign through the region, some locals allegedly took their revenge for earlier French abuses, barbarously slaughtering them in their retreat and, in one case, burying them in the backyard.[10] Such tales, recounted many decades later, corresponded to regionally higher than average rates of crime down to the First World War, confirming for many the violent nature of the impoverished eastern frontier, lending it something of the air of the American 'Wild West.'[11] German authors repeatedly asserted that Prussian rule had brought law and order to this otherwise chaotic region.

This colonial imagery reflected an imperial mindset of many German officials and authors in the nineteenth century who regarded the Prussian east as a territory that needed to be torn out of the past and dragged into modernity, its populace freed from stultifying traditions and detrimental practices. A great many studies of the ethnic conflicts in the region have focused on Prussian efforts to forcibly assimilate its Polish population. Over the course of the nineteenth century, Berlin sought to more fully integrate these territories into the kingdom through a whole series of measures to combat sources of opposition and strengthen those loyal to the dynasty: abrogating the traditional rights and freedoms of the towns and nobility and subordinating them to the absolutist state, limiting the autonomy of the Catholic Church, imposing the German language in schools and administration, favouring German commercial interests, fostering German cultural institutions, encouraging the settlement of German colonists, and generally harassing non-Germans with all manner of bureaucratic impediments.[12] All of these state policies aimed to transform local society, shifting power away from Poles to Germans. Yet despite the fact that this struggle took place in a largely rural society – and came into sharp focus with the Prussian campaign to tilt landownership in the Germans' favour after 1886 – scholars have largely ignored the important role the environment played in this conflict.

Control of the landscape was of critical concern to German nationalists and Prussian officials by the late nineteenth century. The gradually shifting demographics of the region began to alarm them. Germans – disproportionately induced by the pull of industrial jobs and city life – abandoned the countryside, while Poles – with a higher birth rate – bought up land. And not only was the Polish population growing rapidly, but so too was the Polish nationalist movement. Bismarck reportedly worried that a resurrected Poland might 'cut through the best sinews of the Prussian state.'[13] Radical nationalist groups in particular vocalized their desire to secure Germany's eastern borders against possible ethnic revision.[14] To address this issue, the Prussian state created the Royal Settlement Commission (*Königliche Ansiedlungskommission*) in 1886, which sought to buy up the estates of failing Polish nobles for conversion into multiple German farmsteads. Ultimately, however, this endeavour failed to alter the ethnic balance of landownership significantly, as Polish nationalists organized to block the transfer of land into German hands, and the *Ansiedlungskommission* failed to recruit enough settlers to shift the demographic balance.[15]

The story of the *Ansiedlungskommission* is a familiar one, but it was not the only effort by Prussian authorities to secure the eastern landscape. State foresters likewise sought to gain control over large swaths of the countryside and stamp it in the German mould. Indeed, given the apparent environmental degradation of parts of the region, they intended to gain mastery over nature and transform the land and its inhabitants into a rational, productive landscape, well integrated into the German economy and nation. Foresters invoked a discourse of 'environmental chauvinism' to justify their work and imperial rule, identifying a cadre of German technicians as the only people capable of effectively managing the land, very much along the same lines William Rollins has outlined for Germany's overseas colonies.[16] In Pomerelia, as overseas, German foresters prided themselves alone on having the knowledge necessary to make the land productive; as Thaddeus Sunseri has argued for Tanganyika, 'Germans believed that only by controlling the forests would it be possible to relocate people in a manner that facilitated agricultural development.'[17] Whereas the colonial natives (in this case Poles and Kashubs) had apparently destroyed their environment and could now only scratch a meagre living from it, German experts (the foresters) would restore the land to productivity. Unlike colonial natives, however, the inhabitants of the Prussian east were regarded as assimilable, should they learn the right attitudes and behaviours. Above all, forestry officials viewed their 'civilizing mission' as the imposition of discipline on what they regarded as an unruly populace and landscape. Disciplining the land, they believed, would also produce a disciplined and *German* population – one tied intimately to nature, yet not dominated by it.

This chapter is structured in two parts: the first will describe the challenges Prussian foresters perceived in their efforts to 'civilize' the region, and the second will explain their attempts to address these challenges. Above all, Prussian authorities questioned the loyalty of the region and interpreted any resistance to state forestry policy as part of a Polish nationalist campaign of resistance against German rule. Yet despite ongoing (and sometimes violent) struggles between Prussian foresters and the locals, at no point did state policy shift from its goal of cultural assimilation. Given the focus on understanding the German colonial project, the purpose of this chapter is not so much to reconstruct the ethnic conflict in this region as to understand the ways in which German foresters perceived this struggle and the means for its resolution.

Prussian Forestry and Peasant Resistance

Pomerelia suffered from poor agricultural conditions. In the south, the Tuchel Heath was an area of piney woods and desolate sandy wastes that sprawled over approximately 1,900 square kilometres, about 60 kilometres south of Danzig. One local forester described the heath in 1871 as a silent and dismal setting, where crows thrived, songbirds languished, and foxes departed for better hunting elsewhere.[18] Another forester noted that agriculture suffered from frosts as late as May and June.[19] According to an 1878 government survey, the region was 'dry and windy' and generally 'unfavourable' for farming.[20] Conditions were so poor in the region that it took provincial authorities a year to find someone willing to fill the post of county commissioner (*Landrat*) when the Tuchel County (*Kreis*) was formed in 1875, and the eventual appointee had to be forced to stay in the position after just a few days on the job.[21] Neighbouring Kashubia, to the north of the heath, was hillier but suffered from similar conditions. A description from the 1890s indicated that the region was plagued by blowing sand, sterile soil, and a general lack of vegetation, combined with frequent droughts, frosts, and strong winds.[22] These conclusions were not just the self-serving assertions of foresters. Whereas farmers in the Vistula Delta found profit in the late nineteenth century growing wheat and sugar beets, neither could be cultivated in the heath or the Kashubian highlands. And even winter rye failed here. Such conditions meant land values were only a sixth of those in more fertile areas in the province.[23]

As both soil quality and climate could be ameliorated by planting forests, Prussian authorities concluded that the improvement of agriculture necessitated a concerted campaign of reforestation. In particular, foresters, botanists, and other scientists recognized that woodlands provided critical environmental services for agriculture: forests (1) helped moderate temperatures, preventing the earth from gaining or losing heat quickly, (2) regulated the flow of water by holding it in the soil, on the one hand preventing the fall of water tables in areas where swamps had been drained and rivers regulated, and on the other preventing rainwater and snowmelt from inundating lowlands, (3) increased rainfall in arid areas (although not everyone accepted this conclusion), (4) increased the air's humidity and ozone, (5) reduced wind speed and the consequent soil erosion, (6) cleansed the air of dust and bacteria, and (7) returned valuable nutrients to poor soil.[24] Prussian authorities hoped a program of afforestation would provide all of these benefits for local agriculture.

For most of the nineteenth century, this project of reforestation was regarded primarily as a private affair. During the 1870s, under pressure from the *Landtag* to address the ongoing deforestation of the region, the state encouraged landowners to protect stands of trees on their land and form forest cooperatives. Authorities in Berlin also provided funds for reforestation on private and municipal lands and passed laws against deforestation. But these measures appear to have achieved little, and in 1876 the *Landtag* set aside funds for the state's acquisition and afforestation of wasteland. Yet in the coming years legislators increasingly complained that the state did not use these funds.[25]

In the early 1890s, however, the situation seemed to change. By that point, the *Ansiedlungskommission*'s failure to bring about the desired demographic shift was becoming clear to at least some in Berlin. Meanwhile, one state forester's campaign to use forestry to improve the east began to gain attention. In the late 1880s, R. Schütte, chief forester of the Woziwoda forest district in the Tuchel Heath, produced a short book documenting the success of Prussian efforts to revive the local state forests since the 1850s. In it, he argued the introduction of rational forestry had transformed the region and was beginning to create a productive populace and landscape. Schütte financed the publication of his findings himself and distributed copies to senior forestry officials in Berlin. His work received approval from the highest levels. In 1890, the Prussian Ministry of Agriculture compensated Schütte for the publication costs, and the following year he received a promotion. Eventually, the Woziwoda forest district in which he had worked for decades would be renamed in his honour: Schüttenwalde. Schütte republished his work on the heath in 1893, arguing that the model of Woziwoda should be spread throughout the region.

Schütte's message was enthusiastically embraced by Gustav von dem

Borne, a senior official in the Ministry of Agriculture to whom Schütte had sent his book. Borne sought to apply Schütte's methods in neighbouring Kashubia and in 1892 published an article to this effect in a prominent forestry journal. Together, they anticipated transforming this poor, unruly, and ethnically contested region into a 'blossoming stretch of land' on the eastern frontier, well integrated into the nation and its economy. And these plans seemed to capture the imagination of other officials in the Prussian Ministry of Agriculture as well. From 1893 onward, the state began making progressively larger investments in the reforestation of Kashubia and the Tuchel Heath. Hundreds of personnel were deployed to the region and the area of state forests doubled.[26]

This project of afforestation in the Tuchel Heath differed markedly from Prussian policy towards the Lüneburg Heath, in the Province of Hanover. Although both were the product of deforestation and presented similar challenges for agriculture, Prussian officials and nature enthusiasts viewed the regions differently on account of their population. Originally, state authorities anticipated reforesting both areas. In 1900, the rural reformer Heinrich Sohnrey noted that 'while not long ago the Lüneburg Heath constituted a true desert, in which only a few flocks of sheep could find their sustenance, in the last few years reforestation has progressed so far that soon one will need to speak of a Lüneburg Forest.'[27] Another reforestation advocate later predicted that Germany would one day have its largest woodland there.[28] The project of reforestation was not carried out in the west as it was in the east, however. Borne contrasted the two districts directly, arguing that in the Lüneburg Heath one found 'a longstanding, solid farming community [Bauernstand],' which simply needed to plant their own stands of trees and implement better agricultural techniques to improve the land, while in the Tuchel Heath one found peasants incapable of defeating the forces of nature. Consequently, he prescribed private reforestation in the west, and state-led reforestation in the east.[29] This reflected the different attitudes towards the inhabitants of the two regions prevalent among Prussian authorities at the time and fitted in well with the state's overall strategy of shifting state forestry resources from west to east in an effort to consolidate state power in the borderlands.

In keeping with their environmental chauvinism, Prussian foresters universally identified Polish 'mismanagement' as having destroyed this supposedly once healthy woodland.[30] According to Schütte and Borne, when the region passed into Polish hands in 1466 (with the defeat of the Teutonic Knights), the newly installed prefects (starosti) exploited the forests without restraint. The prefects, highly influential nobles, pressured the king into granting them extensive rights over the Crown's woodlands. 'The deciding principle,' Schütte wrote, was 'not so much the common good, but much more the advantage of the *starost*.' He concluded that the result for the heath 'was a remorseless, destructive abuse,' especially along the rivers where wood could be easily transported away. In the interior, peasants cleared forests for agricultural purposes, despite the poor soil quality.[31] Other authors also impugned the Polish prefects, to whom the forests were 'delivered for limitless use,' and whose 'unmanaged sylvan practices' consequently destroyed the woods 'under the capriciousness of the reckless drive for profits.'[32] This discourse essentially equated the local Slavs with colonial natives, who, once having destroyed their environments, stood helpless against them.[33] Only the power of German forestry would restore this desolate landscape to productivity, its practitioners believed.

German depictions of the region identified Friedrich II ('the Great'), the hero of Prussian historiography, as the saviour of the Tuchel Heath and Kashubia. Just as he worked to drain the swampy Oderbruch to create new agricultural settlements, as David Blackbourn has recently described (along with the attendant environmental consequences), so too did he work further to the east to stamp the land with Prussian order.[34] His 'genius' and 'sharp-sightedness' allowed him to halt the damage to the landscape, according to Schütte. In particular, Friedrich was credited with recognizing the need for reforestation and initiating it in many areas, especially along the denuded riverbanks. But Friedrich's concerns were less environmental than economic; on his frequent travels through the heath, he reportedly declared it Prussia's future 'wood reservoir.'[35] Friedrich, a cameralist concerned with making Prussia a more productive land, attempted to impose discipline on this unruly landscape. While Prussian authors hailed Friedrich's struggle to drag the region 'out of chaos and into freedom,' as one commentator put it, not everyone was so keen on German forestry's new techniques and legal sanctions.[36] As on the North American frontier, indigenous people did not welcome the encroachment on their way of life. Therefore, Friedrich placed the heath under the administration of his War Department and installed soldiers and officers in the roles of chief foresters and other forestry officials. While they might have had little idea how to cultivate the stands of timber, they did know how to protect state property.[37]

Friedrich's soldier-foresters maintained a semblance of order in the state forests, according to Borne, but most Pomerelian land was in private hands. With the Crown's woods now inaccessible to the local populace (who along with the *starosti* had used the lands of the Polish monarchs), many ostensibly turned upon their own stands of trees. The West Prussian Forest Ordinance of 1805 attempted to regulate private woodlands, but Borne argued the subsequent liberal property reforms of the Stein-Hardenberg era undermined this measure. He maintained that the forests were 'exposed to the unlimited recklessness of a population unripe for the freedom of using a great sylvan treasure.' Heavy deforestation followed – a problem apparently seriously addressed only after the pregnant year of 1871, Borne asserted.[38] Even on the eve of the First World War, peasants in the Tuchel Heath reportedly continued to engage in suspect forestry practices. One observer described private *Kusselwälder* throughout the heath, consisting of over-exploited and uncultivated trees, pillaged of their branches before they could fully develop.[39] German foresters and other observers told a very similar story about Kashubia, where Berlin 'surrendered' royal forests to the local peasantry in the summer of 1808. The end of state restrictions on land use – meant to promote development – instead unleashed destruction on the woods.

As Schütte explained, 'The population of these territories failed to see that the productivity of their fields, a steady income, and indeed their entire existence depended on the presence of their forests. Often half-drunk, they cast off their timber reserves to wood-dealers one tree or whole plots at a time; what the merchants could not use, they cut into firewood, and they did not stop until their supply was exhausted and the present sorry state had been achieved.'[40]

Confident of their own ability, Prussian foresters emphasized that the peasants of the Tuchel Heath and Kashubia were immature and lacked managerial sense. Rather than conserving their resources, they squandered them 'half-drunk' for quick gain, without regard for the future. Of course, such authors overlooked the many German estate owners who also cut down their own stands of trees in economic hard times.[41] This irresponsibility necessitated state intervention, according to Schütte and Borne, both in the form of reforestation and in the complete reform of local social and economic conditions. The essence of the environmental chauvinist argument was that Germany (and the Prussian foresters in particular) needed to save the Pomerelians from themselves.

The majority of Pomerelians, for the most part Slavic speakers (generally Polish dialects in the south and Kashubian in the north) along with a German-speaking minority, suffered from endemic poverty; the poor soil meant low agricultural productivity and consequently destitute peasants. In particular, German authors often depicted Kashubians as a primitive rural people (unlike their more 'haughty' Polish cousins who sought to assimilate them), living a hardscrabble existence on this marginal land.[42] Ostensibly exacerbating the meagre soil were the Kashubs' flawed farming practices. Borne lamented that their 'agriculture is as planless as their handling of the forest' and characterized the condition of their fields, pastures, livestock, farm buildings, and roads as dismal. The forester Oskar von Riesenthal portrayed the Kashubs as 'simple,' satisfied to subsist on a diet of herring, potatoes, and sauerkraut (bread was apparently a rare luxury).[43] Indeed, in places the land was so unproductive that peasants depended on the many lakes for food. Reportedly, some Kashubian villages lived solely on fish, but as with the forests and the fields, the Kashubs were also charged with overtaxing the waters.[44] The long-term project to reform the landscape and address this poverty became a justification for German rule.

Of course, many German authors considered such impoverished conditions as an impediment to the advance of civilization. The impecunious residents of the Tuchel Heath supposedly stood 'helpless against an unfriendly environment.' Their superstitions, particularly about vampires, struck one German teacher as particularly 'inimical to culture' (*kulturfeindlich*), leading them to adhere desperately to Catholicism; in discussing this backwardness, he proclaimed 'an absolute devotion to the church and a total subordination under the command of the priest rules there, as much as the clinging to old customs and morals.'[45] As a strong advocate for reforestation in Kashubia, Borne likewise complained of the 'unusually low level of culture' there, despite Prussian rule. Both Borne and Schütte dismissed the Kashubs with their 'low level of education,' their 'laziness, drunkenness, and filth,' as well as their lack of 'a sense of order and of industriousness.'[46] From the German point of view, these characteristics made the Kashubs more loathsome than the nationally minded Poles, but at the same time less dangerous. Borne commented, 'The Kashubs lack the national consciousness and the fiery liveliness of the Poles,' suggesting that Kashubian backwardness was an economic problem but not a political one. Yet Prussian officials in Pomerelia had to contend with another vexing characteristic attributed to the Kashubs that threatened the state: their 'tendency towards the theft of wood, fish, and game.'[47]

Many Pomerelians (likely regardless of their ethnicity) seem to have resisted the encroachment of the Prussian state on their territory and livelihoods. According to German sources, as the authority of the old Polish kings eroded, everyone appropriated the fruits of the forest. Prussian foresters perceived a continuation of such practices into their own time. One observer commented, 'The people of the Tuchel Heath regarded the woods for centuries only as property of the Polish king, which one could dispose of as one wished.' Thus, foresters complained of the difficulties in establishing their authority, eager as they were to impose 'law over chaos' and exclude everyone from their rationally managed forests. German authors perceived these limits as especially irritating to the Polish gentry, the *szlachta*, which had enjoyed certain rights to the woods that Prussian foresters now revoked as aspects of 'Polish arbitrariness and mismanagement.'[48] But common Pomerelians – Poles, Kashubs, and Germans alike – also resented their exclusion from forests they had once used and often resorted to surreptitious protest. Schütte complained of the days when 'the cutting down of trees and signposts lining the roads, the knocking down of stacked cordwood and public notices, the disarranging of the sector markers, [and] the tending of livestock in the newly planted areas' vexed local foresters.[49] While some of this resistance – such as pasturing cattle in the forest, or wood theft and poaching, as we shall see – clearly profited the peasantry, most of the acts Schütte identified aimed to sabotage the foresters' work. Indeed, to use James Scott's term, they sought to undermine the 'legibility' of the forest by removing the markers that allowed the foresters to read and control the space.[50] Vandalized signposts no longer guided their way through the woods, rearranged sector markers failed to correlate to maps, toppled cordwood had to be reassessed before it could be sold, and missing public notices blurred the boundaries of where, for instance, one could legally pasture one's animals. These challenges to the foresters' authority made it difficult to impose the order deemed necessary for rational forestry.

Whether as a means to harass Prussian officials, turn swift profits, or simply make ends meet, Pomerelians engaged in a broad range of activities that contravened Prussian law. Royal foresters – as symbols of the advance of capitalism, state authority, and/or German domination – became the object of much resentment.[51] As tensions rose and foresters enforced laws more rigorously at mid-century, violence erupted in the woods. German authors increasingly viewed conflicts over forest practices through a nationalist lens. However, we should be cautious about reading peasant resistance in nationalist terms; one recent study of the region found that nationalism did not emerge from below, and that the voluntary assimilation of Polish peasants was underway before state and religious authorities interrupted it in the late nineteenth century.[52] By the First World War, however, it was probably true that Prussian foresters, 'amid an ill-willed population,' still had 'three enemies in the Tuchel Heath: the poacher, the wood thief, and the forest fire.'[53]

Wood Theft

Pomerelian peasants relied on a wide range of forest resources to sustain themselves in a tough environment. Mushrooms and berries supplemented the human diet; livestock found fodder in the forest undergrowth and clearings; peasants carted away dead leaves and pine needles as feed and bedding for their animals. But above all, wood was a critical resource, necessary as fuel for heating and cooking, as well as material for crafts and construction. Of course, some also sold timber to supplement their incomes. And wood became the source of great conflict between peasants and foresters, given that timber was what the state most prized from the woods. Whereas these resources had once been widely available for the taking, Prussian efforts to enforce new legal limits on public use denied many what were daily necessities. In the name of the common good, foresters criminalized traditional forms of subsistence to maximize profit for the state.[54] Consequently, as the state intensified its control over its territory in the nineteenth century (that is, as more foresters patrolled the woods), reports of theft increased.

Such appropriation constituted an important element of peasant subsistence in the Tuchel Heath, tied to the seasonal rhythms of rural life. Wood theft predominated in the winter, when work was scarce and fuel was in high demand, and declined in the summer and fall, when peasants tended their fields. By contrast, other forms of theft (such as of berries, grass, or mushrooms) rose in the months when these products flourished. Records of the 410 thefts from Schütte's Woziwoda Forest District in 1875 illustrate this seasonal pattern (see figure 4.1).[55] As the graph suggests, wood theft stood as the most prominent form of theft in Woziwoda. Forestry records from the 1870s recorded some personal information about the accused wood thieves. Most of them were local crofters and herders, generally men, although sometimes their wives and daughters were also caught in the act. Moreover, the lists indicated several members of the same families were accused, sometimes multiple times, suggesting they may have depended on the forests more heavily than others.[56]

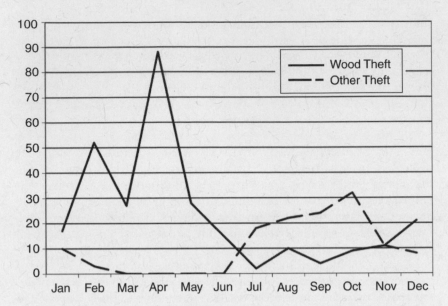

4.1 Cases of forest theft in the Woziwoda Forest District, 1875. From Verzeichniß der vorgefallenen Holzdiebstähle in dem Forst-Revier Woziwodda im Jahr 1875. In APB, Schüttenwalde, Nr.174.

Wood theft had long constituted an enormous problem for the Prussian foresters of the Tuchel Heath. According to Friedrich II's chief tax assessor, the village of Wigonin lived solely from trafficking timber stolen from state forests.[57] In the early nineteenth century, state profits from its timberlands in the region remained meagre as peasants carried off several whole trees nightly, and foresters of the period despaired of ever getting the problem under control.[58] One former forester recalled that wood thieves operated on a commercial level in the 1850s, arriving on dark nights in three or more wagons to help themselves to the sylvan bounty. Local sawmills abetted the pirates, accepting stolen timber without question and declining to inform authorities of irregularities. A state crackdown – including the posting of more foresters to the region and stepped-up patrols – resulted in a rising level of violence, including gunfights.[59]

Archival materials from the early 1870s through the early 1890s illustrate the range of conflicts between foresters and peasants, frequently resulting in physical altercations. Pomerelians continued to resist the state's attempts to limit their access to the forests and persisted in appropriating wood and other resources for themselves. Records from the Czersk state forest district in the Tuchel Heath documented several encounters between foresters and suspected wood thieves, several of which escalated into violence. Often the circumstances were the same: the forester ran across a man in the act of collecting wood and pursued him home, where some deception and/or struggle would ensue. Sometimes the encounter would prove more vexing than violent, as in the 1881 case of the Kartz family. After witnessing Johann Kartz and his son Anton in the act of stealing timber, the forester Kliewert reported tracking them to their home, where he confronted them. They gave him false names, and several days later when Kliewert discovered this deception, he returned to confront them again. Undeterred by the angry official, Johann Kartz claimed Kliewert had miswritten their names in a drunken stupor.[60] Such an accusation likely infuriated Kliewert, undermining as it did the fundamental dichotomy between the industrious Prussian officials and the indolent Polish peasants.

Other episodes in the battle against wood theft threatened more than just irritation. In 1871, for example, the forester Christow chased the alleged wood thief Slominski to his home. Upon arriving at Slominski's cottage, Christow discovered Slominski's horse in its stall. Slominski's wife claimed her husband was away and that the grey mare in the barn was not theirs, but when Christow attempted to seize the horse as collateral, Slominski himself emerged claiming no knowledge of the heist and demanding the return of his mare. When Christow insisted he had evidence, Slominski shoved the forester and ripped the reigns from his hands.[61]

While Christow's encounter proved relatively harmless, other officials faced more stubborn and violent opposition. In 1888, the forester Knop found himself in an altercation involving firearms. Following tracks from the stump of an illegally felled tree, he arrived at the farm of the Kannach brothers. There he discovered what he believed to be the stolen wood, whereupon Stephan Kannach seized the rifle slung over Knop's shoulder. The two struggled for the weapon, attempting to tear it from each other's hands. Desperate, Knop released the trigger, attempting to wound Stephan and regain control of his gun. The shot missed and attracted the attention of Stephan's brother Vincent. Both Kannach brothers managed to wrest the gun from Knop and evict him from the house. The humiliated forester then sought the intervention of the village elder Przytarski, who negotiated the return of his rifle.[62] Knop's struggle illustrates how dangerously close foresters and wood thieves came to killing one another.

Interestingly, violent episodes frequently involved the entire family. In an 1892 incident, the forester Lange along with his assistant Emig attempted to search the farm of the suspected wood thief Johann Grzonka for stolen timber. While they found neither Grzonka nor the wood, they did come upon Grzonka's furious wife, who denounced the two with a variety of insulting names (*'Spitzbuben ..., Räuber, Landstreicher, Louis, Bummler'*) and proceeded to lock the hapless Emig in the barn.[63] Only with force could Lange push the woman aside and free his assistant, he reported, at which point Frau Grzonka came at Emig wielding a log. Lange used the flat of his knife blade to block the attack.[64] In a more serious clash six years earlier, the forester Knop perused the alleged wood thief Johann Wloch home, where he disappeared inside. When Knop demanded entrance, Wloch's children and angry wife Katharina swarmed him. Detecting Wloch under a cover of blankets and cushions, Knop attempted to arrest the man, only to be blocked again by the visibly pregnant Katharina and her children. Knop reported threatening her with his knife, to no avail, and then resorted to beating her with its butt until she released her grasp from her husband (he noted he did this in a way so as not to harm the pregnant woman).[65] Such stories illustrate not only the continuing violence associated with wood theft, but also highlight the role of entire families in confronting Prussian authorities.

Besides confrontations over wood theft, women and children also ran afoul of the authorities for appropriating other sylvan resources. In particular, foresters confronted many locals for allowing their livestock to graze in unauthorized areas, as well as for collecting straw and leaves in the forest for fodder. Prussian forestry regulations strictly controlled these practices, worried that a complete removal of the woods' undergrowth would harm the production of healthy timber. Yet, as with the theft of wood, the local populace felt few constraints. In the summer of 1888, the forester Haase reported that he caught Frau Stamplewski with a forged permit for the collection of straw – a document her husband admitted to altering.[66] While Frau Stamplewski apparently did not offer resistance in this case, other women (like the wives of the accused forest thieves) were more demonstrative. Marianna Wloch embarrassed the infamous forester Knop when he ordered her to dump out her basket of illegally garnered straw and leave state property. She insisted in Polish that he had no right to evict her from the woods and then, according to Knop, 'she lifted her skirts, squatted in my immediate vicinity and

sh— (improved the forest soil).'[67] Similar vexing defiance also found
its way into the forester Oskar von Riesenthal's sketches of the Tuchel
Heath. He grumbled in 1871 about children letting the animals in their
care devour freshly planted saplings. In his drawings of an encounter with
such young herders, the forester berates the children while they 'act as
if they were mute.' During his tirade, a bull charges the forester's horse,
sending the steed galloping off into a bog, to the children's delight.
Riesenthal used the fictional episode to convey a point: 'The people's way
of thinking is reflected in this bovine: / Appearing as innocent as a child,
they seek quietly to do harm; / Perhaps he who shoots at you tomorrow
kisses the hem of your coat today, / 'Be on your guard at all times' – that
is the moral of this picture' (see figure 4.2).[68] Along with male wood
thieves, women and children challenged state control of the forest.

Fortunately for the foresters, incidents of wood theft generally declined
from 1880 onwards. As records from the Ciss forest district indicate,
accusations against wood thieves fell from a high near 1,200 annually
to well below 200 by the First World War (see figure 4.3). This decline
suggests that wood theft became a less generalized problem after about
1893, when the state initiated a reforestation campaign in the Prussian
east. It therefore may have been due to an intensification of sylviculture
in the woods, meaning more foresters, and more locals drawn into the
formal economy of the woods as seasonal labourers in the winter. This effect may also have been compounded by the generally improving economy, both in the industrial and agricultural sectors, drawing seasonal
labourers away from the heath. At the same time, while the number of
accusations sank dramatically, those accused were increasingly likely to
be found guilty. Foresters' growing success in nabbing their foes may indicate the courts' increasing intolerance for suspected wood thieves, but
combined with the decreasing rates of accusation, it seems more likely
foresters had gained better control over their forest districts and could
more effectively monitor them.[69]

A look at the numbers of penal labourers sentenced to work in the
Königsbruch forest district corroborates the apparent decline in forest theft. Courts mandated such penal labour for those who could not
pay the required fines. The fluctuations in the numbers of those condemned to penal labour at Königsbruch (see figure 4.4) corresponded
fairly closely with the numbers of accusations at Ciss. On both graphs,
the rates plunged in the mid-1880s, suddenly rose to a peak in 1889, and
then fell again sharply during the early 1890s. Thereafter, it appears,
despite some gaps in the data, that the numbers gradually declined to a

4.2 Illegal grazing, 1878. From Oskar von Riesenthal, *Bilder aus der Tucheler Heide* (Trier: Fr. Link, 1878), 11.

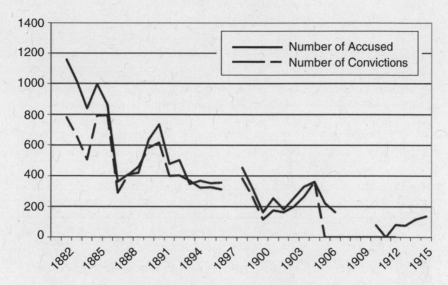

4.3 Criminal statistics, Ciss Forest District, 1880–1915. From Uebersicht der
Geschäfte des Forst-Amtsanwalt Oberförster Feussner zu Cis im Geschäftsjahre
1880–93, 1897–1907, 1911–15. In APB, Czersk, Nr.17.

mere fraction of their 1880s highs. While this trend could indicate a shift
away from the system of penal labour, when combined with the similar
fall in the number of convictions, it seems to confirm the overall waning
of the wood theft problem.

While the problem of commercial-scale forest theft had abated in
the second half of the nineteenth century, anecdotal evidence suggests
many peasants continued to appropriate what they needed from state
forests. As Pastor Johannes Mühlradt, who served a Protestant congrega-
tion on the northern edge of the Heath, reported in 1908, 'Most of the
workers' and crofters' homes in the Tuchel Heath are built from stolen
wood and almost everyone in this region made no secret of how once,
and even still today despite all of my reproaches in this matter, forest
theft is not regarded as a sin; here one regards it as the ancient Spartans,
who allowed their children to steal, so long as they were not caught.'[70] As
one local teacher testified, forest theft continued to vex the heath's care-
takers, who could never quite eliminate the practice.[71] But as frustrating
as the confrontations with forest thieves were, another more dangerous
foe lurked in the forest: the poacher.

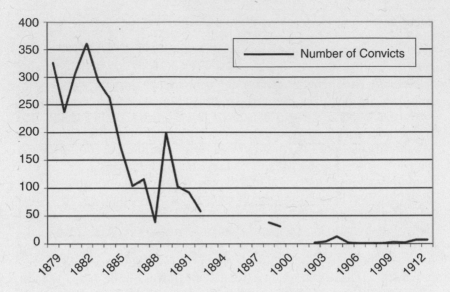

4.4 Penal labour in Königsbruch Forest District, 1878–1913. From Der Ueber-
weisungsliste. In APB, Königsbruch, Nr.145.

Poaching

The Polish gentry had enjoyed hunting rights in the royal forests under
Polish rule, but these rights were denied them by the Prussian state,
which sought to liberate the kingdom's woods from all manner of medieval privileges, asserting the absolute property rights of landowners and
the government in order to carry out new, scientific methods of cultivation. Despite some efforts at monetary compensation, many members
of the *szlachta* insisted on their traditional prerogatives and continued
to pursue game in the state forests. In part, economic imperatives motivated them into defiance; members of the Polish gentry, particularly
in Pomerelia, were hardly distinguishable from their impoverished non-
noble neighbours and therefore used hunting to supplement their income. 'In bands of ten to twenty men, made unrecognizable with black
crosses drawn with coal over their eyebrows and noses,' Schütte recalled,
'the poachers perpetrated their mischief.' Following mass on Sundays and holidays, they strode out into the woods, so disguised, to take
advantage of the foresters' day off.[72] Yet poachers sought not only fresh

game, according to German authors, but also revenge on the Prussian state.

Committed to the memory of the Polish Commonwealth (as well as their lost privileges), so the German narrative ran, some members of the *szlachta* conducted a clandestine campaign against the Prussian interlopers. In the 1870s, the forester Oskar von Riesenthal complained bitterly of poaching in his illustrated book on the Tuchel Heath. He related a fictionalized account of one unlicensed hunter caught in the act: after promising the chief forester to reform, the poacher returned later to steal his geese. 'Even if Madame [Chief Forester] is very angry,' the moustachioed thief gleefully exclaimed as he absconded into a wintry night, 'I really like the taste of roast goose!' (see figure 4.5).[73] Thus poachers pursued their craft not only for economic motives, Riesenthal suggested, but also in a purposeful effort to antagonize Prussian officials.

In a much more pointed representation, an introduction to the region described the poacher, unlike the common wood thief, possessing 'national consciousness … he seems like a red Indian on the warpath; he is a loyalist, who continues his nation's lost war against the Germans; he is irreconcilable, preparing his sons for a greater war that the future will bring.' Indeed, poachers often resorted to violence. In testing the mettle of new officials, poachers at mid-century reportedly turned to torture or even assassination when bribery and intimidation failed.[74] Schütte summoned up (admittedly humorous) incidents of foresters being forced to dance barefoot on pine needles by such malicious bandits.[75] Thus he insisted that duty in the heath demanded 'a constant awareness during one's service in the field, which was not rarely tied to mortal danger,' on account of the hostile locals.[76] And while contraventions of Prussian forest law generally declined to the First World War, they did not disappear altogether. Although poaching both expressed folk resentment and undermined Prussian authority in the region, another perhaps even more treacherous threat lurked in these frequently parched woods: fire.

Arson

While by the 1890s the state had largely imposed its own order on the heath, fire continued to threaten both life and property. The Tuchel Heath was often struck by drought, turning Friedrich II's woodlot into a tinderbox. As Riesenthal commented in the 1870s, 'That the Heath has not yet totally burned is truly a wonder of God' (see figure 4.6).[77] The volatile conditions of the heath led some foresters to suspect that

4.5 Poacher, 1878. From Oskar von Risenthal, *Bilder aus der Tucheler Heide* (Trier: Fr. Link, 1878), 9.

4.6 Forest fire, 1878. From Oskar von Risenthal, *Bilder aus der Tucheler Heide* (Trier: Fr. Link, 1878), 13.

human actors, and not just nature, were behind the blazes. Potentially the most radical form of protest against Prussian rule, arson may have set the timberlands alight, not only destroying state property, but also frustrating Berlin's plans for the region. While some peasants set fires for purely agricultural reasons, such as creating new pastures for their livestock or areas of heather for their bees, in many cases German foresters suspected political motivations dominated. As Schütte observed, wildfires were 'often enough set out of vengeful resistance against the new government.'[78] In most detailed discussions of the Tuchel Heath, authors mentioned the relationship of major forest fires with political unrest.

Schütte apparently first proposed the connection between politics and fire, and the early 1860s, when Russian Poland exploded in unrest, stood out in particular.[79] Schütte himself witnessed particularly large fires in 1862, followed by the calamitous year of the January Uprising itself. On Sunday, 30 August 1863, while most of the community attended church, a blaze erupted that consumed more than twelve square kilometres. Meanwhile, Polish (and even some German) volunteers departed for the Russian frontier to fight the arch-conservative colossus and restore Poland. These partisans waged a guerrilla war against the tsar's army, sometimes ambushing Russian units only a hundred kilometres away. Tensions ran high in the German east, where nationalist Poles and Germans alike anticipated the outcome of the uprising, and the application of such guerrilla techniques as the sabotage of state property would not come as a surprise under these circumstances. Large fires also afflicted the heath the following year, as the insurrection across the border petered out. Smaller infernos also erupted during the height of the *Kulturkampf,* Prussia's 'cultural struggle' against the power of the Catholic Church, altering everyday life in even the remotest schoolhouse and parish. To Schütte, these fires contained a sinister political message.

Schütte proceeded to tabulate the amounts of woodland lost annually and found a strong correlation between periods of ethnic unrest and unusually severe fire seasons (see table 4.1). According to Schütte, between 1860 and 1889, forest fires ravaged an average of 140 hectares per year. In years of political unrest, however, that average rose to 714 hectares. If one excludes those years, however, the annual average falls to a mere 25 hectares. Moreover, he suspected that this pattern had long preceded the records, which had been kept only since 1860. Schütte observed, 'If one considers that the events of 1794 and 1807 – probably also 1846 to 1848 – were burned deep into the memory of the heath, then the

TABLE 4.1   Forest fires in the Tuchel Heath, 1860–89.

Year	Hectares	Average (ha/yr)
1862	349	–
1863*	2,333	–
1864	156	–
1874	622	–
1875	114	–
Total 1860–89	4,206	140
Insurrectionary years	3,574	714
Non-insurrectionary years	632	25

* The fire of 30 August 1863 in Schütte's own forest district (Woziwoda, later renamed Schüttenwalde) consumed more than 1,250 hectares alone. This amounted to more than half the forests in the area burned that year, and more than a quarter of all state forests put to the torch between 1860 and 1889.
Source: Schütte, Die Tucheler Haide, 22–3.

connection with political events leaps before our eyes.'[80] These figures confirmed what he already believed: the fires were politically motivated. The attitude of the local peasantry, as he perceived it, betrayed the origins of the conflagrations: 'They first looked for a long time at the smoke with malicious joy, being pleased at the ruin of state property and the torment of forest officials, before they slowly and reluctantly reported to the fire lines.'[81] Although contemporary accounts did not identify nationalist motives at work in these fires, later authors embraced Schütte's conclusion that they were illustrations of Polish treachery.

Accusations and coercion from the Prussian foresters inspired resentment among the inhabitants of the heath. In May 1888, fourteen residents of the small lumber-mill town of Czersk levelled their own complaints against local foresters. Appealing to district authorities, these peasants claimed that Chief Forester Feußner, in an attempt to extort the name of a local arsonist, refused to allow their animals to graze on state property. While such pressure seems in keeping with Prussian tactics, the Czersk petitioners went on to make a much more serious allegation: the foresters sought to reserve all state pastures for their own livestock, purposefully excluding the peasants. Moreover, they claimed 'the foresters themselves are the arsonists, in order to make room' for more of their own cattle at state expense.[82] Both sides thus traded accusations of arson.

District authorities responded by ordering an investigation of the petitioners, to uncover the sponsors of this 'insult' against state forest officials. After questioning, a number of the petitioners identified a Czersk linen weaver named Radtke as the author. Interviews revealed that he had drawn up the document (in German, which he read to the peasants, with an oral translation into Polish for the two who did not understand the original) based on two pieces of evidence. One petitioner claimed to have witnessed the outbreak of a fire shortly after a forester had passed (although he apparently could not remember the exact circumstances), and three others encountered four cows reportedly belonging to the ill-tempered forester Knop grazing in the forest.[83] While it remained unclear why Radtke in particular initiated the petition, the peasants' resentment of the Prussian forest authorities, and especially Knop (the only forester mentioned by name in the petition), probably contributed to their assent. Indeed, one of the petitioners was Johann Wloch of Czersk, likely the same man whom two years earlier Knop had arrested for wood theft and whose pregnant wife Knop beat with the butt end of his knife. Thus the peasants' claims, while based on thin evidence, illustrate their resentment of the foresters and the increasing politicization of the issue.

By the late 1880s, Schütte claimed the worst period of the forest fires, like forest theft and poaching, lay in the past.[84] The optimistic Pastor Johannes Mühlradt agreed twenty years later, relegating politically motivated arson to times gone by. Forest fires resulted from inattention, he claimed, and 'seldom from malice, in order to fool the forester or make life uncomfortable for him.' Such arson no longer occurred, Mühlradt observed, because the population had come to recognize the state forests as a positive element of the landscape, an institution upon which they had come to depend. They reportedly 'gladly assist and support the foresters' by bringing them beer to quench their thirst during pitched battles with the flames.[85] Fire, like poaching and wood theft, apparently had faded into memory.

Yet Mühlradt's sentimental pictures of harmony on the ethnic frontier belied the continuing seriousness of political arson. In 1912, one observer noted that while incidents of wood theft and poaching had declined, arson remained a problem.[86] And a 1908 review of Mühlradt's work indicated that 'the struggle between the Germans and the Poles' had in fact spilled over into backwaters like the Tuchel Heath and had 'taken on a harshness even in these regions.'[87] According to government statistics, in May 1901 (as the Wreschen/Września school strike commenced in the neighbouring Province of Poznania), one arson fire in the Junkerhof and Taubenfliess forest districts alone ravaged 663 hectares of woodland, more than in all of the heath during the crisis year of 1874.[88] Likewise, in 1910 (following the verdicts in school strike trials), another 400 hectares burned in the Wildungen forest district alone.[89] These major fires, far exceeding the annual average, seem to suggest the foresters' fears were not far fetched. Indeed, comparisons to the rest of Prussia suggest that the forest fires in years of political turmoil may not have been simply caused by climate. Across the kingdom, large forest fires broke out in the dry summers of 1868, 1881, 1892, 1900, 1901, and 1911.[90] The Tuchel Heath's large fires of the early 1860s and mid-1870s therefore seem more inspired by political events than climate. Given that arson, more than poaching and wood theft, presented few if any material gains for its perpetrators, it would seem more likely an act of political resistance. The ongoing episodes of arson suggest resentment of the Prussian state's interference in the woods persisted, whether for nationalist or economic reasons.

Polish firebrands, German nationalists charged, targeted their attacks not only on the Prussian state, but also on order in general. As an anarchic band of thieves unaccustomed to discipline and averse to law, so the argument ran, the Poles naturally rejected Prussian authority and regulations. One guide to the region stated that, 'as Prussian order permeated [the heath], the beekeepers, the poachers, the wood thieves and all manner of other riff-raff could no longer do as they pleased; therefore they gave vent to their grievances in arson.'[91] Neither the *Kulturkampf* against the Catholic Church, the language ordinances against the use of Polish in schools, nor the myriad other intrusions on the daily lives of Slavic speakers in eastern Germany provoked these attacks, such authors implied; rather, the friction between Prussian order and Polish chaos had ignited the woods. Thus from the foresters' perspective, burning state timberlands was not a protest against the abuses of German rule, but instead an act of 'vengeance against the ordered discipline of the Prussian forest authorities.'[92] Another author concluded 'that chaos's hate of the Prussian desire for order led to the forest fires,' characterizing such attacks as the 'senseless vengeance of impotence.'[93] According to this view, Germans countered this reckless lawlessness and imposed civilization. German authors agreed that only once the Slavic population of Pomerelia learned the Prussian virtues of order and discipline, along with the benefits of German rule, would the attacks on the forests and the state come to an end.

While the Prussian foresters approached the local populace with a stern paternalism, these provocations – whether real or imagined – do not seem to have led the foresters or other state officials to embrace the language of race to explain their problems. Only two German authors writing about the Tuchel Heath on the eve of the First World War – Erich Wernicke and Adalbert Luntowski – briefly identified the region's problems as racial in origin. Wernicke, a girls' school headmaster in nearby Marienwerder, described the economic and cultural decline of the heath after the departure of the Teutonic Knights as the result of 'blood mixtures' between German settlers and the indigenous Slavs.[94] Luntowski – a translator of Gobineau into German and a *völkisch* eccentric who would found a spiritual commune during the First World War – echoed Wernicke's 'racial law.'[95] But even with these forthright statements of racism, both authors held out hope for assimilation of the local Slavs. Wernicke seemed to have no problem with the Teutonic Knights' policy of 'the melting together of the German settlers with the Slavic [*wendischen*] inhabitants, as they succeeded in doing on the other side of the Vistula [in East Prussia].'[96] Luntowski, meanwhile, celebrated state efforts to 'improve the land and its people.'[97] Despite momentarily deploying commonplace racial formulas, both authors seemed to believe that German rule could transform the region and assimilate its populace and no one proposed driving the indigenous peasantry off the land. Indeed, reforming the land and populace went hand in hand.

Forestry as Civilization: Discipline and Improvement

Critical to their control of the landscape, Prussian foresters understood, was the control of the local population. One forester who had worked in the Prussian east in the 1870s recalled, 'We protected the forest from fires by forest rangers and by having proper morals in the neighbourhood.'[98] Extending their influence over the forest thus meant policing and reforming its populace. Policing was easy enough; the level of poaching fell, Schütte testified, with the increased patrols of the forest on holiday mornings to prevent this 'bad habit [*Unsitte*].'[99] In 1872 the provincial government in Danzig, perhaps responding to a sense of laxity, reminded foresters in the province to wear their uniforms and to carry weapons in order to effectively enforce forestry regulations.[100] Hundreds of impoverished members of the *szlachta* convicted of violating forest regulations lost their titles.[101] In 1884, provincial police authorities banned all fires (including smoking) from the woods, required permits for all those engaging in economic activities in the forest, and ordered that all timber products being transported from state forests be accompanied by a testament to their origin.[102] In order to elicit (or coerce) cooperation against forest fires from the peasantry, the local forest officials agreed to return a portion of their pasture fees should no large fires break out in the forest district. As Schütte observed, 'With the indolence of the heath's population and their lack of recognition that their own well-being was closely tied to the forest, one turned to their immediate pecuniary interests.'[103]

Schütte's comment suggests the larger goal of Prussian foresters in the region. While policing could limit the financial losses to the state over the short term, overcoming the local peasantry's 'indolence' and 'lack of recognition' of their own welfare stood as an important, ongoing aim. After all, the peasants had been paying the extra pasture fees since the 1830s, yet forest fires continued to erupt in times of crisis through the turn of the century. Fundamentally, the foresters sought to discipline the local Slavs as they were disciplining the landscape: transforming what they saw as an unproductive land and people into a well-regulated part of the national economy. Indeed, already in 1834 the chief forester at Schwiedt had insisted, 'The Polish inhabitants of the Tuchel Heath must be cultivated by all conceivable means, which admittedly in the first years will be as impossible as the planting of trees [*Anlage einer Kultur*] on dead soil.'[104] In this formulation, the connection between the two primary meanings of *Kultur* becomes clear; a flourishing human culture depended on a blossoming agri*culture*. Development of land and people thus would be carried out hand-in-hand.

Disciplining this region had long been a priority. Already in 1773, shortly after Prussia acquired the territory, Friedrich II had built the Bromberg Canal to link the region to the developing Prussian economy. After the military disruptions of the early part of the nineteenth century, the state resumed the major public works program in the region in 1842. Investment in canals, dikes, bridges, roads, and eventually the extension of railways (the Bromberg-Dirschau railway of 1853, the first in the Prussian east, ran through part of the heath) strengthened West Prussia's integration into the kingdom's transportation infrastructure. The Ministry of Agriculture, interested in extracting the heath's timber, sponsored road improvements and new rail depots. The ministry also initiated drainage and irrigation projects in the heath to develop new pastures and cropland. By the 1880s, these efforts encompassed over a thousand hectares.[105] Foresters in particular imposed order on a large part of the province, laying out their forest districts on a grid. They straightened and paved the sandy tracks, planted their pines in neat rows for easier harvesting, and created a huge gridwork of firebreaks visible on maps of the province.[106] At the turn of the century, Pastor Mühlradt commented on the modern sawmills that sprang up around the heath, arguing, 'The wood industry in the Tuchel Heath is indeed highly developed.'[107] The nearby town of Czersk benefited from not only the sawmills, which employed about 390 labourers, but also the picture frame industry. At least one factory employing 400 workers turned the soft pinewood into the ornately carved borders, another gilded them, and yet another provided the glass.[108] Another facility produced railroad ties for German railway expansion, as well as for export to England.[109] Local officials celebrated this modernization; one forester gave a loving description of his forest district with its mixture of trees, scattered settlements, church steeples, and modern railway bridge.[110] Far from a romanticized landscape, German authors revelled in the heath's modernization and looked forward to the growing benefits of Prussian rule.

The expansion of state forests (including the Tuchel Heath) in the Marienwerder administrative district, the southern half of the Province of West Prussia, contributed to the Germanization of the region. According to the Eastern Marches Society, Prussian reforestation efforts meant the state forests in the district had doubled in size between 1867 and 1911, growing by over 180,000 hectares (or 1,800 square kilometres).[111] While in 1874 there were twenty-seven state forest districts organized in four inspectorates, by 1918 their numbers had almost doubled to fifty forest districts in seven inspectorates.[112] In the Tuchel Heath alone between the 1890s and the First World War, the state doubled its landholdings to own a full two-thirds of the land, as well as expanding the number of forest districts from nine in 1886 to twenty-three in 1913. This enormous expansion of both the dimensions and administration of the local state forests occasioned the stationing of extra personnel in the region. The number of forestry officials in the heath doubled during of the 1890s to over two hundred by 1901. Added to this number were at least another hundred watchmen in 1892 (tripling to three hundred by the First World War), not to mention around eight hundred servants and farm hands employed privately by forestry officials.[113] This enlargement of the state forests extended the control of Prussian officials over the landscape and its inhabitants.

While the state maintained only two hundred officials in the Tuchel

Heath by the turn of the century, this relatively small number helped tip the balance of power to the Germans (and the state) in this sparsely populated region.[114] A look at the Tuchel Heath on an ethnic map of the Province of West Prussia from 1905 reveals that in this predominantly Polish area, the state forests tended to be designated as German, while the surrounding fields were not.[115] By 1897, after just a few years of the state's concerted efforts to expand its property, foresters played an important part in local administration. Of the fifteen communities (*Amtsbezirke*) in Tuchel County, chief foresters controlled four and foresters served as deputies in a further four (most of the remaining positions being occupied by local landowners).[116] Foresters, more than private citizens, could be counted on to carry out the agenda of the state. As Prussian state employees working in the German east, foresters were obliged by the Civil Servants Order (*Beamtenerlaß*) of 1898 to work 'in the interest of Germandom.' Specifically, this meant officials could be dismissed for sending their children to Polish schools or voting for Polish candidates. Five years later, in an effort to keep German officials at their posts, the Eastern Marches Subsidy (*Ostmarkenzulage*) provided hardship compensation (a 10 per cent raise) for those government employees who had worked in the settlement zone for more than five years.[117] While foresters did not differ from other state bureaucrats in this regard, they proved of special utility because their influence spread over the countryside, while most other officials were concentrated in the larger towns.

Apparently, foresters fulfilled their political role well. In a meeting of the Prussian cabinet in 1904, several government agencies reported difficulties in getting their staffs to adhere to the regulations set down by Berlin. Minister of Agriculture Victor von Podbielski proudly boasted that 'no official of his ministry has cast his vote in favour of a Polish delegate.' Those who had simply neglected to go to the polls, he announced, had been shifted to other provinces. He justified this administrative procedure by claiming he had never taken measures against any bureaucrat based on his electoral behaviour, but rather used this information to determine 'whether the official proved himself capable and in the appropriate position.'[118] Clearly, the minister regarded voting for German candidates as a mandatory responsibility of all his subordinates, and contravening this expectation had consequences for one's career.

Podbielski's pressure on his local agents to vote German contributed to a shift in the political balance of power in the heath. In the Reichstag elections of 1881, the electoral districts of Neustadt-Karthaus, Berent-Preußisch Stargard, and Konitz-Tuchel – running southward from the

Baltic through the Kashubian highlands to the Tuchel Heath – formed 'a firm bastion of the Poles and the Kashubians, such that a German candidate had absolutely no chance of gaining a seat.'[119] By 1912, however, West Prussia's Polish delegation in the Reichstag had been reduced to defending this electoral fortress. While in 1881 Poles had carried three other constituencies, in 1912 they managed to take only the hills of Kashubia and the pine barrens of the heath.[120] And even there, Polish electoral predominance had eroded. In the Konitz-Tuchel electoral district in particular, German political parties gained significant support. Between 1871 and 1912, German parties more than doubled their number of votes (growing from 2,579 in 1871 to 6,511 in 1912), whereas the Polish party increased its vote by less than half (6,373 in 1871 to 9,104 in 1912). While the Poles continued to carry the Tuchel Heath, they now had to contend with a growing German political presence, rising from 30 per cent of the vote in 1871 to 42 per cent in 1912.[121] While several other factors likely contributed to the Germans' electoral gain, the presence of two hundred loyal Prussian foresters in the region, as well as the labourers under their control, surely contributed to this narrowing gap, particularly in the heath.

Defending the interests of Germandom meant more than just casting one's vote for reliable German candidates; it also meant, according to Podbielski, imposing Germandom on local employees, whose numbers in the heath fluctuated with the season; their total could climb to three thousand during the winter timber harvest.[122] Besides woodsmen, foresters in the 1880s also employed roughly 1,200 workers to transport timber by cart or by river.[123] Altogether, in the Marienwerder administrative district, 13,634 workers laboured·864,974 workdays in 1900.[124] At the same 1904 cabinet meeting mentioned above, Podbielski touted his 1902 order that forestry officials act as 'dependable agents of Germandom,' requiring that they 'not speak Polish with any worker.' Podbielski stressed that he 'could not abide sympathy for the Poles among the foresters and other officials of the eastern provinces' and considered 'severe measures' against any such sympathy as justified.[125] Podbielski's tradition of strident anti-Polonism set a precedent in the ministry, extending not only to the language of seasonal labourers, but also to their politics. According to the Polish politician Bernard Łosiński, a delegate to the Prussian *Landtag*, Polish and Kashubian woodsmen had to endure political harassment by state foresters. In 1907, one group of lumberjacks near Karthaus/Kartuzy had been dismissed despite possessing a six-year contract. The local chief forester first claimed he terminated the contract because they had refused to work and later accused the group of forest theft – a charge that could not be substantiated. According to the woodsmen, the chief forester had abrogated their contract when they refused to sign a declaration in favour of replacing the Polish language with German in religious education in the local schools. Łosiński indicated that there had been similar incidents in the neighbouring Mirchau state forest district.[126] Foresters thus apparently tried to coerce their Slavic employees to support state Germanization in the region.

Beyond the short-term strategies of imposing language restrictions on and political manipulation of its employees, however, the Prussian state still had to achieve its long-term mission of overcoming local 'indolence' and 'ignorance.' Schütte believed he had laid the foundations for this transformation of the inhabitants of the Tuchel Heath. As he commented in 1893, 'The improvement of the inhabitants of the heath – who in their entire lifestyle and civilization [*Lebensweise und Gesittung*] were still very backward only a generation ago – required none other than the opportunity and the education [*Erziehung*] for work.' He described how woodsmen learned the necessary attributes of efficient workers: 'The punctual start of the work day, the specified time for the continuous planting of trees, the necessary alertness in this project, the orderliness of the correct measurement and good positioning of the saws in cutting trees, the proper felling and cleaning of the trunks, in short, all those details upon which the forest administration place great emphasis, provide in their entirety a very important factor in becoming accustomed to orderly, sustained activity.' State employment also meant officials could reward diligent woodsmen for their efforts – perhaps with a garden plot or an inexpensive rate on animal feed – and punish recalcitrant ones – perhaps by cancelling a lease or denying access to pastures.[127] Schütte thus demonstrated the power of the state to modernize its citizens.

As noted earlier, Schütte's apparent success inspired Borne to pursue a similar project in Kashubia. In an 1892 article in a prominent forestry journal, he advocated reforestation as the remedy to the region's socioeconomic maladies. While Prussia had introduced order, military service, and education to the province, Borne contended, there still remained the task of 'healing of all damage that Polish rule has left behind.' That damage consisted not only of abysmal environmental conditions, but also a ruined economy and a populace too mired in tradition and superstition to better itself. As Borne put it, 'The improvement of the conditions totally or substantially on the initiative of the Kashubian population is not possible.' He proposed an expansive project of reforestation, like the one already begun in the neighbouring Tuchel Heath. Such state intervention would 'improve the economically and morally degenerated population. Above all, the habituation to regular activity and the creation of a sufficient earned income contribute to this goal. The extensive cultivation of the wasteland will offer the first opportunity for the employment [*Beschäftigung*] of workers.'[128] Thus reforestation benefited the region not only through its impact on the local environment and economy, but also through the 'moral' education provided by regular work under German supervision.

For Borne, the Tuchel Heath shone out on the eastern landscape like a beacon of social and economic progress. There, he explained somewhat wishfully, 'the barrens are cultivated. The timber planted in the course of the past several years now form a noteworthy source of revenue for the state. The population has accustomed itself to order and work.' The local contingent of foresters had, as he put it 'contributed to the strengthening of Germandom in the Tuchel Heath, encouraged the workers to be industrious and orderly, and served as examples.' Regular work, and inspiration from German authority figures, had apparently led to the decline of taverns and drunkenness, while the state had developed more and better (meaning German) schools. Borne hoped to transform Kashubia in the same way, creating 'a forest out of the wasteland, in which a settled population works and finds reward.' He hoped that such sylvan labour would encourage the Kashubians to 'accustom themselves to order, industriousness, and thriftiness.'[129] Borne's favoured categories of self-improvement, his belief in the moral virtues of work, and his faith in the attractiveness of the Germans' model of behaviour reflected less a conservative agenda than a liberal nationalist attempt to foster the development and integration of Germany's Polish and Kashubian minorities into the national economy.

Borne and Schütte were not alone in their belief that the locals could be educated and moulded into a more prosperous society. Many felt that the provision of regular employment in the Tuchel Heath had transformed the destitute locals into hard-working citizens. One author in 1914 celebrated the 'the cultivating [*erzieherische*] power of work, which the forester generously offers.'[130] In 1901, another account approvingly commented on the state's improvement of the local economy, noting that the inhabitants, largely dependent on the woods for work, understood German and were 'skilful, willing, and able.'[131] Pastor Johannes Mühlradt of Grünthal observed in 1908 that the inhabitants of the village of Wigonin, who once subsisted from wood theft and poaching, now lived from the wages of migrant workers.[132] Indeed, in 1904 the district government reported improving labour conditions in the region, noting a steady increase of forest workers' housing, which by that point accommodated 193 families.[133]

Even the two authors who denigrated the locals for their racial origins – Wernicke and Luntowski – embraced the transformative power of labour on the natives. Wernicke attested that the state forests stood at the heart of the heath's economy, bringing prosperity to the entire region. The growth of state forests and the labour they provided for so many local families made them 'all more or less closely tied to the woods.' Not only men were drawn into the forest's orbit; women and children also supplemented the family income during the spring tree planting. For Wernicke, forestry converted the locals from exploiters of the landscape into conscientious cultivators.[134] And Luntowski, although he dismissed the people of the heath as 'these squalid mongrels [*diese verwahrlosten Mischlingen*],' acclaimed the 'educational [*erzieherische*] power of work, which the forester generously offers.' And it seemed the foresters were succeeding in their task of transforming the natives. 'What was initially coercion to them gradually became a necessary custom,' he averred, 'which carried over into their entire way of life.' Whereas local peasants had once avoided hard work, preferring instead to steal wood, dig up amber, and poach game and fish, 'now serious, ongoing, and regulated activity is demanded of them,' he crowed. Locals learned punctuality and order from the foresters, for 'the rows of cordwood must be well measured and built.' Work, so central to German identity in Luntowski's formulation, became the 'morality-producing [*Sittlichkeitsschaffenden*] centre of their lives.' Despite his initial condemnation of the heath's inhabitants, he celebrated the foresters' work in 'the improvement of the land and its people in the Tuchel Heath.'[135]

Of course, one conceivable way of Germanizing the heath might have been to drive non-Germans off the land. Such a move could have been conceivable. The population of the region was relatively small and poor, squeezing a living from infertile soil. Certainly, a significant number of peasants sold their land to the state for reforestation efforts, and that policy could have been extended to buy out all non-German landowners. Seasonal labourers, so common on the manorial estates of the region, could have been hired for planting and harvesting. At least one prominent agricultural reformer, Heinrich Sohnrey, worried that reforestation throughout Germany was destroying peasant communities and driving farmers off the land.[136] Yet no one appears to have contemplated this solution, even in the ethnically contested Prussian east. Rather than displacing the locals, Prussian policy appeared concerned with (forcibly) integrating them into a healthy economy.

Beyond labour, the woods provided other means of sustenance; peasants leased small fields and pastures, which foresters had reclaimed from swamps or made fertile through irrigation, at low prices. The foresters also offered cheap wood for heating and construction, as well as pine needles for animal bedding. Small farmers earned extra income hauling logs from the woods to the train depots and sawmills around the forest. The woodworking industry employed thousands in the area, particularly in the town of Czersk. The extension of the railways facilitated the sale of the heath's lumber throughout Germany, apparently bringing about a rise in wages (although they remained below the national average). The foresters had transformed the Tuchel Heath, observers commented; without the state forests, Schütte claimed, 'the changing level of culture and growing population of the villages in the heath would be impossible, as otherwise there is no population growth in West Prussia.' With praise for the Prussian administration, he announced in 1893, 'So today the Tuchel Heath stands as a wooded region with a population of mixed blood, capable of education, secure in their existence, and advancing in their well-being, with the large forests in the hands of the state.'[137] Apparently for Schütte, mixed blood was a sign of improvement, not decline. Even Wernicke, ambivalent about the value of mixed blood, declared twenty years later that the heath's residents 'live more contentedly, better and more luxuriously than the urban poor.' All of these factors led him to conclude, 'The forest makes the entire economic life of the Tuchel Heath fertile.'[138]

The forester stood as the champion of this transformation. A review of Mühlradt's work on the heath applauded the foresters' 'German cultural work [*Kulturarbeit*]' in this backward and isolated region.[139] The *völkisch* author Adalbert Luntowski lauded foresters' productive strength (*Kulturkraft*). In glowing terms, he reminded Germans they were to thank the foresters as much as Friedrich II for bringing order to the region: 'The man, upon whom this creation in the Tuchel Heath depends, is primarily the forester. It is he who calls the other residents to take part in this creation.... [He is], so to speak, the law-giving authority for all human effort and for all the activities of these forces all around. The work that he orders has called forth a fruitful reversal in the common condition of culture among the residents of the heath.'[140] In the eyes of these observers, foresters stood out as the heroes of the struggle between chaos and

4.8 'Forester with an owl. (Underneath lies a shot goshawk).' 1908. From Johannes Mühlradt, *Die Tucheler Heide in Wort und Bild. Ein Besuch in Grüntal* (Danzig: Kafemann, 1908), 1:101.

4.7 'An old woman carrying wood in the Tuchel Heath,' 1908. From Johannes Mühlradt, *Die Tucheler Heide in Wort und Bild. Ein Besuch in Grüntal* (Danzig: Kafemann, 1908), 1:37.

order in this forsaken land. Mühlradt's illustrations reflected this message; whereas the old woman in figure 4.7, burdened with a load of firewood, appeared oppressed by nature, the forester in figure 4.8, having tamed an owl and shot a hawk, had conquered it. Likewise, Mühlradt's depictions of German homes – such as the chief forester's residence at Taubenfließ, where presumably the forester's wife waited in the doorway for her husband's return from productive work – demonstrated the domestic order Prussia brought to the heath, quite in contrast to the squalor of the local peasants' dwellings, where male and female inhabitants alike appeared to loaf about (see figures 4.9 and 4.10).

The foresters' intervention in the heath's economy provided positive role models and combated negative cultural influences, commentators believed. Schütte confidently reported in 1893 that, after much effort by Prussian foresters, 'the people learned to protect order in the forest themselves.'[141] The forester Saekel exuded a similar self-assurance: 'The mostly Polish peasants have learned a lot from the Germans in the last century, and so their whole standard of living has not only improved, but today one also sees that some tidy brick farmhouses with hard roofs have been erected.'[142] The Poles owed their rising living standards and new farmhouses less to the expanding economy (or to their own hard work), Saekel contended, than to what they had learned from the Germans. Not only had Prussian officials developed local agriculture and industry, so the story went, but they had turned the Poles away from an exploitative and destructive relationship with nature to a more constructive one, as demonstrated by the foresters and others. Pastor Mühlradt cited the example of a local teacher who, along with a class of spade-toting schoolboys, helped the local forester extinguish a forest fire. The district administration commended the teacher for his efforts 'and for the good example that he provided the population.' While Poles and Kashubs might be inclined to stand aside (if not fan the flames) as state property burned, Prussian officials like the teacher attempted to illustrate the importance of the forest. To his satisfaction, Mühlradt observed, 'Increasingly among the population the realization that their interests are intertwined with those of the woods is gaining ground, and that he who damages the forest also hurts [local interests].'[143] For Mühlradt, it seemed the champions of *Kultur* had achieved some measure of success.

The Failure of Environmental Chauvinism

The self-confidence that foresters and other Prussian officials felt when

4.9 'Chief forester's residence at Taubenfließ,' 1908. From Johannes Mühlradt, *Die Tucheler Heide in Wort und Bild. Ein Besuch in Grüntal* (Danzig: Kafemann, 1908), 1:242.

4.10 'Also a house in the Tuchel Heath,' 1908. From Johannes Mühlradt, *Die Tucheler Heide in Wort und Bild. Ein Besuch in Grüntal* (Danzig: Kafemann, 1908), 1:171.

they looked upon the transformation of the Tuchel Heath could be sustained only with an element of self-delusion. The boundaries of the ethnic communities were generally hardening, not softening, during this period. One study of electoral statistics in the region reveals that ethnicity remained the central factor for the bulk of voters, with few opting for candidates of a different ethnicity.[144] Moreover, although resistance to state intrusion into the woods faded significantly by the early twentieth century, it had by no means disappeared and would flare up again in the crucible of the First World War. Indeed, the war saw a rash of poaching, arson, and violence against foresters, reportedly with the support of the local population.[145] Otto Busdorf, a Berlin chief inspector tasked with combating poaching and the killing of foresters in the eastern provinces, related a sensational account of the poacher Franz Kleinschmidt. Over the course of three years, from 1916 to 1918, Kleinschmidt led an assault against state control of the forests. According to Busdorf's account, Kleinschmidt – a soldier who fled garrison duty in nearby Thorn – led a gang of poachers that 'almost entirely wiped out the abundant game population and set countless forest fires' in the heath. He was also accused of burglaries and train robbery. Even more seriously, however, Busdorf connected him with a campaign of intimidation against Prussian authorities, threatening local officials, terrorizing fire spotters (to the point where no one was willing to staff the isolated observation towers), killing foresters' livestock, and attacking several state functionaries, including four foresters wounded and one local official and four foresters (along with a private estate manager) killed. Busdorf required six months and a contingent of forty soldiers to track Kleinschmidt down in the wilds of the heath, finally killing him in a gun battle in August 1918. Despite a reward of 13,800 marks, no one among the local populace turned him in.[146]

Busdorf portrayed Kleinschmidt as a Polish nationalist (despite his German name), ostensibly because he used Polish newspapers in fabricating handmade cartridges and was apparently popular among the common people. However, his choice of paper may have been purely incidental, and the failure of anyone to denounce him may have been the result of intimidation. After all, Kleinschmidt regularly threatened his opponents with death and administered a severe beating to one elderly tailor who cooperated with police. Moreover, Busdorf provides no evidence of Kleinschmidt's political sentiments, although he might have had other information that led him to this conclusion. Regardless of his ethnic allegiance, however, Kleinschmidt's activities undermined the

Prussian state's forestry apparatus, taking game, setting fires, and intimi-
dating and killing officials. The fact that the public seemed to grant tacit
support to his efforts suggests the failure of Berlin's integration project.

Conclusion

As in Berlin, the Prussian state in Pomerelia sought to impose its will on
an unruly populace in a conflict over forests, and in both cases ultimately
lost the battle. The state's vision of the woods – as orderly, legible, and
productive spaces free of outside intrusion – failed to materialize. In Berlin, intrusions by the masses and public protest – mobilized by the sylvan
discourse – made it difficult for the *Fiskus* to realize profit from the sale
of its lands. At the same time, in Pomerelia, continued peasant recourse
to the woods for all manner of resources, regardless of state sanction,
frustrated Prussian foresters. While these cases bear a similar trajectory,
in Pomerelia it was the foresters, not the public, who called upon the
idea of the 'German forest' – in this version productive and disciplined
– to legitimize their project of reforestation.

Through the lens of environmental chauvinism, the Prussian foresters identified two interlocking problems in Pomerelia: poverty and resistance. Peasants scraped a marginal existence from the poor soil, and
the region contributed little to the national economy. At the same time,
attempts to rationalize production (particularly in forestry) came into
conflict with traditional agricultural practices. Local observers regarded
the resistance to change as inspired by a stubborn Polish nationalism.
As this nationalism had not been quashed by the *Kulturkampf* or the efforts of the *Ansiedlungskommission* – indeed, it seemed only invigorated
by them – Prussian authorities launched a campaign of state reforestation in the 1890s. The growth of state forests, they believed, would help
increase the direct influence of Prussian authority (and hence Germanization) through the ownership of large swaths of ethnically contested
territory, and the employment of a large number of Poles and Kashubians. These two factors allowed the Prussian state to directly discipline
both a wild landscape and an unruly populace. By possessing, developing, and policing the land, Prussian foresters believed they could overcome the long-term economic 'mismanagement' they identified there
and introduce modernity into the region. New transportation and economic infrastructure would gradually pull Pomerelians into the German
nation. Foresters would break the 'bad habits' of Slavic wood thieves
and poachers, and instead of fighting them as intruders, instruct them

as model employers in the bourgeois virtues of orderliness, thrift, hard work, and discipline. Imposing order on Pomerelia would Germanize both the land and its people.

This program of modernization ultimately failed to achieve its main goal: the assimilation of Slavic minorities into the German nation. Although foresters gained increasing control over the landscape and had some success in stamping out most forms of peasant appropriation from the woods, arson remained a problem. Moreover, the foresters' harsh methods and condescension likely spurred the resistance and perhaps even recast it in nationalist terms. Far from erasing the differences between Prussian foresters and Pomerelian peasants, the expansion of the state forests exacerbated long-standing tensions. And the refusal of Pomerelia's Poles and Kashubs to conform to the foresters' expectations, and indeed their apparent sympathy for those who would wilfully destroy the order of the Prussian state forests during the First World War, surely provoked anger and despair. The faith that ethnic minorities could be assimilated to Germandom – a sentiment widely held until the First World War among observers of the region – eroded after the war, when the territory was transferred to Poland. It would only be in the wake of the First World War, following the frustrating loss of broad swaths of Eastern Europe captured from the Russians (not to mention parts of imperial Germany as well), that the German colonial project in the east would be transformed from a program of cultural assimilation to one of racial reordering.[14]

chapter five

Meaningful Woods:
Sylvan Metaphors and Arboreal Symbols

Introduction

An important element of Germany's distinct and aberrant culture, *Sonderweg* historians have argued, was the Germans' rejection of key En-lightenment values (individual freedom, cultural pluralism, represen-tative government, and free-market capitalism) in favour of a *völkisch* ideology (subordination of the individual to the nation, ethnic national-ism, dictatorship, and schemes for national economic self-sufficiency). *Völkisch* thinkers forsook the West, such scholars argue, because they abandoned liberal notions of progress and instead embraced a conser-vative backlash against modernity. Many of the elements of this ideol-ogy shored up the power of traditional elites at the expense of an active citizenry, and much of the rhetoric of the movement called on a ro-manticized medieval past, prior to the onslaught of capitalism and other elements of modern life. Nature – particularly the sylvan ideal – stood as central to this brand of thinking, with organic national communities merely an outgrowth of their ancient, native soil. Leavened with social Darwinism, *völkisch* nationalism became an aggressive force, culminating in the Nazis' policies of expansionism and genocide.

There is much truth in this characterization of the origins of Nation-al Socialist thought, yet historians have questioned the extent to which German nationalism (and the Nazis themselves) rejected modernity and wallowed in pre-Enlightenment irrationalities. Indeed, several have ar-gued that it was precisely its modern elements (eugenics and race sci-ence) that made Nazism so dangerous, and these darker elements of modernity Germans freely borrowed from other modern countries, particularly the United States, suggesting that the Nazis were perhaps not so separate from Western tradition after all.[1] Rather than eschewing modernity altogether, *völkisch* thinkers adopted elements of modernity (particularly nationalist and scientific discourses) they found compatible with their program, while quashing others (personal liberty and free trade) that collided with it. Modernity held within it the seeds of the Nazis' crimes; it was less the Germans' rejection of modernity than the ambivalent nature of modernity itself that led to the catastrophes of the Second World War.

The shadow side of modernity fell over the woods as well. Of course, Germans had already witnessed the rationalization of the forest at the hands of profit-minded states, creating rectilinear monocultures closed to traditional uses. Yet this brand of modernity, increasingly practised around the world by significant numbers of German-trained foresters, was only one part of the story. The changing scientific understanding of the forest, filtered through various ideological lenses, provided another. The 'German forest,' far from being the atavistic retreat of latter-day barbarians, served as inspiration for authors – particularly popular scientists – hoping to explain nature. Some scholars of forest ecology sought to apply the lessons they deduced from the woods to human society, drawing parallels between the biological struggles both waged against their enemies. The woods became a laboratory for social Darwinism, a tendency that would accelerate after the First World War.[2]

Throughout the nineteenth and early twentieth centuries, several German authors used trees and forests as metaphors for society, each of them articulating a different image of the nation. In the 1860s, popular scientists Emil Adolf Roßmäßler and Matthias Jacob Schleiden used social similes to explain the cooperative relationships between the component parts of a tree, as well as between different members of the forest community, that reflected their liberal ideals. The sylvan metaphor seemed to have faded from popular science in 1870s and 1880s, yet it remained in public discourse. The geographer and anthropologist Friedrich von Hellwald first introduced social Darwinism to the forest, depicting the woods engaged in a brutal struggle for survival that was held in check only by human intervention. By contrast, the social reformer Adolf Gumprecht articulated a vision of the woods as a world of social cooperation from which humans could learn. After the turn of the century, however, the metaphor returned in the works of popular scientist Raoul Heinrich Francé and forester Rudolf Düesberg, both of whom used the biological battle of the forest against other forms of vegetation as a means to explain and justify human struggle. Over these years, the scientific and

popular discourse on the woods witnessed a move away from an ideal-
ization of cooperation to an emphasis on conflict, reflecting the rising
influence of social Darwinism on German popular science.

Quite by contrast, the popular debate over the national tree, particularly in the 1870s and 1880s, illustrated that more literary and romantic representations of nature lacked the aggressiveness of scientific
discourse. Trees carried enormous symbolic value, and a long-running
debate emerged after 1871 over which tree best represented the new
German nation: the mighty oak or the graceful linden. Drawing from
literature, poetry, and folklore, advocates for each sought to demonstrate how their favoured tree encapsulated essential German virtues.
This debate, carried out in the mass media and enmeshed in the larger
discourse of the 'German forest,' was far removed from the aggressive
social Darwinism percolating in the world of popular science, even if
popular scientists also participated in the debate. Granted, champions
of the oak styled the tree as martial and manly, but it failed to muscle
out the competition. The graceful linden, coded as female, continued to
stand for many as the true symbol of German nationhood. It was science,
in the search for metaphors, that produced the most violent images of
the woods – images that helped popularize the social Darwinism at the
root of Nazism.

Both the scientific and aesthetic impulses to draw comparisons between men and trees emanated in part from the Enlightenment, which
sought to break down the arbitrary division between humanity and nature. The poet Friedrich Gottlieb Klopstock turned to Germanic myth as
inspiration in the 1760s, with its nature worship and holy trees, prompt-
ing generations of German poets and nationalists to find the national
essence in the woods.[3] Yet as time went on, what exactly the forest and
its trees meant came increasingly into dispute, as conservatives sought to
appropriate nationalism for their own cause. Meanwhile, the renowned
naturalist Alexander von Humboldt identified relations between plants
as social phenomena in his enormously popular *Cosmos* (the first volume
of which appeared in 1845, but which he already had begun to conceive
in 1796), labelling plant groups as 'peoples' (*Völker*). He thus used a
social metaphor to make the relationships between plants more accessible to the general public.[4] Other popular scientists followed his lead,
comparing vegetable and human societies. Gradually, however, these
scientists transformed the sylvan metaphor from a heuristic tool into a
program for reform. They flipped Humboldt's metaphor on its head,
using the model of the forest as means to understand human society,

not the other way around. As they did so, these scientists increasingly applied biological models to society – in the form of social Darwinism – culminating in Düesberg's comparison of the 'racial communities' of the German people and the German forest.[5] Significantly, these ideas developed not among the poets and *Heimat* enthusiasts often maligned as reactionary proto-fascists, but among scientists, attempting to isolate the laws of nature and apply them to society.[6]

While Roßmäßler, Schleiden, Hellwald, Gumprecht, Francé, and Düesberg made connections between Germany's forests and society on several levels, it is worth noting that neither they nor any other forest enthusiast – popular scientist or otherwise – mobilized the forest as a military metaphor in this period. This runs against Elias Canetti's famous statement that 'the crowd symbol of the Germans was the army. But the army was more than just the army; it was the marching forest.' Canetti, and others after him, identified the Germans' love for their forest as a symbol of German militarism, comparing the rows of trees to uniformed ranks of soldiers.[7] This comparison made sense, given the high esteem granted the Prussian military in the *Kaiserreich* and beyond. As Canetti argued, Germany was the only 'modern country' with such a deep affection for the woods, arising from the 'parallel rigidity of the upright trees.' These trees were 'steadfast' and their bark resembled 'a coat of mail,' and where the same trees grew together, they seemed to be uniformed. This comparison, he claimed, appeared in 'countless poems and songs,' and he insisted the influence of this trope 'must never be underestimated.'[8]

Although the Nazis employed the forest metaphor precisely in this way, we must be careful not to ahistorically essentialize these characteristics to Germans in general.[9] Canetti's assertion of woodland militarism does not hold for the *Kaiserreich*. While several authors drew comparisons between the forest and the military, they always employed them to excoriate Germany's commercially oriented forests for their absence of beauty. Poetry likewise lacked images of sylvan armies.[10] While several authors compared sturdy trees with individual warriors, none considered the forest as an army. This distinction is important, as the image of a stubborn, weather-beaten oak doing battle against storms emphasized rugged individuality, and not the uniform quality of the army. Far from embracing the militarized forest, the sylvan discourse rejected it altogether. The woods provided an escape from the strictures of society and an opportunity to return to nature (see chapter 2); the image of an army had no place there.

The negative association of commercial timberlands with uniformed armies arose largely in discussions of nature protection and forest aesthetics, climaxing around the turn of the century. A forest cultivated along 'military' lines (planted in homogeneous formations and stripped of 'needless' undergrowth) received heavy criticism from these reformers. Already in the 1850s, Wilhelm Heinrich Riehl, the ethnographer seminal for so much writing on the forest, positively rejected the military metaphors for nature. Riehl denounced Napoleon's effort to regiment the highly fragmented landscapes of western Germany through the building of long, straight, poplar-lined avenues. The poplar, he complained, was the 'true symbol of centralization imposed from the outside; it is the most uniform tree, which one can have march like a parade of soldiers.'[11] Subsequently, authors denounced the disciplined poplar – or for that matter, any trees planted in rows – as essentially un-German.[12]

Riehl's aesthetic echoed loudly over the decades, with the soldierly forest repeatedly denounced as unappealing, particularly after the turn of the century. A 1900 article on natural monuments praised the preservation of the natural *Wald* and denigrated the timber-producing *Forst*, 'which is a group of trees of the same type, the same height and the same age arranged like soldiers in columns and rows.' Another article five years later presented contrasting photographs of, on one hand, 'A Beautiful Forest (in the Eyes of a Layman)' with luxuriant undergrowth sheltered by trees of different species and ages, and on the other, 'A Beautiful Forest (in the Eyes of a Forester)' with serried ranks of conifers commanded by a uniformed forester. These photos accompanied an article on forest aesthetics that declared only those with 'fully perverted taste' could regard the regimented forest as pleasant.[13] Complaining that the forest without undergrowth appears 'almost menacing and defiant, much like a regiment of soldiers,' an author in the journal of the League for *Heimat* Protection the following year called for a return to more natural forestry methods. Another nature-protection advocate similarly complained, 'How unlovely is the view of a transparent forest without undergrowth, in which the trees are still planted in rows and in straight lines and in measured distances like a regiment of soldiers!' Even a German nationalist complained that this method of afforestation created a discordant picture of nature: 'Like soldiers, [the trees] stand in columns and rows at the same distance, running in straight lines along the roads ... [they] do not please our eye with the regularity of their spacing.' In 1914, the radical nationalist Heinrich Pudor charged that if one found the quadratic forest pleasing, then one had spent too much time in the city.[14] A regimented forest may have appealed to foresters, but not to those espousing the virtues of the 'German forest.' If the forest as a military metaphor carried little currency in public discourse, the woods as a social metaphor found far more resonance.

The Tree of Capitalism: Karl Marx

Although not from a scientist, perhaps the most famous example of a tree deployed as a social metaphor came from Karl Marx, who in 1842 used a tree to describe rural poverty in the Rhineland. Over the course of the 'hungry forties,' peasants throughout Germany took to wood theft to increase their chances of survival. As a result, the Prussian state initiated a campaign to protect private property, inspiring Marx's dissent in the *Rheinische Zeitung*. For Marx, forest trees represented healthy and wealthy citizens who cast off the poor as only so much dead wood. Just as dry branches, no longer productive, fell away from the living tree, so too impoverished peasants found themselves shunted aside by the emerging market economy. This juxtaposition of the dead and the living demonstrated for Marx the 'antithesis of poverty and wealth.' Since the impoverished peasantry felt cast off from society, Marx argued, it sensed an affinity with the dead branches, thus 'deduc[ing] its right to property from this feeling of kinship.' Thus social and dendrological dead wood came together at the margins of capitalism.[15] Marx's arboreal metaphor explained his emerging understanding of the market economy to his audience, and in subsequent years, many other authors, writing from a variety of ideological convictions, would mobilize similar metaphors to convey their social and political critiques of the status quo.

Trees as Social Microcosms: Roßmäßler and Schleiden

Marx was not the only German intellectual at mid-century to liken German society to a tree. The biologists Emil Adolf Roßmäßler and Matthias Jakob Schleiden also made such comparisons in their works on forest protection. Neither was a forestry specialist – Roßmäßler studied molluscs and Schleiden pioneered cell theory – yet both took a keen interest in forest protection, alarmed as they were by deforestation. In widely popular works, they championed conservationism, attempting to reverse the ecological damage caused by the German lands' burgeoning economies during the 1860s. Accustomed to political repression after the Revolutions of 1848, these liberal scholars were no strangers to the use of scientific metaphors to convey political messages, a tradition they continued to varying degrees into the 1860s.

The left-liberal Saxon zoologist and 1848 parliamentarian Emil Adolf Roßmäßler embodied the union of science and politics. Indeed, he believed the spread of scientific knowledge would best advance his liberal goals – securing capitalism, constitutionalism, and national unity – in an age of political censorship and repression. Roßmäßler thus employed natural metaphors to convey his social and political arguments.[16] As an instructor at Saxony's prominent Tharandt Forestry Academy, he developed a keen interest in the woods in particular. However, the revolution had derailed his career, and thereafter he made a living as a popularizer of science and a political activist. His 1863 treatise on forest preservation, *The Forest*, resonated with his active political agenda, drawing implicit parallels between the woods and society, and it found a wide reception in the public, being reprinted in 1870 and 1881.

Starting from Alexander von Humboldt's observation of the social character of plants, Roßmäßler playfully compared vegetable and human societies. Both, he suggested, were influenced by their climate; in Germany's case, this environment was an ideal 'golden mean' promoting social interaction (in contrast to 'the Pole and the Equator, the enemies of sociability'). Roßmäßler invited his readers 'to compare the exclusive social unions of the Germans with those of the German plant world [and] find the fitting comparisons for the cheerful beech wood, the aristocratic oak forest ..., or the plebeian willow thicket of the river bank, among the clubs and associations of men.'[17] Thus the different forms and groupings of vegetation, he suggested, were akin to class divisions. On the one hand, this comparison naturalized the growing class differentiation taking place with the advance of capitalism in Germany (since plants naturally associated with others of their own kind), but on the other, it also justified the acknowledgment of class difference, as well as growth of class-based associations. Indeed, Roßmäßler was a founder of the Leipzig Workers' Association in the 1860s, advocating for the right of labour to organize.[18] His description of the plant world thus not only elucidated the forest for his readers, but also communicated his vision of society.

While Roßmäßler used the social life of plants to normalize the idea of class divisions, he also employed it more subtly to promote national unity. As an 1848 revolutionary committed to national unification, he freighted his descriptions of the woods with suggestions of national significance.[19] He described the forest as 'a beautiful and powerful union of forms and phenomena, in which no part is completely the same as any other, but in which nonetheless everything completely harmonizes in a sublime unison, plucking at the chords of every unspoiled breast.' Indeed, the woods were 'an integrated, organic entity.' One could well have applied this definition to the concept of the nation in the same period. Roßmäßler further explained that the woods stood not simply as a collection of individuals or groups. 'Rather the forest is for us a phenomenon, so rich and many faceted that we, insofar as we surrender ourselves to it, do not think of its divisions.'[20] It is unclear what sylvan divisions Roßmäßler felt he ignored when transported by the beauty of the woods, but like many patriots of his generation, his passion for the nation surely led him to disregard the arbitrary feudal boundaries dividing Germany into so many petty states, or the class divisions that threatened to undermine national unity. Instead, he depicted the forest as a harmonious society united in its endeavours.

For Roßmäßler, not only plant associations, but individual plants themselves, could be compared with human societies. Unlike other authors, who compared trees to individuals, Roßmäßler argued they had more in common with states, comprising leafy and tuberous 'citizens.' Each part of the tree represented a different segment of society, each working individually for the welfare of the whole. The roots represented agriculture, drawing nourishment from the soil for all; the leaves represented the 'thousand working hands of industry,' transforming raw materials (carbon dioxide and light) into useful products; the trunk of the tree represented the market, where the goods of both sectors were exchanged; blossoms and fruit were emigrants who founded colonies, 'which eventually will replicate the Motherland in size and beauty.'[21] Roßmäßler mobilized this dendrological metaphor to envision a harmonious society of citizens, each producing goods for exchange in the market, acting as individuals yet tied together by mutual dependence. The liberal empire he imagined likewise would not be exploitative in his view, but merely a replication of the 'Motherland' on new soil, akin to the republics of the Americas. Through healthy market interactions, the barren soils of the whole world could be made to flourish like a forest.

Like Roßmäßler, Matthias Jakob Schleiden was a liberal popular scientist and veteran of the 1848 revolution who took an interest in ecology and forest protection in the 1860s. His early adoption of Darwinism drew him into controversy; within a year of his appointment as professor of plant chemistry at the University of Dorpat in 1863, the Russian government forced him to give up his post. Thereafter he abandoned academia to compose scientific works for a popular audience, achieving wide regard from the reading public. As a liberal hailing from Hamburg and resident in Saxony in the mid-1860s, Schleiden felt a keen hostility to Prussia. When Prussian troops overran Saxony in 1866, during the Austro-Prussian War, he recoiled at the sight of spiked helmets on the streets of Dresden, penning pacifist and anti-Hohenzollern poetry.[22] The foreword to his plea for nature protection, *For Tree and Forest*, likewise echoed the liberal anxieties of the late 1860s. Writing in December 1869, Schleiden condemned 'the thudding, threatening strides of the approaching Caesarism and military despotism,' the 'fanatically excited priests,' and 'the bluster of the working class spurred on by the insanity of self-serving demagogues.'[23] Clearly, the triumvirate of Prussian militarism, Catholic ultramontanism, and socialist radicalism threatened the 'soft tones of humanity' he saw represented in his liberalism.

Schleiden also shared Roßmäßler's conception of nature. Both subscribed to a Humboldtian world view, which saw the fertile tropics as a land of intense competition between plants, but identified the northern hemisphere, particularly in the Old World, as the 'home of social plants' living in harmony with one another. Only in temperate climes did trees live in exclusive communities, such as oaks, beeches, and firs in pure stands, he claimed.[24] Schleiden imagined these cooperative plant societies much as Hegel viewed the state, as a collection of individual families. Much like Roßmäßler, Schleiden did not regard trees as the equivalent of people. Rather, he preferred to imagine them as 'a living ancestral tree of an entire family, and therefore not subject to the same laws of life as an individual in terms of origins, composition, and decline.... Individual branches of a family can die out, because the branch was too weak,' but the rest of the tree can survive.[25] Here, a certain social Darwinism infiltrates Scheliden's work. Rather than, as in Roßmäßler's view, the tree forming an organic and unified whole, where all parts contributed equally to the strengthening of the communal body, for Schleiden, each family had an inferior branch or two that would have to rot away. Yet, at the same time, his view of society was far more egalitarian than Roßmäßler's. All trees appeared equal in this regard; Schleiden did not lay out a social hierarchy with 'aristocratic oaks' at the top and 'plebeian willows' at the bottom. All families were equally subject to the laws of nature, with some blossoming and others withering, depending on their environmental conditions. Of course, in both Schleiden and Roßmäßler's imagination, this kind of harmonious social organization could best be found in Europe, away from the chaotic struggles of the tropics.

Heavily influenced by the American George Perkins Marsh's land-mark environmental work, *Man and Nature* (1864), Schleiden aimed to raise public consciousness of the forest's ecological function. Marsh argued that ancient Mediterranean societies had been destroyed by deforestation, and Schleiden worried the same fate might befall the rapidly expanding economies of northern Europe. He therefore pled for state intervention, calling for the purchase of wooded watersheds, deforested uplands, sandy coastal areas, and land of poor agricultural quality for the preservation and replanting of forests. Not only would this have the beneficial ecological effects of stabilizing water tables and river levels, reducing strong winds, preventing erosion, and so on, it would also contribute to a pleasing landscape alternating between healthy fields and forests.[26] With this appeal to the public and state in mind, Schleiden could not help but let his politics colour his writing. Deforestation in mountainous areas had a devastating impact on the riparian lowlands below, thus blame for periodic flooding and falling river levels in northern Germany had to be directed upstream. Guiding his reader across the landscape, he noted, 'The more we move into the industrious and intelligent Protestant part of Germany, the more we find an orderly forestry that is concerned with gradually making good the mistakes of earlier times.'[27] The upland areas of Austria and Switzerland, he suggested, were in the hands of lackadaisical Catholics who couldn't be bothered to manage their resources properly, exploiting the landscape carelessly through wanton timber felling and thereby disrupting the otherwise flourishing economy of northern, Protestant Germany.

While this denigration of Catholic indolence did not distinguish Schleiden from other liberals of his day, his anxiety about deforestation and the radical solutions he proposed did. As already noted (chapter 2), Schleiden advocated state ownership of all forests in upland and arid regions. However, since Central Europe's current boundaries meant the headwaters of all major rivers found themselves in different hands from those of the lowlands, he proposed a territorial reorganization of the German lands, diverging from liberal nationalist demands. Since no 'active, industrious people organized into a state' could tolerate having the watersheds of its rivers under the rule of small neighbours who squander their forests, he proposed that river basins would make far more sensible territories for coherent government. After all, 'rivers are the lifeblood of the recent prosperity of every state.' He therefore called for the reorganization of Central Europe into four sovereignties, each concentrated on a major river basin: the Rhine, Danube, Elbe, and Oder.[28] Naturally, this ran counter to the plans of other liberal nationalists, for whom language was far more important than hydrology in determining national boundaries. One suspects Schleiden regarded it as an advantage to this scheme that the Rhine and Danube states would be predominantly Catholic, while those centred on the Elbe and Oder would be predominantly Protestant. Moreover, such a reorganization would partition Prussia among the four different countries, thus ending the 'Caesarism and military despotism' haunting Europe.

Roßmäßler and Schleiden saw in the forest evidence for their liberalism. The arboreal and sylvan communities were defined by the cooperation of distinct elements (roots and leaves, microorganisms and trees) for the progress and benefit of the whole. This harmonious environment, they suggested, paralleled the nation. Indeed, as Schleiden argued, states even ought to be founded on a natural basis, rooted in the geographical unity of river basins, which promoted free commercial expansion and a common concern for the environment. Social Darwinism did play a minor role in Schleiden's work, but far more important for both of these authors was the principal of mutually beneficial cooperation. This would begin to change in the coming decades.

'Plant States' and 'Life Communities': Hellwald and Gumprecht

Liberal scientists did not maintain a monopoly over arboreal and sylvan metaphors. In the 1870s and 1880s, new voices emerged that challenged the social and political order of the *Kaiserreich*. During this period, those writing metaphorically about the forest continued to advocate what they observed in nature as prescriptions for government policy. Given the rising importance of social Darwinism, however, this meant less emphasis on cooperation and more on conflict. Nonetheless, the aggressive world view had not yet won out, and the principle of cooperation remained prevalent.

In early 1871, during the Franco-Prussian War, the popular geographical journal *Foreign Lands* published a series of articles under the heading 'Forest Trees and Forests' that depicted a Darwinist struggle for existence in the woods. Although unattributed, the article was likely authored by Friedrich von Hellwald, an anthropologist and geographer soon to be editor of the journal. An eager and early convert to Darwinism, Hellwald formed a close friendship with Ernst Haeckel, the famous naturalist and popularizer of Darwin's work in Germany. Although a popular scientist like Schleiden and Roßmäßler, Hellwald came from a conservative background, his father serving in the Austrian army and achieving high rank and a patent of nobility upon retirement. From a younger generation, he had not participated in the 1848 Revolution like Schleiden and Roßmäßler. Quite by contrast, Hellwald's father fought men like them, re-conquering Vienna and Hungary from insurgents in the wake of the revolution.[29] He inherited his father's martial conservatism, which in turn undergirded his view of nature.

Not surprisingly, Hellwald's version of Darwinism contrasted sharply with Schleiden's. In the opening of the first article in the series – published as battles raged in eastern France – Hellwald described a classic 'struggle for survival' scenario. Across the landscape, 'plant associations or plant states … like the structured states of men, rise, exist, collapse, and perish…. But even the types of plants constituting these states are those that, as a result of the drive for self-preservation, have succeeded not only in taking possession of their living spaces with great obstinacy and striven to protect it from incursions by other plant states, but they have also been constantly prepared to overrun the territory of other states in conquest as soon as a place cleared of vegetation appears that would satisfy the necessities of life for the invaders.'[30] This dark image was a far cry from Roßmäßler's arboreal harmony, and even from Schleiden's Darwinist vision of the woods. Rather than detailing the inner workings of trees, where different organs (roots, stems, and leaves) collaborated for the common good, or the relationships of mutual dependence between plants in the forest, Hellwald focused on external conflict. Indeed, he marginalized the dynamic relationships within trees and forests that Roßmäßler and Schleiden studied, depicting their inner workings as essentially static. In keeping with his conservative politics, Hellwald believed a 'plant state' perished as 'soon as its constitution [Constitution] is injured or changed in any way.'[31] As in English, the term Constitution has a double meaning in German, indicating either an established political order or the physical composition of an individual. Thus, rather than the more fluid relationships Roßmäßler and Schleiden described, Hellwald conceived of plant (and human) states having rigid internal orders (much like an army) that could not be upset without fatal consequences, in keeping with his conservative worldview.

At the same time, social Darwinism radicalized Hellwald's conservatism. In his articles, cooperation, an important element of Darwinism, became subsidiary. Instead, Hellwald's forest was a world of struggle between 'plant states.' Grasses and mushrooms were invading 'Völker' against which trees must defend themselves.[32] He laid out a new geography of the German lands, with regions defined by their dominant tree types, all in constant flux. In the Alps, for example, 'larger and smaller islands of spruce forest appear as the border posts of a new empire,' as the trees advanced from the lowlands to conquer new territory in the mountains. Without human intervention, the 'forest lords' would overrun the fields and pastures. As such a bleak picture would likely have alienated his bourgeois audience, Hellwald pulled back from a full endorsement of an unlimited natural struggle, ending on a more positive note with a description of a lovely domestic landscape. Anyone comparing the modern German countryside with the primeval wilderness would, he concluded, 'bless the culture that, with wisdom, reigned in the fierce drive to rule of the individual plant states and does not let one gain at the disadvantage of another.'[33] Just as culture prevented human civilizations from constantly launching wars against one another, or elites from ruthlessly exploiting their underlings, Hellwald seemed to suggest, so too culture helped bring order to the landscape, preventing the dominant from exploiting the weak. His bourgeois readers likely appreciated this concession, yet his social Darwinism remained unpalatable for many Germans in the 1870s. As a result, Hellwald had to abandon the editorship of *Foreign Lands* in 1884, complaining to Haeckel that the tide had turned against Darwin. It would not be until the 1890s that social Darwinism would come into vogue.[34]

With Hellwald, the concept of race appears to infiltrate the forest, although it would be decades before others would follow his lead. While neo-romantics posited a special bond between the Germans and their forests, and the historically minded celebrated the ancient struggle between Teutonic tribespeople and their Roman foes, they could interpret the distinction between Germans and others in strictly cultural terms. Hellwald introduced a new factor into the forest discourse: a Darwinistic struggle between species. Identifying the forest as a model for society, and naturalizing violent struggle between societies as a necessary outgrowth of the species' drive for dominance and territory, Hellwald encouraged a racialized understanding of the sylvan metaphor with implications for human society.

Lest we conclude Hellwald's social Darwinism had carried the day by the 1870s, we should consider a very different use of the forest metaphor by the liberal social reformer Adolf Gumprecht in 1883.[35] Writing in the social reform journal *Worker's Friend*, Gumprecht argued the forest taught a lesson of cooperation. He defined the forest as 'not simply a collection of trees, but rather, insofar as it is in good health and its existence is secure, an endlessly complex association, a life community, in which the various beings conclude an alliance against common foes and, at the same time, for the benefit of the people leaving nearby.' Thus the forest was a coherent organism in which 'the whole life community is drawn in compassion to the suffering of one part.' This 'solidarity' ought to serve as a model for human social relations, he believed.

Quite in contrast to Hellwald, who saw human culture keeping a lid on the violence of nature, Gumprecht felt that human intervention in the landscape could at times wreak devastating consequences, leading to a 'disturbance of the harmonious balance' that held the sylvan 'life community' together. Clear-cutting mountain woodlands led to 'ever more frequent and vicious recurring floods,' which 'make fields desolate, ruin the climate, and lead to harvest failures.' These crises indicated an ecology out of balance, and this ecological metaphor he applied to society. Just as agriculture suffered from repeated flooding, so too 'the labour and goods markets suffer from floods of workers and products of industry, and the social climate experiences thunderstorms.' The solution to both of these imbalances, Gumprecht argued, was a broad-ranging public works program: 'Why shouldn't at least a part of the large number of unmarried "excess hands" – who now fill our streets as vagrants and beggars, and fill our hospitals, workhouses, and prisons with physical, moral, and social plagues – serve the admirable purpose of covering grim wastelands with trees and bushes, draining and reclaiming moors, limiting the depletion of the soil, and preventing floods; in short, restoring healthier conditions in the natural realm and human relations?'[36] Demoralized workers, suffering the effects of unemployment, could be restored through healthy labour, at the same time restoring balance to the countryside. Although the reforestation, moor draining, and levee building Gumprecht advocated would likely have their own environmental repercussions, he at least recognized a healthy society's need for a healthy ecosystem.

Rather than social Darwinism, Gumprecht's ecological conception of the forest owed far more to Roßmäßler and Schleiden, who also sought to stave off the dangerous effects of deforestation. He quoted Riehl on the need to preserve forests, worrying Germany might end up like Italy, which, 'once the paradise of Europe, is an exhausted land.' Like Schleiden, Gumprecht endorsed increased state intervention to protect forests. Describing conditions in Tyrol, where he lived, Gumprecht complained that the majority of forests were subject to abuse. An insufficient number of forestry experts oversaw communal forests (half of all Tyrol's woodlands), and another third were left to the 'caprice and ignorance of the peasants,' who razed their stands of timber when the railways arrived. This quick infusion of cash, he noted, 'encouraged luxury, alcoholism, lethargy, and directed countless families to ruin.' Thus the forest avenged itself on those who squandered its value, while at the same time laying waste to innocents downstream. Besides remedying deforestation with reforestation by jobless workers, Gumprecht also proposed better education for the Alpine peasants.[37] Thus, the education of rural folk in the backwoods of Tyrol was of direct concern to those downriver, as Schleiden suggested. Ultimately, the forest – and the German lands as a whole – required a holistic approach, restoring balances within natural and social communities, allowing each member to contribute labour to the common good, and demanding that all parts of the greater community – in this case, the German nation – pay attention to the needs of the least among them.

The contrast between Hellwald's and Gumprecht's visions could not be starker and was undoubtedly related to their politics. Hellwald's social Darwinistic 'struggle for survival' between 'plant states' appears to have been prompted by his military background and conservatism, whereas Gumprecht's emphasis on the 'harmonious balance' of the sylvan 'life community' likely derived from his liberal social reformism. Although he was not a scientist, Gumprecht's concern for the environment – particularly the consequences of deforestation – echoed the sentiments of the 1860s popular scientists he had probably read. Hellwald, on the other hand, who was engaged with popular science, departed from the liberal scientific tradition not only with the weight he gave social Darwinism, but also with his disregard for environmental concerns. Nowhere in his five articles did he express the apprehension over the deforestation, in Germany and abroad, that had prompted Roßmäßler, Schleiden, and Gumprecht to address forests in the first place. Nor did he spend any time discussing the biological mechanisms of the woods, unlike his fellow popular scientists. Instead, perhaps in keeping with his audience at *Foreign Lands*, he was consumed with the geographical distribution of trees and their competition. Nonetheless, his lack of interest in ecology is somewhat surprising, given his friendship with Haeckel, who had coined the term just a few years before. For Hellwald, the forest was not important because it was threatened, but because it could demonstrate principles of social Darwinism in a stark form.

'Plant Sociology': Raoul Francé

After the turn of the century, social Darwinism gained a broader foothold
in German society through the works of the microbiologist and popular
botanist Raoul Heinrich Francé, who sought to decode nature in order to apply its lessons to human life.[38] Between 1906 and 1909, Francé
reached a wide audience through the publication of several works on the
forest underscoring this aim. Citing Darwin and Haeckel, he sought to
tear down the barriers dividing humanity from its environment. Everyone who truly wanted to understand the natural world, Francé insisted,
must recognize '*the complete unity of man with nature.*' Only by bringing
down this barrier, Francé believed, could 'modern' science overcome
the 'medieval remnant' of scholasticism and inaugurate an age when
humankind could 'develop itself fully free and complete.'[39] Francé felt
that, with an understanding of the unity of humans and nature, one
could more easily apply the lessons of nature to human society. Drawing on the same Humboldtian tradition as Roßmäßler and Schleiden,
Francé emphasized the similarities between human and sylvan societies.
'The correspondence between plant and human life is demonstrated by
the fact that plants, like we humans, join one another to create associations, societies, and states,' he insisted.[40] Upon this foundation, Francé
translated Haeckel's concept of ecology into social terms; the ecology
of the forest, he stated, was the study of sylvan social life.[41] Through the
insights of his newly conceived field of 'plant sociology,' Francé claimed,
'one better understands humanity,' initiating 'a new epoch in human
intellectual development.'[42]

Of course, Roßmäßler, Schleiden, Hellwald, and Francé were not
alone in deriving social models from nature. Social Darwinism, positing a struggle of the fittest in human relations, exerted a powerful influence in this period.[43] Francé, however, rejected the crude sort of
social Darwinist 'dogma' that he felt prevailed in both the natural and
social sciences, insisting that 'the great law of mutual aid take an equal
place alongside the other mighty principle of the struggle for survival.'
From his study of plant society, he hoped to demonstrate 'a previously
unknown rule,' stipulating 'a mutual relationship of dependence on
one another, even among distantly situated plants.'[44] Francé's concept
of ecology, understood as the study of social relationships among organisms, thus included cooperation as '*the counterbalance to the struggle
of all against all.*'[45] The union of competition and cooperation, he insisted, 'is the law of the forest and thus a likeness of human life.'[46] His

conception of nature went far beyond Hellwald's caricature of everlasting war.

Francé imagined this cooperation taking place in the 'association' (*Vereinigung*), which, as he stressed, '*is the beginning of mutual assistance.*'[47] Pursuing his social comparisons further, he identified plant associations with social classes, envisioning the forest as a society in which associations both competed and cooperated for the benefit of the whole. While Roßmäßler left the details of his sylvan society to the imagination of his readers, Francé meticulously outlined a woodland class hierarchy. The lowest level consisted of algae and fungi in the soil, essential to the maintenance of the forest but excluded from its elite 'good society.' Above ground, mosses, lichens, lycopods, and grasses formed the next social stratum, the 'cooperative of forest proletarians,' followed by forest herbage and the low undergrowth of heather, milkwort, and ferns, identified by Francé as the woods' 'middle class' (*Bürger*). Standing above them was the 'nobility' of bushes including daphne, roses, blackberries, and juniper. Crowning this social hierarchy were the trees, including a category of 'super plants' (*Überpflanzen*) dominating the woods. In between these levels 'nested a group of beggars and parasites [*Bettler- und Schmarotzervolk*].'[48] The forest, according to Francé, had the most highly evolved social system among all the plant societies; the elaboration of class associations found its 'perfection' in the woods.[49]

This perfect society hardly represented the bourgeois idyll outlined by liberal authors decades earlier. Instead of Roßmäßler's roots and leaves working together as equals, Francé depicted a hierarchical society dominated by apparently Nietzschean 'super-plants' that tower over everyone else (although he denied he meant the term in a Nietzschean sense). The middle class, widely regarded as the backbone of society, is reduced to herbs easily trampled underfoot. Yet this was not a standard conservative vision of the forest, either. He referred rather dismissively to the noble shrubbery flourishing 'only in those places ... where one can live without effort,' and insisted that 'a natural social order begins by supporting ability, not origins or historical rights.'[50] Francé's emphasis on ability echoed liberal demands for a society based on talent, not birth, but in this context, it had a smack of social Darwinism as well, as did his reference to '*Schmarotzervolk.*' Although this term was occasionally used in botany in the 1860s and 1870s to describe particular plants, by the 1890s it had taken on significant racial overtones, being used as a term of abuse for both Jews and Poles by the radical right in Germany and Austria-Hungary. Indeed, the idealized portrait of the sylvan community

Francé painted seemed to correspond with a radical nationalist vision of society, where the subterranean proletariat, meek bourgeoisie, feckless aristocrats, and social parasites would be dominated by an 'oligarchy' of heroes (Nietzschean or otherwise).[51]

Although he laid out a social hierarchy, Francé nevertheless insisted relationships of mutual aid extended across associational boundaries. Many trees had particular species of other plants that accompanied them, known as 'tree companions,' which varied from region to region. In Germany, for instance, the stinging nettle escorted the oak. These relationships developed out of the environmental conditions produced by particular trees. For example, one found plants sensitive to bright light under shadier trees, and those demanding more light under trees with less dense foliage. Mosses and trees developed similar relationships, with the tree shading the moss and the moss holding water for the tree. Nutrition also played a significant role, with trees and their companions drawing on and replenishing to the soil different nutrients, forming what Francé called a 'nutritional cooperative.' Bringing his social comparisons to bear again, he noted, 'In nature and in human life, similar needs bring different comrades together.'[52]

As in any society, Francé intoned, a state united and mediated between its social components; in nature, plant associations cooperated in the form of 'plant formations' (such as a forest, marsh, grassland, etc.). Just like a state, the forest 'succeed[ed] in protecting and promoting the life of the individual,' through cooperation. Since the forest contained all the elements required to perpetuate itself, he noted, it realized 'the ideal of a state.' And like a human state, '*the forest always seeks to preserve itself* against infiltrators and other formations at its margins.[53] Apparently forests girded themselves for battle.

While Francé claimed that cooperation and competition played equal roles in nature, he emphasized cooperation within plant formations and conflict between them. Of course, individual plants within the forest struggled with one another for water, light, and nutrients, 'behav[ing] like job applicants competing for a prized position.' Yet he claimed this struggle differed from 'raw hand-to-hand combat,' not taking place through 'war-like conquering,' but rather through a more 'peaceful competition through the increase of abilities and the improvement of facilities.' Just as manufacturing firms battled one another 'constantly and secretly' for market share, he observed, so too plants engaged in this subtle struggle for advantage. In the end, the 'capable,' not the violent, survived.[54]

Although Francé challenged the crude social Darwinism the day, re-emphasizing cooperation as Roßmäßler and Schleiden had, he nevertheless depicted struggle *between* plant states in terms reminiscent of Hellwald. If competition within society lacked violence, clashes between formations took on martial overtones; Francé cited no examples of cooperation between formations, employed military language in describing their conflicts, and usually presented foreign species as invaders. Friedrich Ratzel's concept of Lebensraum, a term he coined in 1906, hovered just below the surface of Francé's account.[55] Plants, like humans, had long struggled for territory and dominance, he noted, stressing '*even the plant is a historical actor, and even its groups* [Völker] *and societies have a world history,*' with their own 'population migrations [*Völkerwanderungen*], wars, and treaties.'[56] Francé presented the multi-ethnic Danubian basin – where he incidentally spent his childhood – as an important front in the clash between two worlds of vegetation. The region was 'not only the great path of human migration,' he wrote, 'but also the route of plant armies, [where] foreign groups [*Völker*] still mix in the society of the forest.' The species of Central Europe battled those of the Pontian (Black Sea) realm, just as Germans had long battled Turks and Huns in the same region, he explained. Furthermore, on the eastern front, 'the hornbeam, a tree native to Russia, is conquering Prussia.'[57] Francé's vision of vegetable struggle thus mirrored Germany's foreign policy anxieties in the years leading up to the First World War; like the Danubian basin it occupied, the Austro-Hungarian Empire formed a critical zone of great power conflict, while Russia appeared as an insidious enemy quietly building its strength. Or read from a radical nationalist and social Darwinist perspective, these regions constituted zones of conflict between Germans and Slavs (and other non-Germans), with the Slavs depicted as an almost unstoppable force of nature (often depicted as a flood) sweeping over the landscape of the German east. Russian hornbeams and Polish migrant workers were joined in their conquest of the German countryside in a titanic battle between east and west, a radical nationalist might infer from Francé's writings, and it would take a national revolution to bring about the rule of true 'super plants' over German society.

The subtly racist tone of Francé's work also emerged in his discussion of non-native plants. Francé depicted this category of foreigners as weak and susceptible to eradication in the face of pressure from the native population. He sometimes invoked the example of an abandoned garden to illustrate this point. Without the protective hand of the gardener,

Francé explained, a struggle for dominance ensued in which cultivated plants, 'especially the foreign ones unaccustomed to our latitude, disappear first, and their place is taken by native plants, called weeds by the gardener.'[58] He also noted the difficulty of introducing foreign trees into the 'community' of the forest, identifying the Spanish chestnut as a 'guest' from the Mediterranean, and referring to the difficulties in the 'naturalization' (*Einbürgerung*) of the Douglas fir and the American oak.[59] Nature determined foreigners did not fit into the 'German forest.'

Francé repeatedly stressed the importance of his brand of ecology, or 'plant sociology,' in the discovery of natural social laws in nature. The forest, as the most highly developed social organization among plants in his estimation, could provide keys for unlocking these mysteries. What kind of society did Francé imply was natural? One with a clear hierarchy of class divisions based on ability, but in which cooperation within and among classes bound society together, especially in the face of challenges from 'foreign' interlopers. While competition within society ensured the constant improvement of the state, competition between states often manifested itself in violent conflict. Thus, rather than espousing a crude social Darwinist understanding of society stressing the struggle between individuals, Francé proposed instead cooperation among individuals and associations (classes) within the state, with competitive impulses directed outwards. In many ways, this model seems to correspond with the vision of social imperialism espoused by left-leaning social reformers like Friedrich Naumann and the Association for Social Policy during the same period, but in its suspicion of foreigners it also appears to prefigure the concept of the *Volksgemeinschaft* – the people's community – a key term for the Nazis, but already current before the First World War among those on the radical right.[60]

The Sylvan *Volksgemeinschaft*: Rudolf Düesberg

The Pomeranian forester Rudolf Düesberg further racialized Francé's image of the woods. In his 1910 *The Forest as Educator* – half forestry manual and half social reform blueprint – Düesberg championed a new kind of sylviculture and a new kind of society. The German forest, he intoned, arose from the same environment as the German people, and both suffered under the alien forces of capitalism. Praising the social order of woodlands undisturbed by commercial forestry, Düesberg argued they provided a social model for a Germany liberated from industrial capitalism. 'The dominant laws for the cultivation of a forest apply equally to the rationally organized human community,' he insisted. 'In this way the forest becomes an educator.'[61] Although his studies led him to advocate a traditional social hierarchy and a rejection of much of the trappings of modernity, he remained critical of agrarian elites and clung to the liberating potential of science.

Evidently drawing heavily on Francé's attempt, through 'plant sociology,' to decode the laws of nature and apply them to human society, Düesberg explicitly advocated the 'German forest' as a model for German social relations. 'All the imperfections of human institutions,' he maintained, 'arise from the misunderstanding of immutable natural laws.' Thus the true 'German forest,' as a product of nature, would reveal the kind of social conditions nature intended for the German people. In Düesberg's formulation, the forest was more than a metaphor for society, it was an organic companion shaped by the same environmental forces. 'As descendants of a settled *Volksgemeinschaft* of peasants, made great by the iron drive to hard labour in a tough climate on soil of little fertility, the Germans are comparable to the Nordic forest trees,' he claimed.[62] This was quite a departure from Roßmäßler and Schleiden regarding Germany as a pleasant land of natural harmony. Nonetheless, Düesberg, like Francé, believed cooperation was the key to this model. 'The forest in its original condition is the lasting life-community of a great circle of plant and animal life,' he explained, 'which is ruled less by the struggle for existence than by the friendlier picture of mutual adjustment and help.' Düesberg envisioned the woods not as the site of ruthless competition by individuals, but as a place where each tree contributed to the whole. In commercial forests, trees grew to great heights, he averred, 'not as individuals, but only as members of a highly developed community.'[63] The German people, Düesberg asserted, had once belonged to such a community – defined by race and governed by laws corresponding to their racial character – but industrial capitalism had destroyed it. Thus he demanded, 'the social order of the German forests must be a model for the institutions in the economic and social life of the German people.'[64]

Just as the 'essence of the forest' was 'not compatible with the capitalistic means of valuing land,' neither was the essence of the German people suited to capitalism, Düesberg insisted. Capitalism, he claimed, eroded the natural order of both. Drawing on anti-Semitic discourse, he argued capitalism sprang from a 'nomadic' (read Jewish) mentality, which allowed one to accumulate mobile wealth (first livestock, then money) largely divorced from the land. 'The German race,' by contrast,

was rooted in the soil, tending 'towards settled agriculture.' Thus the
introduction of 'alien' capitalism to Germany led to a fundamental disruption of the 'natural' social order, he contended.[65] Like woodland
trees suffering under current forestry methods, which ignored their
'species characteristics' (*Arteigenschaften*), the Germans laboured under
an 'equally incompatible ... world view governing economic and social
life.' Capitalism had regimented social relations in the forest as it had
in society, he explained; whereas trees thrived when allowed to grow of
their own volition in natural forests, capitalist forestry forced trees into
competition with one another, planting them close together in order
to drive them to ever greater productivity (i.e., timber yields) in the
struggle for survival. Ultimately, this practice reduced the productive
elements of sylvan society to 'miserable specimens.' In much the same
way, capitalist industries exploited German workers, Düesberg claimed,
forcing them into regimented urban lives dominated by competition for
survival. Thus he concluded, 'The nomadic world view, hostile to the
German spirit, has over the long term overcome the fundamentally opposed view of the settled peasant and pushed it into the background.'[66]

As a society and a state divorced from its origins and organized around
capitalist industry, imperial Germany earned Düesberg's condemnation.
'The basis of the modern state and the institutions of public life are
neither Christian nor Germanic,' he maintained. 'They represent a nomadic, Jewish *Weltanschauung*.' The ruling 'Jewish and Roman' concepts
of property had eroded German 'law and custom,' driving the rooted
German peasant from the land. Düesberg therefore condemned 'ego-
ism as the driving force behind human economic and social life' and
complained that capitalism's 'free play of forces is responsible for all the
neediness and disgraces, from which the German *Volk* suffers.' Rather
than serving the needs of the German people, the state catered to the interests of industry and trade, spending exorbitant funds on the quest for
world markets. Specifically, he cited military spending, which he claimed
soared to three times the amount necessary for national defence in order to project Germany's influence around the world and subsidize the
armaments industry. The industrial order supported by the German
state had produced an enormous growth of wealth, Düesberg admitted,
but it had also polarized society, resulting in the proletarianization of the
'masses robbed of a *Heimat*' and the spread of socialism.[67]

Rather than supporting Germany's industrialization and the progressive erosion of 'natural' social relations, Düesberg advocated a state-
sponsored return to the land, in particular a vigorous investment in

forestry and wood processing. Like Sohnrey and other conservatives who emphasized the value of woodworking in the rural life, Düesberg regarded the forest as a great social benefactor, providing raw materials and sources of employment for the peasant economy. Indeed, he hoped to shift the German economy towards renewable raw materials to avoid the crisis of dwindling resources industrial economies were bound to face. Peasant woodworking, centred on the farm, would stem the tide of labourers going to the cities. Along with widespread landownership, Düesberg predicted, artisanal production would counteract the corrosive influence of capitalism, preventing proletarianization and negating the socialist threat.[68]

Opposed to capitalism's competitive and socially divisive character, Düesberg drew on nature to find models of social cooperation, where they were more visible than 'in the confusion of human affairs.' He did not try to deny the role of struggle; rather, he attempted to contextualize it. 'The goal of struggle is not so much the benefit of the single being as the welfare of the whole,' he observed; thus the 'social order serves the otherwise senseless, chaotic struggle for existence.' He concluded that, for humans as well as plants, 'all institutions of economic and social life must be directed to the highest goal: to maintain and ennoble the species,' and posited the 'national family' (*Volksfamilie*) as a model for both. In the forest, each member of the community had a special role to play, as Francé described. So too in society, where the differences in strength and ability between men and women, old and young, all complemented one another in the 'labour community of the family.' This conservative notion formed 'the basis for an aristocratic order,' a hierarchy 'with the monarch at the top.' Düesberg called upon the Junkers to revive this national family, which appeared as a strategy to restore Germany's feudal order.[69]

While Düesberg regarded Germany's landed elites as crucial allies in dismantling industrial capitalism, he – like those who insisted the 'German forest' belonged to the public – did not wholeheartedly endorse them. Indeed, he criticized 'many large landowners' for a lacking 'consciousness of social duties,' and charged the Agrarian League, the aggressive agricultural lobby, with the pursuit of landowners' self-interest above the common good. Neither of these traits was compatible with Düesberg's harmonious national family. Furthermore, the Junkers' manors, employing hundreds of landless and seasonal labourers, violated their employees' 'personal freedom,' he charged. The very structure of East Elbian agriculture ran counter to Düesberg's vision of a Germany dominated by small landholders and artisans. Labour had meaning only when one worked for oneself, he insisted; thus he called for the return of workers to the land to counter industrial alienation and the socialism it bred. Only with widespread landownership, Düesberg claimed, would rootedness and patriotism flourish. 'Therefore,' he concluded, 'the possession of land by a few is hurtful to everyone.'[70] Although unlike many agrarian reformers (and out of deference to his prospective Junker allies) he did not propose the break-up of large estates, he did insist on a progressive income tax and the abolition of interest group politics.[71] He recommended that large landowners mechanize their production to avoid recruiting landless labourers. Land for the expanding German population could be won through the purchase of Russian Poland; the Poles (who were chafing under Russian rule anyway) could be resettled in South America in a 'peaceful exchange.'[72] Modern means – including wholesale population transfers – would return Germans to the land and restore the *Volksgemeinschaft*.

Düesberg's belief in science also tempered his anti-modernism, setting him apart from true reactionaries. Although his title drew on Julius Langbehn's 1890 *Rembrandt as Educator* for inspiration, Düesberg did not share Langbehn's hostility to science. Langbehn rejected science, according to Fritz Stern, 'because it presumed to penetrate the mystery of life and nature, to make comprehensible a universe that [he] wanted left shrouded in poetic obscurity.'[73] Düesberg, on the other hand, wholeheartedly embraced the benefits of science, devoting the first part of his work to calculating the efficiency of various sylvicultural methods, and the second to plumbing the forest's mysteries to understand its laws. Like Francé, Düesberg condemned medieval scholasticism, dismissing it as the source of 'the petty spirit of bureaucracy, pedantry, and belief in authority.' Particularly in the forest, one could observe the effects of imposing rigid mathematical models on nature, inspired as they were by commercial interests. The natural sciences, by contrast, offered new methods of 'unconditional critical observation, exact experimentation, and the investigation of connections, interactions, and transformations in the phenomena of the environment,' which defeated this narrow tendency, Düesberg insisted. These new insights inspired his recognition that 'so-called progress is often, if not always, a return to nature, to the recognition of the eternal laws.'[74] For Düesberg, the natural sciences opened the path to enlightenment, revealing immutable natural principles and providing solutions to modern problems. While he embraced an essentially reactionary social order, he did so (at least ostensibly)

neither out of deference to tradition or authority, nor out of a fundamental hostility to technology and science, but out of a belief that such a
society conformed to scientifically discernable natural laws.

Düesberg's racialized image of the woods, and the social conclusions
he drew from it, arose less from aesthetic considerations than from
scientific ones. He clearly desired to unlock the mysteries of nature
through scientific investigation. He demanded the translation of his
dendrological research into social policy. While the society he imagined
looked remarkably similar to that of agrarian romantics, he justified his
arguments in (pseudo-) scientific terms. Thus his plea for a return to
nature emanated more from a belief in the inherent good of organic
social relations (whether for plants or humans) than from nostalgia or a
concern with history or aesthetics. Indeed, when Hugo Conwentz (the
founder of the Prussian nature-protection authority) surveyed German
foresters in 1900, Düesberg (already eleven years at his post in a state
forest) responded that he had undertaken no efforts to preserve rare
trees or rural beauty in his reserve.[75] Thus Düesberg demonstrated little
interest in the widespread passion for trees that dominated the 'German
forest' discourse at the turn of the century. There was little evidence in
his work of the kind of historical or aesthetic interests that animated
Salisch's *Forest Aesthetics*, the *Gartenlaube*'s 'Germany's Remarkable Trees'
series, or the *Heimat* movement's preservation efforts, for example.
Instead, his inspiration was drawn from the popular science tropes of
social Darwinism.

Düesberg's book was embraced by the radical right (it was included
on a list of recommended nationalist books), but attained little popularity.[76] Quite unlike Francé's successful oeuvre, Düesberg's work was far
too fantastic, dark, and explicitly political to earn much consideration
from mainstream readers. Indeed, his employer, the Prussian minister
of agriculture Bernd von Arnim, gave a particularly scathing review in
a private assessment, dismissing his work as commonplace and 'in part
worthless,' concluding, 'I do not believe that Düesberg's often evident
eccentricity and lack of clarity will win his work the regard he hopes for.'
However, in his capacity as chief forester of the royal hunting ground
at Gross Mützelburg, Düesberg did gain the attention of Crown Prince
Wilhelm, which in turn prompted an internal investigation. Officials
from the crown prince's staff, seeking to reduce the influence of radical
nationalists on their impressionable charge, aimed to remove the errant
forester from his position. Although they did not succeed, it was clear
that they eyed his work with suspicion.[77] While this kind of radical social

Darwinism would attain significant appeal after the cataclysm of the First World War, before 1914 it was odd and eccentric. More than social Darwinistic metaphors about the woods, what attracted popular interest in those days was the cultural symbolism of trees.

The German National Tree: Oaks and Lindens

Nationalist iconography across Europe appropriated trees – which had already played a prominent role in mythological and religious symbolism since antiquity – as emblems of the nation and its virtues. In the eighteenth century, the English gentry styled oaks as representations of their deeply rooted political freedom, while French revolutionaries displaced royal and religious statues with liberty trees embodying quite different values. Not surprisingly, the Germans, too, had their own complicated arboreal traditions and meanings, varying from region to region. The French Revolution, however, and the wars that brought it to the German lands, evoked a nationalization of tree symbolism. In this period of strife, the steadfast oak came to represent Germany as it weathered the storms of political turmoil. The oak stood as the antithesis of the French, stubborn and massively rooted, withstanding political change and foreign occupation. With each oak having its own unique character, they could not be regimented by the revolution's supposedly universal laws or the absolutist ambitions of the Napoleonic state. Both the right and left could embrace the tree, as they embraced nationalism in the period, with their own overlapping, yet distinct, interpretations.[78] However, with the advent of the German nation state in 1871, some began to question the pre-eminence of the oak, whose soldierly qualities now seemed to outweigh its democratic tradition.

Particularly in the 1870s and 1880s, several authors considered which tree best symbolized the virtues of the new nation state. Challenging the oak was the linden, representing a very different aspect of German identity. Of course, since the late eighteenth century, the oak stood as the defiant symbol of German nationalism, weathering the storms of warfare that had broken over Europe. The oak – massive, craggy, and solid – represented the exterior nation, the *Vaterland*, Germany ready for battle. Those embracing the oak in the last third of the nineteenth century tended to come from the political right, adopting a more martial nationalism. However, there were those who argued that the oak had usurped the role of national tree from the linden, which – with its heart-shaped leaves – represented the interior nation, the *Heimat*, Germany at home, holding a place dearer to the German people than the oak. These authors tended to come from liberal backgrounds, seeking to maintain some of the early nineteenth-century's idealism in the face of an aggressive realpolitik. At stake was the definition of a new national identity, in flux in this period not only as a result of national unification, but also of the increasing political appropriation of nationalism by the right. In the end, some settled for both representing the nation, complementing the oak's hard exterior with the grace and beauty of the linden.

Historians positing a German *Sonderweg* have tended to regard the oak as an important symbol of Germany's aberrant political culture. As an emblem of the strength and determination of the nation braced for battle, it epitomized the kind of martial, reactionary nationalism that eventually bore fruit under National Socialism. Ulrich Linse regards the oak as an icon of a German 'forest religion' that stood as an anti-modern barrier against the industrializing world. Annemarie Hürlimann writes of the 'xenophobia and racist consciousness ... that the Germans in search of an identity often projected into the oak.'[79] But an analysis of the discourse surrounding the oak in the *Kaiserreich* reveals that neither of these statements seem justified. While the oak may have been associated with historical memory and was usually coded as conservative, it had no particularly reactionary qualities about it. And while it certainly was a nationalist and militarist emblem, the discussions of the oak never exhibited the 'xenophobia and racist consciousness' that Hürlimann describes. Beyond these unsubstantiated assertions, historians have generally overemphasized the importance of the oak as a national symbol. Just as Germany's forests were not made up exclusively of oaks, so too was German nationalism not dominated by '*die deutsche Eiche.*'

In the freewheeling debate over which tree best suited the German national character, those on the right tended to favour the oak, which embodied the strength and longevity of the Fatherland. Perhaps not surprisingly, the conservative and early social Darwinist Friedrich von Hellwald claimed that the ancient Germans had chosen the oak for its 'serious, firm, solid, honest, unbendingly upright character (which would rather be ruined than surrender its will) ... and regarded it as a symbol of German strength and the true German spirit.' Hence, the Teutons 'held their religious assemblies and war councils under them, and decorated their heroes with oak garlands and buried their princes and military leaders under their protection.'[80] According to Hellwald, the weather-beaten oak represented the Germans' essential and unyielding soldierly nature.

The image of an aged, defiant, and battered oak naturally suggested connections to historical memory. In 1884, the Catholic naturalist Carl Berthold contemplated such a tree in his native Westphalia, believing it had witnessed the course of the 'history of our *Volk*.'[81] In the same year, the court gardener Hermann Jäger speculated on the oak as a living monument: 'The things you have experienced, magnificent, lofty oak!' He noted that oaks frequently served as 'memorial trees,' planted to commemorate particular leaders or occasions, such as the two oaks in the palace park at Altenberg named for Saxon princes, or the hundreds of 'Peace Oaks' planted in 1871.[82] Another author cited a variety of historical commemorative trees, such as the oak near Naumburg on the Saale, where Napoleon I ordered his armies to retreat after the momentous Battle of Leipzig, as well as the 'Victory Oaks' commemorating the defeat of Napoleon III.[83] Such trees became monuments to the history of royal houses and their martial exploits.

In rare cases, commemorative oaks could also transport one beyond the nation. Theodor Fontane depicted in his *Journeys through the Mark Brandenburg* the reputedly thousand-year-old Royal Oak in the Brieselang, west of Berlin. In 1873, Fontane described how the tree had become a national symbol in the stormy days of the Napoleonic era, and how recently two comrades-in-arms – veterans of the recent wars of unification – had attached a tablet with a patriotic poem they had written. More interesting, however, was a nationalist ceremony at the oak Fontane detailed. On a pilgrimage to the tree, a party of Berliners raised glasses of Constantia wine from the Cape of Good Hope and recited a toast: 'Oak of a thousand years, we greet you! Here camped the ancient Slav as well as the Berliner, and all sorts of wine, French and German, no less the "fire water" of both Indias, Jamaica and Goa, have been spilled on this spot in your honour. But whether South Africa, or whether the land of the Moors … did homage is at least open to question. Receive this gift from regions in which only [poet Ferdinand] Freiligrath and the Kaffir "lonely ramble through the Karoo," receive this drop of Cape Constantia – the cliffs of Table Mountain greet you and the Brieselang.' The party then turned to singing patriotic songs composed by heroes of the 'Wars of Liberation' against Napoleon I, such as Theodor Körner (killed in battle and buried under an oak) and Ernst Moritz Arndt.[84] These festivities in Fontane's account seamlessly unite the wars against Napoleon I and Napoleon III, as veterans of the latter war honoured the former. But the Royal Oak not only linked the German nation together through time, but also projected it across global spaces. Spirits from the

Caribbean, South Africa, and India all converged on the oak, linking the 'noble savages' of these exotic locales – celebrated in Freiligrath's verse – with the descendants of the Teutonic warriors. The proud oak mediated between past and present, the exotic and the national, trumpeting Germany's strengths and virtues.

With such a prominent role in conjuring the Fatherland's glories, the oak was always gendered male, despite its grammatically feminine name. 'The masculine, heroic character of the oak is expressed by the entire physiognomy of the tree,' commented one author.[85] Likewise, according to folklorist Wilhelm Mannhardt, 'the man in his strength reminds us of the powerful oak, the yielding, graceful woman of the entwining ivy, the perfumed flowers.'[86] An 1879 pamphlet commemorating the golden anniversary of the imperial couple Wilhelm and Augusta explicitly used this oak and ivy metaphor, including cover artwork that depicted Wilhelm's name accompanied by oak leaves and a sprig of ivy over Augusta's.[87] The royal family thus appropriated the oak to legitimize its rule, anchoring it in nationalist symbolism.

It is no coincidence that the state sought to equate the king of Prussia with this 'king of the forest.' As a powerful symbol of strength, the oak was not only represented as a man, but also as a leader. Germans had long 'chosen the oak wreath as the citizens' crown for the man of the people,' noted the count gardener Jäger.[88] According to the conservative nobleman Heinrich von Salisch, 'Often we see the oak standing out above other kinds of trees: it appears to be protecting them regally. It blossoms last: it appears to be the most distinguished of them all. Lower plants make themselves useful as its robes, in order to milden the all-too-great coarseness of its bark with a soft cloak of superb colours. To the many animals of the forest it offers food and shelter.'[89] The oak, like the monarch, protected his realm, while his underlings gave of themselves for his glory.

As the 'king of the forest,' the oak served as a useful emblem of national unity. On 22 March 1871, Wilhelm I's birthday, towns throughout Germany planted oaks in commemoration of their new emperor, the new nation state, and the victory over France. This widespread national celebration surely gratified those imagining a people united. A group of prominent southern German bourgeois took the next step of fashioning the oak into a nationalist emblem, commissioning an enormous centrepiece, entitled 'The German Oak' (figure 5.1), which they presented to their new kaiser in May 1871, and which appeared in the *Illustrierte Zeitung*. The work of the Pforzheim sculptor Karl Siebenpfeiffer,

Figure 5.1 'The German Oak. Gift of Honour for His Majesty the German Kaiser,' 1871. From Rau, Fießler, Auerbach, Ebner, and Ebner, 'Die deutsche Eiche: Ehrengabe für Seine Majestät den Deutschen Kaiser,' *Illustrierte Zeitung* 17 June 1871: 428.

this oak-shaped monument symbolized the unity of the German nation. Above the gnarled roots of the tree, a bas-relief portrayed 'German women and virgins,' led by a princess, handing over the imperial flag to a group of warriors, while enthusiastic Germans of various professions look on. Above them, *Germania* stands accompanied by figures representing religion and art. Further up the trunk we find the branches of the oak, from which sprout the coats-of-arms of the German states, presided over by an eagle. On top of the tree, the Archangel Michael holds his fiery sword aloft while crushing a demonic 'evil enemy' underfoot.[90] In this representation, the oak as Fatherland binds together the various elements. At the root of the tree stand the people (among whom are a mother and a teacher, both essential for the reproduction of the nation) who provide the humus from which German culture, as represented by *Germania* and her handmaidens Art and Religion, springs. Growing from, and providing shelter for, these representatives of German culture are the German states, each a branch of the national tree, and above these branches, the imperial eagle represents the essential unity of the Fatherland. The trunk then reaches further up towards heaven, where it meets Germany's guardian angel, active in his divine protection. As a metaphor for the nation, the oak helped to convey the organic unity of the German people, despite their division into several states.

While this statue might be read by *Sonderweg* historians as a capitulation of southern German liberalism to the imperial might of the Hohenzollerns in the euphoria of unification, it contains a number of democratic elements that challenge this interpretation. First, the fact that the national tree is rooted in the people (the essence of the national idea) would have been disagreeable to a monarch concerned with maintaining his prerogatives in the state. Second, the oak lacked almost any sign of royalty. Note that while the eagle on the Prussian coat-of-arms wears a crown, the German eagle to which it is subordinated most clearly does not. Furthermore, the princess hands the new German flag not to a king, but to a soldier surrounded by a crowd of jubilant commoners. Compare this image to Anton von Werner's famous official painting of the foundation of the Reich, *The Proclamation of the German Empire* (1877), where Emperor Wilhelm I is hailed by his officers. Certainly, the ambiguity of the oak as a national symbol allowed for the blending of liberal nationalism with monarchism at a time when both principles vied for the upper hand.

An oak was similarly used to unite the nation symbolically on the cover of Joseph Kürschner's 1896 picture book *This Is the German Fatherland*

Figure 5.2 Cover of *This Is the German Fatherland*, 1896. From Joseph Kürschner, *Das ist des Deutschen Vaterland* (Berlin: Hermann Hillger, 1896), cover.

(figure 5.2). Here the oak shelters three immediately identifiable German landscapes: the isle of Helgoland, the Wartburg Castle, and the
ruins of the Heidelberg Castle.[91] Besides being sites drawn from northern, central, and southern Germany, each of these landmarks held significant national-historical meaning. Helgoland, a strategic island off
Germany's North Sea coast (acquired by Germany in 1890 from the
British, in exchange for Zanzibar) represented the German naval and
colonial projects, as well as its status as a world power. Moreover, it was
on Helgoland in 1841 that Hoffmann von Fallersleben wrote the anthem
'Deutschland, Deutschland über alles.' The Wartburg, where Luther
translated the Bible into German, represented Germany's Protestant
heritage and its struggles against Rome. Finally, Heidelberg Castle, laid
waste by Louis XIV's troops in 1693, represented the privations suffered
at the hands of the French. It is therefore not surprising that the illustrator chose an oak as a symbol of masculine strength and antipathy for the
French, to link these martial images of the Fatherland.

Yet the oak was not the only option for those who imagined a less
conservative Germany. Among those challenging the oak stood the liberal popular scientist Matthias Jakob Schleiden. Schleiden's rejection of
Prussia's martial character also led him to deny the oak as the German
national tree. While many liberals clung to the oak as a 'freedom tree'
with roots in the revolutionary era, as well as a martial symbol of the
German people mobilized in defence of the nation against outside ag-
gression, conservatives had begun to make increasing use of the tree
themselves.[92] In keeping with his Protestant, liberal, and pacifist vision
of the German lands, Schleiden emphasized that the national tree of
the Germans was not the soldierly oak, which the poet Klopstock had
elevated to iconic status, but the domestic linden. The linden figured
more prominently in medieval poetry than the oak, he noted, and had
been the holy tree of the Teutons (whereas the oak had played that role
for the ancient Celts). The linden also continued to be associated with
religion, he argued, observing that lindens, not oaks, generally graced
the entrances to village churches. Moreover, during the celebrations
surrounding the three-hundredth anniversary of Luther's launch of the
Reformation, villages throughout Saxony planted lindens, not oaks, in
commemoration. With its central place in the community, it followed
that the village linden would be the traditional assembly place for
the people. By contrast, the oak had long been associated with prop-
ertyless servants, he asserted, whereas lindens had symbolized
property ownership.[93] For Schleiden, the linden stood for religion (espe-

cially Protestantism), the village community, and independent property-owners, the ideals of his mid-century liberalism.

Like Schleiden, another popular scientist, Paul Kummer (a mush-room expert and Protestant pastor), praised the national qualities of the linden just weeks before the outbreak of the Franco-Prussian War in the popular family journal *Daheim* (At Home). He identified the oak with the druidic cult of the Celts and claimed the real national tree was the linden: 'It is the tree that always recurs in German folk life.' Imagining a kinder, gentler Germany, Kummer described the linden as a 'tree whose sweet intimacy, whose cosy pleasant fullness corresponds to the German emotional character.' In contrast to the popular image of the German pagans of old, he proclaimed, 'raw power and impetuous violence were not part of the inner nature of our ancestors.' Instead, the linden corre-sponded better to the German essence: 'tenderness of feeling, as it rings out of ancient poetry, the apt contemplativeness, the depth of passion ... the devotion to the religious aspects of life, the struggle for the ideal.' As shade trees, one found lindens in public places, standing as canopies for communal life. Luther preached under such trees, further tying them to Protestant religiosity. This was not to portray the Germans as soft, he interjected, for as historians recorded (with a little too much emphasis for his taste), they had 'used the sword with manly defiance.' Yet Kum-mer observed that 'the man at war is an exceptional case,' just as the era of 'robber barons and all the feuds in the kaiserless, terrible times were only aberrations.' Instead, 'Courtly love, the happy life in nature and the joy of the domestic hearth have most corresponded to the true Ger-man consciousness. And representative of this inner trait was above all the linden, the sweet-scented, golden-bloomed, shady linden with soft, heart-shaped leaves.' The rise of the oak to national importance, stated Kummer, came during the violent storms of the Napoleonic Wars, when Germans sought a symbol of strength and stability. They took their cues from the defiant oaks, he confirmed, but 'this period passed, and the in-ner sympathy came to an end. Defiance and struggle are no longer our goals. There are nobler tasks of the spirit and the mind ahead of us: to bless the work of peace, to enjoy our lives with deep and warm feeling, and to support and promote the ideals of humanity, which have nothing to do with defiance and conflict.' Kummer concluded by once more stat-ing, 'Certainly, the linden is still our tree today, as it once was, according to the voice of our soul ... And thank God, that this is so!'[94] The oak seemed quite outmoded as an emblem of national unity; now the charm-ing grace of the feminine linden appeared much more appropriate.

This assault on the primacy of the oak outraged at least one German nationalist. Karl Strackerjan – an Oldenburg school director, author, and later paranoid nationalist worried about disloyalty amongst Germany's Danish minority – lashed out at Kummer specifically in 1874, furious that 'the opponents of the oak are also making propaganda in popular form' and complaining hysterically that 'modern prophets' sought to 'deny the oak not simply supremacy, but any meaning as a tree of the German people whatsoever.' The gendered characters of these trees made it impossible for him to countenance the rise of the feminine linden in the national pantheon. The oak's 'powerful effect is paternal,' while the linden's 'busy worries are maternal.' With an eye towards other nations, he insisted that if '*the* tree of the German people should be one that fittingly symbolizes the German people's position with regard to other peoples, and if it is to symbolize Germany in its relations with other empires, then it can only be the oak.'[95] Strackerjan's outrage unlikely attracted much attention, however. Writing in his Oldenburg school's annual, his defence of the oak's primacy could not have circulated nearly as widely as Kummer's article in a popular weekly. Moreover, none of the authors touting either tree made any reference to his broadside.

Kummer and Schleiden were not alone in their effort to dethrone the oak. A steady stream of articles following the founding of the empire continued to elevate the linden in the national consciousness. Writing a month after the end of the Franco-Prussian War in the *Illustrierte Zeitung*, the poet Konrad Hofmann von Nauborn continued to depict the linden as the 'true German-national tree,' pushed aside and forgotten during the Napoleonic wars. In Teutonic mythology, the linden was associated with the goddess Herka, a 'masculine woman' wielding a sword and associated with strength, courage, and victory. In the medieval period, the linden embodied both the masculine world of justice and the feminine world of religion and romantic love. No other tree, Hofmann claimed, represented both 'masculine strength and feminine tenderness and charm' as well as the linden. Hence, he sought to replace the martial qualities of the oak with the 'German strength and glory,' as well as the 'German spiritual depth and pious customs' inherent in the linden.[96]

Hofmann's hermaphroditic linden did not have wide appeal. Other authors resolved the tension between the masculine and feminine characteristics by elevating both the oak and the linden to national status. The cultural historian Johannes Scherr, a Württemberg democrat and 1848er, first repeated some of the commonplaces about the linden in the 1879 edition of his *History of German Culture and Customs*. Yet Scherr was unwilling to abandon the oak altogether. The character of the two trees complimented each other, and elements of both could be found in German history, which contained 'beside the ruggedness and hardness also much that is gentle and soft.'[97] In 1888, K.A. von Schulenburg, a Prussian officer, author of hunting stories and amateur ethnographer, published an article in a popular journal likewise celebrating the complimentary virtues of both trees. The oak was the 'symbol of loyalty, patriotism, and the man in his strength,' in this version, while 'like the German woman,' the linden 'stands in charming grace.'[98] The following year, Otto Lohr, an amateur historian in Prague, penned a small booklet that came to much the same conclusion. 'If the oak represents the mighty strength and warlike side of the German people,' he wrote, 'so the linden embodies its spiritual world, its peaceful side.'[99] By the 1880s, a camp had coalesced supporting the elevation of the linden to iconic status, balancing the old belligerent oak with the peaceful and homey linden.

Lohr exhaustively explored the literary and social significance of the linden, reiterating many familiar points. German folk music depended on the linden; indeed, Lohr argued it was 'the *Volk*'s favourite tree.' Village life played out under its branches, where 'the joyful youth dance, while the elders sit at the table in earnest discussion.' Certainly, the entire nation found itself united under the linden, as 'its thick foliage spread itself protectively over the proud knight's castle as over the low cottage of the husbandman.' Lindens were likewise traditionally the trees of love, home, and family, and Lohr rhapsodized about the linden planted by one's ancestors, linking together generations. Also associated with religion, one came across lindens in churchyards and graveyards, accompanying one through all the stations of life.[100]

The linden's association with community and folk culture made it useful in depicting the *Heimat*. A 1910 postcard of Heilbronn (figure 5.3) depicted a linden sheltering the medieval Swabian town.[101] Placed on the tree is a wreath commemorating the poet Friedrich Schiller (born in nearby Marbach), while a child rests at its feet. The roots of the tree extend down into an inset landscape, where a lone hiker surveys a peaceful valley. This image integrated many of the associations of the linden into a bucolic depiction of the Heilbronn *Heimat*. Images of nature combined with local history and culture to nurture the child and the town. Moreover, the postcard advertised the twenty-ninth choral festival of the Swabian Singers' League, a local organization that no doubt aimed to strengthen the feeling for the *Heimat* through its activities. In contrast with the oak on the cover of Kürschner's book on the Fatherland, this

Figure 5.3 Heilbronn postcard, 1910. From Confino, *The Nation as a Local Metaphor*, 207.

linden does not unite scenes of national-historic significance, but rather the local landscape. These two images point to the division of labour between the linden and the oak.

Yet, like the oak, the linden could also function as a tree of imperial ambition, albeit in a less belligerent way. Otto Lohr, secretary of the nationalist Association for the History of the Germans in Bohemia, opened his defence of the linden as a German national tree with a depiction of the ethnic conflict in his province. He described the landscape outside of Prague, including a 'cosy little fir grove' associated with Mozart that stood as a 'beautiful, peaceful island amid the Czech sea.' The 'Slavic flood' engulfing this modest German forest was a violent one, in contrast with the lilting tones of the classical master. Lohr juxtaposed coffee-drinking Mozart devotees gathered for a concert at a German estate with rock-throwing Czech nationalist rabble-rousers. Then he recalled an argument he had with a local Czech, who claimed the linden as his people's national tree, to Lohr's chagrin; Lohr composed his booklet to prove him wrong, providing copious citations from German poetry and folklore, culture high and low.[102] For Lohr, German culture simply outweighed anything the Czechs had to offer. The best way to meet the uncouth Czech nationalist threat, it seemed, was to bury it in citations from German literature.[103] German culture would ultimately carry the day, liberal German nationalists like Lohr were convinced.

The cultural historian August Sach similarly used the linden to envision German cultural supremacy in 1885. Writing just as Germany acquired its first colonial possessions, Sach likened Germany's global influence to a linden. The magnificent lindens that had once animated the culture of the ancient Germans may have disappeared, he claimed, but 'delicious fruits ... are sown like seeds of new learning throughout the lands occupied by the Teutons, and have finally germinated and have then, fertilized from all sides, budded into a high intellectual tree of life, that through its roots draws nourishment from all times and zones, its branches and twigs reaching out over all peoples, offering them intellectually nourishing and refreshing fruits for pleasure, so that they can also be suffused with the new life force of modern education.'[104] Unlike the martial oak, which – like the Royal Oak described by Fontane – received homage from 'noble savages' around the world, the linden spread out its branches 'over all peoples,' offering the fruits of German culture. Like Lohr, Sach envisioned German hegemony in the world of arts and sciences, and eschewed the oak's soldierly symbolism.

Authors continued to address the issue of the national tree over the succeeding decades, but after the 1880s it garnered less attention. Authors on the right continued to favour the oak (geographer Friedrich Ratzel, among others), but the linden still found many advocates who imagined a kinder and gentler Germany. As they suggested, the oak and the linden represented two faces of the nation.

Conclusion

Quite in contrast with Düesberg and Francé, most of those embracing the rhetoric of the 'German forest' – middle-class nature enthusiasts and the *Heimat* movement, among others – did not seek a solution to Germany's problems in the biological sciences. For them, the forest provided an aesthetic experience and an escape from the rigors of everyday life in crowded and polluted industrial cities. The one scientist prominently involved in the *Heimat* movement's leadership, Hugo Conwentz, practised an older brand of botany that focused on the collection, labelling, and preservation of specimens, precisely what Francé and Düesberg rebelled against. Francé insisted botany needed to rise above the facts and engage in 'philosophical speculation,' which he recognized would be difficult for those botanists educated in the 1870s and 1880s (like Conwentz) to accept. Düesberg likewise celebrated the triumph of the natural sciences over the 'petty spirit' of quantification.[105] This flew in the face of Schleiden's mid-century efforts to anchor botany strictly in empiricism. Bourgeois amateurs were content to dream of the past in their local woods, but scientists like Francé and Düesberg wanted to demystify the forest and decode the immutable laws of nature contained in it.

Moreover, the landscapes these scientists imagined differed drastically from the pleasant countryside celebrated by the *Heimat* movement.[106] Hellwald pointed out that the lovely German countryside was a human construct; culture kept normally violent vegetation in check. Francé insisted that 'the songs and legends of the German forest are the sweet lies of the poets. For there are hardly any more forests [*Wälder*].'[107] The popular representations of the ancestral woods, with their cavorting Teutonic tribesmen, are 'painted as a background, as a fairies' realm, in which the highest lushness and beauty compete with the picturesque and magnificently fantastic images of nature.' Yet according to the latest research, Francé explained to his readers, this vision of ancient Germany 'does not hold.' Instead, he conjured an image of 'a totally monstrous world of forests and moors, which has nothing to do with the fantasy world in which [the fairy tale illustrator Moritz von] Schwind presents the German legends so close to our hearts.' Struggle characterized this dark and gloomy dominion, 'full of abnormalities, of horrors'; the lifeless trunks of the defeated litter the forest floor, 'and to this is added the dreadful silence of this wasteland, the almost total lack of flowers and birds.'[108] Düesberg evoked a similar image of arboreal combat, recalling how over thousands of years Germany's forests 'had to undergo a harsh struggle with adverse forces.'[109] Rejecting the gentle fantasies of middle-class nature enthusiasts, embedded in a cheerful cultural landscape, these scientists invoked a biological space predicated on constant struggle. As Thomas Lekan notes, these two radically different representations of nature clashed in the Third Reich, when Nazi officials rode roughshod over the Rhineland's settled countryside, valuing instead the more 'authentic' and 'pure' wilderness.[110] We should be careful, therefore, not to attribute the biologized idea of landscape to the *Heimat* campaigners and nature preservers of the *Kaiserreich*.

Conclusion

This book has two major objectives: first, to explore what the forest meant for the competing factions building the German national identity, and second, to complicate our understanding of the Germans' interest in nature and its connection to politics.

In the national discourse, authors in a variety of genres constructed an entity called the 'German forest' out of Central Europe's sylvan diversity. This *'deutsche Wald'* served as a symbolic green band that tied the nation's splintered geography, history, and society together. Local *Heimat* associations, hiking clubs, nature enthusiasts, museums, schools, and others adopted this belief in the intimate interconnection between the forest and the nation, working to inculcate a sense of local/national identity rooted in nature. Establishing, preserving, and visiting monuments, both natural and constructed, infused the local landscape with emblems that connected Germans across time and space. An excursion to the woods could thus transform the abstract and artificial concept of nation into a tangible and 'natural' experience.

This idealized union of nation and nature belied significant conflicts surrounding the 'German forest.' A wide range of social and political groups contested the implications of the forest as a national symbol. It was one thing to sing the praises of the woods, but quite another to regulate property rights on wooded land. Powerful agrarian interests sought to restrict access to their timberlands, aiming to exclude the urban rambler and impoverished peasant from their property. Motivated by fears of revolution, social reformers, peasant advocates, and radical nationalists each challenged these elite interests, eventually articulating a notion of the woods as 'national property' accessible to all. Radical nationalists, often regarded as the ideological lackeys of 'feudal interests,' instead directly attacked the Junkers' control of the land.

A similar dynamic played out in Berlin, where the municipal government, the local press, and a wide range of citizens' groups confronted the state over its policy of selling, rather than conserving, wooded property near the city. Left liberals (and later socialists) and social reform groups rallied the public to pressure the government through petitions and protest meetings. This political activity crystallized around the Grunewald, a former royal hunting ground. Fearing social unrest among Berlin's working classes, these organizations hoped to alleviate many forms of social suffering, from lung ailments to the collapse of the family, by affording the workers more access to nature. Not only does this example demonstrate the compatibility of the nature discourse with the political left in Germany, it also illustrates the political activism of local government in this period.

By contrast, the Tuchel Heath lay far from Berlin's metropolitan world. And yet this state forest on Germany's periphery also embodied a modernizing ethic. Rather than symbolizing agrarian reaction in this eastern landscape, this forest stood at the centre of a state campaign to erase the social, cultural, and economic legacies of Polish 'mismanagement' and impose a German modernity. State authorities expanded the local transportation infrastructure to draw the region into the German economy, and Prussian foresters represented themselves as models of modern, productive men seeking to inculcate the thoroughly bourgeois values of punctuality, discipline, and order into their Slavic neighbours and labourers. Thus the state pursued a modernization policy without romantic longings for the 'German forest.'

The Germans' passion for nature has often been held accountable for the rise of the Nazis' blood and soil (*Blut und Boden*) ideology. Yet concepts of race played only a marginal role in the woodland discourse during the *Kaiserreich*. Those who sought to introduce a racial analysis into the 'German forest' came from the sciences, not from the *Heimat* movement, and they held a very different view of the landscape. Whereas these scientists occupied themselves reconstructing a primeval forest of biological struggle, nature enthusiasts and *Heimat* activists envisioned a cheerful cultural landscape in which humans lived in harmony with nature. These differences persisted into the Nazi era.

I have tried to explain why Germans turned to the forest to provide national symbolism and at the same time demonstrate that this investment of nature with national sentiment was neither predominantly anti-modern nor proto-fascist. In none of these cases can one identify 'reactionary' elements seeking to uphold an outmoded social and political order through a manipulation of national and natural symbols. As a result, one must refute the ideological *Sonderweg* that sees the Germans' interest in nature as ultimately culminating in the blood and soil ideology of the Nazis. Germans did not stand alone in their love of nature, nor in their assertion of a strong link between landscape and national identity. Indeed, at least among northern Europeans, such sentiments were quite common. Detailed comparisons between Germany and other countries, beyond the scope of this study, would help contextualize the German relationship with nature and clarify its connection to fascism.

For many Germans, France was the foil against which they contrasted their own friendliness to nature. The devastation of forests during French Revolution, cited by several authors, stood out as emblematic of careless French practices. Yet French forestry experts, for their part, quickly appreciated the danger. Already in 1797, a French engineer published an article identifying the consequences of deforestation on rivers. By 1817, a government report urged the state to maintain its forests against destruction, for fear of further erosion and flooding. Like German authors, it cited the desertification of Mediterranean lands as a potential threat.[1] By the mid-nineteenth century, French foresters engaged in the wholesale afforestation of large regions, such as the *Landes de Gascogne,* seeing the rescue of this impoverished region in the development of scientific forestry, just as the Prussians did in the Tuchel Heath.[2]

Likewise, the French had their own civic organizations dedicated to landscape preservation. Danny Trom briefly compares the discourses surrounding nature and nation in France and Germany. Examining the *Bund Heimatschutz* (founded in 1904) and its French equivalent, the *Société pour la protection des paysages de France* (founded in 1901) – as well as several allied groups – Trom discovers a great deal of similarity in their rhetoric and ideology, despite France's common image as a more urbane nation. Both movements incorporated diverse actors in a campaign that viewed the landscape in aesthetic and historical terms, that mediated between regional and national identities, and that sought to protect nature by mobilizing national sentiment.[3]

Although Trom notes the *Société pour la protection des paysages* lacked the interest in hiking so central to German *Heimat* clubs, at least two French associations mirrored German efforts at cultivating a national relationship with the countryside. The *Touring-Club de France* (1890) – a popular middle-class group numbering over 130,000 members by 1913 – aimed to promote hiking throughout France, by organizing trips, calling for the protection of natural sites and monuments, and promoting reforestation to provide more scenic backdrops for hikers. Indeed, reforestation proved so important to its goals, the club sponsored an international conference on forests in Paris. Founded a year later, the *Société des amis des arbres* (1891) sought to endear urbanites to the woods, and by 1895, 'the recreative appeal of forests had become firmly established among the bourgeoisie.' The club went on to intervene in popular alpine hiking areas, attempting to educate peasants in the virtues of the forest. It published texts on forest preservation for local schools and encouraged the institution of *Fêtes de l'arbre* to instil the value of the woods in rural children. The club also helped over four hundred schools establish nurseries in which pupils raised saplings for planting during the *Fêtes.* After the First World War, France instituted its own version of Arbour Day, celebrated on 11 November and intimately bound up with the memory of the war. Popular reforestation had become a patriotic act, and some proposed creating a 'sacred forest' on the battlefields of northeastern France to heal the wounded landscape and commemorate the fallen soldiers.[4] The French thus had organizations dedicated to linking nature and nation, but further investigation of these parallels is necessary.

Some Germans recognized that the French, too, felt themselves bound to their forests. One German author, writing in 1914, cited extensive praise for the woods by contemporary French figures. Reportedly, conservative President Raymond Poincaré identified himself 'as a fanatical friend of the trees and hoped for the right to cut off the heads of those that cut them down.' The nationalist and literary critic Jules Lemaitre likewise condemned the estate owner who razed a grove on the banks for the Loire, while the prominent anti-Semite Maurice Barrès proclaimed, 'We love the trees!'[5] It is interesting to note, however, that each of these statements invoked trees, and not forests, and did not explicitly tie them to the fate of the nation. Moreover, it would be interesting to know whether such expressions of tree-friendliness were limited to the political right.

The relationship between landscape and national identity has an especially strong tradition in Great Britain. Manor houses and their placid parks have long represented a particular version of British 'heritage,' linking together land and nation in a conservative rubric. The persistence of this image of 'old England,' and the social and racial exclusions at its foundation, has prompted much scholarly analysis.[6] This ongoing controversy over the role of the landscape image in the British national identity stems from the success English aristocrats had in asserting their vision of the land as a national icon. In the eighteenth and nineteenth centuries, they reshaped the countryside surrounding their manor houses, obscuring the working land and impoverished villages behind stands of trees, while at the same time extending the view from the manor house as far as possible, visually claiming the countryside. As one landscape architect put it, the changes aimed 'to extend the idea of a seat and appropriate a whole country to a mansion.' Celebrating this appropriation, another landscape architect defined it as 'that charm which only belongs to ownership, the exclusive right of enjoyment, with the power of refusing that others should share our pleasure.' Landscape art of the period likewise celebrated their property as the very image of the nation. This point was not lost on those who sought democratization of the nation and its land. William Cobbett recalled 'a book we used to look at a great deal entitled "A Picture of England." It contained views of County Seats and of fine hills and valleys.... Alas! This was no picture of England, if by England we mean anything more than a certain portion of Houses, Trees and Herbage.'[7] Such a complaint testifies to the powerful political impact of this landscape aesthetic.

Aristocrats likewise appropriated the 'English oak' as both their symbol and the symbol of the nation. Keith Thomas, exploring the history of the English relationship with nature in the early modern period, notes that ancient noble families likened themselves to the oak and cherished those standing on their estates. The conservative Edmund Burke identified the aristocracy as 'the great oaks that shade the countryside,' imagining these old families sheltering the lower classes, as did the magnificent trees in landscape painting. The popularity of oaks stemmed, Thomas suggests, from their sense of massive durability: 'As social change accelerated, the desire to preserve such visible symbols of continuity grew stronger.' In shipbuilding, the foundation of English power and wealth, the oak took on a further patriotic meaning, serving as the 'wooden walls' protecting Britain. Yet these national overtones could not protect the landlords' trees; indeed, their symbolic quality subjected them to attack. Rural rioters felled ornamental trees to strike at their owners, and with the oak serving as an aristocratic, national, and state symbol, it comes as no surprise that Thomas Paine should call on revolutionaries to 'lay the axe to the root and teach Governments humility.'[8] Again, this vocal resistance to aristocratic symbols suggests their power.

The British countryside, clearly, witnessed clashes over the definition and imagery of nationhood. These struggles only increased with the rise of the middle classes and their efforts to attain greater political power. Tourism and other forms of appropriating the landscape 'offered middle-class consumers a way of possessing England (the land) and hence claiming membership in it (the nation) some years before political reforms redefined the conception of property to admit them to the franchise.'[9] For the British – as for the Germans – linking nature and nation was not necessarily conservative or reactionary; indeed, it could stand as part of the fight against the nobility.

However, alternative views of the nation emanated from several sources, not just from those struggling over political power. As in Germany, British industrialization provoked anxieties about urban squalor, disease, and degeneration. The English social critic John Ruskin denounced cities and capitalism, rejecting their destruction of an idealized pastoral landscape.[10] In many ways, Ruskin played the same role as Wilhelm Heinrich Riehl, critiquing the process of modernization.[11] Both these men, writing in the middle of the nineteenth century, expressed a profound hostility to modernity. Yet the writings of both would inspire a generation of reformers reconciled to modernity by the end of the century. William Morris and Edward Carpenter, both on the left of the political spectrum, sought to restore village life. Around them flourished a whole network of reform movements – aimed at changing land tenure, clothing styles, school curricula, and settlement patterns, for example – seeking to dismantle the strictures of over-refined Victorian aesthetics and mores.[12] These movements, like Ruskin himself, inspired Germans to take up the same causes in the *Lebensreform* (life reform) movements.[13] Thus there are several parallels between the British and German experiences.

But the British reform movements linking nature and nation apparently stood more distinctly on the left than their German counterparts (although this conclusion requires more investigation).[14] English radical nationalists seem to have played a less important role in developing the ideology of the countryside than they did in Germany (at least after the First World War). Why did the left wing of the British political spectrum provide the best home for those critical of liberals and conservatives, of urban squalor and industrialization? The alliance of the labour movement with liberalism before the First World War, effective because Britain's comparatively narrow franchise excluded most workers from electoral politics, probably allowed reformist groups to coalesce on the left more easily, without fear of abetting revolution.[15] The persistence of the aristocratic image of countryside and nation, seemingly more powerful than it was in Germany, probably also discouraged bourgeois reformers from moving towards the right.

Even more similarities unite the German and Swedish nature discourses. Swedish authors, very much like their German counterparts, believed a love of nature and the forest in particular was essential to their national identity. A 1910 book on the Swedish national character pronounced, 'The most deeply ingrained trait in the Swedish temperament is a strong love of nature,' which, according to the author, was 'the most profound explanation of the indestructible power and health of the Swedish nation.'[16] Much as in Germany, Swedish nationalists regarded nature as a means to endear the masses to the nation. In 1899, the Swedish natural historian Gustaf Kolthoff noted, 'Few countries are richer or more glorious in nature than our own. The knowledge and love of this nature must greatly assist in increasing the love of our native land – one of the noblest of sentiments.' Ten years later, proposed nature-protection legislation argued that national parks should provide 'visual material for teaching patriotism.' Anthropologist Orvar Löfgren concludes that for contemporary Scandinavians, nature 'has been a very powerful and central theme of national self-understanding.'[17] The parallels between Germany and Sweden thus stand out sharply.

In Sweden, this linkage of nature and nation had an overwhelmingly progressive edge. The turn to nature redefined the nation, challenging conservative jingoism and the dreams of a martial past with an inclusive attempt to transcend class boundaries. The Swedish experience thus appears quite comparable with that of Berlin, where the left-liberal establishment competed with the Social Democrats for the loyalties of urban workers. Swedish nature enthusiasts identified urban parks as 'lungs of the city, a healing force both physically and mentally, a moral resource that was necessary not least for the working-class children of the slums.' One Swedish author worried that workers had been 'taken from the forest and given to the street.' Like German liberals, middle-class Swedes hoped providing accessible forests for the working classes would help them overcome their alienation.[18] Swedes also had an analogous *Heimat* (*Hembygd*) movement, concerned with the preservation of the countryside and peasant life.[19] This group, along with the National Romantic movement in art (allied with the Swedish Social Democratic Party), worked to ensure the survival of an independent peasantry.[20] Thus an interest in nature, even when explicitly linked to the politics of national identity, need not result in an impulse to fascism.

The key difference between Germany and Sweden, of course, was the strain of nature reverence on the German right. Why did efforts to protect the peasantry gravitate to the left in Sweden, and tend to the nationalist right (with Heinrich Sohnrey and Alfred Hugenberg) in Germany? Recent comparisons of Swedish and German society indicate the importance class identities took on in German politics. Whereas the Swedish Social Democrats proved politically flexible and conciliatory vis-à-vis other social groups (especially the peasantry), their German counterparts insisted on the language of revolution and obstructionalism.[21] This explains Swedish socialists' more ready appropriation of the languages of nature and nation. At the same time, the German socialists' militance only strengthened the resolve of the German middle classes, which tenaciously held on to their bourgeois identities, hard won after decades of struggle with conservative elites. The Swedish middle classes, by contrast, lacked this strong bourgeois identity – a result of lower rates of urbanization and the weakness of the Swedish old regime – leading to their increased willingness to work with the socialists.[22] Therefore, while a patriotism rooted in the native landscape helped reconcile the social classes in Sweden, in Germany the bourgeoisie used it to combat socialism. While many bourgeois Germans hoped to use the forest to overcome social cleavages, as did their Swedish neighbours, the greater strain of class tensions in Germany meant that socialists would not or could not cooperate. The woodland discourse thus could not form a bridge to the socialist mass movement in Germany, and instead resulted in varying levels of cooperation between liberals and conservatives in a broad range of reforms meant to forestall revolution. These reforms aimed to modernize society, by rationalizing property rights, eliminating unproductive land, investing resources for the integration of backward regions into the national economy, and bringing about social harmony. These measures were freighted with ambivalence, however. Some groups tended to win, particularly landowners and the state, while others tended to lose, especially peasants and workers. Modernity did not equal progress for everyone.

How did this impulse to modernize the forest proceed beyond 1914? The First World War changed the German relationship with the landscape. The experience of wartime privations made the land, and living from it, an obsession for some. After the trauma of war and defeat, many Germans turned to nature when their faith in the human world had been shattered. All manner of *Lebensreform* movements tied to nature flourished in the Weimar era, from organic farming and nudism to vegetarianism and homeopathy. After the war, communes embracing a wide range of social, cultural, and political values emerged, each seeking to find at least personal, if not national, renewal in the native soil.[23] Those on the left were just as likely as conservatives to turn to nature as a rational response to the problems of military defeat and the ills of industrial modernity, as John Williams has recently illustrated with his analysis of hiking, nudist, and conservation groups.[24] And far from being a tool of the right, the familiar concept of *Heimat* 'played a crucial role in sustaining public loyalty to the republic.'[25] It would therefore be inaccurate to identify a turn to nature as a mainly right-wing phenomenon even after the First World War.

While the First World War did not transform interest in nature into the domain of the political right, it did alter the way radical nationalists looked at the landscape. As some *völkisch* nationalists – like Rudolf Düesberg – anticipated before 1914, nature could provide lessons for the wholesale reform of society. And that reform became all the more urgent with the devastation and dislocation of wartime. With the war increasingly interpreted on the right as a Social Darwinist conflict between the 'races' of Europe, some nature enthusiasts – such as those congregating in the rightward-leaning *Harzklub* hiking group – sought out the 'lesson' the forest could provide as a harmonious community locked in battle against interlopers. After the war, such groups believed a return to nature would revive the *Volk*.[26] Some in the *Heimat* movement – prominent among them the architect Paul Schultze-Naumburg – also began to drift in this direction, arguing for the centrality of their efforts to preserve the local cultural landscape for 'racial' renewal. It comes as no surprise, then, that some nature conservationists would be attracted to Nazism, although far fewer than commonly assumed. As Raymond Dominick points out, of eighteen prominent nature conservationists, only Schultze-Naumburg joined the Nazi Party before 1933. And although after 1933 a disproportionately large number of those involved in the nature-protection movement did join the party, many soon found themselves disillusioned with Nazi policies.[27]

On an ideological level, while both nature conservationists and Nazis agreed on the need to preserve the German landscape as a means to revive the nation, they tended to have different conceptions of that landscape. With a quest for purity being at the heart of the Nazi world view, the government after 1933 conceived of protecting the untrammelled ancient wilderness that supposedly gave rise to the Germanic people, such as the Białowieża Forest (annexed to Germany in 1941). This stood in distinct contrast with the desires of the *Heimat* movement, which had as its object the much more modest goal of preserving the local cultural landscape. Naturally, the Nazis regarded this emphasis on local distinction with some suspicion, intent as they were on centralization under the Führer's leadership.[28] The Nazis' blood and nature protectionists' soil formed a rather unstable ideological solution.

These ideological differences only hinted at the real disillusion those interested in forests would experience as Nazi priorities became apparent. Recent historical research into the environmental policies of the Third Reich have cast significant doubt on the Nazis' green image. While the early years of the regime saw a proliferation of works extolling Germany's forests and their virtues, the Nazi press itself showed little interest in nature preservation, which rarely made the front page of the party's *Völkischer Beobachter*.[29] Likewise, Nazi forestry failed to live up to ecological expectations. Some Nazi foresters, drawing on Düesberg, championed a new kind of forestry – the *Dauerwald* – which advocated more natural methods of production. In reaction against the prevailing practices of scientific forestry (with its emphasis on maximizing wood production through creating evenly aged monocultures of fast-growing softwoods), advocates of the *Dauerwald* proposed creating naturally regenerating forests of mixed species (particularly hardwoods) and mixed ages.[30] While Hermann Goering, in his role as chief of the German forests, officially adopted this more ecologically friendly approach to forestry in 1934, it was quickly abandoned. The same held true for the highly touted landscape aesthetics of the autobahn. Although environmentally sensitive landscape architects like Alwin Seifert were appointed as consultants on the project, their contributions were steadily marginalized by the demand for rapid results.[31] Indeed, it appears Nazi rhetoric of a national renewal arising from nature took a back seat to their more pressing goal: the rearmament of Germany in preparation for war and racial struggle. Almost as quickly as they were proclaimed, measures announcing environmental innovations were gutted in the interest of war industries.[32] By the time of the war, German foresters heavily exploited woodlands, first at home and then especially abroad.[33] Nazi forestry policy thus mirrored other aspects of the recklessly exploitative regime.

As Germany succumbed to defeat in 1945, again the public turned for comfort to nature. As Thomas Lekan has observed, after the Second World War, the German public turned to nature-kitsch to escape the harsh realities of the post-war world. Down came the portraits of Hitler and up went the bucolic landscapes.[34] Yet despite the important rupture of the war years, there remained much continuity in the nature-protection movement. During the 1950s and 1960s, local initiatives at nature protection retained much of the traditional rhetoric, as well as many of the goals and leaders, of the pre-war movement. The *Schutz-gemeinschaft Deutscher Wald* (founded in 1947 to defend Germany's forests against Allied clear-cutting for reparations) helped to keep alive the forest discourse after the war. The concepts of nature and *Heimat* were still intimately intertwined, lending a national meaning to the landscape, and walks in the woods continued to have moral and social meaning; indeed, Sandra Chaney has remarked on the 'striking continuities with the past' in this period.[35]

Yet there were important changes; the old aesthetic discourse and provincial approach gradually gave way to more scientific language and universal campaigns. The *Heimat* began to fade into the background as pollution and other threats took on global proportions. The 1970s in particular marked an important rupture, with the shift in language from nature protection (*Naturschutz*) to environmental protection (*Umwelt-schutz*), indicating a decisive political swing to the left that culminated with the ascendancy of the Green Party. These changes reflected the new concerns embraced by the movement, such as the campaigns against nuclear weapons and energy. Tactics became more confrontational, breaking with the older traditions of public petitions and behind-the-scenes negotiations.[36]

Nevertheless, elements of continuity remain: William Markham has found it significant that – through all of Germany's political regimes of the twentieth century – activists have continued to champion environmental concerns.[37] Albrecht Lehmann has argued that Germans today continue to look at forests in much the same way as their great-grand-parents.[38] The discourse about the impending death of Germany's forests (*Waldsterben*) in the 1980s seems to bear this point out, demonstrating a significant public attachment to the forests, accompanied by national sentiment, with images of iconic German landscapes denuded of forests raising the alarm.[39] At the same time, the radical right in Germany continues to propagate a *völkisch* version of the forest discourse, although it is relegated to the margins of German politics.[40] And recently East Germany's ailing forests have been taken as an indicator of the declining health of the Communist regime.[41] The fates of the German nation and its forests still seem, for the time being, interwoven.

Notes

Introduction

1 Wilhelm Heinrich Riehl, *Die Naturgeschichte des Volkes als Grundlage einer deutschen Social-Politik*, 6th ed. (Stuttgart: Cotta, 1867), 49–50. My italics. All italics are in the original, unless otherwise indicated.

2 Quoted in Alfred Barthelmeß, *Wald als Umwelt des Menschen* (Freiburg: Karl Alber, 1972), 59; T., 'Der Wald als Erzieher,' *Der Kunstwart* 20, no. 5 (1906): 305.

3 For a more detailed discussion of national comparisons, see the conclusion.

4 Benedict Anderson, *Imagined Communities: Reflections on the Origin and Spread of Nationalism*, 2nd ed. (London: Verso, 1991).

5 For contrasting views, see Eric Hobsbawm, *Nations and Nationalism since 1780* (Cambridge: Cambridge University Press, 1990); and Anthony D. Smith, *The Ethnic Origins of Nations* (Cambridge, MA: Blackwell, 1986).

6 See Anderson, *Imagined Communities*; Patrick J. Geary, *The Myth of Nations: The Medieval Origins of Europe* (Princeton, NJ: Princeton University Press, 2002).

7 Anthony D. Smith, *The Ethnic Origins of Nations* (Cambridge, MA: Blackwell, 1986), 183.

8 Orvar Löfgren, 'Landscapes of the Mind,' *Topos* 6 (March 1994): 6.

9 Chandra Mukerji, *Territorial Ambitions and the Gardens of Versailles* (Cambridge: Cambridge University Press, 1997).

10 Stephen Daniels, 'The Political Iconography of Woodland in Later Georgian England,' in *The Iconography of Landscape*, ed. Stephen Daniels and Denis Cosgrove, 43–82 (Cambridge: Cambridge University Press, 1988); Nigel Everett, *The Tory View of Landscape* (New Haven, CT: Yale University Press, 1994); Jill Franklin, 'The Liberty of the Park,' in *Patriotism*, ed.

Raphael Samuel, 141–59 (London: Routledge, 1989); Brigitte Weltman-Aron, *On Other Grounds: Landscape Gardening and Nationalism in Eighteenth-Century England and France* (Albany: State University of New York Press, 2001).

11 Geoff Eley, 'State Formation, Nationalism, and Political Culture,' in *From Unification to Nazism*, 2nd ed., 61–84 (London: Routledge, 1992).

12 Stephen Daniels, 'Mapping National Identities: The Culture of Cartography, with Particular Reference to the Ordnance Survey,' in *Imagining Nations*, ed. Geoffrey Cubitt (Manchester: Manchester University Press, 1998), 112–13.

13 On the relationship of tourism, 'memory landscapes,' and national identity, see Alon Confino, 'The Nation as a Local Metaphor: Heimat, National Memory and the German Empire, 1871–1918,' *History & Memory* 5, no. 1 (1993): 42–86; Confino, *The Nation as Local Metaphor: Württemberg, Imperial Germany, and National Memory, 1871–1918* (Chapel Hill: University of North Carolina Press, 1997); John R. Gillis, ed. *Commemorations: The Politics of National Identity* (Princeton, NJ: Princeton University Press, 1994); Rudy Koshar, *From Monuments to Traces: Artifacts of German Memory, 1870–1990* (Berkeley: University of California Press, 2000); Albrecht Lehmann, 'Der deutsche Wald,' in *Deutsche Erinnerungsorte*, ed. Hagen Schulze and Etienne François (Munich: Beck, 2003), 3:187–200; Pierre Nora, ed. *Realms of Memory: Rethinking the French Past* (New York: Columbia University Press, 1996).

14 Elizabeth Helsinger, *Rural Scenes and National Representation* (Princeton, NJ: Princeton University Press, 1997), 165–6; and Helsinger, 'Turner and the Representation of England,' in *Landscape and Power*, ed. W.T.J. Mitchell, 103–19 (Chicago: University of Chicago Press, 1994).

15 Daniels, 'Mapping National Identities,' 112–26; Wolfgang Kaschuba, 'Die Fußreise: Von der Arbeitswanderung zur bürgerlichen Bildungsbewegung,' in *Reisekultur*, ed. Hermann Bausinger and Gottfried Korff (Munich: Beck, 1991), 170–1.

16 Celia Applegate, *A Nation of Provincials: The German Idea of Heimat* (Berkeley: University of California Press, 1990), 63.

17 George Mosse, *The Crisis of German Ideology: Intellectual Origins of the Third Reich* (New York: Grosset & Dunlap, 1964), 15–19; and Mosse, *The Nationalization of the Masses* (New York: Howard Fertig, 1975), 35–41, 93–4.

18 Fritz Stern, 'Introduction,' in *The Failure of Illiberalism: Essays on the Political Culture of Modern Germany*, ed. Fritz Stern (London: Knopf, 1972), 2; and *The Politics of Cultural Despair: A Study in the Rise of the Germanic Ideology* (Berkeley: University of California Press, 1961).

19 Giselher Klebe and Bernd Weyergraf, 'Vorworte,' in *Waldungen: die Deut-*

schen und ihr Wald, ed. Bernd Weyergraf (Berlin: Akademie der Künste, 1987), 5.

20 Ulrich Linse, 'Der deutsche Wald als Kampfplatz politischer Ideen,' *Revue d'Allemange* 22, no. 2 (1990): 342.

21 Jost Hermand, '"The Death of the Trees Will Be the End of Us All": Protests against the Destruction of German Forests 1780–1950,' in *The Idea of the Forest: German and American Perspectives on the Culture and Politics of Trees*, ed. Karla L. Schultz and Kenneth S. Calhoon (New York: Peter Lang, 1996), 61.

22 Klaus Bergmann, *Agrarromantik und Großstadtsfeindschaft* (Meisenheim am Glan: Anton Hain, 1970), 87.

23 Klaus-Georg Wey, *Umwelt Politik im Deutschland* (Opladen: Westdeutscher Verlag, 1982), 129–30; Heinrich Rubner, *Forstgeschichte im Zeitalter der industriellen Revolution* (Berlin: Duncker & Humblot, 1967), 160.

24 Bartholomäus Grill, 'Deutschland: ein Waldesmärchen,' *Die Zeit*, 25 December 1987, 3. See also Robert Pois, *National Socialism and the Region of Nature* (New York: St. Martin's, 1986).

25 Matthew Jeffries, *Imperial Culture in Germany, 1871–1918* (New York: Palgrave Macmillan, 2003). For more recent *Sonderweg* approaches to the 'German forest,' see Michael Imort, 'A Sylvan People: Wilhelmine Forestry and the Forest as a Symbol of Germandom,' in *Germany's Nature: Cultural Landscapes and Environmental History*, ed. Thomas Lekan and Thomas Zeller, 55–80 (New Brunswick, NJ: Rutgers University Press, 2005); Wolfgang Theilemann, *Adel im grünen Rock: Adliges Jägertum, Grossprivatwaldbesitz und die preußische Forstbeamtenschaft 1866–1914* (Berlin: Akademie Verlag, 2004); and Johannes Zechner, '"Die grünen Wurzeln unseres Volkes": Zur ideologischen Karriere des deutschen Waldes,' in *Völkisch und national. Zur Aktualität alter Denkmuster im 21. Jahrhundert*, ed. Uwe Puschner and G. Ulrich Großmann, 179–94 (Darmstadt: Wissenschaftliche Buchgesellschaft, 2009).

26 Gert Gröning and Joachim Wolschke-Bulmahn, *Natur in Bewegung*, vol. 1 of *Die Liebe zur Landschaft* (Munich: Minerva, 1986); Linse, 'Der deutsche Wald als Kampfplatz politischer Ideen,' 339–50; William T. Markham, *Environmental Organizations in Modern Germany: Hardy Survivors in the Twentieth Century and Beyond* (Oxford: Berghahn, 2008).

27 Simon Schama, *Landscape and Memory* (New York: Alfred A. Knopf, 1995), 115–20.

28 See Dona Brown, *Inventing New England: Regional Tourism in the Nineteenth Century* (Washington, DC: Smithsonian Institution, 1995); Helsinger, *Rural Scenes and National Representation*; Anne Farrar Hyde, *An American Vision: Far Western Landscape and National Culture, 1820–1920* (New York: New York

University Press, 1990); Patricia Jasen, *Wild Things: Nature, Culture, and Tourism in Ontario, 1790–1914* (Toronto: University of Toronto, 1995); David Matless, *Landscape and Englishness* (London: Reaktion, 1998); James Vernon, 'Border Crossings: Cornwall and the English (Imagi)nation,' in *Imagining Nations*, ed. Geoffrey Cubitt, 153–72 (Manchester: Manchester University Press, 1998).

29 W.T.J. Mitchell, 'Introduction,' in *Landscape and Power*, ed. W.T.J. Mitchell, 1–2 (Chicago: University of Chicago Press, 1994).

30 Stephen Daniels and Denis Cosgrove, 'Introduction: Iconography and Landscape,' in *The Iconography of Landscape*, ed. Stephen Daniels and Denis Cosgrove (Cambridge: Cambridge University Press, 1988), 7; see also Stephen Daniels, 'Marxism, Culture and the Duplicity of Landscape,' in *Human Geography*, ed. John Agnew, David Livingstone, and Alisdair Rogers, 329–39 (London: Blackwell, 1997).

31 On the *Heimat* movement, see Applegate, *Nation of Provincials*; Confino, *Nation as Local Metaphor*; Edeltraud Klueting, ed. *Antimodernismus und Reform: Zur Geschichte der deutschen Heimatbewegung* (Darmstadt: Wissenschaftliche Buchgesellschaft, 1991); Andreas Knaut, *Zurück zur Natur! Die Wurzeln der Ökologiebewegung* (Bonn: ABN, 1993); William H. Rollins, *A Greener Vision of Home: Cultural Politics and Environmental Reform in the German Heimatschutz Movement* (Ann Arbor: University of Michigan Press, 1997). For a contrary view, see Werner Hartung, *Konservative Zivilationskritik und regionale Identität* (Hanover: Verlag Hahnische Buchhandlung, 1991).

32 John Alexander Williams, '"The Chords of the German Soul Are Tuned to Nature": The Movement to Preserve the Natural Heimat from the Kaiserreich to the Third Reich,' *Central European History* 29, no. 3 (1996): 340–3; see also his *Turning to Nature in Germany: Hiking, Nudism, and Conservation, 1900–1940* (Palo Alto: Stanford University Press, 2007).

33 Rollins, *Greener Vision of Home*.

34 Lekan, *Imagining the Nation in Nature*. Frank Uekötter makes a similar point in his book on the relationship between the Nazis and those interested in the environment. Uekoetter, *The Green and the Brown*.

35 Detlev Peukert, 'The Genesis of the "Final Solution" from the Spirit of Science,' in *Reevaluating the Third Reich*, ed. Thomas Childers and Jane Caplan, 234–52 (New York: Holmes & Meier, 1993). Peukert originally published the article in German in 1989.

36 Kevin Repp, *Reformers, Critics, and the Paths of German Modernity: Anti-Politics and the Search for Alternatives, 1890–1914* (Cambridge, MA: Harvard University Press, 2000); Thomas Rohkrämer, *Eine andere Moderne? Zivilisationskritik, Natur und Technik in Deutschland 1880–1933* (Paderborn: Schöningh, 1999);

and Rohkrämer, *A Single Communal Faith?: The German Right from Conservatism to National Socialism* (Oxford: Berghahn, 2007).

37 James C. Scott, *Seeing Like a State: How Certain Schemes to Improve the Human Condition Have Failed* (New Haven, CT: Yale, 1998), 11–21.

38 David Blackbourn, *The Conquest of Nature: Water, Landscape, and the Making of Modern Germany* (New York: Norton, 2006).

39 For example, Celia Applegate examines the Bavarian Palatinate (Pfalz), Alon Confino the Duchy of Württemberg, Thomas Lekan the Rhineland, and Werner Hartung the Province of Hanover.

40 In this book, the term *left liberal* applies to members of the liberal political parties standing to the left of the National Liberals: the Deutsche Fortschrittspartei (1861–84), the Deutsche Freisinnige Partei (1884–93), the Freisinnige Vereinigung (1893–1910), the Freisinnige Volkspartei (1893–1910), and the Fortschrittliche Volkspartei (1910–18).

1. National Landscape and National Memory

1 Hans Hausrath, *Der deutsche Wald* (Leipzig: B.G. Teubner, 1907), 1.

2 Friedrich Ratzel, 'Die deutsche Landschaft,' *Dürer Bund: Flugschrift zur Ausdruckskultur* 55 (October 1909): 5.

3 Johannes Trojan, *Unsere deutsche Wälder* (Berlin: Vita Deutsches Verlagshaus, 1911), 7–10.

4 Hausrath, *Der deutsche Wald*, 1.

5 Friedrich Ratzel, *Deutschland: Einführung in die Heimatkunde* (Berlin: Georg Reimer, 1911), 186.

6 Carl Heinrich Edmund Freiherr von Berg, *Geschichte der Deutschen Wälder bis zum Schlusse des Mittelalters* (Dresden: G. Schönfeld, 1871), 5–6.

7 'Normänische Baumriesen,' *Gartenflora: Zeitschrift für Garten- und Blumenkunde* 49, no. 1 (1900): 24–5.

8 F. Brunswick, 'Fest der Bäume in Italien,' *Die Grenzboten* 14 (1902): 53–4; Riehl, *Die Naturgeschichte des Volkes*, 49–50; Carl von Fischbach, 'Der Kulturwert des Waldes,' *Vom Fels zum Meer* 13, no. 2 (1894): 399; Paul Säurich, *Das Leben der Pflanzen im Walde* (Leipzig: Ernst Wunderlich, 1908), 393.

9 Franz Baur, 'Über die Sonderstellung des Waldes im nationalen Wirtschaftsleben,' *Beilage zur Allgemeine Zeitung* 21 December 1895: 4; Raoul H. Francé, *Bilder aus dem Leben des Waldes* (Stuttgart: Kosmos, 1909), 80–1; Konrad Guenther, *Der Naturschutz* (Freiburg: Friedrich Ernst Fehlenfeld, 1910), 50.

10 Adam Schwappach, *Handbuch der Forst- und Jagdgeschichte Deutschlands* (Berlin: Springer, 1886–8), 766–7.

11 F. von Thülmen, 'Wälder unserer Erde,' *Ausland* 58 (1885): 902; v. B., 'Das Neueste über den Stand der Waldungen Rußlands,' *Zeitschrift für Agrarpolitik* 9 (1911): 236–7; Franz Hoermann, *Der deutsche Wald* (Leipzig: F. Dietrich, 1906), 10.

12 Udo Brachvogel, 'Zehntausend Meilen durch den Großen Westen der Vereinigten Staaten,' *Die Gartenlaube* 33 (1885): 619; Adam Schwappach, *Forstwissenschaft* (Leipzig: Göschen'sche, 1899), 8; Heinrich Pudor, 'Wald-Politik,' *Hammer* 8 (1909): 730.

13 Berg, *Geschichte der Deutschen Wälder*, 6; H. Stoetzer, 'Moderne Forstwirtschaft,' *Die Woche* 7, no. 35 (1905): 1504. German foresters established the dominant model of forestry in the nineteenth century. Dietrich Brandis served as the inspector-general of forests in British India, and Bernhard Fernow, among many others, helped import German forestry techniques to the United States. See K. Sivaramakrishnan, *Modern Forests: Statemaking and Environmental Change in Colonial Eastern India* (Stanford, CA: Stanford University Press, 1999); Andrew Denny Rodgers, *Bernhard Eduard Fernow: A Story of North American Forestry* (Princeton, NJ: Princeton University Press, 1951).

14 Arnim to Kaiser Wilhelm II, 7 May 1909. GStAPK, I HA Rep.89, Nr.31280, b.50; Hoermann, *Der deutsche Wald*, 10; speech by Alexander Meyer in AH, 5 December 1879, *Stenographische Berichte über die Verhandlungen des Hauses der Abgeordneten*, 19. Sitzung, Bd. 1 (Berlin, 1879–80): 430; Baur, 'Über die Sonderstellung des Waldes,' 4.

15 Karl Gayer, *Der Wald in Wechsel der Zeiten* (Munich: C. Wolf & Sohn, 1889), 10; Friedrich Simony, 'Schutz dem Walde!,' *Zeitschrift zur Verbreitung naturwissenschaftliche Kenntnisse* 17 (1877): 489–93.

16 On the *Holznot* (wood shortage) debate of the eighteenth century, see Uwe Eduard Schmid, *Der Wald in Deutschland im 18. und 19. Jahrhundert: Das Problem der Ressourcenknappheit dargestellt am Beispiel der Waldressourcenknappheit in Deutschland im 18. und 19. Jahrhundert* (Saarbrücken: Conte-Verlag, 2002).

17 Hansjörg Küster, *Geschichte des Waldes* (Munich: Beck, 1998), 220–33; Henry E. Lowood, 'The Calculating Forester: Quantification, Cameral Science, and the Emergence of Scientific Forestry Management in Germany,' in *The Quantifying Spirit in the 18th Century*, ed. Tore Frängsmyr, J.L. Heilbron, and Robin E. Rider (Berkeley: University of California Press, 1990), 337–42; Scott, *Seeing Like a State*, 11–21.

18 O. Sch., 'Der Verein "Naturschutz,"' *Der Kunstwart* 20, no. 21 (1907): 529–30.

19 Heinrich von Salisch, *Forstästhetik*, 3rd ed. (Berlin: Springer, 1911), 197.

20 Rudy Koshar, *German Travel Cultures* (Oxford: Berg, 2000), 26–8.

21 Kaschuba, 'Die Fußreise,' 168–73. See also Gudrun König, *Eine Kulturgeschichte des Spaziergangs* (Cologne: Böhlau, 1996), 33–7. I use the pronoun *he* intentionally here. As an implicitly political and liberating act, hiking was limited largely to men until late in the nineteenth century. Even at the turn of the century, women's hiking clubs were rare (only two small ones listed in Berlin in 1905), and hiking enthusiasts expressed some concern over mixed-gender hiking. See Erich Baberowsky, 'Damenwandern,' *Die Mark* 2 (1905/6): 17–18; A. Fendrich, *Der Wanderer* (Stuttgart, Frank'sche, 1913), 80–2.

22 Lehmann, 'Der deutsche Wald,' 187–9.

23 Robert Harrison, *Forests: The Shadow of Civilization* (Chicago: University of Chicago Press, 1992), 165–74.

24 Jahn quoted in Georg Eugen Kitzler, 'Ludwig Jahn als Wanderer,' *Die Mark* 7 (1910/1): 292.

25 W.H. Riehl, *Wanderbuch (als zweiter Theil zu "Land und Leute")*, vol. 4 of *Die Naturgeschichte des Volkes als Grundlage einer deutschen Social-Politik*, 6th ed. (Stuttgart: J.G. Cotta, 1869), 3–4. Riehl's use of such civic language (*Einbürgerung*) in writing about the nation suggests a palpable legacy of his liberalism and the modernity of his nationalism.

26 Uli Linke, 'Folklore, Anthropology, and the Government of Social Life,' *Comparative Study of Society and History* 32, no. 1 (1990): 123; Woodruff D. Smith, *Politics and the Sciences of Culture in Germany* (Oxford: Oxford University Press, 1991), 40–4.

27 Emil Adolf Roßmäßler, *Mein Leben und Streben im Verkehr mit der Natur und dem Volke* (Hanover: Carl Rümpler, 1874), 24–127.

28 Emil Adolf Roßmäßler, *Das Gebirgsdorfchen* (Leipzig: Quelle & Meyer, 1909), 5. Originally published in 1876.

29 Ibid., 10.

30 J.C. Hofrichter, 'Der Wandertrieb von politischer Seite betrachtet,' *Der Tourist: Organ für Natur- und Alpenfreunde* 4 (1872): 94–5.

31 Kempe, 'Der Wald als Wanderziel,' *Über Berg und Tal* 31 (1908): 341.

32 From the journal *Wandervogel* (1913): 8. Quoted in Gröning and Wolschke-Bulmahn, *Natur in Bewegung*, 74.

33 E.W. Trojan, 'National-hygienische Grundlagen des Wanderns,' *Heimat und Welt* 1 (1911/12): 292.

34 Fendrich, *Der Wanderer*, 17–18.

35 Gröning and Wolschke-Bulmahn, *Natur in Bewegung*, 81; 'Touristenvereine,' *Meyers Konversationslexikon*, 4th ed. (1885–92), 15:783–4; 'Zur Gründung eines "Allgemeinen deutschen Touristenverbands,"' *Die Gartenlaube* 30 (1882): 488, 740. It is important to note that in this context the term *Tourist* referred to hikers.

36 Zeglin, 'Deutsches Wandern,' *Pädagogische Blätter für Lehrerbildung und Lehrerbildungsanstalten* 12 (1883): 243.

37 Otto Köhler, 'Mitgliederstand etc. der Zweigvereinen,' *Thüringer Monatsblätter* 14 (1906): 51–2; Köhler, 'Übersicht über Mitgliederstand, Kassenverhältnisse etc. der Zweigvereine,' *Thüringer Monatsblätter* 14 (1893): 43.

38 Raymond Dominick, *The Environmental Movement in Germany: Prophets and Pioneers, 1871–1971* (Bloomington: Indiana University Press, 1992), 61; Dieter Kramer, 'Arbeiter als Touristen: Ein Privileg wird gebrochen. Soziale und ökonomische Rahmenbedingungen der Entwicklung der Naturfreunde,' in *Mit uns zieht die neue Zeit,* ed. Jochen Zimmer (Cologne: Pahl-Rugenstein, 1984), 31–65; Augustin Upmann and Uwe Rennspieß, 'Organisationsgeschichte der deutschen Naturfreundebewegung bis 1933,' in Zimmer 66–111; Jochen Zimmer, 'Vom Walzen zum Sozialen Wandern: Fragen an die Einensinnigen Sozialen Praxen des genossenschaftlichen Arbeitertourismus,' in *Studien zur Arbeiterkultur,* ed. Deutsche Gesellschaft für Volkskunde, 141–73 (Münster: F. Coppenrath, 1984).

39 Dominick, *Environmental Movement in Germany,* 57.

40 Baberowsky, 'Damenwandern,' 17–18.

41 Kristen Belgum, 'Displaying the Nation: A View of Nineteenth-Century Monuments through a Popular Magazine,' *Central European History* 26 (1993): 457–74; Koshar, *Monuments to Traces,* 31–5; Thomas Nipperdey, 'Nationalidee und Nationaldenkmal in Deutschland im 19. Jahrhundert,' *Historische Zeitschrift* 206 (1968): 529–85; Charlotte Tacke, *Denkmal im sozialen Raum: Nationale Symbole in Deutschland und Frankreich im 19. Jahrhundert* (Göttingen: Vandenhoeck & Ruprecht, 1995).

42 Tacke, *Denkmal im sozialen Raum,* 68; on the Hermann story as a contested foundational myth of the empire, see Andreas Dörner, 'Der Mythos der nationalen Einheit: Symbolpolitik und Deutungskämpfe bei der Einweihung des Hermannsdenkmals im Jahre 1875,' *Archiv für Kulturgeschichte* 79, no. 2 (1997): 389–416.

43 Both quotations in Lutz Tittel, *Das Niederwalddenkmal* (Hildesheim: Gerstenberg, 1979), 6, 13–14. I should note here, however, that the choice to place the monument in the woods had partly to do with financial considerations, as a structure on the hillside above the Rhine would have to have been much larger to fit into the broader riparian landscape.

44 Mosse, *Nationalization of the Masses,* 35.

45 Hugo Conwentz founded the Prussian State Office for Nature Protection (*Preußische staatliche Stelle für Naturdenkmalpflege*) and authored several works on the subject. I use Conwentz's English translation of the term *Naturdenkmalpflege.* See his *Care of Natural Monuments* (Cambridge: Cam-

bridge University Press, 1909). On the State Office, see Michael Wettengel, 'Staat und Naturschutz 1906–1945: Zur Geschichte der Staatlichen Stelle für Naturdenkmalpflege in Preußen und der Reichstelle für Naturschutz,' *Historische Zeitschrift* 257 (1993): 355–99. On efforts to protect arboreal natural monuments, see F. Moewes, 'Schutz dem deutschen Waldes,' *Die Denkmalspflege* 3 (1901): 62–3.

46 Franz Mammen, 'Forstbotanische Merkbücher,' *Heimatschutz* 4 (1908): 62–70; Mammen, 'Forstbotanische Merkbücher,' *Heimatschutz* 7 (1911): 83–98.

47 Kirsten Belgum, *Popularizing the Nation: Audience, Representation and the Production of Identity in Die Gartenlaube, 1853–1900* (Lincoln: University of Nebraska Press, 1998), 200.

48 'Eine Frage an unser Leser und Freunde,' *Die Gartenlaube* 49 (1901): 272.

49 C.S., 'Die Wendelinuseiche bei Geisfeld,' *Die Gartenlaube* 46 (1898): 668; 'Die Linde zu Grimmenthal;' *Die Gartenlaube* 41 (1893): 36.

50 'Die "tollen Buchen" bei Remilly,' *Die Gartenlaube* 47 (1899): 648, 643; Wilhelm Heun, 'Krausbäumchen bei Homburg,' *Die Gartenlaube* 48 (1900): 376.

51 E. Krause, 'Der Riesenwacholder bei Clossow,' *Die Gartenlaube* 48 (1900): 224.

52 Hugo Kruskopf, 'Die Priorlinde an der Kluse bei Dahl,' *Die Gartenlaube* 44 (1896): 324.

53 'Die Königseiche bei Peisterwitz,' *Die Gartenlaube* 36 (1888): 808; 'Die Linde von Eckersdorf,' *Die Gartenlaube* 46 (1898): 116; 'Der Herzogsbusch zu Neuhäusel,' *Die Gartenlaube* 51 (1903): 316.

54 Mammen, 'Forstbotanische Merkbücher,' 88.

55 A. Janson, 'Eigenartige deutsche Bäume,' *Natur und Haus* 13 (1905): 353–5.

56 Mammen, 'Forstbotanische Merkbücher,' 62–3, 88–9.

57 Ibid., 64–5.

58 Alfred Jentzsch, *Nachweis der beachtenswerten und zu schützenden Bäume, S träucher und erratischen Blöcke in der Provinz Ostpreußen* (Königsberg: Emil Rautenberg, 1900), vii.

59 Fritz Pfuhl, 'Naturdenkmalpflege in der Provinz Posen,' *Aus dem Posener Lande* 6 (1911): 280–2.

60 Hugo Conwentz, *Forstbotanisches Merkbuch* (Berlin: Bornträger, 1900), v–vi.

61 On tourism, see John Urry, *The Tourist Gaze: Leisure and Travel in Contemporary Societies* (London: Sage, 1990); Rudy Koshar, '"What ought to be seen": Tourists' Guidebooks and National Identities in Modern Germany and Europe,' *Journal of Contemporary History* 33, no. 3 (1998): 323–40.

62 For a similar argument, see Helsinger, 'Turner and the Representation of England,' 103–5.

63 Jonas Frykman and Orvar Löfgren have made a similar argument with regard to Sweden. See their *Culture Builders*, trans. Alan Crozier (New Brunswick: Rutgers University Press, 1987), 57–8.

64 William H. Rollins, 'Aesthetic Environmentalism: The Heimatschutz Movement in Germany, 1904–1918' (PhD diss., University of Wisconsin, 1994), 124.

65 Tacke, *Denkmal im sozialen Raum*, 65–7.

66 'Die Schmorsdorfer Linde,' *Die Gartenlaube* 40 (1892): 644.

67 W. Wehrhahn, 'Die alte Linde vor dem Bergthore der Schaumburg,' *Die Gartenlaube* 49 (1901): 528.

68 Bertha Krüger-Ottzenn, 'Die Esche auf dem Friedhofe zu Tilsit,' *Die Gartenlaube* 49 (1901): 832.

69 Robert Geißler, 'Alte Linde auf dem Schloßwalle zu Pyrmont,' *Die Gartenlaube* 37 (1889): 292.

70 'Die Linde zu Bordesholm,' *Die Gartenlaube* 38 (1890): 291.

71 Koshar, *Monuments to Traces*, 27.

72 A.B., 'Der Lutherbaum bei Worms,' *Die Gartenlaube* 31 (1883): 452.

73 Ibid., 454.

74 Ibid., 455.

75 Ibid.

76 'Die vier Linden bei Grotenhof in Westfalen,' *Die Gartenlaube* 51 (1903): 780.

77 'Die 1000 Jährige Linde in Puch,' *Die Gartenlaube* 31 (1883): 300; A. Vogel, 'Die "Dicke Linde" in Reinberg bei Greifswald,' *Die Gartenlaube* 53 (1905): 916.

78 Adolf Ahrens, 'Die Krupeiche bei Völkshagen in Mecklenburg,' *Die Gartenlaube* 49 (1901): 384. Ahrens cites a Dr Bartsch, who identified another two such trees still standing in Mecklenburg.

79 Similarly, forests brought together one's own past and present, evoking memories of childhood. One author asserted that memories of Christmas trees, spring fruits, swinging in the branches, and the carved initials of one's first love tied Germans closely to their trees, concluding that these 'true friends' thus became lifelong companions. See K.G., 'Mensch und Baum,' *Deutsche Welt* (1903/4): 340–2. Likewise, just as the forest made one think of the past and present of the nation, so the individual tree provoked reflection on one's own youth. Interestingly, the concept of *Heimat* functioned in much the same way.

80 August Bernhardt, *Die Waldwirthschaft und der Waldschutz* (Berlin: Springer, 1869), 1:44.

81 Trojan, *Unsere deutsche Wälder*, 66.

82 Hoermann, *Der deutsche Wald*, 3.

83 Konrad Guenther, *Der Naturschutz*, 54.

84 K. Mischke, 'Naturdenkmäler,' *Mutter Erde* 4 (1900): 324.

85 Theodor Cotta, *Die Heimatkunde für Berlin* (Berlin: Georg Reimer, 1873), 227.

86 J.J. Egli, 'Über die Fortschritte in der geographischen Namenkunde,' *Geographische Jahrbuch* 12 (1888): 26.

87 Brent Maner, 'The Search for a Buried Nation: Prehistoric Archaeology in Central Europe, 1750–1945' (PhD diss., University of Illinois, 2001).

88 Hoermann, *Der deutsche Wald*, 2.

89 Harrison, *Forests*, 167.

90 Johannes Scherr, *Deutsche Kultur- und Sittengeschichte* (Leipzig: O. Wigand, 1887), 17–18.

91 Berg, *Geschichte der Deutschen Wälde*, 1.

92 Ibid., 2. One should note, however, that this system of forest protection arose not out of economic need, as Berg suggested, but from the nobility's passion for the hunt.

93 Hoermann, *Der deutsche Wald*, 2.

94 Ernst Rudorff, 'Über das Verhältniß des modernen Lebens zur Natur,' *Preußische Jahrbücher* 45 (1880): 276.

95 K.A. von Schulenburg, 'Deutsche Eichen und Linden,' *Über Land und Meer* 30, no. 2 (1888): 1082.

96 Riehl, *Die Naturgeschichte des Volkes*, 49–50.

97 Carl Fraas, *Geschichte der Landbau- und Forstwissenschaft* (Munich: Cott-aschen Buchhandlung, 1865), 649–58; Simony, 'Schutz dem Walde!,' 452–3; Heinrich Jösting, *Der Wald, seine Bedeutung, Verwüstung und Wiederbegründung* (Berlin: Parey, 1898), 4.

98 'Wald bäume und Wälder,' *Ausland* 44 (1871): 73, 226–7.

99 Theodor Fontane, 'Am Wannsee,' *Neue Preußische Zeitung*, 4 December 1861. Reproduced in vol. 3 of *Wanderungen durch die Mark Brandenburg*, div. 2 of *Theodor Fontane: Werke, Schriften und Briefe*, ed. Walter Keitel (Munich: Karl Hanser, 1977), 494–98.

100 Raoul H. Francé, *Das Pflanzenleben Deutschlands und seiner Nachbarländer*, vol. 1 of *Das Leben der Pflanze* (Stuttgart: Kosmos, 1906), 7.

101 Raoul H. Francé, 'Der deutsche Urwald,' *März* (December 1907): 488.

102 Francé, *Das Pflanzenleben Deutschlands*, 4. Also cited in Franz Mammen and Fritz Brumm, 'Heimatschutz im Walde und Waldschönheitspflege,' *Mitteilungen des Landesvereins Sächsischer Heimatschutz* 1 (1908): 41.

103 'Die Schöpfung des deutschen Waldes,' *Die Gartenlaube* 53 (1905): 568;

Friedrich Knauer, *Der Niedergang unserer Tier- und Pflanzenwelt* (Leipzig: Theodor Thomas, 1912), 83.

104 Ratzel, *Deutschland*, 188; Ratzel, 'Die deutsche Landschaft,' 8.

105 August Sach, *Die deutsche Heimat, Landschaft und Volkstum* (Halle: Buchhandlung des Waisenhauses, 1885), 15.

106 Schwappach, *Handbuch*, 1:33–4; Schwappach, *Forstwissenschaft*, 9–10.

107 For a contemporary synopsis of Ratzel's work in the field, see Richard Marek, 'Zur Anthropogeographie des Waldes,' *Geographische Zeitschrift* 18 (1912): 1–15.

108 Robert Gradmann, 'Das mitteleuropäische Landschaftsbild nach seiner geschichtlichen Entwicklung,' *Geographische Zeitschrift* 7 (1901): 368–76.

109 Johannes Hoops, *Waldbäume und Kulturpflanzen im Germanischen Altertum* (Strassburg: Karl J. Trübner, 1905), 91.

110 Moritz Buesgen, *Der deutsche Wald* (Leipzig: Quelle & Meyer, 1908), 3; Konrad Guenther, *Der Naturschutz*, 51; Xaver Siefert, *Der Deutsche Wald* (Karlsruhe: Braunschen Hofbuchdruckerei, 1905), 6; Josef Wimmer, *Geschichte des deutschen Bodens mit seinem Pflanzen- und Tierleben* (Halle: Buchhandlung des Waisenhauses, 1905). Interestingly enough, scholars have turned against this view, now believing that the German lands were in fact covered with forests in ancient times.

111 Paul David Fischer, *Germany and the Germans: Containing the Greater Part of P.D. Fischer's Betrachtungen eines in Deutschland Reisenden Deutschen*, ed. A. Lodeman (New York: Silver, Burdett, 1901), 37–51 (out of a total ninety-four pages of text); Sidney Whitman, *Teuton Studies* (Leipzig: Bernhard Tauchnitz, 1896), 74.

112 Theilemann, *Adel im grünen Rock*, 203–6.

113 See, for instance, Uwe Eduard Schmidt, 'Waldfrevel contra staatliche Interessen,' *Der Bürger im Staat* 51, no. 1 (2001): 17–23; Heinrich Sohnrey and Ernst Löber, *Das Glück auf dem Lande: Ein Wegweiser, wie der kleine Mann auf einen grünen Zweig kommt* (Berlin: Deutsche Buchhandlung, 1906).

114 Adolf Levenstein, *Die Arbeiterfrage* (Munich: Ernst Reinhardt, 1912). On Levenstein's study, see Joan Campbell, *Joy in Work, German Work* (Princeton: Princeton University Press, 1989), 92–7.

115 Levenstein, *Die Arbeiterfrage*, 358–81.

2. Contested Forests

1 David Blackbourn, 'The Politics of Demagogy in Imperial Germany,' *Past and Present* 113 (1987): 152–84; Geoff Eley, 'Nationalism and Social History,' *Social History* 6 (1981): 83–107; Eley, *Reshaping the German Right: Radical*

Nationalism and Political Change after Bismarck, 2nd ed. (Ann Arbor: University of Michigan Press, 1991); Wolfgang Mock, '"Manipulation von Oben" oder Selbsorganisation an der Basis? Einige neuere Ansätze in der englischen Historiographie zur Geschichte des deutschen Kaiserreichs,' *Historische Zeitschrift* 232 (1982): 358–75.

2 For those who dismiss the agrarian reformers and the *Heimat* movement as organizations that stabilized the empire, and thus elite interests, see Arne Andersen, 'Heimatschutz: Die bürgerliche Naturschutzbewegung,' in *Besiegte Natur: Geschichte der Umwelt im 19. und 20. Jahrhundert*, ed. Franz-Josef Brüggemeier and Thomas Rommelspacher, 143–57 (Munich: Beck, 1987); Bergmann, *Agrarromantik und Großstadtsfeindschaft*; Ina-Maria Greverus, *Auf der Suche nach Heimat* (Munich: Beck, 1979); Hartung, *Konservative Zivilationskritik*; Hans-Jürgen Puhle, *Agrarische Interessenpolitik und preussischer Konservatismus im Wilhelminischen Reich (1893–1914): Ein Beitrag zur Analyse des Nationalismus in Deutschland am Beispiel des Bundes der Landwirte und der Deutsch-Konservativen Partei* (Hanover: Verlag für Literatur und Zeitgeschehen, 1966); Winfried Speitkamp, 'Denkmalpflege und Heimatschutz in Deutschland zwischen Kulturkritik und Nationalsozialismus,' *Archiv für Kulturgeschichte* 70 (1988): 149–93.

3 On the idea of nature as a site of freedom in the eighteenth century, see Gotthardt Frühsorge, *Die Kunst des Landlebens: vom Landschloss zum Campingplatz: eine Kulturgeschichte* (Munich: Koehler & Amelang, 1993), 183–94.

4 Riehl, *Die Naturgeschichte des Volkes*, 49–50. Other authors quoted Riehl's comparison. See Sach, *Die deutsche Heimat*, 58; Salisch, *Forstästhetik*, 195.

5 Riehl, *Die Naturgeschichte des Volkes*, 52–3 (also quoted in Salisch, *Forstästhetik*, 195).

6 Ibid., 58.

7 Ibid., 52–3. Later authors often cited this passage. See Richard Haupt, *Über die Erhaltung der Fußwege und das Recht der Nation am Walde* (Schleswig: Schleswiger Nachrichten, 1910), 7; Salisch, *Forstästhetik*, 194–5; T., 'Der Wald als Erzieher,' *Der Kunstwart* 20, no. 5 (1906): 305. Sigmund Freud theorized in his *General Introduction to Psychoanalysis* (1920) that an unspoiled landscape provides us 'freedom from the grip of the external world.' He even converted this idea into a simile, comparing human fantasy life with a nature park, both of which are free to grow undisturbed, but are surrounded by disciplined landscapes. Quoted in Leo Marx, *The Machine in the Garden: Technology and the Pastoral Ideal in America* (Oxford: Oxford University Press, 1964), 8.

8 Riehl, *Die Naturgeschichte des Volkes*, 52–3. Echoing Riehl's comments about modern forest freedom, some authors identified such liberty as a key

characteristic of the ancient Germanic tribesmen. See August Bernhardt, *Geschichte des Waldeigenthums, der Waldwithschaft und Forstwissenschaft* (Berlin: Springer, 1872), 1:12–13; Anton Thümer, 'Die Erhaltung der Pflanzenwelt,' *Dürer Bund: Flugschrift zur Ausdruckskultur* 69 (1913): 1–2.

9 Marx rejected the idea of sylvan freedom, complaining, 'German nationalists [*Deutschtümler*] by blood and free-thinkers by reflection seek our history of freedom in the history of the primeval Teutonic woods. But what distinguishes our history of freedom from the wild boar's, if it is only to be found in the forests?' Quoted in Joachim Radkau, 'The Wordy Worship of Nature and the Tacit Feeling for Nature in the History of German Forestry,' in *Nature and Society in Historical Context*, ed. Mikulas Teich, Roy Porter, and Bo Gustafsson (Cambridge: Cambridge University Press, 1997), 234–5.

10 The German language distinguishes between the ideal forest (*der Wald*) and the productive forest (*der Forst*). One always spoke of *der deutsche Wald* and never of *der deutsche Forst*. Fairy tales were always set in the *Wald*, while foresters usually spoke of their field as *Forstwissenschaft* (forest science).

11 Baur, 'Über die Sonderstellung des Waldes,' 2–3. On the conditions of forest labour, see Rubner, *Forstgeschichte*, 164–6.

12 *Agrarische Interessenpolitik und* , 241. In 1896, the recovery of the economy and a new wave of industrialization pushed wood prices upwards, making forestry even more profitable. See Friedrich-Wilhelm Henning, *Handbuch der Wirtschafts- und Sozialgeschichte Deutschlands* (Munich: Ferdinand Schönigh, 1996), 3:963–7.

13 Baur, 'Über die Sonderstellung des Waldes,' 2–4; Max Eckert, *Deutsche Kulturgeographie* (Halle: Hermann Schroedel, 1912), 85–7; Jösting, *Der Wald*, 6–7, 28–9; Fr. Köllner, 'Wald in Volks- und Naturhaushalt,' *Die Natur* 50, no. 15 (1901): 170–1; Säurich, *Das Leben der Pflanzen im Walde*, 379.

14 Eckert, *Deutsche Kulturgeographie*, 85–7; Säurich, *Das Leben der Pflanzen im Walde*, 378–9, 388.

15 Indeed, Germany's wood-processing and paper industries employed more workers than the dynamic chemical sector and grew faster than textiles, clothing, and food processing during the *Kaiserreich*. Theilemann, *Adel im grünen Rock*, 9; Frank B. Tipton, 'Technology and Industrial Growth,' in *Imperial Germany: A Historiographical Companion*, ed. Roger Chickering (Westport, CT: Greenwood, 1996), 71–2.

16 Historians have hotly debated whether the impending wood shortage was real or imagined. See Joachim Radkau, 'Holzverknappung und Krisenbewusstsein im 18. Jahrundert,' *Geschichte und Gesellschaft* 9 (1983): 513–43; Radkau, 'Wood and Forestry in German History: In Quest of an Environ-

mental Approach,' *Environment and History* 2 (February 1996): 67; Schmid, *Der Wald in Deutschland.*

17 Lowood, 'Calculating Forester,' 340–2. At the same time, the forester Wilhelm Pfeil announced, 'Material needs make it ever less permissible for forestry to take into consideration the sense of beauty.' See Hermand, '"Death of the Trees,"' 54.

18 Scott, *Seeing Like a State*, 11–21; see also Walther Schoenichen, *Der deutsche Wald* (Bielefeld: Velhagen & Klasing, 1913), 15–16.

19 Karl Hasel, *Zur Geschichte der Forstgesetzgebung in Preussen* (Frankfurt am Main: Sauerländer, 1974), 116–19.

20 Dirk Blasius, *Bürgerliche Gesellschaft und Kriminalität: zur Sozialgeschichte Preussens im Vormärz* (Göttingen: Vandenhoeck & Ruprecht, 1976), 104–5; Josef Moser, 'Property and Wood Theft: Agrarian Capitalism and Social Conflict in Rural Society, 1800–50. A Westphalian Case Study,' in *Peasants and Lords in Modern Germany: Recent Studies in Agricultural History*, ed. Robert G. Moeller, 52–80 (Boston: Allen & Unwin, 1986); Schmidt, 'Waldfrevel contra staatliche Interessen,' 17–23.

21 On rural protest in 1848, see Christof Dipper, 'Rural Revolutionary Movements: Germany, France, Italy,' in *Europe in 1848: Revolution and Reform*, ed. Dieter Dowe, 416–442 (Oxford: Berghahn Books, 2001). On the forest conflict in 1848, see Alfred Barthelmeß, *Landschaft: Lebensraum des Menschen* (Freiburg: Karl Alber, 1988), 99; Regina Schulte, *The Village in Court: Arson, Infanticide, and Poaching in the Court Records of Upper Bavaria, 1848–1910*, trans. Barrie Selman (Cambridge: Cambridge University Press, 1994), 130, 179; Jonathan Sperber, *Rhineland Radicals: The Democratic Movement and the Revolution of 1848–1849* (Princeton: Princeton University Press, 1991), 72–8. In many Prussian provinces, cases of wood theft doubled during the early nineteenth century, and investigations of repeat offenders tripled. Blasius, *Bürgerliche Gesellschaft und Kriminalität*, 140–6.

22 Riehl, *Die Naturgeschichte des Volkes*, 58.

23 Ibid., 45–7.

24 Ludwig Heiß, *Der Wald und die Gesetzgebung* (Berlin: Springer, 1875), 2.

25 Richard Heß, *Der Forstschutz* (Berlin: B.G. Teubner, 1898), 1:64–6. First published in 1878.

26 Indeed, between 1873 and 1880, wood prices fell 15–30 per cent, and state forest income fell 30–40 per cent. See Rubner, *Forstgeschichte im Zeitalter der industriellen Revolution*, 150–60.

27 Feld- und Forstpolizeigesetz, *Anlagen zu den Stenographischen Berichten über die Verhandlungen des Hauses der Abgeordneten* (Berlin, 1881), 351–3.

28 Speech by August Bernhardt in AH, 10 January 1878, *Stenographische Berichte*, 43. Sitzung (Berlin: 1878): 1111–12. Bernhardt had switched allegiance from the National Liberal Party the previous year.

29 Speeches by Alexander Meyer in AH, 16 December 1879, *Stenographische Berichte*, 26. Sitzung (Berlin: 1880): 649–51; Hermann Fiebiger in AH, 23 January 1880, 1152; Albert Träger in AH, 23 January 1880, *Stenographische Berichte*, 44. Sitzung (Berlin: 1880): 1146–7; Ernst von Eynern in AH, 31 January 1880, *Stenographische Berichte*, 50. Sitzung (Berlin: 1880): 1329–30.

30 Speeches by Peter Reichensperger in AH, 4 November 1879, *Stenographische Berichte*, 4. Sitzung (Berlin: 1880): 28–9; Robert von Ludwig in AH, 15 December 1879, *Stenographische Berichte*, 25. Sitzung (Berlin: 1880): 639–40; Johann Franke in AH, 22 January 1880, *Stenographische Berichte*, 43. Sitzung (Berlin: 1880): 1119–22; Robert von Ludwig and Ludwig Windthorst in AH, 31 January 1880, *Stenographische Berichte*, 50. Sitzung (Berlin: 1880): 1328–9, 1331.

31 Speech by Peter Reichensperger in AH, 4 November 1879, *Stenographische Berichte*, 4. Sitzung (Berlin: 1880): 28–9; see also speeches by Ernst von Eynern and Alexander Meyer in AH, 16 December 1879, *Stenographische Berichte*, 26. Sitzung (Berlin: 1880): 649–52; Johann Franke in AH, 22 January 1880, *Stenographische Berichte*, 43. Sitzung (Berlin: 1880): 1119–22.

32 Speech by Wilhelm Seelig in AH, 16 December 1879, *Stenographische Berichte*, 26. Sitzung (Berlin: 1880): 645–6. Indeed, this contrast in tradition is demonstrated by the higher levels of communal forests in western Germany. See 'Gemeindewaldbesitz,' *Das Land* 19 (1911): 272.

33 Speech by Karl Grimm in AH, 16 December 1879, *Stenographische Berichte*, 26. Sitzung (Berlin: 1880): 652. Grimm's warnings were more than rhetoric. Robert von Friedberg notes that these restrictions did lead to many Hessians freezing to death after 1880. See *Ländliche Gesellschaft und Obrigkeit* (Göttingen: Vandenhoeck & Ruprecht, 1997), 142–4.

34 Speeches by Wilhelm Seelig in AH 16 December 1879, *Stenographische Berichte*, 26. Sitzung (Berlin: 1880): 645–6; Hermann Fiebiger in AH, 23 January 1880, *Stenographische Berichte*, 44. Sitzung (Berlin: 1880): 1152.

35 Speech by Alexander Meyer in AH, 16 December 1879, *Stenographische Berichte*, 26. Sitzung (Berlin: 1880): 649–51.

36 Speech by Julius von Mirbach-Sorquitten in HH, 3 February 1880, cited in Ewald Berger, *Das deutsche Waldesideal* (Lissa i.P.: Ebbecke, 1907), 99; speeches by Wilhelm von Heydebrand und der Lasa in AH, 15 December 1879, *Stenographische Berichte*, 25. Sitzung (Berlin: 1880): 636–7; Jordan von

Kröcher in AH, 23 January 1880, *Stenographische Berichte*, 44. Sitzung (Berlin: 1880): 1147–8; Robert von Ludwig in AH, 18 February 1880, *Stenographische Berichte*, 65. Sitzung (Berlin: 1880): 1847–8.

37 Speeches by Robert von Lucius in AH, 23 January 1879, *Stenographische Berichte*, 44. Sitzung (Berlin: 1880): 1153; Bernhard Schmidt in AH, 4 November 1879, *Stenographische Berichte*, 4. Sitzung (Berlin: 1880): 30–1; Sigismund Leonhardt in AH, 15 December 1879, *Stenographische Berichte*, 25. Sitzung (Berlin: 1880): 638.

38 Speech by Robert Jacobs in AH, 23 January 1880, *Stenographische Berichte*, 44. Sitzung (Berlin: 1880): 1154–5.

39 Speeches by Peter Yorck von Wartenburg in AH, 15 December 1879, *Stenographische Berichte*, 25. Sitzung (Berlin: 1880): 1122–4; Julius von Mirbach-Sorquitten in HH, 3 February 1880, cited in Berger, *Das deutsche Waldesideal*, 99–102.

40 Speeches by Julius von Mirbach-Sorquitten in HH, 3 February 1880, cited in Berger, *Das deutsche Waldesideal*, 99–102; Wilhelm von Heydebrand und der Lasa and Robert Jacobs in AH, 23 January 1880, *Stenographische Berichte*, 44. Sitzung (Berlin: 1880): 1145–6, 1154–5.

41 Rolf Hennig, *Bismarck und die Natur* (Suderburg: Nimrod, 1998): 69–82, 142–3.

42 Theilemann, *Adel im grünen Rock*, 53–148.

43 See Staatsministerium meeting of 5 March 1880, in Hartwin Spenkuch, ed., *Die Protokolle des Preussischen Staatsministeriums 1817–1934/38* (Hildesheim: Olms-Weidmann, 1999), 7:59.

44 'Fortschrittliche Agitation. I,' *Provinzial-Correspondenz* 18, no. 32 (4 August 1880): 1–2.

45 Karl Dickel, *Deutsches und Preußisches Forstzivilrecht* (Berlin: Franz Vahlen, 1917), 711–16; Arnold Freymuth, *Das Betreten des Waldes* (Neudamm: Neumann, 1912).

46 'Die deutsche Forstwirthschaft und die Zölle auf Bauholz,' *Provinzial-Correspondenz* 17, no. 17 (23 April 1879): 3–4.

47 'Die deutschen Nutzholzzölle.' *Provinzial-Correspondenz* 21, no. 10 (7 March 1883): 5–6.

48 'Parlaments-Bericht. II,' *Neueste Mittheilungen* 2, no. 38 (4 April 1883): 4.

49 'Die Ablehnung des Holzzolles,' *Provinzial-Correspondenz* 21, no. 20 (17 May 1883): 2.

50 'Schutz dem deutschen Walde,' *Neueste Mittheilungen* 4, no. 24 (26 February 1885): 1.

51 Max Endres, *Handbuch der Forstpolitik* (Berlin: Springer, 1905): 694–5.

52 Bernhardt, *Die Waldwirthschaft und der Waldschutz*, 47.

53 Karl Böhmert, 'Zurück aus den Großstädten aufs Land!,' *Die Gartenlaube* 35 (1887): 554–5.

54 Lorenz Wappes, 'Über die ästhetische Bedeutung des Waldes,' *Forstwissenschaftliches Zentralblatt* 9 (1887), 329–32.

55 Ibid., 341–2.

56 Kisch, 'Zur Wahl der Sommerfrischen,' *Die Gartenlaube* 37 (1889): 352–5.

57 Endres, *Handbuch der Forstpolitik*, 200–1; Kempe, 'Der Wald als Wanderziel,' 343.

58 Fischbach, 'Der Kulturwert des Waldes,' 397.

59 See Adam Schwappach, *Forstpolitik, Jagd- und Fischereipolitik* (Leipzig: C.L. Hirschfeld, 1894), 66–8.

60 On the concept of nervousness, see Joachim Radkau, *Das Zeitalter der Nervosität* (Munich: Carl Hanser, 1998).

61 'Waldbäume und Wälder,' *Ausland* 44 (1871): 73.

62 K. Mischke, 'Naturdenkmäler,' *Mutter Erde* 4 (1900): 325.

63 Endres, *Handbuch der Forstpolitik*, 200–2.

64 Alexander von Padberg, 'Pflege der Waldschönheit,' *Kosmos* 4, no. 9 (1907): 274.

65 Speech by Ströbel in AH, 30 January 1911, *Stenographische Berichte*, 44. Sitzung (Berlin: 1911): 967–8.

66 König, *Eine Kulturgeschichte des Spaziergangs*, 35–7.

67 Ein eifriger Anhänger des Wanderns, 'Das Wandern,' *Die Mark* 2 (1905/6): 105–6.

68 Konrad Guenther, *Der Naturschutz*, 10–13.

69 *Magdeburger Zeitung*, 28 June 1906; *Magdeburgische Generalanzeiger*, 13 July 1906; *Preußisch-Litauische Zeitung*, 11 July 1906; *Die Post*, 16 July 1906; *Hamburger Nachrichten*, 17 July 1906; *Wild und Hund* 34 (24 August 1906); *Die Post*, 27 July 1906; *Schlesische Zeitung*, 18 August 1906; *Liegnitzer Tageblatt*, 24 July 1906; *Rheinische Courier*, 27 July 1906, all cited in Berger, *Das deutsche Waldesideal*, 9–23.

70 *Dortmunder Zeitung*, 24 July 1906; *Königsberger Hartungsche Zeitung*, 28 July 1906; *Hannoverscher Courier*, 9 August 1906; *Berliner Tageblatt*, 17 August 1906; *Breslauer Zeitung*, 19 August 1906, all cited in Berger, *Das deutsche Waldesideal*, 20–4.

71 *Deutsche Tageszietung*, 26 July 1906; *Deutsche Zeitung*, 29 July 1906, both cited in Berger, *Das deutsche Waldesideal*, 19–21. The radical nationalist *Tägliche Rundschau*, on the other hand, endorsed Lehfeld's position in late August, calling for the protection of landowners near big cities, 'who have to suffer much due to the rights of the excursionist.' The divergence of the

Tägliche Rundschau from the other right-wing papers might be explained by its rivalry with Lange's *Deutsche Zeitung*. A decade previously, Lange had been removed from the editorial board of the *Rundschau* and responded by starting his own paper. See *Tägliche Rundschau*, 26 August 1906, cited in Berger, *Das deutsche Waldesideal*, 21.

72 It is significant that several of these figures followed interesting political trajectories in the late nineteenth century, often moving between liberalism and conservatism. See Kenneth D. Barkin, *The Controversy over German Industrialization, 1890–1902* (Chicago: University of Chicago Press, 1970): 138–47; Erik Grimmer-Solem, *The Rise of Historical Economics and Social Reform in Germany, 1864–1894* (Oxford: Oxford University Press, 2003): 229–32; Dankwart Guratzsch, *Macht durch Organisation: Die Grundlegung des Hugenbergschen Presseimperius* (Düsseldorf: Bertelsmann Universitätsverlag, 1974), 48–52; Hans Herzfeld, *Johannes von Miquel; sein Anteil am Ausbau des Deutschen Reiches bis zur Jahrhundertwende* (Detmold: Meyersche Hofbuchhandlung, 1938): 64–8, 315–17; Dieter Lindenlaub, *Richtungskämpfe im Verein für Sozialpolitik: Wissenschaft und Sozialpolitik im Kaiserreich vornehmlich vom Beginn des 'Neuen Kurses' bis zum Ausbruch des 1. Weltkrieges (1890–1914)* (Wiesbaden: F. Steiner, 1967), 42; Wolfgang J. Mommsen, *Max Weber and German Politics, 1890–1920*, trans. Michael S. Steinberg (Chicago: University of Chicago Press, 1984), 21–34, 41–8; Fritz Ringer, *Max Weber: An Intellectual Biography* (Chicago: University of Chicago Press, 2004), 41–8.

73 See, for example, Wagner's *Allgemeine oder theoretische Volkswirtschaftslehre* (Leipzig: C.F. Winter'sche Verlagshandlung, 1876), 681–3; and his letter to the *National-Zeitung* 19 March 1878, reprinted in Heinrich Rubner, ed., *Adolph Wagner: Briefe, Dokumente, Augenzeugenberichte, 1851–1917* (Berlin: Duncker & Humblot, 1978): 167–9.

74 Bergmann, *Agrarromantik und Großstadtsfeindschaft*, 63–70. On the Agrarian League as a venue for peasant politics, see Geoff Eley, 'Anti-Semitism, Agrarian Mobilization, and the Conservative Party: Radicalism and Containment in the Founding of the Agrarian League, 1890–1893,' in *Between Reform, Reaction, and Resistance: Studies in the History of German Conservatism from 1789 to 1945*, ed. James Retallack and Larry Eugene Jones, 187–227 (Oxford: Berg, 1993).

75 Bergmann, *Agrarromantik und Großstadtsfeindschaft*, 70–7; Karlheinz Rossbacher, *Heimatkunstbewegung und Heimatroman: zu eine Literatursoziologie der Jahrhundertwende* (Stuttgart: Klett, 1975).

76 Hartung, *Konservative Zivilationskritik und regionale Identität*, 148–53. The most explosive growth for the *Zentralverband der Forst-, Land- und Weinbergsarbeiter* came between 1909 and 1910, coinciding with the strengthening

of the SPD in the Reichstag, the collapse of the Bülow administration, and the foundation of the *Bauernbund*, a liberal counterweight to the Agrarian League.

77 On Sohnrey's role in the *Bund Heimatschutz*, see the recollections by his friend and collaborator Robert Mielke: 'Meine Beziehungen zu Ernst Rudorff und die Gründung des Bundes Heimatschutz,' *Brandenburgia* 38 (1929): 6.

78 Bergmann, *Agrarromantik und Großstadtsfeindschaft*, 101; Heinrich Kröger, 'Sohnrey, Heinrich,' in *Biographisch-Bibliographisches Kirchenlexikon*, ed. Traugott Bautz (Herzberg: Traugott Bautz, 1995), 10:745–9.

79 Heinrich Sohnrey, *Wegweiser für Ländliche Wohlfahrts- und Heimatpflege* (Berlin: Deutscher Dorfschriftenverlag, 1900), 157–8; Sohnrey, *Wegweiser für Ländliche Wohlfahrts- und Heimatpflege* (Berlin: Deutsche Buchhandlung, 1908), 111–13; Sohnrey and Löber, *Das Glück auf dem Lande*, 138–41.

80 Indeed, the Prussian state actively sought to dissolve traditional communal use rights to the woods. Where this was not possible, it shifted those rights to either distant or degraded forests, rendering them useless. See Friedberg, *Ländliche Gesellschaft und Obrigkeit*, 142–4.

81 Adolf Korell, 'Kampf um das Waldrecht,' *Das Land* 10 (1902): 112–14.

82 Sohnrey, *Wegweiser für Ländliche Wohlfahrts- und Heimatpflege* (1900), 145–8, 157–8, 160; Sohnrey, *Wegweiser für Ländliche Wohlfahrts- und Heimatpflege* (1908), 15–16. On Fuchsmühl, see Konrad Köstlin, 'Der Ethnisierte Wald,' in *Der Wald: Ein deutscher Mythos?*, ed. Albrecht Lehmann and Klaus Schriewer (Berlin: Dietrich Reimer, 2000), 61; Walter Stelzle, 'Die wirtschaftlichen und sozialen Verhältnisse der bayerischen Oberpfalz um die Jahrhundertwende vom 19. zum 20. Jahrhundert: Der Streit von Fuchsmühl,' *Zeitschrift für bayerische Landesgeschichte* 37 (1976): 487–539.

83 Franz Hoermann, *Wald und Waldverwüstung* (Leipzig: Felix Dietrich, 1905), 13–15; see also his *Der deutsche Wald*.

84 Jeffrey K. Wilson, 'Environmental Chauvinism in the Prussian East: Forestry as a Civilizing Mission on the Ethnic Frontier, 1871–1914,' *Central European History* 41 (2008): 32.

85 Mathias Jakob Schleiden, *Für Baum und Wald: eine Schutzschrift an Fachmänner und Laien gerichtet* (Leipzig: Engelmann, 1870), 131–6.

86 Friedrich Freiherr von Löffelholz-Colberg, *Die Bedeutung und Wichtigkeit des Waldes: Ursachen und Folgen der Entwaldung*, iv.

87 Friedrich Simony, 'Schutz dem Walde!' *Zeitschrift zur Verbreitung naturwissenschaftliche Kenntnisse* 17 (1877): 502.

88 Hugo Conwentz, 'Die deutschen Wälder einst und jetzt,' speech given 29 September 1883. SBPK, Nachlaß Conwentz, Kiste 11 Mappe 20.

89 Rudorff published an article in the Free Conservative *Die Post* in 1878. See Mielke, 'Meine Beziehungen zu Ernst Rudorff,' 5.

90 Rudorff's criticism of modern agriculture is particularly prescient. Fearing livestock would increasingly be raised in pens, Rudorff remarked, 'Is it imaginable that the consumption of the meat and the milk of such livestock must gradually have a negative effect on the human organism? Nature will hardly here set aside the revenge that she takes everywhere, where one contradicts her laws.' Ernst Rudorff, 'Über das Verhältniß des modernen Lebens zur Natur,' *Preußische Jahrbücher* 45 (1880): 274–6.

91 Ibid.

92 Ernst Rudorff, *Der Schutz der landschaftlichen Natur und der geschichtlichen Denkmäler Deutschlands* (Berlin: Allgemeiner Deutscher Verein, 1892), 14.

93 Ibid., 21.

94 Salisch, *Forstästhetik*, 7–8.

95 Throughout the *Kaiserreich*, many forestry experts – along with other agricultural interests – called for increased tariffs (dropped in 1865 but reinstated in 1879) to protect the German market. In part, they justified this position by arguing that foreign forest reserves were dramatically dwindling and that a concerted reforestation of Germany's wastelands could cover most of Germany's demands for imports. See Eckert, *Deutsche Kulturgeographie*, 85–7; Rubner, *Forstgeschichte im Zeitalter der industriellen Revolution*, 150–60; Jösting, *Der Wald*, 6–7, 28–9; Heinrich Mayr, 'Die Bedeutung der fremdländischen Holzarten für den deutschen Wald,' Wissenschaftliche Beilage zur *Allgemeinen Zeitung* (1885), GStAPK, I HA 87D, Nr.3332; Minister of Agriculture von Arnim to the kaiser, 7 May 1909, in GStAPK, I HA Rep.89, Nr.31280, b.46–8; Säurich, *Das Leben der Pflanzen im Walde*, 387–8; speech by Wallenborn in AH, 25 February 1909, *Stenographische Berichte*, 13. Sitzung (Berlin: 1909): 2.

96 Fischbach, 'Der Kulturwert des Waldes,' 406.

97 Bieder, 'Zweite Jahresversammlung der Landesgruppe Brandenburg am 20. und 21 Juni 1908 in Frankfurt a/O,' *Heimatschutz in Brandenburg* 1 (1909): 15.

98 Rudorff to Mielke, 16 January 1903, in SBPK, Nachlass Mielke, Mappe 38.

99 Padberg, 'Pflege der Waldschönheit,' 274–6.

100 'Pflegt die Wälder,' *Wanderers Freund* 10 (1904): 71–2.

101 Barthelmeß, *Wald als Umwelt des Menschen.*

102 'Hans Thoma und die Pflege des Waldes,' *Mitteilungen des Bundes Heimatschutz* 2 (1906): 99.

103 Haupt, *Über die Erhaltung der Fußwege*, 4–7.

104 Ibid., 8–11.

105 Ibid., 15–16.

106 C., 'Feld- und Waldfreiheit,' *Volkswohl* 31 (1907): 227–8.

107 Speech by Ströbel in AH, 30 January 1911; *Stenographische Berichte*, 15. Sitzung (Berlin: 1911): 967–8.

108 *Kölnische Volkszeitung* 21 July 1912, cited in Hermann Graf zu Stolberg, 'Waldbesitzer und Publikum,' Mitteilungen der Deutschen dendrologischen Gesellschaft 21 (1912): 107–8.

109 For details on this organization, see Jeffrey K. Wilson, 'Nature and Nation: The "German Forest" in the National Imagination, 1871–1914' (PhD diss., University of Michigan, 2002), 221–3.

110 Georg Eugen Kitzler, 'Allüren märkischer Gutsbesitzer,' *Die Mark* 6 (1909/10): 97–8.

111 Article from *Berlin Lokal-Anzeiger* 7 September 1909, cited in ibid., 97–8.

112 Georg Eugen Kitzler, 'Laßt uns den Wald,' *Die Mark* 6 (1909/10): 129–30. Kitzler later expressed the suspicion that the state, like private landowners, was closing paths in order to avoid the possibility of their being legally transformed into public roads (which could occur after thirty years of public use). See Georg Eugen Kitzler, 'Verbotener Weg,' *Die Mark* 10 (1913/14): 12.

113 K.B., 'Achtung "Verbotene Wege"!' *Die Mark* 8 (1911/12): 63–4.

114 A.S., 'Achtung "Verbotene Wege"!' *Die Mark* 8 (1911/12): 91–2.

3. Environmental Activism in the Kaiserreich

1 This discourse conforms with what Dan Mattern calls 'urban modernism,' which sought 'to create a new city that was efficient, rational, and humane.' Brian Ladd agrees that the turn-of-the-century reform movements, including the *Heimat* enthusiasts, were 'far from … antiurban or anti-industrial.' Rather, 'Their goal was to promote the continued growth and prosperity of the big cities.' See Brian Ladd, *Urban Planning and Civic Order in Germany, 1860–1914* (Cambridge, MA: Harvard University Press, 1990), 231; Dan Mattern, 'Creating the Modern Metropolis: The Debate over Greater Berlin, 1890–1920' (PhD diss., University of North Carolina, 1991), 7–8.

2 Jan Palmowski, *Urban Liberalism in Imperial Germany: Frankfurt am Main, 1866–1914* (Oxford: Oxford University Press, 1999), 19–20. Ursula Bartelsheim makes a similar argument in her *Bürgersinn und Parteiinteresse: Kommunalpolitik in Frankfurt am Main 1848–1914* (Frankfurt am Main: Campus Verlag, 1997), 255–9. See also Rudy Koshar, *Social Life, Local Politics, and Nazism* (Chapel Hill: University of North Carolina Press, 1986).

3 George Steinmetz, *Regulating the Social: The Welfare State and Local Politics in*

Imperial Germany (Princeton, NJ: Princeton University Press, 1993), 150, 186.

4 Andrew Lees, *Cities, Sin, and Social Reform in Germany, 1880s–1914* (Ann Arbor: University of Michigan Press, 2002).

5 This attempt to integrate Berlin's working class through nature paralleled similar efforts in Hamburg focused on encouraging working-class interest in the arts. See Jennifer Jenkins, *Provincial Modernity: Local Culture and Liberal Politics in Fin-de-siècle Hamburg* (Ithaca, NY: Cornell University Press, 2003).

6 Palmowski, *Urban Liberalism in Imperial Germany*, 322. See also Repp, *Reformers, Critics, and the Paths of German Modernity*, 38–9; Steinmetz, *Regulating the Social*, 215–20.

7 Michael Erbe, 'Berlin im Kaiserreich,' in *Geschichte Berlins*, ed. Wolfgang Ribbe (Munich: Beck, 1987), 2:745–9; Ladd, *Urban Planning and Civic Order in Germany*, 50–60.

8 Ulrich Linse, Reinhard Falter, Dieter Rucht, and Winfried Kretschmer, 'Ein Vergleich,' in *Von der Bittschrift zur Platzbesetzung: Konflikte um technische Grossprojekten: Laufenburg, Walchensee, Wyhl, Wackersdorf*, ed. Ulrich Linse, Reinhard Falter, Dieter Rucht, and Winfried Kretschmer (Berlin: JHW Dietz, 1988), 231, 237, 240, 248, 254. This sort of dismissal of early environmental efforts is common. See, for example, Andersen, 'Heimatschutz,' 143–57.

9 Werner Hegemann, a Berlin urban planner involved with the purchase of the greenbelt, bitterly recalled the episode in his *Das steinerne Berlin: Geschichte der grössten Mietkasernenstadt der Welt* (Berlin: G. Kiepenheuer, 1930). He accused the Berlin city government of not being resolute enough in the face of government pressure, yet does not suggest what the municipal authorities should have done. Felix Escher's work on Berlin urban planning appropriates Hegemann's criticisms. See his *Berlin und sein Umland* (Berlin: Colloquium, 1985). For a critique of Hegemann's harsh assessment of his colleagues, see Ernst Kaeber, 'Werner Hegemanns Werk: "Das steinerne Berlin. Geschichte der größten Mietskassernenstadt der Welt" oder: der alte und der neue Hegemann,' in *Beiträge zur Berliner Geschichte*, ed. Ernst Kaeber, 204–33 (Berlin: De Gruyter, 1964).

10 Dan Mattern argues with regard to the creation of Greater Berlin that 'without reforming the Prussian three-class suffrage, movement on the provincial and state levels were [*sic*] foreclosed.' The example of the campaign to save the Grunewald, part of the struggle to create a Greater Berlin, reveals the power of public protest under municipal leadership. Mattern, 'Creating the Modern Metropolis,' 196.

11 Raymond Dominick very briefly discusses the Berliner's campaign for the

woods as a success in his book on the early German environmental movement. See his *Environmental Movement in Germany*, 43–5.

12 W. von D., 'Sankt Hubertus-Fest im Grunewald bei Berlin,' *Über Land und
    Meer* 33 (1874): 255; August Trinius, *Die Umgebung der Kaiserstadt Berlin* (Ber-
    lin: Lehmann, 1889), 208; Karl Schmedes, ed., *Grunewald*, vol. 4 of *Fontane's
    Führer durch die Umgegend Berlin*, ed. Touristen-Club für die Mark Branden-
    burg (Berlin: F. Fontane, 1894), 28; Freiherr von Dincklage-Campe, 'Der
    Kaiser als Jäger und Heger,' *Wild und Hund* 19, no. 24 (1913): 458; Katha-
    rine Lerman, 'Hofjagden: Royal Hunts and Shooting Parties in the Imperial
    Era,' in *Das politische Zeremoniell im Deutschen Kaiserreich, 1871–1918*, ed.
    Andreas Biefang, Michael Epkenhans, and Klaus Tenfelde (Düsseldorf:
    Droste, 2008), 6, 14; Theilemann, *Adel im grünen Rock*, 17–19.

13 Theilemann, *Adel im grünen Rock*, 25.

14 Lerman, 'Hofjagden,' 6.

15 Trinius, *Die Umgebung der Kaiserstadt Berlin*, 209.

16 Heinrich Prinz von Schönburg-Waldenburg, 'Parforcejagd im Grunewald,'
    in *Geist und Gesellschaft der Bismarckzeit*, ed. Karl Heinz Höfele (Göttingen:
    Musterschmidt, 1967), 263.

17 Schmedes, *Grunewald*, 28.

18 Andreas Gautschi, *Wilhelm II. und das Waidwerk: Jagen und Jagden des letzten
    Deutschen Kaisers. Eine Bilanz* (Hanstedt: Nimrod Verlag, 2000), 19–20, 43.

19 Berdrow, *Der Grunewald*, 94.

20 Andreas Gautschi, *Wilhelm II*, 43; Regina Hanemann & Jürgen Julier,
    'Zur Baugeschichte des Jagdschlosses Grunewald II. Von 1708 bis in die
    Gegenwart,' in *450 Jahre Jagdschloss Grunewald, 1542–1992*, vol. 1: *Aufsätze*,
    ed. Staatliche Schlösser und Gärten Berlin, (Berlin: Staatliche Schlösser
    und Gärten Berlin, 1992), 71–3.

21 G. Albrecht, 'Aus der Vergangenheit des Grunewalds,' *Brandenburgia* 16
    (1907/8): 254–255.

22 Berdrow, *Der Grunewald*, 98–100.

23 G. Koch, 'Kremserpartie im Grunewald,' *Die Gartenlaube* 47 (1899). Re-
    printed in Magdelene Zimmermann, *Die Gartenlaube als Dokument ihrer Zeit*
    (Munich: Heimeran Verlag, 1963), 162–3.

24 On Carstenn, see Christoph Bernhardt, *Bauplatz Groß-Berlin* (Berlin: Walter
    de Gruyter, 1998), 199; Erbe, 'Berlin im Kaiserreich,' 2:704–8; Escher, *Berlin
    und sein Umland*, 219–26; Hegemann, *Das steinerne Berlin*, 343–52.

25 Carstenn to Wilhelm I, 25 September 1872, GStAPK I HA Rep.89, Nr.31820,
    b.19–20. On Berlin city planning, see Escher, *Berlin und sein Umland*, 243–9;
    Jutta Lubowitzki, 'Der "Hobrechtplan": Probleme der Berliner Stadtent-
    wicklung um die Mitte des 19. Jahrhunderts,' in *Berlin Forschungen*, ed.

Wolfgang Ribbe (Berlin: Colloqium, 1990), 5:11–130; Günther Richter, 'Zwischen Revolution und Reichsgründung,' in *Geschichte Berlins*, ed. Wolfgang Ribbe (Munich: Beck, 1987), 2:605–87, 662–7.

26 Carstenn to Wilhelm I, 25 September 1872, GStAPK I HA Rep.89, Nr.31820, b.17–18.

27 Carstenn to Bismarck, 6 October 1872, GStAPK, I HA Rep.90, Nr.1632, b.4–5.

28 Carstenn to Wilhelm I, 25 September 1872, GStAPK I HA Rep.89, Nr.31820, b.23.

29 Carstenn to Bismarck, 6 October 1872, GStAPK I HA Rep.90, Nr.1632, b.8–10.

30 Ibid., b.5; Carstenn to Wilhelm I, 25 September 1872, GStAPK I HA Rep.89, Nr.31820, b.26.

31 Carstenn to Bismarck, 6 October 1872, GStAPK I HA Rep.90, Nr.1632, b.11.

32 Carstenn to Wilhelm I, 25 September 1872, GStAPK, I HA Rep.89, Nr.31820, b.26–8.

33 Ministers of trade (Heinrich von Itzenplitz) and finance (Otto von Camphausen), 20 November 1872, GStAPK, I HA Rep.89, Nr.31820, b.32–4.

34 Ibid., b.36–7. In order to pay for the road-building, however, he recommended the sale of roughly 165 hectares along the Havel south of Schildhorn, in the middle of the Grunewald's riverbank. So while state officials sought to protect the forest for public health reasons, at the same time they were willing to sell valuable parts of the Grunewald for development, presaging the conflict with the public after the turn of the century. At the same time, however, the press lauded the Fiskus's effort to protect the Grunewald from developers, perhaps having caught wind of the Carstenn plan. See W. von D., 'Sankt Hubertus-Fest im Grunewald bei Berlin,' 255.

35 Escher, *Berlin und sein Umland*, 236–7, 242–3. On the state's role in promoting and profiting from private real estate development, see 293–5, 299–300.

36 For her concern for the working classes, Heinrich von Treitschke tarred Dohna-Poninski as a socialist. Arminius [Countess Adelheid Dohna-Poninski], *Die Grosstädte in ihrer Wohnungsnoth und die Grundlagen einer durchgreifenden Abhilfe* (Leipzig: Duncker & Humblot, 1874), 149. See also Hegemann, *Das steinerne Berlin*, 369–72, 377; Hegemann, 'Stadt und Wald,' *Die Woche* 15, no. 7 (1913): 256.

37 Even when *Kreis* Teltow imposed limits the size of new construction in 1891, the state intervened in 1895, under the pressure of developers, to restrict these limits only to the most distant suburbs. Escher, *Berlin und sein Umland*, 243–5, 246–9; H.J. Mielke, *Die kulturlandschaftliche Entwicklung des Grunewaldgebiets* (Berlin: Dietrich Reimer, 1971).

38 Erbe, 'Berlin im Kaiserreich,' 2:700–4; Ladd, *Urban Planning*, 89–90, 224–6.

39 Dieter Hennebo, 'Öffentlicher Park und Grünplanung als kommunale Aufgabe in Deutschland,' in *Kommunale Leistesverwaltung und Stadtentwicklung vom Vormärz bis zur Weimarer Republik*, ed. Hans Heinrich Blotevogel, 169–82 (Cologne, Böhlau, 1990); Norbert Schindler, 'Gartenwesen und Grünordnung in Berlin,' in *Gartenwesen*, vol. 11 of *Berlin und seine Bauten*, ed. Klaus Konrad Weber (Berlin: Wilhelm Ernst & Sohn, 1972), 1–50; Rainer Stürmer, *Freiflächenpolitik in Berlin in der Weimarer Republik* (Berlin: Berlin Verlag, 1990), 1–35.

40 See Theodor Köhn, *Über die Einverleibung der Vororte in Berlin* (Berlin, 1892), cited in Escher, *Berlin und sein Umland*, 314. On Vienna, see Robert Rothenburg, *Landscape and Power in Vienna* (Baltimore: Johns Hopkins University Press, 1995), 148–87.

41 Meetings of the Magistrat, 13 and 20 September, 13 and 21 October 1892, LAB, STA Rep.01-02, Nr.1814, b.6–10; speech by AH Delegate and Berlin Stadtrat Fischbeck in the AH, 13 February 1907, *Stenographische Berichte*, 9. Sitzung (Berlin: 1907): 579–80; LAB, STA Rep.01-02, Nr.1814, b.40.

42 Marggraff to O.B. [these are not initials, but an abbreviation for Oberbürgermeister] Forckenbeck, 2 November 1891, LAB, STA Rep.01-02, Nr.1814, b.1. Köhn's speech and Marggraff's proposal are mentioned in Mielke, *Die kulturlandschaftliche Entwicklung des Grunewaldgebiets*, 223.

43 Carstenn circulated his views in an 'Open Letter to the Members of the Reichstag and the Prussian Landtag,' and he even published a short book explaining his vision of the future Berlin. In neither, however, did he explicitly repeat his desire to divide Berlin along class lines. See his 'Offenen Breif an die Mitglieder des Reichstages und des Preußischen Landtages,' sent to the Berlin Magistrat, 22 May 1892, LAB, STA Rep.01-02, Nr.1814, b.2; Johann Anton Wilhelm von Carstenn, *Die Zukünftige Entwicklung Berlins* (Berlin: Hugo Steinitz, 1892).

44 Ministry of Agriculture to Berlin Magistrat, 15 November 1892, LAB, STA Rep.01-02, Nr.1814, b.11; Staatsministerium meeting, 16 November 1892, GStAPK, I HA Rep.90, Nr.1632, b.21–2.

45 Magistrat to Ministry of Agriculture, 13 January 1893, LAB, STA Rep.01-02, Nr.1814, b.13–14; speech by AH Delegate and Stadtrat Fischbeck in the AH, 13 February 1907, *Stenographische Berichte*, 9. Sitzung (Berlin: 1907): 581; LAB, STA Rep.01-02, Nr.1814, b.40.

46 Oliver Ohmann, 'Die Berliner bauen ihre Berge selber,' *Berlinische Monatsschrift* 6 (1999): 32–4.

47 HH motion by Count Mortimer von Tschirschky-Renard, 15 May 1897,

GStAPK I HA Rep.169 C 23, Nr.39, b.1; R.S., 'Zur Erhaltung des Grunewaldes,' *Die Post*, 22 May 1897.

48 Speech by Robert Lucius von Ballhausen in HH, 21 May 1897, GStAPK, I
HA Rep.169 C 23, Nr.39, b.2–3.

49 HH, 31 May 1897, GStAPK, I HA Rep.169 C 23, Nr.39, b.4.

50 HH, Session 1898, document Nr.9, GStAPK I HA Rep.169 C 23, Nr.39, b.5;
Staatsministerium meeting, 6 January 1898, GStAPK, I HA Rep.90, Nr.1632,
b.37.

51 C.G., 'Der Grunewald zum Volkspark umgeschaffen,' *Deutsche Warte*, 19
January 1902. In 1904, the paper reported in more detail on Geitner's
plan, observing that athletic facilities, refreshments stands, an outdoor
museum, and a zoo were included in the development package. See 'Der
Grunewald als Volkspark,' *National Zeitung*, 12 March 1902; 'Die Umwandlung des Grunewalds in einen Volkspark,' *Der Tag*, 12 March 1902; 'Der
Volkspark Grunewald,' *Der deutsche Blatt*, 18 March 1902; 'Zur Umwandlung
des Grunewalds in Bauterrain und Volkspark,' *Deutsche Warte,*, 25 November
1904. LAB, STA Rep.01-02 Nr.1814, b.16-21 and envelope 2.

52 'Die Umwandlung des Grunewaldes,' *Tägliche Rundschau*, 12 March 1902;
'Vom Grunewald,' *Berliner Neueste Nachrichten*, 24 November 1904.

53 'Zu dem Grunewald-Volksparkprojekt,' *Volks-Zeitung*, 14 March 1902.

54 See speech by Luwdig Jablonski in *Der Kampf um unserer Wälder*, ed. Der
Berliner Zentralausschuß für die Wald- und Ansiedlungsfrage (Berlin: Julius
Springer, 1909), 10.

55 Escher, *Berlin und sein Umland*, 308; Wilson, 'Nature and Nation,' 238–310.

56 Podbielski and Rheinbaben to the kaiser, 21 December 1904, GStAPK, I HA
Rep.89, Nr.31820, b.179–81. On the issue of Podbielski's vision for a woodland defence, see chapter 4.

57 The kaiser to Podbielski and Rheinbaben, 3 January 1905 and 15 February
1905, GStAPK, I HA Rep.89, Nr.31820, b.182, 184; Podbielski to the kaiser,
16 June 1906, GStAPK, I HA Rep.89, Nr.31820, b.204–5.

58 'Forstverwaltung,' *Berliner Correspondenz*, 14 January 1903. GStAPK, I HA
Rep.90 Nr.1632 b.40; 'Zur Bebauung von Teilen des Grunewaldes,' *Der Tag*,
17 May 1903. LAB, STA Rep.01-02 Nr.1814, envelope 2.

59 'Wenn der Grunewald "Volkspark" wird,' *Volks-Zeitung*, 23 September
1904.

60 Stutz, 'Pod der Waldverwüster,' *Kladderadatsch*, 9 October 1904: 164. Apparently Podbielski tired of such portrayals in the press. Following another
Kladderadatsch lampoon, the minister had his secretary cancel an appointment with a complaining citizen on the grounds that 'he had to go to the
Grunewald in order to cut down a few more trees.' Recounted by Ober-

landforstmeister Wesener in the AH, 13 February 1907, *Stenographische Berichte*, 9. Sitzung (Berlin: 1907): 593; LAB, STA Rep.01-02, Nr.1814, b.40.
61 'Gegen die Verstümmelung des Grunewaldes,' *Volks-Zeitung*, 12 November 1904. LAB, STA Rep.01-02 Nr.1814 envelope 2.
62 'Das Schiksal des Grunewaldes,' *Tägliche Rundschau*, 14 November 1904, in SBPK, Nachlaß Conwentz, Kiste 12, Zeitungsausschnitte zum Natur- schutz; 'Schicksal des Grunewaldes,' *Volks-Zeitung*, 14 November 1904; and 'Schicksal des Grunewaldes,' *Berliner Tageblatt*, 14 November 1904. LAB, STA Rep.01-02 Nr.1814 b.26-27; 'Unsere Information bezüglich des Grune- waldes,' *Berliner Neueste Nachrichten*, 14 November 1904. LAB, STA Rep.01-02 Nr.1814 envelope 2.
63 'Schicksal des Grunewaldes,' *Berliner Tageblatt*; 'Schicksal des Grunewaldes,' *Volks-Zeitung*.
64 'Der Kampf um den Grunewald,' *Berliner Tageblatt*, 15 November 1904.
65 'Wenn der Grunewald "Volkspark" wird.'
66 'Der Kampf um den Grunewald.'
67 On Berlin politics, see Erbe, 'Berlin im Kaiserreich,' 2:759–75; Sheehan, *German Liberalism*, 230.
68 A similar dynamic unfolded in other German cities, where the socialists' entry into municipal politics spurred left liberals to propose social reforms. See Bartelsheim, *Bürgersinn und Parteiinteresse)*, 255–9; Steinmetz, *Regulating the Social*, 186.
69 'Das Schiksal des Grunewaldes,' *Tägliche Rundschau*.
70 'Unsere Information bezüglich des Grunewaldes.'
71 'Noch einmal Berlin und der Grunewald,' *Neue Preußische Zeitung* 15 November 1904.
72 Speech by Podbielski in AH, 28 January 1905, *Stenographische Berichte*, 127. Sitzung (Berlin: 1907): 9118–20; GStAPK, I HA Rep.169 C 23, Nr.39. Ironi- cally, this was precisely what James Hobrecht, who planned Berlin's expan- sion in 1861, had in mind. Moreover, state building authorities, not the municipalities, regulated the dimensions of buildings, and they regularly sought to increase their size in order to maximize land values. See Escher, *Berlin und sein Umland*, 246–9.
73 Speeches by Wesener in AH, 18 January 1907, *Stenographische Berichte*, 5. Sitzung (Berlin: 1907): 13; and 13 February 1907, *Stenographische Berichte*, 5. Sitzung (Berlin: 1907): 591–3; LAB, STA Rep.01-02, Nr.1814, b.39–40.
74 Ibid.
75 Speech by Kreitling in AH, 28 January 1905, *Stenographische Berichte*, 127. Sitzung (Berlin: 1905): 9121.
76 Speech by Fischbeck in AH, 13 February 1907, *Stenographische Berichte*, 5.

Sitzung (Berlin: 1907): 579–80; LAB, STA Rep.01-02, Nr.1814, b.40. Indeed, the suburbs had significantly lower taxes than the capital. Local taxes were assessed as a percentage of state income tax rates. According to 1902/3 statistics, the luxury suburb of Grunewald levied taxes equivalent to only 15 per cent of state taxes, while Berlin asked its residents to pay 100 per cent (working-class suburbs had even higher rates: Rixdorfers paid 150 per cent of state income tax rates, and their neighbours in Britz paid 233.33 per cent). Tax statistics cited in Mielke, *Die kulturlandschaftliche Entwicklung des Grunewaldgebiets*, 77n117.

77 Speech by Bender in HH, 30 March 1908; LAB, STA Rep.01-02, Nr.1814, b.79. Bender himself contended with a recalcitrant Fiskus when attempting to secure forests for Breslau. On Bender, see Hartwin Spenkuch, *Das Preußische Herrenhaus: Adel und Bürgertum in der Ersten Kammer des Landtages, 1854–1918* (Düsseldorf: Droste, 1998): 343–51.

78 Speech by Hermann Müller in AH, 13 February 1907, *Stenographische Berichte*, 5. Sitzung (Berlin: 1907): 589; LAB, STA Rep.01-02, Nr.1814, b.40.

79 Speeches by Henry von Böttinger and Robert Friedberg in AH, 13 February 1907, *Stenographische Berichte*, 5. Sitzung (Berlin: 1907): 597–8, 600; LAB, STA Rep.01-02, Nr.1814, b.40.

80 Speech by Hammer in AH, 1 February 1906, *Stenographische Berichte*, 15. Sitzung (Berlin: 1906): 952–3; GStAPK, I HA Rep.169 C 23, Nr.39.

81 Petitions from the Berliner deutschkonservative Wahlverein (A.B. Wagner) to the Ministry of Agriculture, 28 June 1906 and December 1906, GStAPK, I HA Rep.90, Nr.1632, b.42, 43.

82 See speeches by Hans von Brandstein and Karl von Pappenheim in AH, 13 February 1907, *Stenographische Berichte*, 5. Sitzung (Berlin: 1907): 579, 586–7; LAB, STA Rep.01-02, Nr.1814, b.40.

83 Speech by Brandstein in AH, 13 March 1909, *Stenographische Berichte*, 53. Sitzung (Berlin: 1909): 3980–2; GStAPK, I HA Rep.169 C 23, Nr.39.

84 AH, 13 March 1909, *Stenographische Berichte*, 53. Sitzung (Berlin: 1909): 4017; GStAPK, I HA Rep.169 C 23, Nr.39.

85 Petition from the vereinigten kommunalen Vereine von Zehlendorf to the HH, 1907, LAB, STA Rep.01-02, Nr.1814, b.77.

86 For a brief depiction, see Dominick, *Environmental Movement in Germany*, 44; Escher, *Berlin und sein Umland*, 316.

87 Invitation to the first Waldschutztag from the Berliner Waldschutzverein to the Magistrat Berlin, December 1907, LAB, STA Rep.12, Nr.485, b.13.

88 For more on Brandenburgia, see chapter 4.

89 HH Commission for Agricultural Relations meeting, 1 April 1908, GStAPK, I HA Rep.191, Nr.185, b.5–6.

90 HH, 6 April 1908, GStAPK, I HA Rep.169 C 23, Nr.39.

91 *Übersicht der Entschließungen der Königlichen Staatsregierung auf Beschlüße des Herrenhauses aus der 20. Legislaturperiode*, Nr. 19, GStAPK, I HA Rep.169 C 23, Nr.39.

92 Berliner Zentralausschuß, ed., *Der Kampf um unserer Wälder*, 6.

93 Ibid., 5. On Damaschke and the *Bund Deutscher Bodenreformer*, see Nicholas Bullock and James Read, *The Movement for Housing Reform in Germany and France, 1840–1914* (Cambridge: Cambridge University Press, 1985), 159–63, 178–9; Ladd, *Urban Planning*, 177–8; Elisabeth Meyer-Renschhausen and Hartwig Berger, 'Bodenreform,' in *Handbuch der deutschen Reformbewegungen, 1880–1933*, ed. Diethart Kerbs and Jürgen Reulecke, 265–76 (Wupperthal: Peter Hammer, 1998); Repp, *Reformers, Critics, and the Paths of German Modernity*, 69–91; Josef Seemann, 'Bund Deutsche Bodenreformer (BDB) 1898–1945,' in *Lexikon zur Parteiengeschichte*, ed. Dieter Fricke et al. (Leipzig: VEB Bibliographisches Institut Leipzig, 1983), 282–8;

On Francke and the *Büro für Sozialpolitik*, see Rüdiger vom Bruch, ed., *Weder Kommunismus noch Kapitalismus: bürgerliche Sozialreform in Deutschland vom Vormärz bis zur Ära Adenauer* (Munich: Beck, 1985), 130–9; Holger J. Tober, *Deutscher Liberalismus und Sozialpolitik in der Ära des Wilhelminismus* (Husum: Matthiesen, 1999).

On Kampffmeyer and the *Deutsche Gartenstadt-Gesellschaft*, see Bergmann, *Agrarromantik und Großstadtsfeindschaft*, 135–64; Kristiana Hartmann, *Deutsche Gartenstadtbewegung: Kulturpolitik und Gesellschaftsreform* (Munich: H. Moos, 1976); Hartmann, 'Gartenstadtbewegung,' in *Handbuch der deutschen Reformbewegungen, 1880–1933*, ed. Diethart Kerbs and Jürgen Reulecke (Wupperthal: Peter Hammer, 1998), 289–300.

On Wetekamp and the *Bund Heimatschutz*, see 'Wie Wilhelm Wetekamp zum Naturschutz kam,' *Heimatblätter* (supplement of *Der Patriot*) (8 October 1929); Knaut, *Zurück zur Natur!*; Rollins, *A Greener Vision of Home*; Friedemann Schmoll, *Erinnerung an die Natur: Die Geschichte des Naturschutzes im deutschen Kaiserreich* (Frankfurt am Main: Campus, 2004). Little is known about the *Zentralkommission der Krankenkassen Berlins und der Vororte*.

94 Included here were: the Ansiedlungsverein Groß-Berlin, Berliner Zentralausshuß für die Wald- und Ansiedlungsfrage, Freie Vereinigung Grunewald, Mieterbund Groß-Berlin, Verein der Vororte Berlins zur Wahrung gemeinsamer Interessen; the Gewerk-Verein der Heimarbeiterinnen, Hirsch-Duncker Gewerbeverein, Verband der Deutschen Gewerkvereine, and the Kartell der Christlichen Gewerkschaften Berlins und Umgegend; the Berlin branch of the Gesellschaft für soziale Reform and the Jacob Plaut-Stiftung Berlin; and the Verbündete Frauenvereine Groß-Berlin.

95 Included here were: the Berliner medizinischen Gesellschaft, the Berlin branch of the Deutsche Zentrale für Volkshygiene, the Verein öffentlicher Gesundheitspflege, and the Vereinigung der Walderholungsstätten vom Roten Kreuz; the Berliner Zentralverband zur Bekämpfung des Alkoholismus, Brandenburgischer Distrikt des Internationalen Guttempler Ordens, and Deutscher Verein gegen Mißbrauch geistiger Getränke; the Ausschuß der Berliner Turngaue and Berliner Hochschulsportvereinigung; and the Bund der Verein für Naturgemäße Lebens- und Heilweise (Naturheilkunde).

96 Included here were: the Berliner Gymnasiallehrer-Verein, Berliner Gymnasiallehrer-Gesellschaft, Berliner Lehrerverein; the Berlin branch of the Verein zur Förderung des mathematischen und naturwissenschaftlichen Unterrichts; and the Deutsche Zentrale für Jugendfürsorge.

97 Included here were: the Verein für die Geschichte Berlins, Deutscher Botanischen Gesellschaft, and the Ausschuß der wissenschaftlichen und gemeinnützigen Vereine zur Erhaltung der Grunewald-Moore.

98 Berliner Zentralausschuß, ed., *Der Kampf um unserer Wälder*, 32.

99 *Jahresbericht der Berliner Waldschutzverein* (1909): 25–6, quoted in Mattern, 'Creating the Modern Metropolis,' 188–91.

100 Erich Neuhaus, 'Berliner Waldschutztag,' *Bodenreform* 20 (1909): 70–5; 'Zum Schutze der Wälder um Groß-Berlin,' *Soziale Praxis* (1909): 436–7; 'Zur Grunewald-Frage,' *Heimatschutz in Brandenburg* 1 (1909): 48–53.

101 Berliner Zentral-Ausschuss für die Wald- und Ansiedlungsfrage to Magistrat Berlin, 15 January 1910, LAB, STA Rep.01-02, Nr.1814, b.127.

102 Magistrat Berlin to the cities of Charlottenburg, Schöneberg, Spandau, Wilmersdorf, Grunewald, Schmargendorf, Steglitz, Zehlendorf, Groß Lichterfelde, Wannsee, and the Kreis Teltow, 25 March 1907, LAB, STA Rep.01-02, Nr.1814, b.43.

103 Summary of the confidential meeting of representatives of Berlin-area cities, 4 April 1907, LAB, STA Rep.01-02, Nr.1814, b.44–5. Of those invited, only Schmargendorf and Steglitz failed to send a representative. Those in attendance agreed to invite Potsdam and Friedenau to further discussions.

104 Petition from the Magistrat Berlin and the cities of Potsdam, Charlottenburg, Schöneberg, Spandau, Wilmersdorf, Grunewald, Schmargendorf, Steglitz, Friedenau, Zehlendorf, Groß Lichterfelde, Wannsee, and the Kreis Teltow to the kaiser, 1 May 1907, LAB, STA Rep.01-02, Nr.1814, b.46–7.

105 Arnim to the kaiser, 4 July 1907, GStAPK, I HA Rep.89, Nr.31820, b.235–8.

106 Ministry of Agriculture to Magistrat Berlin, 26 August 1907, LAB, STA Rep.01-02, Nr.1814, b.54.

107 *Vorlage – zum Kentnissmachen – betr. die Erhaltung des Grunewaldes als Volkserho-lungsstätten,* 6 September 1907, LAB, STA Rep.01-02, Nr.1814, b.55–6.

108 Speeches by Rosenow and Cassel, *Stenographische Berichte über die öffentlichen Sitzungen der Stadtverordnetenversammlung der Haupt- und Residenzstadt Berlin* 34 (Berlin: Loewenthal, 1907), 293–5.

109 Kirschner's interview in the *Berliner Tageblatt* was read to the City Assembly by Dr Weyl. *Stenographische Berichte über die öffentlichen Sitzungen der Stadtver-ordnetenversammlung,* 294. Kirschner, a prominent left liberal in Berlin civic circles, gained prominence earlier in his career as a lawyer for defending members of the SPD in court, and earned the ire of the monarch for vo-ting to restore the graves of 1848 revolutionaries on the fiftieth anniversa-ry of the event. See Erbe, 'Berlin im Kaiserreich,' 2:759–63; Hans Tigges, *Das Stadtoberhaupt: Porträts im Wandel der Zeit* (Baden-Baden: Nomos, 1988).

110 *Stenographische Berichte über die öffentlichen Sitzungen der Stadtverordnetenver-sammlung,* 296.

111 Ibid., 294. Dr Weyl's positions were largely in keeping with an article in *Vorwärts* of the same day. See 'Die Erhaltung des Grunewaldes,' *Vorwärts,* 19 September 1907, LAB, STA Rep.01-02 Nr.1814, b.57.

112 Stadtverordnete zu Berlin to Berlin Magistrat, 19 September 1907, LAB, STA Rep.01-02, Nr.1814, b.62.

113 B.H., 'Die schönste Stadt,' *Berliner Tageblatt,* 17 March 1907.

114 Mayor Kirschner to the Parks Department, 18 April 1906, LAB, STA Rep.12, Nr.485, b.1. Vienna bought a significant amount of forests on 24 May 1905 for 50 million crowns.

115 Erbe, 'Berlin im Kaiserreich,' 741–3; Hermann Jansen, *Vorschlag zu einem Grundplan für Gross-Berlin* (Munich: Callwey, 1910).

116 Professor Otto Morgenstern, Gemeindevorsitzender Raeke, and Redaktur J. Lazarus of Groß Lichterfelde to Berlin Magistrat, 1 March 1907, LAB, STA Rep.01-02, Nr.1814, b.42.

117 'Neue Verkaufsobjekte,' *Volks-Zeitung,* 21 February 1907. The *Berliner Ta-geblatt* claimed the idea of a *Zweckverband* as its own. See 'Die Zukunft des Grunewaldes,' *Berliner Tageblatt,* 22 February 1907.

118 *Entwurf für den der Kommission zu erstattenden Bericht,* LAB, STA Rep.01-02, Nr.639, b.17–18.

119 *Denkschrift betreffend die Erhaltung des Waldbestandes um Berlin* (ca. 1909), LAB, STA Rep.01-02, Nr.639, b.12–15. For comparison, the OB commissio-ned a study of parks in and around other European capitals. See Clauswitz to OB, 26 April 1909, LAB, STA Rep.01-02, Nr.1814, b.96–105.

120 Oberstadtsekretär to OB, 26 April 1909, LAB, STA Rep.01-02, Nr.1814, b.111–12.

121 See Magistrat Berlin to Minister of Agriculture von Arnim, 13 April 1909,

LAB, STA Rep.01-02, Nr.1814, b.117; Minister of Agriculture von Arnim to Magistrat Berlin, 5 May 1909, LAB, STA Rep.01-02, Nr.1814, b.119; Oberstadtsekretär to OB Berlin, 2 September 1909, LAB, STA Rep.01-02, Nr.1814, b.113–14.

122 'Landrat v. Stubenrauch über den Wald- und Wiesengürtel,' *Berliner Tageblatt*, 2 April 1907); Vorsitzende des Kreis-Ausschusses des Kreises Niederbarnim to OBM Kirschner, 11 June 1909, LAB, STA Rep.01-02, Nr.639, b.1–2; 'Provinziallandtag und Waldschutz,' *Berliner Lokal-Anzeiger*, 3 March 1910.

123 'Zum Schutz des Waldbestandes in und um Berlin,' *Berliner Lokal-Anzeiger*, 29 March 1910.

124 Denkschrift from OB Kirschner to RP zu Potsdam, 12 March 1910, LHAB, Pr. Br. Rep.2A I Kom, Nr. 3208, b.3–5.

125 Staatsministerium Notiz, GStAPK, I HA Rep.90, Nr.1632, b.126.

126 Minister of the Interior von Moltke to minister of agriculture, 27 April 1910, GStAPK, I HA Rep.191, Nr.185, b.87.

127 Minister of Agriculture von Arnim to Magistrat Berlin, 13 April 1910, LAB, STA Rep.01–02 Nr.639 b.47.

128 Ministry of Agriculture meeting, 12 October 1912, GStAPK, I HA Rep.90, Nr.1632, b.262–74.

129 For accounts of the *Zweckverband* and its tasks, see Bernhardt, *Bauplatz Groß-Berlin*, 273; Erbe, 'Berlin im Kaiserreich,' 2:749–54; Escher, *Berlin und sein Umland*, 318–20; Mattern, 'Creating the Modern Metropolis,' 255ff.; Jürgen von Reuß, 'Freiflächenpolitik als Sozialpolitik,' in *Martin Wagner, 1885–1957: Wohnungsbau und Weltstadtplanung: die Rationalisierung des Glücks*, ed. Akademie der Künste (Berlin: Akademie der Künste, 1985): 49–65.

130 'Eröffnungssitzung der vereinigten beiden Häuser des Landtags,' 10 January 1911, 3; and *Übersicht der Entschließungen der Königlichen Staatsregierung auf Beschluße des Herrenhauses aus der 21. Legislaturperiode*, 8 January 1911, GStAPK, I HA Rep.169 C 23, Nr.39.

131 Speech by Maltzahn in AH, 30 January 1911, *Stenographische Berichte*, 15. Sitzung (Berlin: 1911): 1004.

132 Report on the negotiations with the *Zweckverband*, 18 November 1911, GStAPK, I HA Rep.90, Nr.1632, b.173.

133 Hegemann complained Berlin had fewer than a third of the votes in the *Zweckverband*, although its population made up half of the total, and the city's citizens paid more in taxes than those of the suburbs. At the same time, however, the suburbs looked to Berlin for leadership. Given the growing convergence of conservative, liberal, and socialist attitudes towards the forest question among Berlin's municipal and state political representatives, it is difficult to see how the *Zweckverband* constrained

Berlin's options. Hegemann, *Das steinerne Berlin*, 458–9. On Hegemann's career, see Kaeber, 'Werner Hegemanns Werk: "Das steinerne Berlin,"' 204–33.

134 Minister of agriculture to the Ministry of Public Works, 4 May 1912, GStAPK, I HA Rep.90, Nr.1632, b.189.

135 Bernhard Dernburg, 'Ein Kritischer Moment in der Entwicklung Groß-Berlins,' *Berliner Tageblatt*, 6 July 1912; 'Die Vorlage über die Groß-Berliner Waldkäufe,' *Berliner Tageblatt*, 9 October 1912, morning edition.

136 Memorandum by former Verbandsdirektor Steiniger in 1938, reprinted in Rainer Stürmer, *Freiflächenpolitik in Berlin*, 348–9. See also Steiniger to the minister of agriculture, 31 July 1912, GStAPK, I HA Rep.90, Nr.1632, b.205–11.

137 Bender quoted the resolution made by the HH on 30 March 1908. Speech by Bender in HH (25 May 1909): 306–7, LAB, STA Rep.01-02, Nr.1814, b.116.

138 Verbandsdirektor Steiniger to the Staatsministerium, 31 July 1912, GStAPK, I HA Rep.90, Nr. 1633, b.8–10.

139 Staatsministerium meeting, 18 May 1914, GStAPK, I HA Rep.84a, Nr.6108, b.126–33. The RP of Potsdam, Rudolf von der Schulenburg, likewise feared such a breakdown would play into the hands of the socialists, 'forcing the royal government to drop its objection to suburban annexation across the board.' RP Potsdam von der Schulenburg to minister of the interior, 2 May 1914, GStAPK, I HA Rep.84a, Nr.6108, b.93–5.

140 Staatsministerium meeting, 30 November 1908, GStAPK, I HA Rep.90, Nr.1632, b.67–8.

141 OP Brandenburg to Staatsministerium, 20 October 1911, GStAPK, I HA Rep.90, Nr.1632, b.170–2.

142 Staatsministerium Notiz, 6 June 1912, GStAPK, I HA Rep.90, Nr.1632, b.194.

143 Ministry of Agriculture meeting, 12 October 1912, GStAPK, I HA Rep.90, Nr.1632, b.271–3.

144 Ibid., b.266–7, 275–6.

145 See Staatsministerium meetings, 29 October, 11 November 1912, 4, 11, 22 January 1913, I HA Rep.90, Nr. 1633, b.18–25, 43–52, 92–7, 102–4, 118–23.

146 Ministries of Agriculture and Finance to the Staatsministerium, 24 April 1913; Ministries of Public Works and Interior to Staatsministerium, 5 May 1913, GStAPK, I HA Rep.90, Nr. 1633, b.162–4, 167–8.

147 For the Zweckverband's offer, see 'Zur Walderwerbsfrage,' *Korrespondenz Horn*, 16 October 1912. The verity of this report is underlined by the fact that Verbandsdirektor Steiniger cited this article as evidence of leaks

from the *Zweckverband*. See Verbandsdirektor des Verbandes Groß-Berlin (Steiniger) to an unnamed Unterstaatssekretär in the Staatsministerium, 16 October 1912, GStAPK, I HA Rep.90, Nr.1632, b.239.

148 He credited this move for driving down the price. Adolf Wermuth, *Ein Beamtenleben* (Berlin: Scherl, 1922), 340–6.

149 On the falling water table, see Mielke, *Die kulturlandschaftliche Entwicklung des Grunewaldgebiets*, 87–96. Arguments relating the condition of the Grunewald to its cost include: C.E., 'Der Zweckverband auf der Wanderfahrt,' *Berliner Tageblatt*, 1 October 1912, morning edition; 'Der Gefährdete Baumbestand des Grunewalds,' *Vossische Zeitung*, 4 April 1914; 'Grunewaldsorgen,' *Berliner Lokal-Anzeiger*, 21 April 1914; 'Grunewaldfragen,' *Vossische Zeitung*, 23 April 1914.

150 'Der Fiskus als Bauspekulant,' *Vorwärts*, 23 February 1913.

151 C.E., 'Die Unannehmbarkeit der Regierungsförderung,' *Berliner Tageblatt*, 12 February 1913, evening edition; C.E., 'Das Rückkaufsrecht auf 300 Jahre,' *Berliner Tageblatt*, 16 February 1913, morning edition. The Magistratsassessor Kurt Riess made many of the same arguments in an article in the *Berliner Tageblatt*. See Kurt Riess, 'Der Preis des Waldgürtels,' *Berliner Tageblatt*, 1 April 1913, morning edition.

152 'Der Fiskus als Bauspekulant,' *Vorwärts*.

153 Bernhard Dernburg, 'Die Waldverkauf,' *Berliner Tageblatt*, 14 February 1913, morning edition.

154 P.B., 'Berlin,' *Deutsche Tageszeitung*, 6 March 1913, morning edition.

155 H.K., 'Großprotzendorf,' *Hallesche Zeitung* 19 March 1913.

156 Nachweisung des forstfiskalischen Besitzes in einem Umkreise von 20km um Berlin (Leipziger Platz) am 1. Januar 1901 sowie das in der Zeit vom 1. Januar 1901 bis 31. Dezember 1909 in dem gleicher Umkreise veräußerten und mit Abholzungsbefugnis verpachteten bezw. an die Eisenbahnverwaltung abgetretenen Staatsforstgeländes nebst einer Überschrift für den 25km Umkreis. In GStAPK, Pr. Br. Rep.2A, III F, Nr.3094.

157 Carl von Tyszka, 'Vor der Entscheidung,' *Berliner Tageblatt*, 25 April 1914, evening edition, LHAB, Pr. Br. Rep.2A, III F, Nr.3101.

158 'Die Waldfrage im Zweckverband,' *Vossische Zeitung*, 2 May 1914. *Vorwärts* attacked Wermuth for his vote in favour of the deal (he had opposed it until the day of the decision). See 'Gegen den Oberbürgermeister Wermuth,' *Vorwärts*, 6 May 1914, morning edition.

159 See Staatsministerium meeting, 18 May 1914, GStAPK, I HA Rep.84a, Nr.6108, b.127.

160 RP Potsdam Rudolf von der Schulenburg to minister of the interior, 2 May 1914, GStAPK, I HA Rep.84a, Nr.6108, b.93–5.

161 C., 'Waldvernichtung und Volksgesundheit,' *Volkswohl* 31 (1907): 55–6;

Hermann Kötschke, *Die Berliner Waldverwüstung und verwandte Fragen* (Berlin: Ansiedlungsverein Groß-Berlin, 1910), 97; Karl von Mangoldt, 'Großstadt und Waldschutz,' *Die Hilfe* (1910): 265–7; Henriette Meynen, *Die Kölner Grünanlagen: Die städtebauliche und gartenarchitektonische Entwicklung des Stadtgrüns und das Grünsystem Fritz Schumachers* (Düsseldorf: Schwann, 1979); City of Vienna, *Der Wald- und Wiesengürtel und die Höhenstrasse der Stadt Wien* (Vienna: Verlag der Gemeinde Wien, 1905), 17, 26; 'Waldpflege,' *Tägliche Rundschau*, 30 August 1904.

162 The secondary literature on this topic is woefully inadequate. Much of the scholarship on parks had focused on their aesthetics or social benefits, and not on the politics surrounding their creation. I assume, in the absence of scholarship and contemporary references, that similar campaigns did not develop elsewhere. See, for example, Hennebo, 'Öffentlicher Park,' 169–82; Renate Kastorff-Viehmann, 'Die Stadt und das Grün 1860 bis 1960,' in *Die grüne Stadt: Siedlungen, Parks, Wälder, Grünflächen 1860–1960 im Ruhrgebiet*, ed. Renate Kastorff-Viehmann and Hermann Josef Bausch, 49–141 (Essen: Klartext, 1998); Hans Walden, *Stadt, Wald: Untersuchungen zur Grüngeschichte Hamburgs* (Hamburg: DOBU, Wissenschaftlicher Verlag Dokumentation & Buch, 2002).

163 Wermuth, *Ein Beamtenleben*, 317–40.

164 *Kaufantrag mit dem Verband Groß-Berlin*, GStAPK, X HA 2B III, Nr.1514.

165 Memorandum by the former Verbandsdirektor Steiniger in 1938, reprinted in Stürmer, *Freiflächenpolitik in Berlin*, 348–9.

4. Reforestation as Reform

1 Karl Pernin, *Wanderungen durch die sogen: Kassubei und die Tucheler Haide* (Danzig: A.W. Kafemann, 1886), 87; Wilhelm Schwandt, 'Zur Geschichte des Marienparadieses,' in *Karthaus und die Kassubische Schweiz*, ed. Wilhelm Schwandt (Danzig: Kafemann, 1913), 119.

2 Gustav von dem Borne, 'Die Oedlands-Ankäufe und Aufforstungen der Preußischen Staatsforst-Verwaltung mit besonderer Berücksichtigung der westpreußischen Kassubei.' *Zeitschrift für Forst- und Jagdwesen* 24 (1892): 399–400.

3 F.W.F. Schmitt, *Land und Leute in Westpreußen*, vol. 2 of *Die Provinz Westpreußen* (Thorn: Ernst Lambeck, 1879), 56.

4 Pernin, *Wanderungen durch die sogen*, 187–90.

5 Indeed, the term *Kultur* can often refer to agriculture.

6 G. Nentwig, 'Deutsche Pioniere im Osten,' *Die Gartenlaube* 29 (1881): 830–2.

7 A. Keller, 'Karthaus in der Kassubischen Schweiz,' *Die Gartenlaube* 49 (1901): 409–10.
8 Prof. Heidenhain rejected draft of the *Festschrift zum 10 jährigen Stiftungsfest for the Ostmarkenverein* (Marienburg, 1907), GStAPK, I HA Rep.195, Nr.35, b.9; Baeck, *Heimatskunde der Provinz Posen* (Königsberg: Bon, 1882), 9–10.
9 Margarete Boie, *Hugo Conwentz und seine Heimat: Ein Buch der Erinnerungen* (Stuttgart: Steinkopf, 1940), 176–8.
10 Adalbert Luntowski, *Westpreußische Wanderungen* (Berlin: G. Westermann, 1914), 79; Schmitt, *Land und Leute in Westpreußen,* 56–8; R. Schütte, *Die Tucheler Haide, vornehmlich in forstlicher Beziehung* (Danzig: Th. Bertling, 1893), 13–14.
11 Eric A. Johnson, 'Urban and Rural Crime in Germany, 1871–1914,' in *The Civilization of Crime,* ed. Eric A. Johnson and Eric H. Monkkonen, 217–57 (Chicago: University of Illinois Press, 1996).
12 Richard Blanke, *Prussian Poland in the German Empire* (Boulder: East European Monographs, 1981); Martin Broszat, *Zweihundert Jahre deutsche Polenpolitik* (Frankfurt am Main: Suhrkamp, 1986); Norman Davies, *God's Playground: A History of Poland* (New York: Columbia University Press, 1982); Geoff Eley, 'German Politics and Polish Nationality: The Dialectic of Nation-Forming in the East of Prussia,' in *From Unification to Nazism,* ed. Geoff Eley, 200–30 (London: Routledge, 1992); Karin Friedrich, *The Other Prussia: Royal Prussia, Poland and Liberty, 1569–1772* (Cambridge: Cambridge University Press, 2000); William W. Hagen, *Germans, Poles, and Jews: The Nationality Conflict in the Prussian East, 1772–1914* (Chicago: University of Chicago Press, 1980); Lech Trzeciakowski, *The Kulturkampf in Prussian Poland* (Boulder: East European Monographs, 1990); Piotr Wandycz, *The Lands of Partitioned Poland* (Seattle: University of Washington Press, 1993); Mathias Niendorf, *Minderheiten an der Grenze: Deutsche und Polen in den Kreisen Flatow (Złotów) und Zempelburg (Sępólno Krajeńskie) 1900–1939* (Wiesbaden: Harrassowitz, 1997).
13 Cited in Roland Baier, *Die deutsche Osten als soziale Frage: Eine Studie zur preußischen und deutschen Siedlungs- und Polenpolitik in den Ostprovinzen während des Kaiserreichs und der Weimarer Republik* (Cologne: Böhlau, 1980), 5.
14 Brigitte Balzer, *Die preußische Polenpolitik 1894–1908 und die Haltung der deutschen konservativen und liberalen Parteien* (Frankfurt am Main: Peter Lang, 1990), 290.
15 Balzer, *Die preußische Polenpolitik,* 144; Hagen, *Germans, Poles, and Jews,* 184–5.
16 William Rollins, 'Imperial Shades of Green: Conservation and Environmental Chauvinism in the German Colonial Project,' *German Studies Review* 22, no. 2 (1999): 187–213.

17 Thaddeus Sunseri, 'Reinterpreting a Colonial Rebellion: Forestry and Social Control in German East Africa, 1874–1915,' *Environmental History* 8, no. 3 (2003): 443.

18 Oskar von Riesenthal, *Bilder aus der Tucheler Heide*, 2nd ed. (Trier: Fr. Link, 1878), 1.

19 Schütte, *Die Tucheler Haide*, 4.

20 *Nachweisung über den Ankauf und die Aufforstung von Ländereien im Interesse der Landeskultur* (Regierungsbezirk Marienwerder, 17 September 1878), GStAPK, I HA Rep.87D, Nr.2412.

21 Ursula Hannelore Wagner, *Die preussische Verwaltung des Regierungsbezirks Marienwerder 1871–1920* (Cologne: Grote, 1982), 41.

22 Borne, 'Die Oedlands-Ankäufe und Aufforstungen,' 399–400.

23 Hans-Jürgen Bömelburg, 'Westpreußische Gutsbesitzer "auf der Höhe,"' in *Polen, Deutsche und Kaschuben … Alltag, Brauchtum und Volkskultur auf dem Gut Hochpaleschken in Westpreußen um 1900*, ed. Bernhard Lauer (Kassel: Brüder Grimm-Gesellschaft, 1997), 28–30; Christoph Nonn, *Eine Stadt sucht einen Mörder: Gerücht, Gewalt und Antisemitismus im Kaiserreich* (Göttingen: Vandenhoeck & Ruprecht, 2002), 103–10.

24 See, for example, Francé, *Bilder*, 78; 'Klimatologische Bedeutung des Waldes,' *Das Ausland* 45 (1872): 601–3; Köllner, 'Wald,' 170–1; Löffelholz-Colberg, *Die Bedeutung*, v; Säurich, *Das Lebe*, 392–6; Schwappach, *Handbuch*, 773–4; Jösting, *Der Wald*, 1–3; Friedrich Simony, 'Schutz dem Walde!' *Zeitschrift zur Verbreitung naturwissenschaftliche Kenntnisse* 17 (1877): 466–98.

25 Wilson, 'Nature and Nation,' 271–83.

26 Ibid., 283–307.

27 Sohnrey, *Wegweiser* (1900), 162.

28 Säurich, *Das Leben der Pflanzen im Walde*, 395–6.

29 Borne, 'Die Oedlands-Ankäufe,' 395–6.

30 For a historical treatment of the concept of 'Polish mismanagement,' see Hubert Orlowski, *'Polnische Wirtschaft': Zum deutschen Polendiskurs der Neuzeit* (Wiesbaden: Harrassowitz, 1996).

31 Borne, 'Die Oedlands-Ankäufe,' 399–400; Schütte, *Die Tucheler Haide*, 10.

32 Luntowski, *Westpreußische Wanderungen*, 71–3; Hans Preuß, 'Die Entwicklung der staatlichen Forstwirtschaft in Westpreußen,' in *Lesebuch*, part 2 of *Die Provinz Westpreußen in Wort und Bild*, ed. Paul Gehrke, Robert Hecker, and Hans Preuss (Danzig: Kafemann, 1912), 105–6; Preuß, 'Drei Tage in der Tucheler Heide,' in *Lesebuch*, 98.

33 Rollins, 'Imperial Shades of Green'; Sunseri, 'Reinterpreting a Colonial Rebellion,' 430–51.

34 Blackbourn, *Conquest of Nature*, 21–75.

35 Borne, 'Die Oedlands-Ankäufe,' 393–5; Preuß, 'Drei Tage in der Tucheler Heide,' 98; Schütte, *Die Tucheler Haide*, 11–12.

36 Luntowski, *Westpreußische Wanderungen*, 74–6.

37 Ibid.; Preuß, 'Die Entwicklung der staatlichen Forstwirtschaft in Westpreußen,' 105–6.

38 Borne, 'Die Oedlands-Ankäufe,' 399–400.

39 Erich Wernicke, *Wanderung durch die Tucheler Heide* (Danzig: Kafemann, 1913), 9–10.

40 Schütte, *Die Tucheler Haide*, 50.

41 During the agricultural crisis years of 1874–98, the German-owned Altpaleschken estate reduced its forest from roughly fifty-nine to thirteen hectares.. See Bömelburg, 'Westpreußische Gutsbesitzer "auf der Höhe,"' 28–30.

42 On the Kashubians, see H. Lingenberg, 'Die Kaschuben,' *Westpreußen-Jahrbuch* 35 (1985): 133–8; Richard Breyer, 'Die kaschubische Bewegung vor dem Ersten Weltkrieg,' in *Studien zur Geschichte des Preussenlandes; Festschrift für Erich Keyser zu seinem 70. Geburtstag dargebracht von Freuden und Schülern*, ed. Ernst Bahr, 327–41 (Marburg: N.G. Elwert, 1963).

43 Riesenthal, *Bilder aus der Tucheler Heide*, 2.

44 Schmitt, *Land und Leute in Westpreußen*, 55; Schütte, *Die Tucheler Haide*, 49.

45 Wernicke, *Wanderung durch die Tucheler Heide*, 12.

46 Borne, 'Die Oedlands-Ankäufe,' 398–400; Schütte, *Die Tucheler Haide*, 49.

47 Borne, 'Die Oedlands-Ankäufe,' 398.

48 Luntowski, *Westpreußische Wanderungen*, 61–3; Wernicke, *Wanderung durch die Tucheler Heide*, 16–17.

49 Schütte, *Die Tucheler Haide*, 44.

50 See Scott, *Seeing Like a State*, 11–22.

51 Scholarship on wood theft emphasizes peasant resistance to market forces, arguing rural folk challenged the rationalization of commercial production by asserting their 'traditional' rights to their environment. In this case, it is difficult to disentangle incipient anti-capitalism from national resentments. See Ramachandra Guha, *The Unquiet Woods: Ecological Change and Peasant Resistance in the Himalaya* (Berkeley: University of California Press, 2000); Peter Sahlins, *Forest Rites: The War of the Demoiselles in Nineteenth-Century France* (Cambridge, MA: Harvard University Press, 1994); Moser, 'Property and Wood Theft,' 75–7.

52 Niendorf, *Minderheiten an der Grenze*.

53 Luntowski, *Westpreußische Wanderungen*, 61.

54 For a parallel case in Indonesia, see Nancy Peluso, *Rich Forests, Poor People: Resource Control and Resistance in Java* (Berkeley: University of California Press, 1992).

55 K. Sivaramakrishnan points to a similar seasonal pattern of wood theft in colonial Bengal, as does Josef Moser in Westphalia. See Moser, 'Property and Wood Theft,' 66; Sivaramakrishnan, *Modern Forests*, 39.

56 Unfortunately, it is impossible to deduce ethnicity from the lists. Verzeich- niß der vorgefallenen Holzdiebstähle in dem Forst-Revier Woziwodda im Jahr 1875, Archiwum Panstwowe w Bydgoszczy (hereafter APB), Schütten- walde, Nr.174; Verzeichniß der vorgefallenen Forst-Contraventionen in dem Forst-Revier Czersk während des Monats Mai im Jahre 1878. Ciss, 18 June 1878, APB, Czersk, Nr.19; Verzeichniß der vorgefallenen Forst-Contraven- tionen in dem Forst-Revier Czersk während des Monats Juni im Jahre 1878. Ciss, 10 July 1878, APB, Czersk, Nr.19.

57 Luntowski, *Westpreußische Wanderungen*, 54; Johannes Mühlradt, *Ein Besuch in Grüntal*, vol. 1 of *Die Tucheler Heide in Wort und Bild* (Danzig: Kafemann, 1908), 80.

58 Schütte, *Die Tucheler Haide*, 17; Wernicke, *Wanderung durch die Tucheler Heide*, 16–17.

59 Luntowski, *Westpreußische Wanderungen*, 62–3.

60 F. Kliewert to O.F. Feußner, 2 February 1881, APB, Czersk, Nr.16.

61 F.M. Christow to O.F. Feußner, 12 November 1871, APB, Czersk, Nr.16.

62 F.A. Knop to O.F. Feußner, 22 February 1888, APB, Czersk, Nr.16.

63 It seems here again a local peasant attempted to invert the foresters' mental hierarchy, characterizing them as thieves and vagrants instead of upstanding officials.

64 F. Lange to O.F. Feußner, 8 March 1892, APB, Czersk, Nr.16.

65 Knop notes that he managed to beat her in a way that did no harm to the pregnant woman, although this seems hard to believe. F.A. Knop to O.F. Feußner, 3 March 1886, APB, Czersk, Nr.16.

66 F. Haase to O.F. Feußner, 13 June 1888, APB, Czersk, Nr.16.

67 F.A. Knop to O.F. Feußner, 30 June 1888, APB, Czersk, Nr.16.

68 Riesenthal, *Bilder aus der Tucheler Heide*, 11.

69 Interestingly, British foresters had an entirely different experience in colonial Bengal over roughly the same period. From 1880 to 1905, the unauthorized felling of trees rose sharply from 37 cases to 1,984 (over fifty times), while cases of illegal grazing of livestock leaped from 6 to 860 (over 140 times). While environmental factors (such as the size and topography of the territory in question) contributed to these diverging experiences, the more recent assertion of state control over Bengal's previously unregulated forests plays a key role. While Prussia had already invested a century in battling wood thieves, British authorities had only just extended their con- trol to the forests. See Sivaramakrishnan, *Modern Forests*, 39; Guha, *Unquiet Woods*, 186–8.

70 Mühlradt, *Ein Besuch in Grüntal*, 231–2.
71 Wernicke, *Wanderung durch die Tucheler Heide*, 16–17.
72 Schütte, quoted in Wernicke, *Wanderung durch die Tucheler Heide*, 16–17;
    Luntowski, *Westpreußische Wanderungen*, 61–3. It is interesting to speculate
    about the significance of the black crosses. While the French peasants
    whom Sahlins describes cloaked themselves in women's garb – potentially
    symbolizing a 'feminine' disruption of the state's imposition of a rational,
    'masculine' order on the forest – these Polish poachers perhaps chose
    the cross as a religious symbol. Given the alliance of the Catholic church
    and the Polish nationalist movement, and that the poachers operated on
    Sundays directly after mass, it is conceivable that their disguise carried a
    religious-cum-national message. Indeed, one could imagine these poachers
    arguing they were simply taking what God had given them and the Prussian
    state unjustly had taken away. Bavarian poachers understood their work
    similarly. See Sahlins, *Forest Rites*, 24–8, 54; Schulte, *Village in Court*, 121–77.
73 Riesenthal, *Bilder aus der Tucheler Heide*, 7–9.
74 Schmitt, *Land und Leute in Westpreußen*, 56–8.
75 Schütte, cited in Mühlradt, *Ein Besuch in Grüntal*, 71.
76 Luntowski, *Westpreußische Wanderungen*, 79. We should not conclude that
    violent clashes between foresters and poachers were limited to the Prus-
    sian east, however. For examples from Bavaria and Hessia, see Friedberg,
    Ländliche Gesellschaft und Obrigkeit, 142–4; Köstlin, 'Der Ethnisierte Wald,' 62;
    Schulte, *Village in Court*, 179–87.
77 Ibid., 13.
78 Schütte, *Die Tucheler Haide*, 13. Little historical literature has been written
    on the topic of arson in the German context. Regina Schulte's historical an-
    thropological study of rural life in Upper Bavaria touches on the issue, iden-
    tifying arson as a personal act of vengeance (i.e., burning homes or barns)
    within village society. Such attacks, she argues, did not aim to upset the local
    social order but to undermine the economic welfare of a particular family.
    Setting state forests alight, while certainly a different undertaking in scale
    and intent, bore some similarity to village arson. Both intended to destroy
    the property of those seen as having perpetrated injustice according to local
    mores. Thus these assaults on state property had much in common with the
    German peasant's attacks on forested property in the 1848 Revolution. See
    Schulte, *Village in Court*.
79 Other accounts of forest fires in the Tuchel Heath did not attribute political
    or nationalist motives to the forest fires. The local forester Kohli's lengthy
    first-hand report of the fires made no mention of Polish hostility to the
    foresters and indeed indicates local villagers were extremely worried the fire
    might threaten their own homes. He also notes that Schütte was away at his

father-in-law's funeral when the fires broke out. Likewise, Riesenthal's work, the first detailed account of the heath in this period, did not suggest that forest fires stemmed from political malice. See Kohli, 'Drei Waldbrände in der Tucheler Haide,' *Forstliche Blätter* 8 (1864): 146–66, and Riesenthal, *Bilder aus der Tucheler Heide*, 13.

80 Schütte, *Die Tucheler Haide*, 22–3. The radical nationalist Adalbert Luntowski attempted to fill in the gaps Schütte left. Despite a lack of official statistics, Luntowski stated that an astounding 16,000 hectares had burned during the Kościuszko Uprising of 1794, and at least another 30,000 hectares went up in smoke following Napoleon's defeat of Prussia and the erection of the Duchy of Warsaw in the years 1807–8. See Luntowski, *Westpreußische Wanderungen*, 63–6.

81 Schütte, *Die Tucheler Haide*, 22–3.

82 Czersk petitioners to K.R. Marienwerder, 21 May 1888, APB, Czersk, Nr.16.

83 K.R. Marienwerder to O.F. Feußner, 23 May 1888; O.F. Feußner to K.R. Marienwerder, 16 June 1888, APB, Czersk, Nr.16.

84 Schütte, *Die Tucheler Haide*, 41.

85 Mühlradt, *Ein Besuch in Grüntal*, 39–44.

86 Luntowski, *Westpreußische Wanderungen*, 61.

87 Review of Mühlradt, *Die Tucheler Heide in Wort und Bild*, in the *Deutsche Forstzeitung* 8 (August 1908), cited in Johannes Mühlradt, *Die 'Tucheler Heide in Wort und Bild' in Beurteilung der Presse* (Grünthal: Selbstverlag, 1915), 14.

88 *Denkschrift betreffend die Ergebnisse der Forstverwaltung im Regierungsbezirk Marienwerder in den Jahre 1901, 1902 und 1903* (Marienwerder, 1 November 1904). RB Marienwerder, Abt. für direkte Steuern, Domänen und Forsten, 12–16, APB, Bülowsheide, Nr.67.

89 Luntowski, *Westpreußische Wanderungen*, 63–6. On the school strikes, see John J. Kulczycki, *School Strikes in Prussian Poland, 1901–1907: The Struggle over Bilingual Education* (Boulder: East European Monographs, 1981).

90 Stephen J. Pyne, *Vestal Fire: An Environmental History, Told through Fire, of Europe and Europe's Encounter with the World* (Seattle: University of Washington Press, 1997), 199–200.

91 Wernicke, 'Erdkundliche und naturwissenschaftliche Schülerwanderungen in der Tucheler Heide,' *Monatshefte für den naturkundlichen Unterricht* 5, no. 1 (1912): 14.

92 Wernicke, *Wanderung durch die Tucheler Heide*, 13. The limits on the use of Polish in schools from the 1870s were eased during the Caprivi era, but returned in 1894. State pressure on Polish speakers and Catholics in the region cancelled any goodwill Prussia gained with its economic initiatives.

Balzer, *Die preußische Polenpolitik*, 230; Kulczycki, *School Strikes in Prussian Poland*, 210.

93 Luntowski, *Westpreußische Wanderungen*, 63–6.

94 Wernicke, *Wanderung durch die Tucheler Heide*, 26–7.

95 Luntowski, *Westpreußische Wanderungen*, 74.

96 Wernicke, *Wanderung durch die Tucheler Heide*, 26.

97 Luntowski, *Westpreußische Wanderungen*, 85–6.

98 Bernhard Fernow, who went on to become one of the founders of American forestry, cited in Rodgers, *Bernhard Eduard Fernow*, 16.

99 Schütte, quoted in Wernicke, *Wanderung durch die Tucheler Heide*, 16–17; Luntowski, *Westpreußische Wanderungen*, 61–3. Poachers, unlike wood thieves, could operate only in daylight.

100 R.B. Danzig to OFs, 14 July 1872, APG, Nr.92/17.

101 Schmitt, *Land und Leute in Westpreußen*, 56–8.

102 Polizei-Verordnung, 23 March 1884, BAK, B245/175, b.96–100.

103 Schütte, *Die Tucheler Haide*, 22–3; Luntowski, *Westpreußische Wanderungen*, 63–6. Schütte noted that this practice had been instated already in the 1830s. Luntowski observed that it continued at the time of his writing.

104 Quoted in Luntowski, *Westpreußische Wanderungen*, 78. Friedrich II had also recognized this goal, seeking to inculcate in 'the common man … a Prussian character' by releasing Polish peasants from serfdom (although he did not accomplish this in his lifetime). He also hoped that a few diligent German farmers and schoolmasters, through their interactions with the Poles, would be able to enlighten the locals. We should be clear, however, his project was a 'civilizing,' not a Germanizing, one. Hagen, *Germans, Poles, Jews*, 43–4.

105 Schmitt, *Land und Leute in Westpreußen*; Wagner, *Die preussische Verwaltung des Regierungsbezirks Marienwerder*, 102–9; Wernicke, *Wanderung durch die Tucheler Heide*, 34–6.

106 Borne, 'Die Oedlands-Ankäufe und Aufforstungen,' 404.

107 Mühlradt, *Ein Besuch in Grüntal*, 17–18.

108 Schütte, *Die Tucheler Haide*, 44; Johann Ziesemer, *Die Provinzen Ost- und Westpreußen* (Berlin: W. Spemann, 1901), 12.

109 Schütte, *Die Tucheler Haide*, 48.

110 Saekel, 'Aus der Tucheler Heide,' *Deutsche Forstzeitung* 21 (1906): 438–9.

111 Hermann Wagner, 'Die Land- und Forstwirtschaft,' in *Die deutsche Ostmark*, ed. Deutsche Ostmarkenverein (Lissa i.P.: Eulitz, 1913), 328.

112 Ursula Hannelore Wagner, *Die preussische Verwaltung des Regierungsbezirks Marienwerder*, 102–3.

113 In 1892, there were about 136 foresters working in the Heath. See Borne,

'Die Oedlands-Ankäufe und Aufforstungen,' 406; Luntowski, *Westpreußische Wanderungen*, 6; Schütte, *Die Tucheler Haide*, 44; Wernicke, *Wanderung durch die Tucheler Heide*, 121; Ziesemer, *Die Provinzen Ost- und Westpreußen*, 12.

114 The county of Tuchel, almost entirely covered by the heath, contained only 27,000 inhabitants in 1878. See *Nachweisung über den Ankauf und die Aufforstung von Ländereien im Interesse der Landeskultur* (Regierungsbezirk Marienwerder, 17 September 1878), GStAPK, I HA Rep.87D, Nr.2412.

115 Paul Langhans, 'Karte der Tätigkeit der Ansiedlungskommission fuer die Provinz Westpreußen und Posen, 1886–1896,' *Petermanns Geographische Mitteilungen* 42 (1896): table 9.

116 *Bericht übder die Verwaltung und den Stand der Angelegenheiten des Kreises Tuchel für das Rechnungsjahr 1896/7* (Tuchel, 1897), 6.

117 Balzer, *Die preußische* Polenpolitik, 231.

118 Report on the meeting of the *Staatsministerium*, 8 June 1904, GStAPK, I HA Rep.87ZB, Nr.152, b.93–4. Podbielski had a reputation as a zealous enemy of the Poles. In his previous position as imperial postmaster general, Podbielski refused to allow the delivery of mail using Polish place names instead of German (or Germanized) ones. See records relating to Podbielski's libel case against the Polish publisher Casimir von Rakowski, GStAPK, I HA Rep.87ZB, Nr.368, b.53–8.

119 Bernhart Jähning, 'Die Bevölkerung Westpreußens um 1900,' *Westpreußen Jahrbuch* 42 (1992): 16–20; Helmut Neubach, 'Reichstagswahlen 1881 in Westpreußen,' *Westpreußen Jahrbuch* 31 (1981): 121–6.

120 Jähning, 'Die Bevölkerung Westpreußens um 1900,' 16–20.

121 Szczepan Wierzchoslawski, *Polski Ruch Narodowy w Prusach Zachodnich w Latach 1860–1914* (Warsaw: Polska Akademia Nauk, 1980), 73, 131, 187. At the same time, the Prussian three-class voting system likewise returned improving results for German parties. In the 1903 *Landtag* elections, for example, left liberals won in the urban centres (Danzig, Elbing, Thorn), while National Liberals, Free Conservatives, and Conservatives succeeded in the countryside (indeed, a National Liberal represented the Polish bastion of Tuchel in the heart of the heath). No Centre delegates managed to win a seat in the provincial delegation, because there were few German Catholics, and the Poles managed to win only a few seats. See Report from the Ministry of the Interior (Anlage zu Ib. 4668) on the *Ansiedlungskommission*, GStAPK, I HA Rep.87B, Nr.9694.

122 Wernicke, *Wanderung durch die Tucheler Heide*, 12.

123 Schütte, *Die Tucheler Haide*, 44.

124 'Summarische Nachweisung über die bei der Staatsforstverwaltung

vorgekommenen Erkrankungen von Arbeitern … 1900,' *Sammlung der Druckschriften des Preußischen Hauses der Abgeordneten, 19 Legislaturperiode, IV. Session, 1902.* (Berlin: W. Moeser, 1902), 2:172–3.

125 Meeting of the *Staatsministerium*, 8 June 1904, GStAPK, I HA Rep.87ZB, Nr.152, b.93–4. In GStAPK, I HA Rep.87ZB, Nr.368, b.53–8.
126 Speech by Łosiński in AH, 13 February 1907, *Stenographische Berichte*, 9. Sitzung (Berlin: 1907): 640–1; LAB, STA Rep.01-02, Nr.1814, b.40.
127 Schütte, *Die Tucheler Haide*, 47–8.
128 Borne, 'Die Oedlands-Ankäufe,' 399–401. Borne's proposal received the endorsement of Conservative West Prussian Landtag delegate Bernhard von Puttkamer-Plauth in the 1897 forestry budget debate. See speech by Puttkamer-Plauth, AH, 8 March 1897, *Stenographische Berichte*, 44. Sitzung (Berlin: 1897): 1399–1400.
129 Borne, 'Die Oedlands-Ankäufe,' 405–6.
130 Luntowski, *Westpreußische Wanderungen*, 81.
131 Ziesemer, *Die Provinzen Ost- und Westpreußen*, 12.
132 Mühlradt, *Ein Besuch in Grüntal*, 80. Not everyone saw migrant labour as a necessarily bad thing. Schütte noted that money sent home by girls working in domestic service infused needed cash into the local economy, and while they sometimes returned home pregnant and averse to agricultural labour, they also gained a solid knowledge of the German language and expanded their horizons. See Schütte, *Die Tucheler Haide*, 47.
133 *Denkschrift betreffend die Ergebnisse der Forstverwaltung im Regierungsbezirk Marienwerder in den Jahre 1901, 1902 und 1903* (Marienwerder, 1 November 1904). RB Marienwerder, Abt. für direkte Steuern, Domänen und Forsten, APB, Bülowsheide, Nr.67, 5.
134 Wernicke, *Wanderung durch die Tucheler Heide*, 12.
135 Luntowski, *Westpreußische Wanderungen*, 81–6.
136 Heinrich Sohnrey, 'Der Zug vom Lande,' *Das Land* 1 (1893): 192–3.
137 Schütte, *Die Tucheler Haide*, 47–8.
138 Wernicke, *Wanderung durch die Tucheler Heide*, 34–6.
139 Mühlradt, *Die 'Tucheler Heide in Wort und Bild' in Beurteilung der Presse*, 14.
140 Luntowski, *Westpreußische Wanderungen*, 67–70.
141 Schütte, *Die Tucheler Haide*, 44.
142 Saekel, 'Aus der Tucheler Heide,' 438–9. Such assessments were not limited to the impoverished heath. In 1907, an author describing the achievements of Prussia's Polish policy wrote, 'Earlier one was able to recognize even at a great distance which village or house was Polish and which was German. This has completely changed. The Poles have become

diligent, thrifty, and sober.' Hugo Ganz, *Die Preußische Polenpolitik* (1907), cited in Harry K. Rosenthal, *German and Pole: National Conflict and Modern Myth* (Gainesville: University Presses of Florida, 1976), 44.

143 Mühlradt, *Ein Besuch in Grüntal*, 39–44.

144 Oliver Steinert, 'Reichstagwahlen und Nationalitätenkonflikt: Eine Untersuchung anhand der Wahlergebnisse zwischen 1871 und 1912 im Regierungsbezirk Marienwerder,' *Beiträge zur Geschichte Westpreußens* 16 (1999): 125–219.

145 For further accounts of resistance during the war, see Wiktor Zybajło, 'Ruch oporu w Borach Tucholskich w latach I wojny światowej,' *Szkice Człuchowskie* 2, nos. 2–6 (1991-6): 66–72; and the reports in GStAPK, XIV HA Rep.180, Nr.19181.

146 Otto Busdorf, 'Der Schrecken der Tucheler Heide,' in *Jahrhundertmorde: Kriminalgeschichte aus erster Hand*, ed. Peter Heiss and Christian Lunzer, 198–218 (Vienna: Edition S, 1994).

147 Vejas Gabriel Liulevicius, *War Land on the Eastern Front: Culture, National Identity and German Occupation in World War I* (Cambridge: University of Cambridge Press, 2000).

5. Meaningful Woods

1 Stefan Kühl, *The Nazi Connection: Eugenics, American Racism, and German National Socialism* (Oxford: Oxford University Press, 2002).

2 Sarah Jansen has explored the parallel story of entomology during this period, which shifted from discussing measures against 'damaging insects' in the 1840s to the wholesale campaigns against undifferentiated 'pests' after the turn of the century. She argues modern entomology's constant efforts to sustain monocultures in agriculture and forestry led to ever-more drastic measures against what were seen as 'abnormal' disruptions of production, culminating in an ideology that justified the use of chemical agents not only against insects, but also foreign soldiers during the First World War, and ultimately against human 'pests' during the Nazi era. See her '*Schädlinge': Geschichte eines wissenschaftlichen und politischen Konstrukts 1840–1920* (Frankfurt am Main: Campus Verlag, 2003).

3 On Klopstock as an Enlightenment figure, see Harro Zimmermann, *Freiheit und Geschichte: F.G. Klopstock als historischer Dichter und Denker* (Heidelberg: Winter, 1987).

4 On Humboldt's influence on the idea of social relationships in nature, see Andreas Daum, *Wissenschaftspopularisierung im 19. Jahrhundert: bürgerliche*

Kultur, naturwissenschaftliche Bildung und die deutsche Öffentlichkeit, 1848–1914 (Munich: Oldenbourg, 1998), 459–64.

5 On social Darwinism, see Richard J. Evans, 'In Search of German Social Darwinism: The History and Historiography of a Concept,' in *Medicine and Modernity: Public Health and Medical Care in Nineteenth- and Twentieth-Century Germany*, ed. Manfred Berg and Geoffrey Cocks, 55–79 (Cambridge: Cambridge University Press, 1997); Sabine Maasen and Peter Weingart, *Metaphors and the Dynamics of Knowledge* (London: Routledge, 2000), 43–62.

6 Detlev Peukert has argued forcefully for the centrality of 'scientific' racism to the Nazis' brutal policies against 'community aliens.' See his 'Genesis of the "Final Solution,"' 234–52. Paul Weindling uses Peukert's observation to locate the origins of Nazi racial policies in the rising network of welfare and public health authorities from 1871 onward. See his *Health, Race, and German Politics between National Unification and Nazism, 1870–1945* (Cambridge: Cambridge University Press, 1989).

7 See Bartholomäus Grill, 'Deutschland: ein Waldesmärchen,' *Die Zeit* 25 December 1987: 3; Annemarie Hürlimann, 'Die Eiche, heiliger Baum deutscher Nation,' in *Waldungen: die Deutschen und ihr Wald*, ed. Bernd Weyergraf (Berlin: Akademie der Künste, 1987), 67; Marcus Termeer, *Verkörperungen des Waldes: Eine Körper-, Geschlechter-, und Herrschaftsgeschichte* (Bielefeld: transcript, 2005), 277. Although not specifically mentioning the military metaphor, Michael Imort claims that 'Germans celebrate the evident order, straightness, and tidiness of the managed forest landscape as an embodiment of "typical German" characteristics.' Imort, 'A Sylvan People,' 56.

8 Elias Canetti, *Crowds and Power*, trans. Carol Stewart (New York: Noonday, 1991), 173–4. James Scott notes that a rationally managed forest 'quickly became a powerful aesthetic as well.' While this might have been true for foresters, it failed to gain much ground among the public. See Scott, *Seeing Like a State*, 15–18.

9 On the National Socialists' mobilization of the forest as a martial metaphor, see Ulrich Linse, 'Der Film "Ewiger Wald" – oder: Die Überwindung der Zeit durch den Raum,' *Zeitschrift für Pädigogik* (Beiheft 31, 1993): 57–75.

10 A collection of hundreds of forest poems compiled by Otto Boeckel, the Hessian folklorist and anti-Semitic politician, contained no obvious comparisons to the military. See Einem deutschen Waldfreund [Otto Boeckel], *Der deutsche Wald im deutschen Lied* (Berlin: H. Walter, 1899).

11 Wilhelm Heinrich Riehl, *Die Naturgeschichte des Volkes als Grundlage einer deutschen Social-Politik* (Stuttgart: Cotta, 1854), 1:48.

12 Brüning, 'Moderne Forstwirtschaft ist die Grab Altwürdigen Eichen und Buchen,' *Jahresbericht der westfälischen Provinzialvereins für Wissenschaft und Kunst* 18 (1889): 127; Heinrich Pudor, 'Von der Schönheit des Baumes,' *Heimat und Welt* 2 (1911/12): 349–52; Pudor, *Waldpolitik* (Gautzsch bei Leipzig: Felix Dietrich, 1914), 21–2.

13 'Forstästhetik,' *Die Umschau* 9 (1905): 554–5.

14 Ibid., 553; Konrad Guenther, *Der Naturschutz*, 59; 'Hans Thoma und die Pflege des Waldes,' *Mitteilungen des Bundes Heimatschutz* 2 (1906): 101; K. Mischke, 'Naturdenkmäler,' *Mutter Erde* 4 (1900): 323–4; Johannes Mühlradt, *Die 'Tucheler Heide in Wort und Bild,'* 1:94–5; Pudor, *Waldpolitik*, 18.

15 See Harrison, *Forests*, 176–7; Peter Linebaugh, 'Karl Marx, the Theft of Wood, and Working-Class Composition,' *Crime and Social Justice* 6 (1976): 7.

16 On Roßmäßler, see his autobiography, *Mein Leben*; the introduction by W. Kobelt-Schwanheim to Roßmäßler's *Das Gebirgsdorfchen*; Daum, *Wissenschaftspopularisierung*, 138–61; and Alfred Kelly, *The Descent of Darwin: The Popularization of Darwinism in Germany, 1860–1914* (Chapel Hill: University of North Carolina Press, 1981), 18–19.

17 Emil Adolf Roßmäßler, *Der Wald* (Leipzig: C.F. Winter'sche Verlagshandlung, 1863), 1–2.

18 Daum, *Wissenschaftspopularisierung*, 158.

19 On Roßmäßler's role in the national movement, see ibid., 160–1.

20 Roßmäßler, *Der Wald*, 9–10; Roßmäßler, quoted in Dominick, *Environmental Movement in Germany*, 36–8. Roßmäßler's idea of nature functioning as a united community, articulated in 1863, came very close to the biologist Ernst Haeckel's concept of ecology, which he formally introduced in 1866. See Haeckel, *Generellen Morphologie der Organismen* (Berlin, 1866), 286, quoted in Barthelmeß, *Landschaft*, 11.

21 Roßmäßler, *Der Wald*, 20–1.

22 Ilse Jahn and Isolde Schmidt, *Matthias Jacob Schleiden (1804–1881): Sein Leben in Selbstzeugnissen* (Halle: Deutscher Akademie der Naturforscher Leopoldina e.V., 2005), 204–15; Marianne Scholz, *Letzte Lebensstationen: Zum postakademischen Wirken des deutschen Botanikers Matthias Jacob Schleiden (1804–1881)* (Berlin: Verlag für Wissenschafts- und Regionalgeschichte, 2001), 29–35.

23 Schleiden, *Für Baum und Wald*, v–vi.

24 Ibid., 37–8.

25 Ibid., 19–20.

26 Ibid., 139–44.

27 Ibid., 105–6.

28 Ibid., 108–9. Schleiden did join with other German nationalists on the

question of Alsace, however. In a portentous move, he condemned the French for asserting the Rhine as their natural boundary, arguing the Vosges Mountains and the Ardennes formed the natural boundary of German-speaking peoples in the west, strengthening his argument for the political unity of the Rhine basin. He did not address the role of the Netherlands in his discussion, however.

29 On Hellwald, see Kelly, *Descent of Darwin*, 104; Maasen and Weingart, *Metaphors and the Dynamics of Knowledge*, 45–6.

30 Friedrich von Hellwald [?], 'Waldbäume und Wälder,' *Das Ausland* 44 (1871): 73.

31 Ibid.

32 Ibid., 139.

33 Ibid., 224–7.

34 Maasen and Weingart, *Metaphors and the Dynamics of Knowledge*, 46, 52–3.

35 On Gumprecht, see 'Zur Erinngerung an Adolf Gumprecht,' *Der Arbeiterfreund* 37 (1899): 373–5; H. Ellissen, 'Gumprecht, Adolf,' in *Biographisches Jahrbuch und deutscher Nekrolog*, ed. Anton Bettelheim (Berlin: Georg Reimer, 1900), 4:188.

36 Adolf Gumprecht, 'Arbeitsgelegenheit durch Wald-, Moor-, und Heidekultur,' *Der Arbeiterfreund* 21 (1883): 225–6.

37 Ibid., 230–1.

38 Francé, along with Roßmäßler, stands as a key figure in the popularization of science in Germany. Together with Wilhelm Bölsche, he founded Kosmos, Germany's first natural science book society (which had its own journal of the same name), in 1903. By 1912, Kosmos membership reached 100,000, although Francé had broken with this group to start his own venture, the Deutsche Naturwissenschaftliche Gesellschaft, in 1909. Within a year, it had 15,000 members. See Daum, *Wissenschaftspopularisierung*, 316–17. For more on Francé, see his *Lebenserinnerungen* (Leipzig: Alfred Kröner, 1927); and Ulrich Linse, 'Der deutsche Wald als Kampfplatz politischer Ideen,' *Revue d'Allemange* 22, no. 2 (1990): 341–45.

39 Raoul H. Francé, *Das Pflanzenleben Deutschlands und seiner Nachbarländer*, vol. 1 of *Das Leben der Pflanze* (Stuttgart: Kosmos, 1906), 370. The publishers of *Das Leben der Pflanze* included several positive reviews from the mass media in the book, including praise for its 'completely modern foundation,' from the liberal *Hamburger Fremdenblatt*, and tribute for its granting public access to 'modern knowledge' of the plant world, from Basel's *Nationalzeitung*.

40 Francé, *Das Pflanzenleben Deutschlands*, 370. See also Raoul H. Francé, *Bilder aus dem Leben des Waldes* (Stuttgart: Kosmos, 1909), 13; Francé, 'Gesetz des Waldes,' *Kosmos* 5, no. 1 (1908): 7.

41 Francé, *Bilder aus dem Leben des Waldes*, 37.

42 Raoul H. Francé, 'Naturgesetz und Kulturleben,' *Kosmos* (1907): 245–6; Francé, 'Soziologie im Walde,' *März* 2 (November 1908): 217–18. *März* was a periodical supported by Hermann Hesse and prominent left-liberal politicians. See David Blackbourn, *The Long Nineteenth Century* (Oxford: Oxford University Press, 1998), 388.

43 On social Darwinism, see Evans, 'In Search of German Social Darwinism,' 55–79.

44 Francé, *Das Pflanzenleben Deutschlands*, 374–5. Indeed, Francé explicitly rejected Social Darwinism, insisting that plants' bitter struggle for survival had no analogue among humans, for 'in human society almost everyone finds his place, even if it is more modest than the his capacities allow; in the forest, however, the social struggles are of shocking violence and bitterness.' Francé, 'Soziologie im Walde,' 217.

45 Francé, *Bilder aus dem Leben des Waldes*, 38; see also 15–16.

46 Francé, 'Gesetz des Waldes,' 8. Francé repeatedly emphasized the social utility of his insights. He believed that the study of arboreal associations would aid anthropologists and economists to understand the principle of cooperation in socialism, as well as the 'conditions of the human masses.' Francé, *Das Pflanzenleben Deutschlands*, 375.

47 Francé, *Bilder aus dem Leben des Waldes*, 38; Francé, 'Soziologie im Walde,' 217.

48 Francé, *Das Pflanzenleben Deutschlands*, 374; Francé, 'Gesetz des Waldes,' 8–9; Francé, 'Soziologie im Walde,' 217–18; Francé, *Bilder aus dem Leben des Waldes*, 38–39.

49 Francé, *Das Pflanzenleben* Deutschlands, 524–5. Francé observed that foresters disrupted this natural social order when they cleared away the underbrush, leaving only the organisms in the soil, the mosses and lichens, and the trees. He concluded in tautological fashion, 'That this artificially limited social order cannot be healthy and harmonious, however, is demonstrated by the frequency of human suffering.' Francé, 'Soziologie im Walde,' 217–18.

50 Francé, 'Soziologie im Walde,' 217–18; Francé, *Das Pflanzenleben Deutschlands und seiner Nachbarländer*, 374.

51 Plant societies could have a variety of forms of government, ranging from democratic republics to aristocratic free states. 'The forest,' according to Francé, 'is an oligarchy … The patrician order of the trees rules outright, and the rest of the vegetation satisfies itself with subordinate roles.' Francé, *Das Pflanzenleben Deutschlands*, 524–5.

52 Francé, 'Soziologie im Walde,' 215; Francé, *Das Pflanzenleben* Deutschlands, 374.

53 Francé, *Das Pflanzenleben Deutschlands*, 542.

54 Francé, 'Gesetz des Waldes,' 8.

55 On Ratzel and the concept of *Lebensraum*, see Woodruff D. Smith, *Politics and the Sciences of Culture*, 223–7.

56 Francé, *Das Pflanzenleben Deutschlands*, 382; Francé, *Bilder aus dem Leben des Waldes*, 36; Francé, 'Soziologie im Walde,' 214–215.

57 Francé, 'Soziologie im Walde,' 216. Francé's background embodied the ethnic diversity of the Austro-Hungarian Empire. Born in Vienna to a Bohemian German father (of French descent) and a Czech mother (whose family included Polish and Hungarian branches), he spent his childhood both in Hungarian lowlands and the Tyrolean Alps. See his *Lebenserinnerungen*.

58 Francé, *Das Pflanzenleben Deutschlands*, 401; Francé, 'Gesetz des Waldes,' 8.

59 Francé, *Das Pflanzenleben Deutschlands*, 534. It is interesting to note that Francé almost exclusively used the term *society* (*Gesellschaft*) to describe the social relationships among plants. In this case, however, highlighting the differences between the foreigners and the natives, he chose to describe the plants as belonging to a 'community' (*Gemeinschaft*).

60 See Geoff Eley, 'Social Imperialism in Germany: Reformist Synthesis or Reactionary Sleight of Hand?' in *From Unification to Nazism*, ed. Geoff Eley, 2nd ed. (London: Routledge, 1992), 154–70. Francé's relationship with the radical right remains unclear. Although he was friends with Franz Hartmann and Max Seiling (both members of the *völkisch* and occultist Guido-von-List-Gesellschaft), Francé's only biographer claims he was apolitical. Moreover, the Nazis appear to have taken an ambivalent attitude towards his work, and he spent the Nazi period (until his death in 1943) resident outside of Germany. See René Romain Roth, *Raoul H. Francé and the Doctrine of Life* (N.d.: self-published, 2000): 133–41.

61 Rudolf Düesberg, *Der Wald als Erzieher* (Berlin: Parey, 1910), 138–39.

62 Ibid., 202, 138.

63 Ibid., 17, 42.

64 Ibid., 138–9.

65 Ibid., 193, 182.

66 Ibid., 138–43.

67 Ibid., 147–52.

68 Ibid., 152–4, 185.

69 Ibid., iii–iv, 144–5, 158.

70 Ibid., 157, 145–6.

71 Ibid., 158–73, 183–4.

72 Ibid., 192–3. Elsewhere, Düesberg regarded a lack of settlement space as justifiable grounds for war: ibid., 146.

73 Fritz Stern, *The Politics of Cultural Despair: A Study in the Rise of the German Ideology* (Berkeley: University of California Press, 1961), 122.

74 Düesberg, *Der Wald als Erzieher*, 141, 202. Surprisingly, Düesberg displayed none of Francé's hostility to foreign species. Ibid., 8.

75 Survey submitted by Düesberg to Conwentz, 12 October 1900, SBPK, Nachlass Conwentz.

76 See Rudolf Rüsten, *Was tut Not? Ein Führer durch die gesamte Literatur der Deutschbewegung* (Leipzig: G. Hedeler, 1914).

77 The effort to remove Düesberg foundered on the reluctance of the Ministry of Agriculture to transfer him. The ministry feared crossing the prince, who had previously promised Düesberg could stay in his position, despite his apparent subsequent approval of Düesberg's reassignment. See correspondence between the Ministry of Agriculture and the Hofmarschallamt, 22 April 1909 to 1 July 1912, GStAPK, I HA Rep.87D, Nr.969, Düesberg.

78 See Matthew Levinger, *Enlightened Nationalism: The Transformation of Prussian Political Culture, 1806–1848* (Oxford: Oxford University Press, 2000).

79 Linse, 'Der deutsche Wald als Kampfplatz politischer Ideen,' 341–5; Hürlimann, 'Die Eiche, heiliger Baum deutscher Nation,' 67. Neither of these authors cites any evidence for what have become commonplace assertions about the oak.

80 Hellwald, 'Waldbäume und Wälder,' 201–2.

81 Carl Berthold, *Darstellungen aus der Natur* (Cologne: J.P. Bachem, 1884), 177–8.

82 Hermann Jäger, 'Die Eiche,' *Vom Fels zum Meer* (September 1884): 671–5. Jäger was the court gardener for the Grand Duke of Saxe-Weimar-Eisenach.

83 Schulenburg, 'Deutsche Eichen und Linden,' 1083.

84 Theodor Fontane, 'Die Königseiche,' in *Theodor Fontane: Werke, Schriften und Briefe*, div. 2: *Wanderungen durch die Mark Brandenburg*, vol. 2, ed. Walter Keitel (Munich: Karl Hanser, 1977), 120–3.

85 The art historian Max Schasler quoted in Jäger, 'Die Eiche,' 676.

86 Wilhelm Mannhardt, *Der Baumkultus der Germanen und ihrer Nachbarstämme*, vol. 1 of *Wald- und Feldkulte*, 2nd ed. (1875; Berlin: Bornträger, 1904–5), 2.

87 *Wilhelm und Augusta: Ein Eichen und Epheu-Kranz um unser allverehrtes und allgeliebtes Deutsches Kaiser- und Preußisches Königs-Paar zu der Jubelfeier Allerhöchstihrer Goldenen Hochzeit den 11. Juni 1879* (Berlin: Wilhelm Schultze, 1879)., AP Gdansk, Nr.10/1658, b.104–10.

88 Jäger, 'Die Eiche,' 675.

89 Salisch, *Forstästhetik*, 83.

90 Rau, Fießler, Auerbach, Ebner, and Ebner, 'Die deutsche Eiche: Ehrengabe für Seine Majestät den Deutschen Kaiser,' *Illustrierte Zeitung* 17 June 1871: 428.

91 Joseph Kürschner, *Das ist des Deutschen Vaterland* (Berlin: Hermann Hillger, 1896), cover.

92 Hürlimann, 'Die Eiche, heiliger Baum deutscher Nation,' 62–6. And just as Germans of various political stripes contested the oak, so too the ancient hero Arminius (Hermann) found himself a national symbol subject to claims by liberals, conservatives, and socialists. See Andreas Dörner, 'Der Mythos der nationalen Einheit: Symbolpolitik und Deutungskämpfe bei der Einweihung des Hermannsdenkmals im Jahre 1875,' *Archiv für Kulturgeschichte* 79, no. 2 (1997): 389–416.

93 Schleiden, *Für Baum und Wald*, 30–1.

94 Paul Kummer, 'Der Baum des deutschen Volkes,' *Daheim* 6 (25 June 1870): 623–4. In his 1885 book on the German *Heimat*, August Sach plagiarized many of these passages from Kummer. See Sach, *Die deutsche Heimat*, 64–5.

95 Karl Strackerjan, 'Ist die Eiche oder die Linde der Baum des deutschen Volkes?' in *Einunddreißigstes Programm der Vorschule und der Realschule zu Oldenburg* (Oldenburg: Gerhard Stalling, 1874), cited in Uwe Hentschel, 'Der Lindenbaum in der deutschen Literatur des 18. und 19. Jahrhunderts,' *Orbis Litterarum* 60, no. 5 (2005): 359–61. On Strackerjan, see Eric Kurlander, '*Völkisch* Nationalism and Universalism on the Margins of the Reich: A Comparison of Majority and Minority Liberalism in Germany, 1898–1913,' in *German History from the Margins: Visions of Community between Nationalism and Particularism, 1850–1933* (Bloomington: Indiana University Press, 2006), 88.

96 K. Hofmann von Nauborn, 'Linde als nationaler Baum der Deutschen,' *Illustrierte Zeitung* 10 June 1871: 403.

97 Johannes Scherr, *Deutsche Kultur- und Sittengeschichte*, 7th ed. (Leipzig: O. Wigand, 1879), 8. In his 1885 book on the German *Heimat*, August Sach plagiarized this passage from Scherr. See Sach, *Die deutsche Heimat, Landschaft und Volkstum*, 69.

98 Schulenburg, 'Deutsche Eichen und Linden,' 1082–3.

99 Otto Lohr, *Die Linde, ein deutscher Baum* (Spandau: Gustav Schob, 1889), 1.

100 Ibid., 2–6, 20–1.

101 Confino, *The Nation as a Local Metaphor*, 207. Confino misidentifies the linden in the postcard as an oak (181), which indicates the extent to which the linden has been forgotten by historians.

102 Lohr, *Die Linde, ein deutscher Baum,* vii.
103 On the mentality of Prague Germans, see Gary Cohen, *The Politics of Ethnic Survival: Germans in Prague, 1861–1914* (Princeton: Princeton University Press, 1981). Lohr's work was panned in a review article for its 'stupid collection of citations,' a method by which, according to the critic, one could prove even the palm was essentially German. See Ernst Kossmann, quoted in Alfred Biese, 'Zur Literatur der Geschichte des Naturgefühls,' *Zeitschrift für vergleichende Literaturgeschichte* 7 (1894): 339.
104 Sach, *Die deutsche Heimat, Landschaft und Volkstum,* 71.
105 Düesberg, *Der Wald als Erzieher,* 141; Francé, *Das Pflanzenleben Deutschlands,* 223.
106 Edward Dickinson argues that the Alps, with their dramatic and violent physiognomy, provided a more suitable venue for nineteenth-century racists to infuse the landscape with racial meaning. See his 'Germanizing the Alps and Alpinizing the Germans, 1875–1935,' *German Studies Review* 33, no. 3 (2010): 579–602.
107 Francé, *Die Welt der Pflanze: Eine Volkstümliche Botanik* (Berlin: Ullstein, 1912), 287.
108 Francé, 'Der deutsche Urwald,' 485, 488–90.
109 Düesberg, *Der Wald als Erzieher,* 138.
110 Lekan, *Imagining the Nation in Nature.*

Conclusion

1 Barthelmeß, *Landschaft,* 96–8.
2 Samuel Temple, 'The Natures of Nation. Negotiating Modernity in the Landes de Gascogne,' *French Historical Studies* 32 (2009): 419–46.
3 Danny Trom, 'Natur und nationale Identität: Der Streit um den Schutz der "Natur" um die Jahrhundertwende in Deutschland und Frankreich,' in *Nation und Emotion,* ed. Etienne François, Hannes Siegrist, and Jakob Vogel, 147–67 (Göttingen: Vandenhoeck & Ruprecht, 1995). For a comparison of German and Italian attitudes towards the forest, see Reinhard Johler, 'Wald, Kultur, Nation: Ein deutsch-italienische Vergleich,' in *Der Wald: Ein deutscher Mythos?,* ed. Albrecht Lehmann and Klaus Schriewer (Berlin: Dietrich Reimer, 2000), 83–96.
4 Tamara L. Whited, *Forests and Peasant Politics in Modern France* (New Haven, CT: Yale University Press, 2000), 181–91.
5 E. Klein, *Heimatschutz und Heimatpflege* (Berlin: C. Spiethoff, 1914), 45–6.
6 Robert Hewison, *The Heritage Industry* (London: Methuen, 1987); John Rennie Short, *Imagined Country: Environment, Culture and Society* (London:

Routledge, 1991), 77–81; Ken Worpole, 'Village School or Blackboard
Jungle?,' in *Patriotism*, ed. Raphael Samuel, 125–40 (London: Routledge,
1989); Patrick Wright, *On Living in an Old Country: The National Past in
Contemporary Britain* (London: Verso, 1985).

7 Daniels, 'Political Iconography of Woodland,' 45–7.

8 Keith Thomas, *Man and the Natural World: Changing Attitudes in England,
1500–1800* (New York: Pantheon Books, 1983), 217–22; Daniels, 'Political
Iconography of Woodland,' 43, 52–3.

9 Helsinger, 'Turner and the Representation of England,' 106; see also her
Rural Scenes.

10 On Ruskin, see Daniels and Cosgrove. 'Introduction: Iconography and
Landscape,' 5–6; Peter Fuller, 'The Geography of Mother Nature,' in *The
Iconography of Landscape*, ed. Stephen Daniels and Denis Cosgrove, 11–31
(Cambridge: Cambridge University Press, 1988); Jan Marsh, *Back to the
Land: The Pastoral Impulse in England, 1880–1914* (New York: Quartet, 1982);
Jeffrey L. Spear, *Dreams of an English Eden: Ruskin and His Tradition in Social
Criticism* (New York: Columbia University Press, 1984); Short, *Imagined
Country*, 45.

11 Indeed, several *Heimat* activists identified Ruskin as inspiration for both
Riehl and the movement. See Karl Johannes Fuchs, 'Naturschutz und Indu-
strie,' *Die Woche* 7, no. 38 (1905): 1636–7; Conwentz, *Care of Natural Monu-
ments*, 4–5; Eugen Gradmann, *Heimatschutz und Landschaftspflege* (Stuttgart:
Stecker & Schröder, 1910), 4; Georg Minde-Pouet, 'Naturdenkmalpflege,'
Aus dem Posener Lande 6 (1911): 164.

12 Other such reformers on the left included George Stuart (radical), and
Cecil Sharp and Vaughan Williams (socialists). See Marsh, *Back to the Land*,
1–22; Alun Howkins, 'The Discovery of Rural England,' in *Englishness:
Politics and Culture, 1880–1920*, ed. Robert Colls and Philip Dodd (London:
Croom Helm, 1986), 68–9, 74–5.

13 See Rollins, *Greener Vision of Home*; Diethart Kerbs and Jürgen Reulecke, eds.
Handbuch der deutschen Reformbewegungen, 1880–1933 (Wupperthal: Peter
Hammer, 1998).

14 Karl Ditt, 'Nature Conservation in England and Germany 1900–70: Forerunner of Environmental Protection?,' *Contemporary European History* 5, no.
1 (1996): 1–28.

15 For a comparison of British and German liberalism, see Geoff Eley, 'Putting
German (and British) Liberalism into Context: Liberalism, Europe, and the
Bourgeoisie 1840–1914' (unpublished Comparative Study of Social Trans-
formations paper, Ann Arbor, 1990).

16 Gustav Sundbärg, quoted in Frykman and Löfgren, *Culture Builder*, 42.

17 Löfgren, 'Landscapes of the Mind,' 11–12.

18 Ibid., 10.

19 Frykman and Löfgren, *Culture Builders*, 57–64.

20 Michelle Facos, *Nationalism and the Nordic Imagination: Swedish Art of the 1890s* (Berkeley: University of California Press, 1998).

21 Sheri Berman, *The Social Democratic Moment: Ideas and Politics in the Making of Interwar Europe* (Cambridge, MA: Harvard University Press, 1998).

22 Madeleine Hurd, *Public Spheres, Public Mores, and Democracy: Hamburg and Stockholm, 1870–1914* (Ann Arbor: University of Michigan Press, 2000).

23 Ulrich Linse, *Zurück, o Mensch, zur Mutter Erde: Landkommunen in Deutschland 1890–1933* (Munich: DTV: 1983).

24 Williams, *Turning to Nature in Germany*.

25 Applegate, *A Nation of Provincials*, 151.

26 Susanne Ude-Koeller, *Auf gebahnten Wegen: Zum Naturdiskurs am Beispiel des Harzklubs e.V.* (Berlin: Waxmann, 2004), 144–8.

27 Dominick, *Environmental Movement in Germany*, 113.

28 Thomas Lekan, 'Regionalism and the Politics of Landscape Preservation in the Third Reich,' *Environmental History Review* 4 (July 1999): 384–404.

29 Dominick, *Environmental Movement in Germany*, 91.

30 Imort, 'Sylvan People, 55–80; Michael Imort, '"Eternal Forest – Eternal *Volk*": The Rhetoric and Reality of National Socialist Forest Policy,' in *How Green Were the Nazis? Nature, Environment, and Nation in the Third Reich*, ed. Franz-Josef Brüggemeier, Mark Cioc, and Thomas Zeller, 43–72 (Athens, OH: Ohio University Press, 2005).

31 Thomas Zeller, *Driving Germany: The Landscape of the German Autobahn, 1930–1970* (Oxford: Berghahn Books, 2007).

32 Uekoetter, *The Green and the Brown*. See also the excellent collection of essays that take a range of different approaches to the issue of Nazi environmentalism: Brüggemeier, Cioc, and Zeller, eds., *How Green Were the Nazis?*

33 Imort, 'Sylvan People.'

34 Lekan, *Imagining the Nation in Nature*.

35 Sandra Chaney, *Nature of the Miracle Years: Conservation in West Germany, 1945–1975* (Oxford: Berghahn Books, 2008), 98, 243.

36 Ibid., 243–5; Thomas Rohkrämer, 'Contemporary Environmentalism and Its Links with the German Past,' in *The Culture of German Environmentalism: Anxieties, Visions, Realities*, ed. Axel Goodbody, 47–62 (Oxford: Berghahn, 2002).

37 Markham, *Environmental Organizations in Modern Germany*.

38 Albrecht Lehmann, 'Mythos Deutscher Wald,' *Der Bürger im Staat* 51, no. 1 (2001): 4–9.

39 Franz-Josef Brüggemeier, '*Waldsterben*: The Construction and Deconstruction of an Environmental Problem,' in *Nature in German History*, ed. Christof Mauch (Oxford: Berghahn, 2004), 118–31.

40 Johnathan Olsen, *Nature and Nationalism: Right-Wing Ecology and the Politics of Identity in Contemporary Germany* (New York: St Martin's, 1999).

41 Arvid Nelson, *Cold War Ecology: Forests, Farms, and People in the East German Landscape, 1945–1989* (New Haven, CT: Yale University Press, 2005).

Works Cited

Archival Sources

Archiwum Państwowe w Bydgoszczy (APB)

Nadleśnictwa z terenu woj. pomorskiego

Nadleśnictwo Czersk/Oberförsterei Czersk
  Nr.16 – Beleidigung und Wiedersetzlichkeit gegen Forstbeamten
  Nr.17 – Die alljährlich der Oberstaats-Anwaltschaft einzureichenden Übersi-
  chten an Holzdiebstählen pp.

Nadleśnictwo Przewodnik/Oberförsterei Bülowsheide
  Nr.67 – Ergebnisse der Forstverwaltung im Regierungsbezirk Marienwerder
  in den Jahren 1901–3
  Nr.75 – Historische Funde

Nadleśnictwo Woziwoda/Oberförsterei Schüttenwalde
  Nr.23 – Ergebnisse der Forstverwaltung im Regierungsbezirk Marienwerder
  in den Jahren 1901–3
  Nr.31 – Defraudations-Liste pro 1873
  Nr.32 – Defraudations-Liste pro 1874
  Nr.33 – Defraudations-Liste pro 1876

Archiwum Państwowe w Gdańsku (APG)

Regierungsbezirk Marienwerder – Nr.10
  /1658 – Empfohlene Schriften
  /8722 – Holz-Verkauf-Taxe 1880/5

/8723 – Holz-Verkauf-Taxe 1903–9
/10143 – Walderholungsstätte des Vaterländischen Frauenvereins in
  Graudenz
/10209 – Verzeichnis der polnischen Vereine im Kreis Tuchel

Nadleśnictwo Bartel Wielke (Gross Bartel) – Nr.90
  /9 – Forstbeamten Vereinswesen

Oberförsterei Sobbowitz (Nadleśnictwo w Sobowidzach) – Nr.92
  /97 – Inexegieble Forststrafen; Verwendung fer Forststrafarbeiter
  /99 – Verstärkung des Forstschutzes durch Jäger- und Forstschutzmänner

Bundesarchiv Koblenz (BAK)

Bundesforschungsamt für Naturschutz und Landschaftsökologie – B245
  /76 – Grunewald
  /108 – Einzelmaßnahmen in Brandenburg
  /141 – Kreis Teltow
  /175 – Naturschutz Angelegenheiten im Reichsgau Danzig-Westpreußen
  /176 – Kreise Konitz, etc.
  /177 – Kreisen Bromberg, Kulm, Schwetz, Thorn, Tuchel
  /256 – Umfrage der Kommission zur Herausgabe eines forstbotanischen
    Merkbuches für die Mark Brandenburg
  /257 – Umfrage der Kommission zur Herausgabe eines forstbotanischen
    Merkbuches für die Mark Brandenburg

Nachlaß Alfred Hugenberg – N1231
  /111 – Reden, Aufsätze

Geheimes Staatsarchiv Preußischer Kulturbesitz (GStAPK)

Abgeordnetenhaus – I HA Rep.169 C
  23 Nr.39 – Erhaltung der Wälder … in der Nähe von Großstädten
  23 Nr.52 – Walderhaltung bei Berlin

Anhang Nr.71 – Festschrift zum 10 jährigen Stiftungsfest

Ansiedlungskommission – I HA Rep.212
  Nr.5222 – Zwanzig Jahre deutscher Kulturarbeit

Geheime Zivilkabinet – I HA Rep.89
  Nr.31279–80 – Forstwirtschaft und Forstbeamte
  Nr.31820–1 – Der Grunewald bei Berlin

Justizministerium – I HA Rep.84a
  Nr.577 – Forstdiebstahlsgesetz und Forstkontraventionen (Fiche Nr.12969–74)
  Nr.10716–8 – Forstdiebstahlsgesetz und Forstkontraventionen
  Nr.11484 – Grunewald bei Berlin
  Nr.11489 – Bestrafung der Widersetzlichkeit bei Forst- und Jagdverbrechen
  Nr.11493 – Befugnis der Forstbeamten zum gebrauch der Waffen gegen Forstkontraventen
  Nr.15736 – Generalberichte zum Forstdiebstahlsgesetz und über Forstvergehen

Landratsamt Berent – XIV HA Rep.184
  Nr.49 – Miscellanea
  Nr.68 – Baumfrevel

Ministerium des Innern – Rep.77
  Tit.1433 Forsten
  Nr.14 – Die Verhütung von Holzdiebstählen in der Nähe der Stadt Berlin

Ministerium für Landwirtschaft, Domänen und Forsten – I HA Rep.87

Ministerium für Landwirtschaft …, Forstabteilung – I HA Rep.87 D
  Nr.48–9 – Forstbereisungen durch die Oberlandforstmeister
  Nr.103 – Erteilung von Nachrichten und Informationen
  Nr.969 – Personalakten, Düesberg 1879–1922
  Nr.1511 – Personalakten, Schütte 1853–1890
  Nr.2412–14 – Ankauf von Ödländereien und Aufforstung (1878–80)
  Nr.3332 – Fremdländische Bäume

Ministerium für Landwirtschaft …, Landwirtschaftsabteilung – I HA Rep.87 B
  Nr.34 – Beschäftigung erwerbsoloser Arbeiter aus Berlin
  Nr.211–22 – Beschäftigung ausländischer Arbeiter
  Nr.3131–4 – Naturschutz
  Nr.3144–5 – Naturschutzparks
  Nr.3149 – Zeitungsausschnitte über Naturschutzgebiete
  Nr.9486 – Kredit für Domänen- und Forstankäufe
  Nr.9491 – Verschiedene Eingaben
  Nr.9581 – Die meliorationstechn. Angelegenheiten der Ansiedlungskommission
  Nr.9637–40 – Eingaben, Vorschläge etc. über die Maßnahmen
  Nr.9694 – Ansiedlungspolitik in den Ostprovinzen

Ministerium für Landwirtschaft …, Zentralbüro – I HA Rep.87 ZB

Nr.152–3 – Verhalten der Staatsbeamten bei Wahlen

Nr.190 – Maßnahmen gegen die Ausbreitung des Polentums (Eingaben)

Nr.368 – Podbielski Personalakten

Nr.370–4 – Zeitungsausschnitte Podbielski

Ministerium für Volkswohlfahrt – I HA Rep.191

Nr.185 – Erhaltung des Waldbestandes

Ostmarkenverein – I HA Rep.195

Nr.35, v.2 – Ortsgruppe Berlin

Nr.37, v.1 – Ortsgruppe Beuthen

Nr.115 – Reiseberichte Voßburgs

Nr.314 – Zeitungen, Berichte, Jahresabrechnung, usw

Regierungsforstamt Potsdam – X HA Rep.2 B III

Nr.1514 – Verkauf von Flächen

Regierung Danzig – XIV HA Rep.180

Nr.15053 – Waldschutz

Nr.16776 – Deutscher Heimatbund für den Osten (1910)

Nr.17497 – Verschiedenes (incl. Ostmarkenverein) (1908–20)

Nr.17579 – Denkmalpflege

Nr.17715 – Patriotische Feiern (1895–1917)

Nr.19181 – Unruhen im Walde (1918)

Regierung Marienwerder – XIV HA O Rep.A181

Nr.30320 – Bau eines Museums in Graudenz

Nr.31606 – Deutscher Heimatbund für den Osten

Nr.31817 – Statistik des nationalen Besitzstandes

Nr.31890 – Ansiedlungen im Kreis Tuchel

Nr.32108 – Deckung der Sandscholle

Nr.32130 – Aufforstung von Ödländereien in Kr. Flatow

Nr.32250 – Geschäftskalender für die Kgl. Oberförstereien des RB
Marienwerder

Staatsministerium – I HA Rep.90

Nr.1632–3 – Grunewald

Landesarchiv Berlin (LAB)

Forstverwaltung – STA Rep.12

Nr.604 – Wald und Wiesengürtel

Fotosammlung – STA Rep.370-09
   Postkarten aus dem Grunewald

Generalbüro – STA Rep.01-02
   Nr.639 – Massnahmen zur Erhaltung eines ausreichenden Waldbestandes
   Nr.1814 – Kauf des Grunewaldes durch die Stadt Berlin

Nachlaß Gunter Thiel – STA Rep.200 Acc.3647
   Nr.1 – Doktorarbeit
   Nr.7 – Literaturverzeichnis

Stadtveroretenversammlung zu Berlin – STA Rep.00-02/1
   Nr.272 – Stenographische Berichte über die öffentlichen Sitzungen der SVV
      1908
   Nr.1580 – Die Erhaltung der Wälder und Seen in der Umgebung Berlins
   Nr.1581 – Schutz der Stadt Berlin gegen Verunstaltungen

Landeshauptarchiv Brandenburg (LHAB)

Pr. Br. Rep.2A – Regierung Potsdam
   I P Präsidialregistatur
      8. Finanzverwaltung, Forst-S.
         Nr.1068–70 – Volkspark Grunewald & Heerstraße
         Nr.1071 – Waldzweckverband

   II Abteilung für Kirchen- und Schulwesen
      Gen.
         Nr.1746 – Naturdenkmalpflege in Preußen
         Nr.1747 – Naturdenkmalpflege in Preußen

   III F Abteilung für direkte Steuern, Domänen und Forsten
      Jüngere Forstregistratur
         Nr.3094 – Walderhaltung in der Umgebung Berlins
         Nr.3095 – Walderhaltung in der Umgebung Berlins
         Nr.3101 – Walderhaltung in der Umgebung Berlins
         Nr.3645–6 – Naturdenkmalpflege
         Nr.3867–8 – Armenpflege, Beerdigung Leichen
      Oberförsterei Grunewald
         Nr.9147 – Friedhof in Schildhorn
         Nr.9176 – Fürsorgeverein
         Nr.9327 – Kaiser-Wilhelm-Turm
         Nr.9428 – Verschiedene Polizeiangelegenheiten

Pr. Br. Rep.30 Berlin C – Polizeipräsidium Berlin
  Politische Polizei
    Tit.94 Geheime Präsidialregistratur
      Nr.1112 – Bernhard Kampffmeyer
      Nr.9983 – den Redakteur Dr. phil. Ernst Francke
  Schutzpolizei
    Tit.89 Polizei-, Sicherheits- und Strafsachen
      Nr.7426 – Sicherheitszustand Berlins und Umgebung
      Nr.7431 – Sicherheitsdienst in Vororten Berlins
      Nr.7432 – Sicherheitsdienst in Vororten Berlins

Staatsbibliothek Preußischer Kulturbesitz,
Handschriften Abteilung (SBPK)

Nachlaß Hugo Conwentz
Nachlaß Robert Mielke
Sammlung Darmstaedter

Newspapers and Periodicals (with more than three articles cited)

Aus dem Posener Lande
Das Ausland
Berliner Lokal-Anzeiger
Berliner Tageblatt
Bodenreform
Brandenburgia
Dürer Bund: Flugschrift zur Ausdruckskultur
Forstwirtschaftliche Zentralblatt
Gartenflora
Die Gartenlaube
Geographische Zeitschrift
Die Grenzboten
Heimat und Welt
Heimatschutz
Heimatschutz in Brandenburg
Kosmos
Der Kunstwart
Das Land
Die Mark
Mitteilungen des Bundes Heimatschutz

Mitteilungen des Landesvereins Sächsischer Heimatschutz
Mittheilungen des Touristen-Klub für die Mark Brandenburg
Monatsblätter des Touristen-Klub für die Mark Brandenburg
Die Natur
Neueste Mittheilungen
Die Ostmark
Provinzial-Correspondenz
Der Tag
Tägliche Rundschau
Thüringer Monatsblätter
Volkswohl
Volks-Zeitung (Berlin)
Vom Fels zum Meer
Vorwärts
Vossische Zeitung
Wissenschaftliche Beilage der Leipziger Zeitung
Die Woche
Zeitschrift für Forst- und Jagdwesen

Primary Sources

Arminius [Countess Adelheid Dohna-Poninski]. *Die Grosstädte in ihrer Wohnungsnoth und die Grundlagen einer durchgreifenden Abhilfe*. Leipzig: Duncker & Humblot, 1874.

Baeck. *Heimatskunde der Provinz Posen*. Königsberg: Bon, 1882.

Baedeker, Karl. *Berlin und Umgebung*. Leipzig: Karl Baedecker, 1906.

– *Nord-Ost Deutschland*. Leipzig: Karl Baedeker, 1908.

Berdrow, Hermann. *Der Grunewald*. Berlin: Hermann Eichblatt, 1902.

Berg, Carl Heinrich Edmund Freiherr von. *Geschichte der Deutschen Wälder bis zum Schlusse des Mittelalters*. Dresden: G. Schönfeld, 1871.

Berger, Ewald. *Das deutsche Waldesideal*. Lissa i.P.: Ebbecke, 1907.

Bernhardt, August. *Die Waldwirthschaft und der Waldschutz*. Berlin: Springer, 1869.

– *Geschichte des Waldeigenthums, der Waldwithschaft und Forstwissenschaft*. Vol. 1. Berlin: Springer, 1872.

Berthold, Carl. *Darstellungen aus der Natur*. Cologne: J.P. Bachem, 1884.

Boie, Margarete. *Hugo Conwentz und seine Heimat: Ein Buch der Erinnerungen*. Stuttgart: Steinkopf, 1940.

Buesgen, Moritz. *Der deutsche Wald*. Leipzig: Quelle & Meyer, 1908.

Busdorf, Otto. 'Der Schrecken der Tucheler Heide.' In *Jahrhundertmorde:*

Kriminalgeschichte aus erster Hand, ed. Peter Heiss and Christian Lunzer, 198–218. Vienna: Edition S, 1994.

Carstenn, Johann Anton Wilhelm von. *Die Zukünftige Entwicklung Berlins.* Berlin: Hugo Steinitz, 1892.

City of Vienna. *Der Wald- und Wiesengürtel und die Höhenstrasse der Stadt Wien.* Vienna: Verlag der Gemeinde Wien, 1905.

Clemenz, Bruno. *Naturdenkmalpflege und Schule.* Breslau: Phönix, 1909.

Conwentz, Hugo. *The Care of Natural Monuments.* Cambridge: Cambridge University Press, 1909.

– *Forstbotanisches Merkbuch.* Berlin: Bornträger, 1900.

Cotta, Theodor. *Die Heimatkunde für Berlin.* Berlin: Georg Reimer, 1873.

Der Berliner Zentralausschuß für die Wald- und Ansiedlungsfrage, ed. *Der Kampf um unserer Wälder.* Berlin: Julius Springer, 1909.

Dickel, Karl. *Deutsches und Preußisches Forstzivilrecht.* Berlin: Franz Vahlen, 1917.

Dincklage-Campe, Freiherr von. 'Der Kaiser als Jäger und Heger.' *Wild und Hund* 19, no. 24 (1913): 457–69.

Düesberg, Rudolf. *Der Wald als Erzieher.* Berlin: Parey, 1910.

Eckert, Max. *Deutsche Kulturgeographie.* Halle: Hermann Schroedel, 1912.

Einem deutschen Waldfreund [Otto Boeckel], ed. *Der deutsche Wald im deutschen Lied.* Berlin: H. Walter, 1899.

Endres, Max. *Handbuch der Forstpolitik.* Berlin: Springer, 1905.

Feld- und Forstpolizeigesetz. *Anlagen zu den Stenographischen Berichten über die Verhandlungen des Hauses der Abgeordneten.* Berlin, 1881.

Fendrich, A. *Der Wanderer.* Stuttgart: Frank'sche, 1913.

Fischer, Paul David. *Germany and the Germans: Containing the Greater Part of P.D. Fischer's Betrachtungen eines in Deutschland Reisenden Deutschen.* Edited by A. Lodeman. New York: Silver, Burdett, 1901.

Fontane, Theodor. 'Am Wannsee.' *Neue Preußische Zeitung*, 4 December 1861. Reproduced in vol. 3 of *Wanderungen durch die Mark Brandenburg*, div. 2 of *Theodor Fontane: Werke, Schriften und Briefe*, ed. Walter Keitel, 494–98. Munich: Karl Hanser, 1977.

– *Wanderungen durch die Mark Brandenburg.* Div. 2 of *Theodor Fontane: Werke, Schriften und Briefe*, ed. Walter Keitel. Munich: Karl Hanser, 1977.

Fraas, Carl. *Geschichte der Landbau- und Forstwissenschaft.* Munich: Cottaschen Buchhandlung, 1865.

Francé, Raoul H. *Bilder aus dem Leben des Waldes.* Stuttgart: Kosmos, 1909.

– *Das Pflanzenleben Deutschlands und seiner Nachbarländer.* Vol. 1 of *Das Leben der Pflanze.* Stuttgart: Kosmos, 1906.

– *Die Welt der Pflanze: Eine Volkstümmliche Botanik.* Berlin: Ullstein, 1912.

– *Lebenserinnerungen.* Leipzig: Alfred Kröner, 1927.

Freymuth, Arnold. *Das Betreten des Waldes.* Neudamm: Neumann, 1912.

Gayer, Karl. *Der Wald in Wechsel der Zeiten.* Munich: C. Wolf & Sohn, 1889.

Gradmann, Eugen. *Heimatschutz und Landschaftspflege.* Stuttgart: Stecker & Schröder, 1910.

Grimm, Jacob, and Wilhelm Grimm. *Deutsches Wörterbuch.* Leipzig: S. Hirzel, 1922.

Guenther, Konrad. *Der Naturschutz.* Freiburg: Friedrich Ernst Fehlenfeld, 1910.

Haupt, Richard. *Über die Erhaltung der Fußwege und das Recht der Nation am Walde.* Schleswig: Schleswiger Nachrichten, 1910.

Hausrath, Hans. *Der deutsche Wald.* Leipzig: B.G. Teubner, 1907.

Heiß, Ludwig. *Der Wald und die Gesetzgebung.* Berlin: Springer, 1875.

Heß, Richard. *Der Forstschutz.* Vol. 1. Berlin: B.G. Teubner, 1898.

Hoermann, Franz. *Der deutsche Wald.* Leipzig: F. Dietrich, 1906.

– *Wald und Waldverwüstung.* Leipzig: Felix Dietrich, 1905.

Hoops, Johannes. *Waldbäume und Kulturpflanzen im Germanischen Altertum.* Strassburg: Karl J. Trübner, 1905.

Hugenberg, Alfred. 'Der preußische Staat als Polonisator.' In *Streiflichter aus Vergangenheit und Gegewart,* ed. Alfred Hugenberg, 300–6. Berlin: Scherl, 1927.

Jansen, Hermann. *Vorschlag zu einem Grundplan für Gross-Berlin.* Munich: Callwey, 1910.

Jentzsch, Alfred. *Nachweis der beachtenswerten und zu schützenden Bäume, Sträucher und erratischen Blöcke in der Provinz Ostpreußen.* Königsberg: Emil Rautenberg, 1900.

Jösting, Heinrich. *Der Wald, seine Bedeutung, Verwüstung und Wiederbegründung.* Berlin: Parey, 1898.

Klein, E. *Heimatschutz und Heimatpflege.* Berlin: C. Spiethoff, 1914.

Knauer, Friedrich. *Der Niedergang unserer Tier- und Pflanzenwelt.* Leipzig: Theodor Thomas, 1912.

Königliche Statistische Landesamt, ed. *Statistisches Jahrbuch für den Preußischen Staat.* Berlin: Königliche Statistische Landesamt, 1903 and 1917.

Kötschke, Hermann. *Die Berliner Waldverwüstung und verwandte Fragen.* Berlin: Ansiedlungsverein Groß-Berlin, 1910.

Kohli. 'Drei Waldbrände in der Tucheler Haide.' *Forstliche Blätter* 8 (1864): 146–66.

Kürschner, Joseph. *Das ist des Deutschen Vaterland.* Berlin: Hermann Hillger, 1896.

Levenstein, Adolf. *Die Arbeiterfrage.* Munich: Ernst Reinhardt, 1912.

Löffelholz-Colberg, Friedrich Freiherr von. *Die Bedeutung und Wichtigkeit des Waldes: Ursachen und Folgen der Entwaldung.* Leipzig: H. Schmidt, 1872.

Lohr, Otto. *Die Linde, ein deutscher Baum.* Spandau: Gustav Schob, 1889.

Luntowski, Adalbert. *Westpreußische Wanderungen.* Berlin: G. Westermann, 1914.

Mannhardt, Wilhelm. *Der Baumkultus der Germanen und ihrer Nachbarstämme.* Vol. 1 of *Wald- und Feldkulte.* Berlin: Bornträger, 1904–5.

Mühlradt, Johannes. *Die 'Tucheler Heide in Wort und Bild' in Beurteilung der Presse.* Vol. 13 of *Die Tucheler Heide in Wort und Bild.* Grünthal: Selbstverlag, 1915.

– *Ein Besuch in Grüntal.* Vol. 1 of *Die Tucheler Heide in Wort und Bild.* Danzig: Kafemann, 1908.

Pernin, Karl. *Wanderungen durch die sogen: Kassubei und die Tucheler Haide.* Danzig: A.W. Kafemann, 1886.

Pfuhl, Fritz. 'Das Pflanzenkleid, das den Boden des Posener Landes schmückt.' In *Die deutsche Ostmark,* ed. Deutsche Ostmarkenverein, 119–40. Lissa i.P.: Eulitz, 1913.

Preuß, Hans. 'Die Entwicklung der staatlichen Forstwirtschaft in Westpreußen.' In *Lesebuch.* Part 2 of *Die Provinz Westpreußen in Wort und Bild,* ed. Paul Gehrke, Robert Hecker, and Hans Preuss, 105–6. Danzig: Kafemann, 1912.

– 'Drei Tage in der Tucheler Heide.' In *Lesebuch.* Part 2 of *Die Provinz Westpreußen in Wort und Bild,* ed. Paul Gehrke, Robert Hecker, and Hans Preuss, 96–105. Danzig: Kafemann, 1912.

Pudor, Heinrich. *Waldpolitik.* Gautzsch bei Leipzig: Felix Dietrich, 1914.

Radtke, Richard. *Handbuch für den preussischen Förster enthaltend sämtliche, die Betriebs- und Schutzbeamten des Staats-, Kommunal- und Privat-Forstdienstes angehenden Gesetze, Verordnungen usw.* 4th ed. Neudamm: J. Neumann, 1908.

Ratzel, Friedrich. *Deutschland: Einführung in die Heimatkunde.* Berlin: Georg Reimer, 1911.

Riehl, Wilhelm Heinrich. *Die Naturgeschichte des Volkes als Grundlage einer deutschen Social-Politik.* 6th ed. Stuttgart: Cotta, 1867.

– *Wanderbuch.* Part 2 of *Land und Leute.* Vol. 4 of *Die Naturgeschichte des Volkes als Grundlage einer deutschen Social-Politik.* Stuttgart: J.G. Cotta, 1869.

Riesenthal, Oskar von. *Bilder aus der Tucheler Heide.* Trier: Fr. Link, 1878.

Roßmäßler, Emil Adolf. *Das Gebirgsdorfchen.* Leipzig: Quelle & Meyer, 1909.

– *Der Wald.* Leipzig: C.F. Winter'sche Verlagshandlung, 1863.

– *Mein Leben und Streben im Verkehr mit der Natur und dem Volke.* Hanover: Carl Rümpler, 1874.

Rubner, Heinrich, ed. *Adolph Wagner: Briefe, Dokumente, Augenzeugenberichte, 1851–1917.* Berlin: Duncker & Humblot, 1978.

Rudorff, Ernst. *Der Schutz der landschaftlichen Natur und der geschichtlichen Denkmäler Deutschlands.* Berlin: Allgemeiner Deutscher Verein, 1892.

Rüsten, Rudolf. *Was tut Not? Ein Führer durch die gesamte Literatur der Deutsch-bewegung.* Leipzig: G. Hedeler, 1914.

Sach, August. *Die deutsche Heimat, Landschaft und Volkstum.* Halle: Buchhandlung des Waisenhauses, 1885.

Salisch, Heinrich von. *Forstästhetik.* 3rd ed. Berlin: Springer, 1911.

Säurich, Paul. *Das Leben der Pflanzen im Walde.* Leipzig: Ernst Wunderlich, 1908.

Scherr, Johannes. *Deutsche Kultur- und Sittengeschichte.* Leipzig: O. Wigand, 1887.

Schleiden, Matthias Jakob. *Für Baum und Wald: eine Schutzschrift an Fachmänner und Laien gerichtet.* Leipzig: Engelmann, 1870.

Schmedes, Karl, ed. *Grunewald.* Vol. 4 of *Fontane's Führer durch die Umgegend Berlin*, ed. Touristen-Club für die Mark Brandenburg. Berlin: F. Fontane, 1894.

Schmitt, F.W.F. *Land und Leute in Westpreußen.* Vol. 2 of *Die Provinz Westpreußen.* Thorn: Ernst Lambeck, 1879.

Schoenichen, Walther. *Der deutsche Wald.* Bielefeld: Velhagen & Klasing, 1913.

Schönburg-Waldenburg, Heinrich Prinz von. 'Parforcejagd im Grunewald.' In *Geist und Gesellschaft der Bismarckzeit*, ed. Karl Heinz Höfele, 261–4. Göttingen: Musterschmidt, 1967.

Schultze-Naumburg, Paul. *Die Entstellung unseres Landes.* Meinigenen: Bund Heimatschutz, 1909.

Schütte, R. *Die Tucheler Haide, vornehmlich in forstlicher Beziehung.* Abhandlungen zur Landeskunde der Provinz Westpreußen, no. 5. Danzig: Th. Bertling, 1893.

Schwandt, Wilhelm, ed. *Karthaus und die Kassubische Schweiz.* Danzig: Kafemann, 1913.

Schwappach, Adam. *Forstpolitik, Jagd- und Fischereipolitik.* Leipzig: C.L. Hirsch-feld, 1894.

– *Forstwissenschaft.* Leipzig: Göschen'sche, 1899.

– *Handbuch der Forst- und Jagdgeschichte Deutschlands.* Berlin: Springer, 1886–8.

Schwarz, Paul. *Heimatkunde der Provinz Brandenburg und der Stadt Berlin.* Breslau: Ferdinand Hirt, 1899.

Siefert, Xaver. *Der Deutsche Wald.* Karlsruhe: Braunschen Hofbuchdruckerei, 1905.

Sohnrey, Heinrich. *Wegweiser für Ländliche Wohlfahrts- und Heimatpflege.* Berlin:

– *Wegweiser für Ländliche Wohlfahrts- und Heimatpflege.* 2nd, rev. ed. Berlin: Deutsche Buchhandlung, 1908.

Sohnrey, Heinrich, and Ernst Löber. *Das Glück auf dem Lande: Ein Wegweiser, wie der kleine Mann auf einen grünen Zweig kommt.* Berlin: Deutsche Buchhand-lung, 1906.

Trinius, August. *Die Umgebung der Kaiserstadt Berlin.* Berlin: Lehmann, 1889.

Trojan, Johannes. *Unsere deutsche Wälder.* Berlin: Vita Deutsches Verlagshaus, 1911.

Wagner, Adolph. *Allgemeine oder theoretische Volkswirtschaftslehre.* Leipzig: C.F. Winter'sche Verlagshandlung, 1876.

Wagner, Hermann. 'Die Land- und Forstwirtschaft.' In *Die deutsche Ostmark,* ed. Deutsche Ostmarkenverein, 270–329. Lissa i.P.: Eulitz, 1913.

Wermuth, Adolf. *Ein Beamtenleben.* Berlin: Scherl, 1922.

Wernicke, Erich. *Wanderung durch die Tucheler Ḥeide.* Danzig: Kafemann, 1913.

Whitman, Sidney. *Teuton Studies.* Leipzig: Bernhard Tauchnitz, 1896.

Wilhelm II. *The Kaiser's Memoirs.* Translated by Thomas R. Ybarra. New York: Harper & Brothers, 1922.

Wimmer, Josef. *Geschichte des deutschen Bodens mit seinem Pflanzen- und Tierleben.* HalleBuchhandlung des Waisenhauses, 1905.

Ziesemer, Johann. *Die Provinzen Ost- und Westpreußen.* Berlin: W. Spemann, 1901.

Secondary Sources

Andersen, Arne. 'Heimatschutz: Die bürgerliche Naturschutzbewegung.' In *Besiegte Natur: Geschichte der Umwelt im 19. und 20. Jahrhundert,* ed. Franz-Josef Brüggemeier and Thomas Rommelspacher, 143–57. Munich: Beck, 1987.

Anderson, Benedict. *Imagined Communities: Reflections on the Origin and Spread of Nationalism.* 2nd ed. London: Verso, 1991.

Applegate, Celia. *A Nation of Provincials: The German Idea of Heimat.* Berkeley: University of California Press, 1990.

Baier, Roland. *Die deutsche Osten als soziale Frage: Eine Studie zur preußischen und deutschen Siedlungs- und Polenpolitik in den Ostprovinzen während des Kaiserreichs und der Weimerer Republik.* Cologne: Böhlau, 1980.

Balzer, Brigitte. *Die preußische Polenpolitik 1894–1908 und die Haltung der deutschen konservativen und liberalen Parteien.* Frankfurt am Main: Peter Lang, 1990.

Barkin, Kenneth D. *The Controversy over German Industrialization, 1890–1902.* Chicago: University of Chicago Press, 1970.

Bartelsheim, Ursula. *Bürgersinn und Parteiinteresse: Kommunalpolitik in Frankfurt am Main 1848–1914.* Frankfurt am Main: Campus Verlag, 1997.

Barthelmeß, Alfred. *Landschaft: Lebensraum des Menschen.* Munich: Karl Alber, 1988.

– *Wald als Umwelt des Menschen.* Munich: Karl Alber, 1972.

Belgum, Kirsten. *Popularizing the Nation: Audience, Representation and the Production of Identity in Die Gartenlaube, 1853–1900.* Lincoln: University of Nebraska Press, 1998.

Bergmann, Klaus. *Agrarromantik und Großstadtsfeindschaft.* Meisenheim am Glan: Anton Hain, 1970.

Berman, Sheri. *The Social Democratic Moment: Ideas and Politics in the Making of Interwar Europe.* Cambridge, MA: Harvard University Press, 1998.

Bernhardt, Christoph. *Bauplatz Groß-Berlin.* Berlin: de Gruyter, 1998.

Bessel, Richard. 'Eastern Germany as a Structural Problem in the Weimar Republic.' *Social History* 3 (1978): 199–218.

Blackbourn, David. *The Conquest of Nature: Water, Landscape, and the Making of Modern Germany.* New York: Norton, 2006.

– *The Long Nineteenth Century.* New York: Oxford University Press, 1998.

– 'The Politics of Demagogy in Imperial Germany.' *Past and Present* 113 (1987): 152–84.

Blanke, Richard. *Prussian Poland in the German Empire.* Boulder: East European Monographs, 1981.

Blasius, Dirk. *Bürgerliche Gesellschaft und Kriminalität: zur Sozialgeschichte Preussens im Vormärz.* Göttingen: Vandenhoeck & Ruprecht, 1976.

Bömelburg, Hans-Jürgen. 'Westpreußische Gutsbesitzer "auf der Höhe."' In *Polen, Deutsche und Kaschuben … Alltag, Brauchtum und Volkskultur auf dem Gut Hochpaleschken in Westpreußen um 1900,* ed. Bernhard Lauer, 25–33. Kassel: Brüder Grimm-Gesellschaft, 1997.

Breyer, Richard. 'Die kaschubische Bewegung vor dem Ersten Weltkrieg.' In *Studien zur Geschichte des Preussenlandes; Festschrift für Erich Keyser zu seinem 70. Geburtstag dargebracht von Freuden und Schülern,* ed. Ernst Bahr, 327–41. Marburg: N.G. Elwert, 1963.

Brown, Dona. *Inventing New England: Regional Tourism in the Nineteenth Century.* Washington: Smithsonian Institution, 1995.

Bruch, Rüdiger vom, ed. *Weder Kommunismus noch Kapitalismus: bürgerliche Sozial-reform in Deutschland vom Vormärz bis zur Ära Adenauer.* Munich: Beck, 1985.

Brüggemeier, Franz-Josef. '*Waldsterben*: The Construction and Deconstruction of an Environmental Problem.' In *Nature in German History,* ed. Christof Mauch, 118–31. Oxford: Berghahn, 2004.

Bullock, Nicholas, and James Read. *The Movement for Housing Reform in Germany and France, 1840–1914.* Cambridge: Cambridge University Press, 1985.

Campbell, Joan. *Joy in Work, German Work.* Princeton, NJ: Princeton University Press, 1989.

Canetti, Elias. *Crowds and Power.* Translated by Carol Stewart. New York: Noonday, 1991.

Chaney, Sandra. *Nature of the Miracle Years: Conservation in West Germany, 1945–1975.* Oxford: Berghahn Books, 2008.

Cohen, Gary. *The Politics of Ethnic Survival: Germans in Prague, 1861–1914.* Princeton: Princeton University Press, 1981.

Confino, Alon. 'The Nation as a Local Metaphor: Heimat, National Memory and the German Empire, 1871–1918.' *History & Memory* 5, no. 1 (1993): 42–86.

– *The Nation as Local Metaphor: Württemberg, Imperial Germany, and National Memory, 1871–1918.* Chapel Hill: University of North Carolina Press, 1997.

Daniels, Stephen. 'Mapping National Identities: The Culture of Cartography, with Particular Reference to the Ordnance Survey.' In *Imagining Nations*, ed. Geoffrey Cubitt, 112–31. Manchester: Manchester University Press, 1998.

– 'Marxism, Culture and the Duplicity of Landscape.' In *Human Geography*, ed. John Agnew, David Livingstone, and Alisdair Rogers, 329–39. London: Blackwell, 1997.

– 'The Political Iconography of Woodland in Later Georgian England.' In *The Iconography of Landscape*, ed. Stephen Daniels and Denis Cosgrove, 43–82. Cambridge: Cambridge University Press, 1988.

Daniels, Stephen, and Denis Cosgrove. 'Introduction: Iconography and Landscape.' In *The Iconography of Landscape*, ed. Stephen Daniels and Denis Cosgrove, 1–10. Cambridge: Cambridge University Press, 1988.

Daum, Andreas. *Wissenschaftspopularisierung im 19: Jahrhundert: bürgerliche Kultur, naturwissenschaftliche Bildung und die deutsche Öffentlichkeit, 1848–1914.* Munich: Oldenbourg, 1998.

Davies, Norman. *God's Playground: A History of Poland.* Vol. 2. New York: Columbia University Press, 1982.

Dickinson, Edward Ross. 'Germanizing the Alps and Alpinizing the Germans, 1875–1935.' *German Studies Review* 33, no. 3 (2010): 579–602.

Dipper, Christof. 'Rural Revolutionary Movements: Germany, France, Italy.' In *Europe in 1848: Revolution and Reform*, ed. Dieter Dowe, 416–42. Oxford: Berghahn Books, 2001.

Ditt, Karl. 'Nature Conservation in England and Germany 1900–70: Forerunner of Environmental Protection?' *Contemporary European History* 5, no. 1 (1996): 1–28.

Dominick, Raymond. *The Environmental Movement in Germany: Prophets and Pioneers, 1871–1971.* Bloomington: Indiana University Press, 1992.

Dörner, Andreas. 'Der Mythos der nationalen Einheit: Symbolpolitik und Deutungskaempfe bei der Einweihung des Hermannsdenkmals im Jahre 1875.' *Archiv für Kulturgeschichte* 79, no. 2 (1997): 389–416.

Eley, Geoff. 'Anti-Semitism, Agrarian Mobilization, and the Conservative Party: Radicalism and Containment in the Founding of the Agrarian League, 1890–1893.' In *Between Reform, Reaction, and Resistance: Studies in the History of*

German Conservatism from 1789 to 1945, ed. James Retallack and Larry Eugene Jones, 187–227. Oxford: Berg, 1993.

– 'German Politics and Polish Nationality: The Dialectic of Nation-Forming in the East of Prussia.' In *From Unification to Nazism*, ed. Geoff Eley, 200–30. 2nd ed. New York: Routledge, 1992.

– 'Nationalism and Social History.' *Social History* 6 (1981): 83–107.

– 'Putting German (and British) Liberalism into Context: Liberalism, Europe, and the Bourgeoisie 1840–1914.' Unpublished Comparative Study of Social Transformations paper, Ann Arbor, 1990.

– *Reshaping the German Right: Radical Nationalism and Political Change after Bismarck.* 2nd ed. Ann Arbor: University of Michigan Press, 1991.

– 'Social Imperialism in Germany: Reformist Synthesis or Reactionary Sleight of Hand?' In *From Unification to Nazism*, ed. Geoff Eley, 154–70. 2nd ed. New York: Routledge, 1992.

– 'State Formation, Nationalism, and Political Culture.' In *From Unification to Nazism*, ed. Geoff Eley, 61–84. 2nd ed. London: Routledge, 1992.

Erbe, Michael. 'Berlin im Kaiserreich.' In *Geschichte Berlins*, ed. Wolfgang Ribbe, 2:691–793. Munich: Beck, 1987.

Escher, Felix. *Berlin und sein Umland.* Berlin: Colloquium, 1985.

Evans, Richard J. 'In Search of German Social Darwinism: The History and Historiography of a Concept.' In *Medicine and Modernity: Public Health and Medical Care in Nineteenth- and Twentieth-Century Germany*, ed. Manfred Berg and Geoffrey Cocks, 55–79. Cambridge: Cambridge University Press, 1997.

Everett, Nigel. *The Tory View of Landscape.* New Haven, CT: Yale University Press, 1994.

Facos, Michelle. *Nationalism and the Nordic Imagination: Swedish Art of the 1890s.* Berkeley: University of California Press, 1998.

Franklin, Jill. 'The Liberty of the Park.' In *Patriotism*, ed. Raphael Samuel, 141–59. London: Routledge, 1989.

Friedberg, Robert von. *Ländliche Gesellschaft und Obrigkeit.* Göttingen: Vandenhoeck & Ruprecht, 1997.

Friedrich, Karin. *The Other Prussia: Royal Prussia, Poland and Liberty, 1569–1772.* Cambridge: Cambridge University Press, 2000.

Frühsorge, Gotthardt. *Die Kunst des Landlebens: vom Landschloss zum Campingplatz: eine Kulturgeschichte.* Munich: Koehler & Amelang, 1993.

Frykman, Jonas, and Orvar Löfgren. *Culture Builders.* Translated by Alan Crozier. New Brunswick, NJ: Rutgers University Press, 1987.

Fuller, Peter. 'The Geography of Mother Nature.' In *The Iconography of Landscape*, ed. Stephen Daniels and Denis Cosgrove, 11–31. Cambridge: Cambridge University Press, 1988.

Gautschi, Andreas. *Wilhelm II. und das Waidwerk. Jagen und Jagden des letzten Deutschen Kaisers. Eine Bilanz.* Hanstedt: Nimrod Verlag, 2000.

Geary, Patrick J. *The Myth of Nations: The Medieval Origins of Europe.* Princeton, NJ: Princeton University Press, 2002.

Gillis, John R., ed. *Commemorations: The Politics of National Identity.* Princeton, NJ: Princeton University Press, 1994.

Greverus, Ina-Maria. *Auf der Suche nach Heimat.* Munich: Beck, 1979.

Grill, Bartholomäus. 'Deutschland: ein Waldesmärchen.' *Die Zeit,* 25 December 1987, 3.

Grimmer-Solem, Erik. *The Rise of Historical Economics and Social Reform in Germany, 1864–1894.* Oxford: Oxford University Press, 2003.

Gröning, Gert, and Joachim Wolschke-Bulmahn. *Natur in Bewegung.* Vol. 1 of *Die Liebe zur Landschaft.* Munich: Minerva, 1986.

Guha, Ramachandra. *The Unquiet Woods: Ecological Change and Peasant Resistance in the Himalaya.* Berkeley: University of California Press, 2000.

Guratzsch, Dankwart. *Macht durch Organisation: Die Grundlegung des Hugenbergschen Presseimperiums.* Düsseldorf: Bertelsmann Universitätsverlag, 1974.

Hagen, William W. *Germans, Poles, and Jews: The Nationality Conflict in the Prussian East, 1772–1914.* Chicago: University of Chicago Press, 1980.

Hanemann, Regina, and Jürgen Julier. 'Zur Baugeschichte des Jagdschlosses Grunewald II. Von 1708 bis in die Gegenwart.' In *450 Jahre Jagdschloss Grunewald, 1542–1992,* ed. Staatliche Schlösser and Gärten Berlin, 1:57–81. Berlin: Staatliche Schlösser und Gärten Berlin, 1992.

Harrison, Robert. *Forests: The Shadow of Civilization.* Chicago: University of Chicago Press, 1992.

Hartmann, Kristiana. *Deutsche Gartenstadtbewegung: Kulturpolitik und Gesellschaftsreform.* Munich: H. Moos, 1976.

– 'Gartenstadtbewegung.' In *Handbuch der deutschen Reformbewegungen, 1880–1933,* ed. Diethart Kerbs and Jürgen Reulecke, 289–300. Wupperthal: Peter Hammer, 1998.

Hartung, Werner. *Konservative Zivilationskritik und regionale Identität.* Hanover: Verlag Hahnische Buchhandlung, 1991.

Hasel, Karl. *Zur Geschichte der Forstgesetzgebung in Preussen.* Frankfurt am Main: Sauerländer, 1974.

Hegemann, Werner. *Das steinerne Berlin: Geschichte der grössten Mietkasernenstadt der Welt.* Berlin: G. Kiepenheuer, 1930.

Helsinger, Elizabeth. 'Turner and the Representation of England.' In *Landscape and Power,* ed. W.T.J. Mitchell, 103–19. Chicago: University of Chicago Press, 1994.

Helsinger, Elizabeth K. *Rural Scenes and National Representation*. Princeton, NJ: Princeton University Press, 1997.

Henderson, W.O. *The Rise of German Industrial Power, 1834–1914*. Berkeley: University of California Press, 1975.

Hennebo, Dieter. 'Öffentlicher Park und Grünplanung als kommunale Aufgabe in Deutschland.' In *Kommunale Leistesverwaltung und Stadtentwicklung vom Vormärz bis zur Weimarer Republik*, ed. Hans Heinrich Blotevogel, 169–82. Cologne: Böhlau, 1990.

Hennig, Rolf. *Bismarck und die Natur*. Suderburg: Nimrod, 1998.

Henning, Friedrich-Wilhelm. *Handbuch der Wirtschafts- und Sozialgeschichte Deutschlands*. Vol. 3. Munich: Ferdinand Schönigh, 1996.

Hermand, Jost. '"The Death of the Trees Will Be the End of Us All': Protests against the Destruction of German Forests 1780–1950.' In *The Idea of the Forest: German and American Perspectives on the Culture and Politics of Trees*, ed. Karla L. Schultz and Kenneth S. Calhoon, 49–71. New York: Peter Lang, 1996.

Herzfeld, Hans. *Johannes von Miquel: sein Anteil am Ausbau des Deutschen Reiches bis zur Jahrhundertwende*. Detmold: Meyersche Hofbuchhandlung, 1938.

Hewison, Robert. *The Heritage Industry*. London: Methuen, 1987.

Hobsbawm, Eric. *Nations and Nationalism since 1780*. Cambridge: Cambridge University Press, 1990.

Howkins, Alun. 'The Discovery of Rural England.' In *Englishness: Politics and Culture, 1880–1920*, ed. Robert Colls and Philip Dodd, 62–88. London: Croom Helm, 1986.

Hurd, Madeleine. *Public Spheres, Public Mores, and Democracy: Hamburg and Stockholm, 1870–1914*. Ann Arbor: University of Michigan Press, 2000.

Hürlimann, Annemarie. 'Die Eiche, heiliger Baum deutscher Nation.' In *Waldungen: die Deutschen und ihr Wald*, ed. Bernd Weyergraf, 62–7. Berlin: Akademie der Künste, 1987.

Hyde, Anne Farrar. *An American Vision: Far Western Landscape and National Culture, 1820–1920*. New York: New York University Press, 1990.

Imort, Michael. '"Eternal Forest – Eternal *Volk*': Rhetoric and Reality of National Socialist Forest Policy.' In *How Green Were the Nazis? Nature, Environment and Heimat in the Third Reich*, ed. Franz-Josef Brüggemeier, Mark Cioc, and Thomas Zeller, 43–72. Athens, OH: Ohio University Press, 2005.

– 'A Sylvan People: Wilhelmine Forestry and the Forest as a Symbol of Germandom.' In *Germany's Nature: Cultural Landscapes and Environmental History*, ed. Thomas Lekan and Thomas Zeller, 55–80. New Brunswick, NJ: Rutgers University Press, 2005.

Jahn, Ilse, and Isolde Schmidt. *Matthias Jacob Schleiden (1804–1881): Sein Leben in Selbstzeugnissen.* Halle: Deutscher Akademie der Naturforscher Leopoldina e.V., 2005.

Jähning, Bernhart. 'Die Bevölkerung Westpreußens um 1900.' *Westpreußen Jahrbuch* 42 (1992): 5–22.

Jansen, Sarah. *'Schädlinge': Geschichte eines wissenschaftlichen und politischen Konstrukts 1840–1920.* Frankfurt am Main: Campus Verlag, 2003.

Jasen, Patricia. *Wild Things: Nature, Culture, and Tourism in Ontario, 1790–1914.* Toronto: University of Toronto Press, 1995.

Jeffries, Matthew. *Imperial Culture in Germany, 1871–1918.* New York: Palgrave Macmillan, 2003.

Jenkins, Jennifer Louise. "Provincial Modernity: Culture, Politics and Local Identity in Hamburg, 1885–1914." PhD diss., University of Michigan, 1997.

– *Provincial Modernity: Local Culture and Liberal Politics in Fin-de-siècle Hamburg.* Ithaca, NY: Cornell University Press, 2003.

Johler, Reinhard. 'Wald, Kultur, Nation: Ein deutsch-italienische Vergleich.' In *Der Wald: Ein deutscher Mythos?*, ed. Albrecht Lehmann and Klaus Schriewer, 83–96. Berlin: Dietrich Reimer, 2000.

Johnson, Eric A. 'Urban and Rural Crime in Germany, 1871–1914.' In *The Civilization of Crime*, ed. Eric A. Johnson and Eric H. Monkkonen, 217–57. Chicago: University of Illinois Press, 1996.

Kaeber, Ernst. 'Werner Hegemanns Werk: "Das steinerne Berlin. Geschichte der größten Mietskassernenstadt der Welt" oder: der alte und der neue Hegemann.' In *Beiträge zur Berliner Geschichte*, ed. Ernst Kaeber, 204–33. Berlin: de Gruyter, 1964.

Kaschuba, Wolfgang. 'Die Fußreise: Von der Arbeitswanderung zur bürgerlichen Bildungsbewegung.' In *Reisekultur*, ed. Hermann Bausinger and Gottfried Korff, 165–73. Munich: Beck, 1991.

Kastorff-Viehmann, Renate. 'Die Stadt und das Grün 1860 bis 1960.' In *Die grüne Stadt: Siedlungen, Parks, Wälder, Grünflächen 1860–1960 im Ruhrgebiet*, ed. Renate Kastorff-Viehmann and Hermann Josef Bausch, 49–141. Essen: Klartext, 1998.

Kelly, Alfred. *The Descent of Darwin: The Popularization of Darwinism in Germany, 1860–1914.* Chapel Hill: University of North Carolina Press, 1981.

Klebe, Giselher, and Bernd Weyergraf. 'Vorworte.' In *Waldungen: die Deutschen und ihr Wald*, ed. Bernd Weyergraf, 5. Berlin: Akademie der Künste, 1987.

Klueting, Edeltraud. 'Vorwort.' In *Antimodernismus und Reform: Zur Geschichte der deutschen Heimatbewegung*, ed. Edeltraud Klueting, vii–xi. Darmstadt: Wissenschaftliche Buchgesellschaft, 1991.

Knaut, Andreas. *Zurück zur Natur! Die Wurzeln der Ökologiebewegung.* Bonn: ABN, 1993.

König, Gudrun. *Eine Kulturgeschichte des Spaziergangs.* Cologne: Böhlau, 1996.

Koshar, Rudy. *From Monuments to Traces: Artifacts of German Memory, 1870–1990.* Berkeley: University of California Press, 2000.

German Travel Cultures. Oxford: Berg, 2000.

– *Social Life, Local Politics, and Nazism.* Chapel Hill: University of North Carolina Press, 1986.

– '"What ought to be seen": Tourists' Guidebooks and National Identities in Modern Germany and Europe.' *Journal of Contemporary History* 33, no. 3 (1998): 323–40.

Köstlin, Konrad. 'Der Ethnisierte Wald.' In *Der Wald: Ein deutscher Mythos?,* ed. Albrecht Lehmann and Klaus Schriewer, 53–65. Berlin: Dietrich Reimer, 2000.

Kramer, Dieter. 'Arbeiter als Touristen: Ein Privileg wird gebrochen. Soziale und ökonomische Rahmenbedingungen der Entwicklung der Naturfreunde.' In *Mit uns zieht die neue Zeit,* ed. Jochen Zimmer, 31–65. Cologne: Pahl-Rugenstein, 1984.

Kröger, Heinrich. 'Sohnrey, Heinrich.' In *Biographisch-Bibliographisches Kirchenlexikon,* ed. Traugott Bautz. Herzberg: Traugott Bautz, 1995), 10:745–9.

Kulczycki, John J. *School Strikes in Prussian Poland, 1901–1907: The Struggle over Bilingual Education.* Boulder: East European Monographs, 1981.

Kurlander, Eric. '*Völkisch* Nationalism and Universalism on the Margins of the Reich: A Comparison of Majority and Minority Liberalism in Germany, 1898–1913.' In *German History from the Margins: Visions of Community between Nationalism and Particularism, 1850–1933,* 84–103. Bloomington: Indiana University Press, 2006.

Küster, Hansjörg. *Geschichte des Waldes.* Munich: Beck, 1998.

Ladd, Brian. *Urban Planning and Civic Order in Germany, 1860–1914.* Cambridge, MA: Harvard University Press, 1990.

Lees, Andrew. *Cities, Sin, and Social Reform in Germany, 1880s–1914.* Ann Arbor: University of Michigan Press, 2002.

Lehmann, Albrecht. 'Der deutsche Wald.' In *Deutsche Erinnerungsorte,* ed. Etienne François and Hagen Schulze, 3:187–200. Munich: Beck, 2003.

– 'Mythos Deutscher Wald.' *Der Bürger im Staat* 51, no. 1 (2001): 4–9.

Lekan, Thomas M. *Imagining the Nation in Nature: Landscape Preservation and German Identity, 1885–1945.* Cambridge, MA: Harvard University Press, 2004.

– 'Regionalism and the Politics of Landscape Preservation in the Third Reich.' *Environmental History Review* 4 (July 1999): 384–404.

Lerman, Katharine Anne. 'Hofjagden: Royal Hunts and Shooting Parties in the

Imperial Era.' In *Das politische Zeremoniell im Deutschen Kaiserreich, 1871–1918*, ed. Andreas Biefang, Michael Epkenhans, and Klaus Tenfelde, 115–38. Düsseldorf: Droste, 2008.

Levinger, Matthew. *Enlightened Nationalism: The Transformation of Prussian Political Culture, 1806–1848.* Oxford: Oxford University Press, 2000.

Lindenlaub, Dieter. *Richtungskämpfe im Verein für Sozialpolitik: Wissenschaft und Sozialpolitik im Kaiserreich vornehmlich vom Beginn des 'Neuen Kurses' bis zum Ausbruch des 1. Weltkrieges (1890–1914).* Wiesbaden: F. Steiner, 1967.

Linebaugh, Peter. 'Karl Marx, the Theft of Wood, and Working-Class Composition.' *Crime and Social Justice* 6 (1976): 5–16.

Lingenberg, H. 'Die Kaschuben.' *Westpreußen-Jahrbuch* 35 (1985): 123–50.

Linke, Uli. 'Folklore, Anthropology, and the Government of Social Life.' *Comparative Study of Society and History* 32, no. 1 (1990): 117–48.

Linse, Ulrich. 'Der deutsche Wald als Kampfplatz politischer Ideen.' *Revue d'Allemange* 22, no. 2 (1990): 339–50.

– 'Der Film "Ewiger Wald" – oder: Die Überwindung der Zeit durch den Raum.' *Zeitschrift für Pädigogik* (Beiheft 31, 1993): 57–75.

– *Zurück, o Mensch, zur Mutter Erde: Landkommunen in Deutschland 1890–1933.* Munich: DTV, 1983.

Linse, Ulrich, Reinhard Falter, Dieter Rucht, and Winfried Kretschmer. 'Ein Vergleich.' In *Von der Bittschrift zur Platzbesetzung. Konflikte um technische Grossprojekten: Laufenburg, Walchensee, Wyhl, Wackersdorf,* ed. Ulrich Linse, Reinhard Falter, Dieter Rucht, and Winfried Kretschmer, 219–56. Berlin: JHW Dietz, 1988.

Liulevicius, Vejas Gabriel. *War Land on the Eastern Front: Culture, National Identity and German Occupation in World War I.* Cambridge: University of Cambridge Press, 2000.

Löfgren, Orvar. 'Landscapes of the Mind.' *Topos* 6 (March 1994): 6–14.

Lowood, Henry E. 'The Calculating Forester: Quantification, Cameral Science, and the Emergence of Scientific Forestry Management in Germany.' In *The Quantifying Spirit in the 18th Century,* ed. Tore Frängsmyr, J.L. Heilbron, and Robin E. Rider. Berkeley: University of California Press, 1990.Lubowitzki, Jutta. 'Der "Hobrechtplan": Probleme der Berliner Stadtentwicklung um die Mitte des 19. Jahrhunderts.' In *Berlin Forschungen,* ed. Wolfgang Ribbe, 5:11–130. Berlin: Colloqium, 1990.

Maasen, Sabine, and Peter Weingart. *Metaphors and the Dynamics of Knowledge.* London: Routledge, 2000.

Maner, Brent. "The Search for a Buried Nation: Prehistoric Archaeology in Central Europe, 1750–1945." PhD diss., University of Illinois, 2001.

Markham, William T. *Environmental Organizations in Modern Germany: Hardy Survivors in the Twentieth Century and Beyond.* Oxford: Berghahn, 2008.

Marsh, Jan. *Back to the Land: The Pastoral Impulse in England, 1880–1914.* New York: Quartet, 1982.

Marx, Leo. *The Machine in the Garden: Technology and the Pastoral Ideal in America.* Oxford: Oxford University Press, 1964.

Matless, David. *Landscape and Englishness.* London: Reaktion, 1998.

Mattern, Dan. "Creating the Modern Metropolis: The Debate over Greater Berlin, 1890–1920." PhD diss., University North Carolina, 1991.

Meyer-Renschhausen, Elisabeth, and Hartwig Berger. 'Bodenreform.' In *Handbuch der deutschen Reformbewegungen, 1880–1933*, ed. Diethart Kerbs and Jürgen Reulecke, 265–76. Wupperthal: Peter Hammer, 1998.

Mielke, H.J. *Die kulturlandschaftliche Entwicklung des Grunewaldgebiets.* Berlin: Dietrich Reimer, 1971.

Meynen, Henriette. *Die Kölner Grünanlagen: Die städtebauliche und gartenarchitektonische Entwicklung des Stadtgrüns und das Grünsystem Fritz Schumachers.* Düsseldorf: Schwann, 1979.

Mitchell, W.T.J. 'Introduction.' In *Landscape and Power*, ed. W.T.J. Mitchell, 1–4. Chicago: University of Chicago Press, 1994.

Mock, Wolfgang. '"Manipulation von Oben" oder Selbsorganisation an der Basis? Einige neuere Ansätze in der englischen Historiohraphie zur Geschichte des deutschen Kaiserreichs.' *Historische Zeitschrift* 232 (1982): 358–75.

Mommsen, Wolfgang J. *Max Weber and German Politics, 1890–1920.* Translated by Michael S. Steinberg. Chicago: University of Chicago Press, 1984.

Moser, Josef. 'Property and Wood Theft: Agrarian Capitalism and Social Conflict in Rural Society, 1800–50. A Westphalian Case Study.' In *Peasants and Lords in Modern Germany: Recent Studies in Agricultural History*, ed. Robert G. Moeller, 52–80. Boston: Allen & Unwin, 1986.

Mosse, George. *The Crisis of German Ideology: Intellectual Origins of the Third Reich.* New York: Grosset & Dunlap, 1964.

– *The Nationalization of the Masses.* New York: Howard Fertig, 1975.

Mukerji, Chandra. *Territorial Ambitions and the Gardens of Versailles.* Cambridge: Cambridge University Press, 1997.

Nelson, Arvid. *Cold War Ecology: Forests, Farms, and People in the East German Landscape, 1945–1989.* New Haven, CT: Yale University Press, 2005.

Neubach, Helmut. 'Reichstagswahlen 1881 in Westpreußen.' *Westpreußen Jahrbuch* 31 (1981): 121–6.

Niendorf, Mathias. *Minderheiten an der Grenze: Deutsche und Polen in den Kreisen*

Flatow (Złotów) und Zempelburg (Sępólno Krajeńskie) 1900–1939. Wiesbaden: Harrassowitz, 1997.

Nipperdey, Thomas. 'Nationalidee und Nationaldenkmal in Deutschland im 19. Jahrhundert.' *Historische Zeitschrift* 206 (1968): 529–85.

Nonn, Christoph. *Eine Stadt sucht einen Mörder: Gerücht, Gewalt und Antisemitismus im Kaiserreich.* Göttingen: Vandenhoeck & Ruprecht, 2002.

Nora, Pierre, ed. *Realms of Memory: Rethinking the French Past.* New York: Columbia University Press, 1996.

Ohmann, Oliver. 'Die Berliner bauen ihre Berge selber.' *Berlinische Monatsschrift* 8, no. 6 (1999): 32–9.

Olsen, Jonathan. *Nature and Nationalism: Right-Wing Ecology and the Politics of Identity in Contemporary Germany.* New York: St Martin's, 1999.

Orlowski, Hubert. *'Polnische Wirtschaft': Zum deutschen Polendiskurs der Neuzeit.* Wiesbaden: Harrassowitz, 1996.

Palmowski, Jan. *Urban Liberalism in Imperial Germany: Frankfurt am Main, 1866–1914.* Oxford: Oxford University Press, 1999.

Peluso, Nancy. *Rich Forests, Poor People: Resource Control and Resistance in Java.* Berkeley: University of California Press, 1992.

Peukert, Detlev. 'The Genesis of the "Final Solution" from the Spirit of Science.' In *Reevaluating the Third Reich,* ed. Thomas Childers and Jane Caplan, 234–52. New York: Holmes & Meier, 1993.

Pois, Robert. *National Socialism and the Region of Nature.* New York: St Martin's, 1986.

Puhle, Hans-Jürgen. *Agrarische Interessenpolitik und preussischer Konservatismus im wilhelminischen Reich, 1893–1914: Ein Beitrag zur Analyse des Nationalismus in Deutschland am Beispiel des Bundes der Landwirte und der Deutsch-Konservativen Partei.* Hanover: Verlag für Literatur und Zeitgeschehen, 1966.

Pyne, Stephen J. *Vestal Fire: An Environmental History, Told through Fire, of Europe and Europe's Encounter with the World.* Seattle: University of Washington Press, 1997.

Radkau, Joachim. *Das Zeitalter der Nervosität.* Munich: Carl Hanser, 1998.

– 'Wood and Forestry in German History: In Quest of an Environmental Approach.' *Environment and History* 2 (February 1996): 63–76.

– 'The Wordy Worship of Nature and the Tacit Feeling for Nature in the History of German Forestry.' In *Nature and Society in Historical Context,* ed. Mikulas Teich, Roy Porter, and Bo Gustafsson, 228–39. Cambridge: Cambridge University Press, 1997.

Repp, Kevin. *Reformers, Critics, and the Paths of German Modernity: Anti-Politics and the Search for Alternatives, 1890–1914.* Cambridge, MA: Harvard University Press, 2000.

Reuß, Jürgen von. 'Freiflächenpolitik als Sozialpoliitk.' In *Martin Wagner, 1885–1957: Wohnungsbau und Weltstadtplanung: die Rationalisierung des Glücks*, ed. Akademie der Künste, 49–65. Berlin: Akademie der Künste, 1985.

Richter, Günther. 'Zwischen Revolution und Reichsgründung.' In *Geschichte Berlins*, ed. Wolfgang Ribbe, 2:605–87. Munich: C.H. Beck, 1987.

Ringer, Fritz. *Max Weber: An Intellectual Biography*. Chicago: University of Chicago Press, 2004.

Rodgers, Andrew Denny. *Bernhard Eduard Fernow: A Story of North American Forestry*. Princeton, NJ: Princeton University Press, 1951.

Rohkrämer, Thomas. *Eine andere Moderne? Zivilisationskritik, Natur und Technik in Deutschland 1880–1933*. Paderborn: Schöningh, 1999.

– *A Single Communal Faith?: The German Right from Conservatism to National Socialism*. New York: Berghahn, 2007.

Rohkrämer, Thomas. 'Contemporary Environmentalism and Its Links with the German Past.' In *The Culture of German Environmentalism: Anxieties, Visions, Realities*, ed. Axel Goodbody, 47–62. Oxford: Berghahn, 2002.

Rollins, William H. "Aesthetic Environmentalism: The Heimatschutz Movement in Germany, 1904–1918." PhD diss., University of Wisconsin, 1994.

– *A Greener Vision of Home: Cultural Politics and Environmental Reform in the German Heimatschutz Movement*. Ann Arbor: University of Michigan Press, 1997.

– 'Imperial Shades of Green: Conservation and Environmental Chauvinism in the German Colonial Project.' *German Studies Review* 22, no. 2 (1999): 187–213.

Rosenthal, Harry K. *German and Pole: National Conflict and Modern Myth*. Gainesville: University Presses of Florida, 1976.

Rossbacher, Karlheinz. *Heimatkunstbewegung und Heimatroman: zu eine Literatursoziologie der Jahrhundertwende*. Stuttgart: Klett, 1975.

Roth, René Romain. *Raoul H. Francé and the Doctrine of Life*. N.d.: self-published, 2000.

Rothenburg, Robert. *Landscape and Power in Vienna*. Baltimore: Johns Hopkins University Press, 1995.

Rubner, Heinrich. *Forstgeschichte im Zeitalter der industriellen Revolution*. Berlin: Duncker & Humblot, 1967.

Rueschemeyer, Dietrich, and Ronan van Rossem. 'The *Verein für Sozialpolitik* and the Fabian Society: A Study in the Sociology of Policy-Relevant Knowledge.' In *States, Social Knoweldge, and the Origins of Modern Social Policies*, ed. Dietrich Rueschemeyer and Theda Skocpol, 117–62. Princeton: Princeton University Press, 1996.

Sahlins, Peter. *Forest Rites: The War of the Demoiselles in Nineteenth-Century France*. Cambridge, MA: Harvard University Press, 1994.

Schama, Simon. *Landscape and Memory*. New York: Knopf, 1995.

Schindler, Norbert. 'Gartenwesen und Grünordnung in Berlin.' In *Gartenwesen*. Vol. 9 of *Berlin und seine Bauten*, ed. Klaus Konrad Weber, 1–50. Berlin: Wilhelm Ernst & Sohn, 1972.

Schmidt, Uwe Eduard. *Der Wald in Deutschland im 18. und 19. Jahrhundert: Das Problem der Ressourcenknappheit dargestellt am Beispiel der Waldressourcenknappheit in Deutschland im 18. und 19. Jahrhundert. Eine historisch-politische Analyse*. Saarbrücken: Conte-Verlag, 2002.

– 'Waldfrevel contra staatliche Interessen.' *Der Bürger im Staat* 51, no. 1 (2001): 17–23.

Schmoll, Friedemann. *Erinnerung an die Natur: Die Geschichte des Naturschutzes im deutschen Kaiserreich*. Frankfurt am Main: Campus, 2004.

Scholz, Marianne. *Letzte Lebensstationen: Zum postakademischen Wirken des deutschen Botanikers Matthias Jacob Schleiden (1804–1881)*. Berlin: Verlag für Wissenschafts- und Regionalgeschichte, 2001.

Schulte, Regina. *The Village in Court: Arson, Infanticide, and Poaching in the Court Records of Upper Bavaria, 1848–1910*. Translated by Barrie Selman. Cambridge: Cambridge University Press, 1994.

Schulze, Hagen, and Etienne François, eds. *Deutsche Erinnerungsorte*. Munich: Beck, 2001.

Scott, James C. *Seeing Like a State: How Certain Schemes to Improve the Human Condition Have Failed*. New Haven, CT: Yale University Press, 1998.

Seemann, Josef. 'Bund Deutsche Bodenreformer (BDB) 1898–1945.' In *Lexikon zur Parteiengeschichte*, ed. Dieter Fricke, 282–8. Leipzig: VEB Bibliographisches Institut Leipzig, 1983.

Sheehan, James J. *German Liberalism in the Nineteenth Century*. Atlantic Hights, NJ: Humantities, 1995.

Short, John Rennie. *Imagined Country: Envirnoment, Culture and Society*. London: Routledge, 1991.

Sivaramakrishnan, K. *Modern Forests: Statemaking and Environmental Change in Colonial Eastern India*. Stanford, CA: Stanford University Press, 1999.

Smith, Anthony D. *The Ethnic Origins of Nations*. Cambridge, MA: Blackwell, 1986.

Smith, Woodruff D. *Politics and the Sciences of Culture in Germany*. Oxford: Oxford University Press, 1991.

Spear, Jeffrey L. *Dreams of an English Eden: Ruskin and His Tradition in Social Criticism*. New York: Columbia University Press, 1984.

Speitkamp, Winfried. 'Denkmalpflege und Heimatschutz in Deutschland zwischen Kulturkritik und Nationalsozialismus.' *Archiv für Kulturgeschichte* 70 (1988): 149–93.

Spenkuch, Hartwin. *Das Preußische Herrenhaus: Adel und Bürgertum in der Ersten Kammer des Landtages, 1854–1918*. Düsseldorf: Droste, 1998.

Sperber, Jonathan. *Rhineland Radicals: The Democratic Movement and the Revolution of 1848–1849*. Princeton, NJ: Princeton University Press, 1991.

Steinmetz, George. *Regulating the Social: The Welfare State and Local Politics in Imperial Germany*. Princeton, NJ: Princeton University Press, 1993.

Stelzle, Walter. 'Die wirtschaftlichen und sozialen Verhältnisse der bayerischen Oberpfalz um die Jahrhundertwende vom 19. zum 20. Jahrhundert: Der Streit von Fuchsmühl.' *Zeitschrift für bayerische Landesgeschichte* 37 (1976): 487–539.

Stern, Fritz, ed. *The Failure of Illiberalism: Essays on the Political Culture of Modern Germany*, ed. Fritz Stern. London: Knopf, 1972.

– *The Politics of Cultural Despair: A Study in the Rise of the Germanic Ideology*. Berkeley: University of California Press, 1961.

Stürmer, Rainer. *Freiflächenpolitik in Berlin in der Weimarer Republik*. Berlin: Berlin Verlag, 1990.

Sunseri, Thaddeus. 'Reinterpreting a Colonial Rebellion: Forestry and Social Control in German East Africa, 1874–1915.' *Environmental History* 8, no. 3 (2003): 430–51.

Tacke, Charlotte. *Denkmal im sozialen Raum: Nationale Symbole in Deutschland und Frankreich im 19. Jahrhundert*. Göttingen: Vandenhoeck & Ruprecht, 1995.

Temple, Samuel. 'The Natures of Nation: Negotiating Modernity in the Landes de Gascogne.' *French Historical Studies* 32 (2009): 419–46.

Theilemann, Wolfram G. *Adel im Grünen Rock: Adliges Jägertum, Grossprivatwaldbesitz und die preußische Forstbeamtenschaft 1866–1914*. Berlin: Akademie Verlag, 2004.

Thomas, Keith. *Man and the Natural World: Changing Attitudes in England, 1500–1800*. New York: Pantheon Books, 1983.

Tigges, Hans. *Das Stadtoberhaupt: Porträts im Wandel der Zeit*. Baden-Baden: Nomos, 1988.

Tipton, Frank B. 'Technology and Industrial Growth.' In *Imperial Germany: A Historiographical Companion*, ed. Roger Chickering, 62–96. Westport, CT: Greenwood, 1996.

Tittel, Lutz. *Das Niederwalddenkmal*. Hildesheim: Gerstenberg, 1979.

Tober, Holger J. *Deutscher Liberalismus und Sozialpolitik in der Ära des Wilhelminismus*. Husum: Matthiesen, 1999.

Trom, Danny. 'Natur und nationale Identität: Der Streit um den Schutz der "Natur" um die Jahrhundertwende in Deutschland und Freankreich.' In *Nation und Emotion*, ed. Etienne François, Hannes Siegrist, and Jakob Vogel, 147–67. Göttingen: Vandenhoeck & Ruprecht, 1995.

Trzeciakowski, Lech. *The Kulturkampf in Prussian Poland.* Boulder: East European Monographs, 1990.

Ude-Koeller, Susanne. *Auf gebahnten Wegen: Zum Naturdiskurs am Beispiel des Harzklubs e.V.* Berlin: Waxmann, 2004.

Uekoetter, Frank. *The Green and the Brown: A History of Conservation in Nazi Germany.* Cambridge: Cambridge University Press, 2006.

Upmann, Augustin, and Uwe Rennspieß. 'Organisationsgeschichte der deutschen Naturfreundebewegung bis 1933.' In *Mit uns zieht die neue Zeit,* ed. Jochen Zimmer, 66–111. Cologne: Pahl-Rugenstein, 1984.

Urry, John. *The Tourist Gaze: Leisure and Travel in Contemporary Societies.* London: Sage, 1990.

Vernon, James. 'Border Crossings: Cornwall and the English (Imagi)nation.' In *Imagining Nations,* ed. Geoffrey Cubitt, 153–72. Manchester: Manchester University Press, 1998.

Wagner, Ursula Hannelore. *Die preussische Verwaltung des Regierungsbezirks Marienwerder, 1871–1920.* Cologne: Grote, 1982.

Walden, Hans. *Stadt, Wald: Untersuchungen zur Grüngeschichte Hamburgs.* Hamburg: DOBU, Wissenschaftlicher Verlag Dokumentation & Buch, 2002.

Wandycz, Piotr. *The Lands of Partitioned Poland.* Seattle: University of Washington Press, 1993.

Weindling, Paul. *Health, Race, and German Politics between National Unification and Nazism, 1870–1945.* Cambridge: Cambridge University Press, 1989.

Weltman-Aron, Brigitte. *On Other Grounds: Landscape Gardening and Nationalism in Eighteenth-Century England and France.* Albany: State University of New York Press, 2001.

Wettengel, Michael. 'Staat und Naturschutz 1906–1945: Zur Geschichte der Staatlichen Stelle für Naturdenkmalpflege in Preußen und der Reichstelle für Naturschutz.' *Historische Zeitschrift* 257 (1993): 355–99.

Wey, Klaus-Georg. *Umwelt Politik im Deutschland.* Opladen: Westdeutscher Verlag, 1982.

Whited, Tamara L. *Forests and Peasant Politics in Modern France.* New Haven, CT: Yale University Press, 2000.

Wierzchoslawski, Szczepan. *Polski Ruch Narodowy w Prusach Zachodnich w Latach 1860–1914.* Warsaw: Polska Akademia Nauk, 1980.

Williams, John Alexander. '"The Chords of the German Soul Are Tuned to Nature": The Movement to Preserve the Natural Heimat from the Kaiserreich to the Third Reich.' *Central European History* 29, no. 3 (1996): 339–84.

– *Turning to Nature in Germany: Hiking, Nudism, and Conservation, 1900–1940.* Palo Alto: Stanford University Press, 2007.

Wilson, Jeffrey K. 'Nature and Nation: The "'German Forest'" in the National Imagination, 1871–1914' (PhD diss., University of Michigan, 2002).

Worpole, Ken. 'Village School or Blackboard Jungle?' In *Patriotism*, ed. Raphael Samuel, 125–40. London: Routledge, 1989.

Wright, Patrick. *On Living in an Old Country: The National Past in Contemporary Britain* London: Verso, 1985.

Zechner, Johannes. '"Die grünen Wurzeln unseres Volkes": Zur ideologischen Karriere des ‚deutschen Waldes.' In *Völkisch und national. Zur Aktualität alter Denkmuster im 21. Jahrhundert*, ed. Uwe Puschner and G. Ulrich Großmann, 179–94. Darmstadt: Wissenschaftliche Buchgesellschaft, 2009.

Zeller, Thomas. *Driving Germany: The Landscape of the German Autobahn, 1930–1970*. Oxford: Berghahn Books, 2007.

Zimmer, Jochen. 'Vom Walzen zum Sozialen Wandern: Fragen an die Einensinnigen Soxialen Praxen des genossenschaftlichen Arbeitertourismus.' In *Studien zur Arbeiterkultur*, ed. Deutsche Gesellschaft für Volkskunde, 141–73. Münster: F. Coppenrath, 1984.

Zimmermann, Harro. *Freiheit und Geschichte: F.G. Klopstock als historischer Dichter und Denker*. Heidelberg: Winter, 1987.

Zimmermann, Magdalene. *Die Gartenlaube als Dokument ihrer Zeit*. Munich: Heimeran Verlag, 1963.

Zybajło, Wiktor. 'Ruch oporu w Borach Tucholskich w latach I wojny światowej.' *Szkice Człuchowskie* 2, nos. 2–6 (1991/6), 66–72.

Index

acid rain, 15, 24
Adriatic Sea, 24
afforestation. *See* reforestation
Agrarian League (*Bund der Land-wirte*), 71, 72, 74, 197, 245n76
agrarian reform, 71–5

Allgäu (Bavaria), 20–1
Allgemeines Landrecht, 56
Alps, 3, 21, 22, 31, 187, 280n106
Alsace, 274n23
Altenberg (Saxony), 202
Altpaleschken (West Prussia), 265n41
Anderson, Benedict, 6
Ansiedlungskommission. See Royal Settlement Commission
Ansiedlungsverein Groß-Berlin, 256n94
anti-capitalism, 4–5, 9, 11, 15, 220, 265n65; Düesberg's, 194–7; Marx', 180; Riehl's, 26–7; Rudorff's, 76–8
anti-modernism. *See Sonderweg*
anti-Semitism, 50, 82, 191, 195–6, 218
Archangel Michael, 205
Arminius. *See* Hermann the Cherusker
Arndt, Ernst Moritz, 4, 26, 202
Arnim, Bernd von, 105, 119, 124, 199

arson. *See* Tuchel Heath
Asia Minor, 43
Association for Social Policy (*Verein für Sozialpolitik*), 71, 194
Association for the History of Berlin (*Verein für Geschichte Berlins*), 118
Association for the History of the Germans in Bohemia (*Verein für Geschichte der Deutschen in Böhmen*), 212
Ausschuß der Berliner Turngaue, 257n95
Ausschuß der wissenschaftlichen und gemeinnützigen Vereine zur Erhaltung der Grunewald-Moore, 257n97
Austria-Hungary, 20, 21, 184, 191
Austro-Prussian War, 183

Babylonia, 43
Bad Homburg (Grand Duchy of Hessia), 33
Baden (Grand Duchy), 80, 81
Baltic Sea, 3, 20, 21
Barmen (Rhineland), 64
Barrès, Maurice, 218
Bastei, Die (Saxony), 30
Battle of Leipzig (1813), 202
Bauernbund, 245

Baumbücher, 32–3, 35–6
Bavaria, Upper, 20, 267n78
Beamtenerlaß. See Civil Servants Order
    (1898)
beech, 3, 20, 181
beekeeping, 156, 159
Belgium, 65
Belt, 20, 24
Bender, Georg, 113, 125
Bengal, 266n55
Berdrow, Hermann, 94
Berg, C.H. Edmund von, 42
Berlin, 97–8. *See also* Grunewald
Berlin Architects Association (*Berliner
    Architekten Verein*), 121
Berlin Central Committee for the
    Forest and Settlement Question
    (*Berliner Zentralausschuß für die
    Wald- und Ansiedlungsfrage*), 118
Berlin's Conservative Voters' Associa-
    tion (*deutschkonservative Wahlver-
    ein*), 113
Berliner Gymnasiallehrer-Gesellschaft,
    257n96
Berliner Gymnasiallehrer-Verein, 257n96
Berliner Hochschulsportvereinigung,
    257n95
Berliner Lehrerverein, 257n96
Berliner Tageblatt, 70, 120, 121,
    124, 127; campaign to save the
    Grunewald, 106–10
*Berliner Zentralausshuß für dieWald-und
    Ansiedlungsfrage*, 256n94
*Berliner Zentralverband zur Bekämpfung
    des Alkoholismus*, 257n95
Bernhardt, August, 40, 59, 64–5
Berthold, Carl, 202
Bethmann Hollweg, Theobald von,
    122
Białowieża Forest, 223

Bieder, Hermann, 80
Birkholz (Brandenburg), 112
Bismarck, Otto von, 7, 16, 61; as a
    Holznarr, 62; on Polish nationalism,
    136–7
Bismarck towers, 30
Blackbourn, David, 12, 141
blood-and-soil ideology. *See* Nazism
Boeckel, Otto, 273n10
Bohemia, 20, 21, 31, 210–12
Böhmert, Karl Viktor, 65
Bölsche, Wilhelm, 275n38
Bordesholm (Holstein), 38
Borne, Gustav von dem, 140–3, 165–6
Botanical Association of the Province
    of Brandenburg (*Botanischer Verein
    der Provinz Brandenburg*), 35, 115
Brandenburg (Prussian province),
    44, 126, 202. *See also* trespassing
Brandenburgia, 115
*Brandenburgischer Distrikt des Internatio-
    nalen Guttempler Ordens*, 257n95
Brandis, Dietrich, 232n13
Brandstein, Hans von, 114
Brentano, Lujo, 71
Breslau, 129
Brieselang (Brandenburg), 202
Britain, 21, 23, 200; as a land without
    forests, 53, 57, 65; landscape and
    national identity, 7, 218–21
Britz (Brandenburg), 255n76
Brocken (Harz), 30, 31
Bromberg Canal (West Prussia), 161
Bromberg-Dirschau railway (West
    Prussia), 161
Buch (Brandenburg), 112
Bülow, Bernhard von, 113
Bund der Landwirte. See Agrarian
    League
Bund der Verein für Naturgemäße Lebens-

und Heilweise (*Naturheilkunde*),
257n95
Bund Heimatschutz. See League for
Heimat Protection
Bureau for Social Policy (*Büro für Sozi-
alpolitik*), 117–18
Burke, Edmund, 219
Burkhardt, Heinrich, 33
Busdorf, Otto, 172

cameralism, 141
Canada. *See* North America
Canetti, Elias, 178
capitalism, 5–6, 51, 144, 175, 181
Caribbean, 202–3
Carpenter, Edward, 220
Carstenn, Johann Anton Wilhelm
von, 97–102, 251n34, 252n43
Catholics, 7, 17; in the Prussian east,
136, 143, 156, 159, 267n72, 268n92;
Schleiden's critique of, 184. *See also*
Centre Party, *Kulturkampf*
Celts, 207–8
Central Commission of Health Insur-
ance Companies of Berlin and Its
Suburbs (*Zentralkommission der Kan-
kenkassen Berlins und der Vororte*),
117
Centre Party, 114, 270n121; critique
of Field and Forest Law, 13, 49,
59–62, 82
Chaney, Sandra, 225
Charlottenburg (Brandenburg), 88,
98, 108, 121, 129
chemical warfare, 272
Christow (forester), 147
Ciss/Cis (West Prussia), 149, 151
Civil Servants Order (*Beamtenerlaß*,
1898), 163
Clossow (forester), 34

Cobbett, William, 219
Cologne (Rhineland), 129
Committee for the Cultivation of Ru-
ral Welfare and *Heimat* (*Ausschuß
für ländliche Wohlfahrts- und Heimat-
pflege*), 72, 78
Communal Association of Greater
Berlin (*Zweckverband Groß-Berlin*),
122, 124–30, 259–60n133
Confino, Alon, 17
Conrad, Alfred von, 126
Conservative Party, 60, 115
Conwentz, Hugo, 32, 35, 76, 199, 213
Crown Prince Wilhelm, 199, 278n77
cultural landscape vs. wilderness,
213–14
Czersk (West Prussia), 147, 151, 157–
8, 162, 168

Dahl (Westphalia), 34
Daily Telegraph affair, 126
Dalmatia, 20
Damaschke, Adolf, 117
Daniels, Stephen, 8
Danish minority, 209
Danube River, 184
Darwinism, 182, 185–7, 190
Das Land, 72–3
Dauerwald, 224
deforestation, 22–3, 43, 132, 217; in
Germany, 75–6, 139–42, 180, 184,
188–9
Denmark, 38
Dernburg, Bernhard, 127
*Deutsche Naturwissenschaftliche Gesell-
schaft*, 275n38
Deutsche Tageszeitung, 71, 128
Deutsche Zeitung, 71, 244
Deutsche Zentrale für Jugendfürsorge,
257n96

Deutsche Zentrale für Volkshygiene,
257n95

Deutscher Botanischen Gesellschaft,
257n97

*Deutscher Verein gegen Mißbrauch geisti-
ger Getränke,* 257n95

Deutschlandlied, 17, 20–1, 24, 207

Dickinson, Edward, 280n106

Döhlauer Heath (Halle), 129

Dohna-Poninski, Adelheid von, 100–3

Dominick, Raymond, 223

Douglas fir, 194

Dresden (Saxony), 183

Duchy of Warsaw, 156, 268n80

Düesberg, Rudolf, 176, 178, 194–200,
213–14, 223–4, 278nn72, 74, 77

Düsseldorf (Rheinland), 129

East Prussia, 20, 34, 35, 69, 160

East Prussian Natural Science Association
(*Naturwissenschaftlicher Verein der
Provinz Ostpreussen*), 35

Eastern Marches Society (*Ostmarkenverein*), 162

Eastern Marches Subsidy (*Ostmarkenzulage*), 163

Eberswalde Forestry Academy, 22

Eckersdorf (East Prussia), 34

Eichendorff, Joseph von 20, 43

Eifel Mountains (Rhineland), 23, 112

Elbe River, 31, 184

Elberfeld (Rhineland), 64, 129

Eley, Geoff, 50

Emig (forester), 148

Enclosure Act (*Gemeinheitsteilungs-
Ordnung,* 1821), 74

entomology, 272n2

environmental chauvinism, 132, 137,
140–2, 173

environmental damage, 5, 12, 22–3,

165; Mediterranean as site of, 23,
43, 184, 217; Polish "mismanagement," 140–4, 165, 173, 216. *See also*
environmental chauvinism

environmental determinism, 42

environmental services, 63, 72, 138,
139

environmentalism, 5, 9, 11, 15,
224–5; in campaign to save the
Grunewald, 88, 131; Schleiden's,
76, 184

Erzgebirge (Saxony), 23, 33

Escher, Felix, 102

Essen (Rhineland), 129

ethnography, 26

Etsch/Adige River, 20, 24

Ewald, Karl Anton, 116

Feld- und Forstpolizeigesetz. See Field and
Forest Law (1880)

Fernow, Bernhard, 232

Feußner (forester), 157

Field and Forest Law (*Feld- und Forstpolizeigesetz,* 1880), 49, 56, 103,
110–11; debated in newspapers
(1906), 69–71; debated in Prussian Landtag, 58–64; and 'national
property,' 73–7

fir, 3, 20, 24, 183

First World War, 172, 174, 222–3

Fischbeck, Otto, 112, 119

Fiskus. See Prussian Ministry of Agriculture

Fontane, Theodor, 44, 202, 212

forest: aesthetic value, 5, 66, 79–82,
179, 224; as antidote to nervousness, 67–8; as a bridge between
classes, 67–8; economic role, 54–5;
as German national symbol, 4–5,
18–19; health benefits, 5, 60, 66,

76; as a hedge against revolution, 65–6; as marker of national landscape, 19–36; as 'national property,' 50, 75–84, 215; nobles' attitudes towards, 46, 61; as a site of freedom, 52–4; as site of national memory, 30, 35–45; working-class attitudes towards, 46–7

forest fires, 22, 57, 170, 172. *See also* Tuchel Heath

forest grazing, 58, 60, 150, 158, 266n69

forest history, 5, 9, 21, 37, 41–3

Forest Protection Conference (*Waldschutztag*), 114–19

forest theft, 148–50. *See also* wood theft

Forest Theft Law (*Forstdiebstahlgesetz,* 1878), 59

forestry, 23–4, 55–6, 160–3, 196

Forstdiebstahlgesetz. See Forest Theft Law

Forstfiskus. See Prussian Ministry of Agriculture

Frammersbach (Bavaria), 73

France, 20, 21, 25, 57; French Revolution, 22, 200, 217–18; landscape discourse, 217–18. *See also* Franco-Prussian War, Napoleonic Wars

Francé, Raoul Heinrich, comparison with Düesberg, 195, 197, 198, 199, 213–14, 275, 276, 277, 278; on "plant sociology," 178, 190–4, on *Urwald,* 44

Francke, Ernst, 117

Franco-Prussian War (1870–71), 30, 39, 185–6, 202–3, 208–9

Frankfurt am Main, 87

Franz I (Austrian Emperor), 28

Freie Vereinigung Grunewald, 256n94

Freiligrath, Ferdinand, 202–3

Freud, Sigmund, 239n7

Freytag, Gustav, 134

Friedenau (Brandenburg), 257nn103, 104

Friedrich I, Barbarossa, 31

Friedrich II, the Great, 37, 39; and Pomerelia, 132–3, 141–2, 146, 161, 168, 269n104

Friedrich Wilhelm IV, 90

Friedrich, Caspar David, 4

Friends of Nature (*Naturfreunde*), 29

Fuchsmühl (Bavaria), 74

Gartenlaube, 33–4, 36–40

Gascony, 217

Geißler, Robert, 37–8

Geitner, Hermann, 103, 119, 253

Gemeinheitsteilungs-Ordnung. See Enclosure Act (1821)

German Association for the Cultivation of Rural Welfare and *Heimat* (*Deutscher Verein für ländliche Wohlfahrts- und Heimatpflege*), 72

German Botanical Society (*Deutsche Botanische Gesellschaft*), 118

German Entomological Society (*Deutsche Entomologische Gesellschaft*), 115

German Garden City Society (*Deutsche Gartenstadt-Gesellschaft*), 117

Gesellschaft für soziale Reform, 256n94

Gewerk-Verein der Heimarbeiterinnen, 256n94

Gobineau, Arthur de, 160

Goering, Hermann, 224

Goethe, Johann Wolfgang von, 31, 37, 43

Goldschmidt, 118

Göttingen Grove League (*Göttinger Hainbund*), 4
Gradmann, Robert, 45
Greece, 40, 43
Green Party (Germany), 15, 225
Grimm brothers, Jakob and Wilhelm, 25–6, 41
Grimm, Karl, 242n33
Grimmenthal (Thuringia), 33
Gröning, Gert, 10
Gross Mützelburg (Pommerania), 199
Grotenhof (Westphalia), 40
Grunewald, 13–14; Berlin proposes to buy, 101–2, 119–24; conservative plans to protect, 102–3; description, 86–7; developers' plans, 97–100; negotiations over sale to Communal Association, 124–30; parliamentary campaign to protect, 110–14; popular campaign to protect, 114–19; press campaign to save, 71, 104–10; and public health 87–8, 100, 110, 113, 114, 116–18, 120, 126, 131, 251n34; as a site of recreation, 88–97; *Volkspark* plan, 103–4, 111, 119, 120, 126. *See also* *Hubertusjagd.*
Grunewald (suburb), 255
Grünthal (West Prussia), 166
Grzonka, Johann, 148
Guenther, Konrad, 68–9
Guido-von-List- Gesellschaft, 277n60
Gumprecht, Adolf, 176, 178, 187–9
Gwinner, Arthur von, 115

Haase (forester), 148
Haeckel, Ernst, 185, 187, 189, 190, 274n20
Halle (Prussian Saxony), 129

Hamburg, 97, 183, 249n5
Hammer, Friedrich, 113
Hanover (kingdom), 33
Hanover (Prussian province), 73, 140
Hartmann, Franz, 277n60
Harz Mountains, 31, 33, 70
Harzklub, 223
Hasbruch Forest (Oldenburg), 41
Haupt, Richard, 81
Havel River, 88, 96, 98, 114, 119, 251n34
Heerstrasse project, 104, 108, 119–20, 126
Hegel, Wilhelm Friedrich, 183
Hegemann, Werner, 124, 249n6, 259n133
Heidelberg Castle, 30, 31, 207
Heilbronn (Württemberg), 210
Heimat movement (*Bund Heimatschutz*), comparison with *Société pour la protection des paysages de France*, 217; historiography, 10–11; modernity, 248n1; "national property," 80–2; property rights, 50, 51, 84–5; relationship to Nazism, 223–4; relationship to Ruskin, 281n11; resistance to social Darwinism, 178, 179, 213; Sohnrey 72; *Waldschutztag* and, 116, 117, 118. *See also* Brandenburgia, *Hembygd* movement, League for *Heimat* Protection, Rudorff
Helgoland Island, 207
Hellwald, Friedrich von, 176, 178, 185–97, 201, 213
Hembygd movement, 221
Henting (teacher), 115
Herder, Johann Gottfried, 4, 25, 42
Herka, 209
Hermann Monument, 16, 30, 31, 32, 101

Hermann the Cherusker, 4, 279n92
Hermannsdenkmal. See Hermann
  Monument
Hess, Richard, 58
Hesse, Hermann, 276n42
Hessia (Grand Duchy), 60, 73, 74,
  80, 81
Hessia-Nassau (Prussian province),
  60, 242n33, 267n76
hiking, 24–36, 233n21. *See also* tres-
  passing
Hirsch-Duncker Gewerbeverein, 256n94
Hobrecht, James, 101, 254n72
Hoermann, Franz, 75
Hofmann von Nauborn, Konrad, 209
Holstein (Prussian province), 38
Holznot. See wood crisis
hornbeam, 193
Hubertusjagd, 89–96, 103
Hugenberg, Alfred, 71
Humboldt, Alexander von, 43, 177,
  181, 183, 190
Humboldt, Wilhelm von, 32
Hungary, 186
hunting, 46, 62, 70; poaching, 152–3.
  See also Hubertusjagd
Hürlimann, Annemarie, 201

India, 23, 202–3, 232
Indonesia, 265
Italy, 21–2, 40, 43, 188
Itzenplitz family, 83

Jacob Plaut-Stiftung, Berlin, 256n94
Jäger, Hermann, 202–3, 278n82
Jahn, Friedrich Ludwig, 26
Jansen, Hermann, 121
Jansen, Sarah, 272n2
January Uprising (1863), 156
Jentzsch, Alfred, 35

Junkerhof/Trzebciny (West Prussia),
  159

Kampffmeyer, Bernhard, 117
Kannach brothers, Stephan and Vin-
  cent, 147
*Kartell der Christlichen Gewerkschaften
  Berlins und Umgegend*, 256n94
Karthaus/Kartuzy (West Prussia),
  164
Kartz, Johann, 147
Kaschuba, Wolfgang, 25, 36
Kashubia, 132, 138–45, 164–6; plans
  for reforstation, 165–7
Kirschner, Max, 120–4, 129, 258n109
Kitzler, Georg Eugen, 83–4, 248nn112
Kladderadatsch, 20, 104, 106, 253n60
Kleinschmidt, Franz, 172
Kleist, Heinrich von, 4
Kliewert (forester), 147
Klopstock, Friedrich Gottlieb, 4, 177,
  207
Knapp, Georg Friedrich, 71
Knop (forester), 147–8, 158, 266n65
Knorr, Eduard von, 115
Koblenz (Rhineland), 34
Koch, Georg, 92–5
Köckeritz family, 83
Kohli (forester), 267n79
Köhn, Theodor, 102
Kölnische Volkszeitung, 82
Kolthoff, Gustaf, 221
Königsbruch/Lipowa (West Prussia),
  149, 152
Königstädten (Grand Duchy of Hes-
  sia), 73
Königs-Wüsterhausen (Branden-
  burg), 83
Korell, Adolf, 73–4
Körner, Theodor, 202

Kościuszko Uprising (1794), 156, 268n80

Koshar, Rudy, 38

Kosmos, 275n38

Kreitling, Robert, 112

Kulturkampf, 17, 22, 39, 156, 159, 173

Kummer, Paul, 208–9

Kürschner, Joseph, 205–6, 210

Kusselwälder, 142

Kyffhäuser Monument, 30, 32

Ladd, Brian, 248n1

Landwehr Canal (Berlin), 98

Langbehn, Julius, 198

Lange (forester), 148

Lange, Friedrich, 71, 244n71

League for *Heimat* Protection. *See Heimat* movement

League of German Land Reformers (*Bund Deutscher Bodenreformer*), 117, 118

League of German Unions (*Verband der Deutschen Gewerkvereine*), 118

Lebensreform (life reform) movement, 220, 222

Lehfeld (legal scholar), 244n71

Lehnitz (Brandenburg), 90

Leipzig Workers' Association (*Leipziger Arbeiterverein*), 181

Leistikow, Walter, 115

Lekan, Thomas, 11, 214, 224

Lemaitre, Jules, 218

Lerman, Katharine, 90

Levant, 43

Levenstein, Adolf, 46

linden, 14, 279n101; as symbol of empire, 212; as symbol of femininity, 203, 208–10; as symbol of nation, 200, 207–13; as symbol of national memory 37–40, as symbol of prop-

erty, 207–8; as symbol of Protestantism, 207–8

Linse, Ulrich, 10, 201

Loebell, Friedrich Wilhelm von, 125

Löfgren, Orvar, 7, 221

Lohr, Otto, 210–12, 280n103

Loire River, 218

Łosiński, Bernhard, 164–5

Louis XIV, 7, 207

Lucius von Ballhausen, Robert, 84

Lüneburg Heath, 140

Luntowski, Adalbert, 160, 167–8, 268n80, 269n103

Luther Elm, 38–9

Luther, Martin, 31, 38–9, 207–8

Maas River, 20, 21

Maltzahn, Hans von, 124

Mangoldt, Karl von, 118, 124

Mannhardt, Wilhelm, 203

Marienwerder (administrative district), 162, 164

Marienwerder/Kwidzyn (West Prussia), 160

Markham, William T., 10, 225

Marsh, George Perkins, 184

Marx, Karl, 180, 240n9

Marxism, 47

Mattern, Dan, 248n1, 249n10

Mecklenburg (Grand Duchy), 20, 40

Memel/Klaipėda (East Prussia), 20

Meyer, Alexander, 60

Middle Ages, 17, 38

Mieterbund Groß-Berlin, 256n94

Mietskasernen (rental barracks), 87, 101

Miquel, Johannes von, 71, 120, 124

Mirchau/Mirachowo (West Prussia), 165

Mitchell, W.T.J., 10
Moltke, Friedrich von, 122
Moltke, Helmuth von, the Elder, 79
Morris, William, 220
Mosse, George, 8–10, 32
Mozart, Wolfgang Amadeus, 212
Mühlradt, Johannes, 151, 158, 162, 166, 168–9, 171
Mukerji, Chandra, 7
Münchgesang, F., 126
Munich (Bavaria), 24

Napoleonic Wars, and German national identity 4, 25, 39; and the oak, 200, 202, 208–9; in Prussian east 134, 136, 268n80
national identity, 3–4, 16–19, 26–7, 60–1, 201; and hiking, 24–36; and landscape, 5–12, 19–24, 75–82, 216–25; and national monuments, 30–2; and sites of memory, 36–47. See also environmental chauvinism, radical nationalism
National Liberal Party, 69, 113, 115
natural monument (Naturdenkmal), 32, 35, 202
Naumann, Friedrich, 71–3, 194
Naumburg an der Saale, 202
Nazism, 10; blood and soil 9, 116–17; and environmentalism, 11, 15, 214; and forests as military metaphor, 178; forests under, 223–4; Volksgemeinschaft, 194–5, 198
Niederwald Monument, 16, 30, 32
Nietzsche, Friedrich, 191–2
Normandy, 20
North Africa, 43
North America, 22, 53, 131–2, 141
North Sea, 19, 24, 81, 207
Norway, 21

oak, English, 210; as national symbol, 4, 43, 200–7, 212–13; as a site of memory, 37; as symbol of empire, 202–3; as symbol of masculinity, 178, 203, 208–10; as symbol of monarchy, 203–5
Oberpfalz (Bavaria), 74
Oder River, 184
Oderbruch, 141
Oeynhausen (Westphalia), 33
Oldenburg (Grand Duchy), 41, 209

Palestine, 43
Palmowski, Jan, 87
Pan-German League, 115
Paris Commune (1871), 97
peasant use-rights. See use-rights
Peisterwitz (Silesia), 34
Persia, 43
Peukert, Detlev, 11, 273n6
Pfeil, Wilhelm, 56
Pfuhl, Fritz, 35
Pichelswerder (Grunewald), 119
pine, 11, 24, 55
poaching. See hunting
Podbielski, Viktor von, and the Grunewald, 104, 106, 108, 110–12, 253n60; and the Prussian east, 163–4, 270n118
Poincaré, Raymond, 218
Polish Commonwealth, 132, 153
Polish gentry. See szlachta
Polish nationalism, 136–8, 156–60, 172–3
Pomerelia. See Tuchel Heath, Kashubia
poplar, 179
Potonié, Hans, 115
Potsdam (Brandenburg), 98, 257n103

Poznania (Prussian province), 132, 159

Poznanian Natural Science Association (*Naturwissenschaftlicher Verein der Provinz Posen*), 35

Prague, 210–12

Protestantism, and German national identity, 3–4, 16–17, 31, 36–9, 207–8; Schleiden's, 184–5

Provence, 20

Prussian Department of Forestry (*Forstfiskus*). *See* Prussian Ministry of Agriculture

Prussian Ministry of Agriculture, assessment of Düesberg, 199, 278n77; and the Grunewald, 100, 104, 108, 110–14, 251n34; negotiations over sale of the Grunewald 119–22, 123–30; property rights, 58–9, 75, 83–4; reforestation of Pomerelia, 139–41, 161, 173

Prussian Ministry of Culture, 35, 127

Prussian Ministry of Finance, 100, 125–7

Prussian Ministry of Interior, 122, 125–8

Prussian Ministry of Justice, 127

Prussian Ministry of Public Works, 126–7

Prussian Ministry of Trade, 100, 127

Prussian War Department (*Kriegskammer*), 141

Przytarski (village elder), 147

Pudor, Heinrich, 179

Pyrmont (Waldeck-Pyrmont), 33, 37

Quitzow family, 83

race, 14–15, 201, 280n106; in Düesberg's work, 195–6, 199; in England, 218; forest as a metaphor for, 175, 178; in Francé's work, 191–3; in Hellwald's work, 186–7; and Nazism, 216–17, 223–4, 273n6; in Pomerelia, 160, 167, 174

radical nationalism (*völkisch* nationalism), 8–9, 175–6, 215–16; in Francé's work, 191–3, 277n60; in Pomerelia, 160, 168. *See also* Rudolf Düesberg, Nazism , Heinrich Pudor

Radtke (weaver), 158

Rangsdorf Lake (Brandenburg), 84

Ratzel, Friedrich, 20–1, 25, 44–5, 193, 213, 231n2

recreation, public right to, 81; and social reform, 5, 13, 29, 60, 64–7. *See also* Grunewald, hiking, hunting

reforestation, critique of, 167–8, 179; and environment, 138–40; in France, 6, 22, 217–18; in Prussian east, 14, 113, 141–2, 162–3, 165–6, 173; and social reform, 188–9; and wood supply, 247n95

Reformation, Protestant, 3, 17, 39, 207

Remilly (Lorraine), 33

Repiczno (West Prussia), 134

Repp, Kevin, 11

Revolution of 1848, forests in, 26–7, 267n78; graves of revolutionaries, 258n109; in Prussian east, 134–6, 156; influence on Hellwald, 186; influence on Riehl, 26–7; influence on Roßmäßler and Schleiden, 56–7, 180–2

Revolution of 1905, 22

Rheinbaben, Georg von, 126

Rhine River, as a site of tourism, 30, 32, 33, 44; as basis for state, 184–5, 274n23

Rhineland, 11, 20, 39, 180, 214

Rhön Mountains, 23

Riehl, Wilhelm Heinrich, comparison
to Ruskin, 220, 281n11; critique of
capitalism, 9; decline of Mediterranean, 43; as ethnographer, 26–7;
forest aesthetic, 179; forest as national symbol, 3, 4, 5; influence on
Gumprecht, 188; influence of 1848,
26–7, 57; inspiration for Rudorff,
75, 78; inspiration for Salisch, 24,
79; inspiration for Sohnrey, 72; liberalism, 233n25; social role of forest, 49, 57, 59; sylvan freedom, 52–3

Riesengebirge (Silesia), 20, 21, 31, 79

Riesenthal, Oskar von, 143, 149–50,
153, 267n79

Rixdorf (Brandenburg), 255n76

Rohkrämer, Thomas, 11

Rollins, William, 11, 36, 137

Roman Empire, 3, 4, 19, 43, 47

Roman Law, 31, 76, 81

Romance peoples, 21–2

Rome (city), 22

Roßmäßler, Emil Adolf, 27–8, 176,
180–3, 275n38; comparison to
Francé, 191, 193, 195; comparison
to Hellwald, 185–6, 188, 189

Rothschild family, 81

Royal Settlement Commission, 137,
139, 173

Rubner, Max, 115

Rudelsburg Castle (Thuringia), 30,
31

Rüdesheim (Rhineland), 30

Rudorff, Ernst, 43, 77–80, 82, 86,
247n90

Ruhr (Rhineland), 17

Ruskin, John, 220

Russia, 21, 22, 57

Russian Poland, 134, 156, 198

Sach, August, 45, 212, 279nn94–7

Sachsenwald, 62

Saekel (forester), 170

Sahlins, Peter, 267

Salisch, Heinrich von, 24, 79, 86, 199,
203; reception, 80–1

Savigny, Friedrich Karl von, 25

Saxon Switzerland, 28, 31

Saxony, 17, 55, 181, 183, 207

Scandinavia, 23

Schama, Simon, 10

Schasler, Max, 278n85

Schaumburg (Hessia, Prussian province), 34, 37

Scherr, Johannes, 209, 279

Schildhorn (Grunewald), 96, 119,
251n34

Schiller, Friedrich, 210

Schlachtensee (Grunewald), 104

Schleiden, Matthias Jakob, 213;
comparison to Francé, 193, 195;
comparison to Hellwald, 185–6,
188, 189; forest protection, 76, 184;
liberalism, 182–3, 184–5, 274n23;
tree as a social metaphor, 176, 178,
180, 182–3; view of oaks, 207–8

Schleswig-Holstein Natural Science
Association (*Naturwissenschaftlicher
Verein für Schleswig-Holstein*), 35

Schmargendorf (Brandenburg),
257n103

Schnackenburg, Bernhard, 115

Schneekoppe (Silesia), 30, 31

Schönaich-Carolath, Heinrich zu, 115

Schönburg-Waldenburg, Heinrich
von, 92

Schöneberg (Brandenburg), 121

Schulenburg, K.A. von, 210

Schulenburg, Rudolf von der, 260n139

Schulte, Regina, 267

Schultze-Naumburg, Paul, 223

Schütte, R., on arson, 156–8, 267n79; on disciplining populace, 160–1, 165–6, 168, 170; on Kashubs, 143; on migrant labor, 271n132; on peasant resistance, 144; on poaching, 152, 153; on reforestation 139–40, 140–1, 142

Schüttenwalde/Woziwoda (West Prussia), 139, 145–6, 157

Schutzgemeinschaft Deutscher Wald, 225

Schwappach, Adam, 45, 66–7

Schwarzwald (Württemberg), 27

Schwiedt/Świt (West Prussia), 161

Schwind, Moritz von, 213

Scott, James, 11, 144, 273n8

seasonal labour, 149, 164, 167, 197

Sedan Day, 17

Seifert, Alwin, 224

Seiling, Max, 277n60

Sering, Max, 71

Servituten, 58. See use-rights

Sharp, Cecil, 281n12

Siebenpfeiffer, Karl, 203

Silesia (Prussian province), 17, 21, 31, 34, 71

Silesian Society for Patriotic Culture (Schlesische Gesellschaft für Vaterländische Kultur), 35

Simanowski (insurance representative), 117

Slominski (wood thief), 147

Smith, Anthony, 6

Smolensk, 22

social Darwinism, 175–8, 183, 185–91, 193, 199–200, 276n44

Social Democratic Party, in campaign to save Grunewald, 109, 120, 124, 128, 130; on 'national property,' 82; as threat to nation, 17–18, 78, 80; view of nature, 10, 221–2

social reform, 64–9, 86–8, 109–10

Societas Hiking Club, 84

Société des amis des arbres, 218

Société pour la protection des paysages de France, 217

Sohnrey, Heinrich, 72–5, 140, 167, 197, 222

Sonderweg, 9–10, 18, 90, 175, 217; interpretation of oak, 201, 205; in property rights debate, 50–1, 71, 85

South Africa, 202–3

South America, 198

Spain, 43

Spanish chestnut, 194

Spickermann (landowner), 84

Spree River, 98

spruce, 187

Stamplewski (forest thief), 148

Steglitz (Brandenburg), 100, 257n103

Stein-Hardenberg reforms, 56, 142

Steiniger, Karl, 124–5, 129–30

Stern, Fritz, 9, 198

Strackerjan, Karl, 209

Ströbel, Heinrich, 67–8, 82, 124

Stuart, George, 281n12

Sunseri, Thaddeus, 137

Swabian Singers' League, 210

Sweden, 21, 221–2

Switzerland, 34, 184

Sylt (Schleswig-Holstein), 81

Syria, 43

szlachta, 136, 144, 152–3, 160

Tacitus, 3–4, 41, 42, 45

Tacke, Charlotte, 31, 36

Tanganyika, 137

Taubenfließ/Gołąbek (West Prussia), 159, 170, 171

Teich, Otto, 102

Teltow (Brandenbrug), 251n37

Teutoburg Forest (Hanover), 4, 30

Teutonic Knights, 140, 160

Tharandt Forestry Academy, 181

Theilemann, Wolfram G., 46, 90, 96

Thirty Years' War (1618–48), 31, 37, 39

Thoma, Hans, 81

Thomas, Keith, 219

Thorn/Toruń (West Prussia), 172, 270n121

Thuringian Forest Association (*Thüringerwald Verein*), 29

Tiergarten (Berlin), 103

Touring-Club de France, 217

tourism. *See* hiking

tree symbolism, comparisons with humans, 177–8; as metaphors for capitalism, 180; as metaphors for society, 181–200; as metaphors for soldiers, 178–80; as national symbols, 177, 200; as symbols of liberty, 200, 207. *See also* oak, linden

trespassing, 82–4

Trinius, August, 92

Trojan, E.W., 29

Trojan, Johannes, 20–1, 40, 104

Trom, Danny, 217

Tuchel (county), 138, 163, 270n21

Tuchel Heath, 14, 216–17; arson and forest fires, 153–9, 172–3, 267n79; description, 138–45, elections, 163–5; ethnic relations, 132–8; forestry and development, 138–45; Germanization policies, 162–5, 173–4; infrastructure building in, 161–2; labor, 164–5; map, 135; poaching, 152–3, 172–3; racism and assimilation, 159–60, 167–9; wood and forest theft, 145–52

Tyrol, 188–9

Union of Brandenburg Hiking Associations (*Verband märkischer Touristen-Vereine*), 82

Union of German Hiking Associations (*Verband deutscher Touristenvereine*), 29

United Communal Associations of Zehlendorf (*Vereinigten kommunalen Vereine Zehlendorf*), 115

United States. *See* North America

Urwald, 11, 43, 44, 45, 102

use-rights (*Servituten*), 27, 49, 56–7, 72–8, 246n80

Verband der Deutschen Gewerkvereine, 256n94

Verbündete Frauenvereine Groß-Berlin, 256n94

Verein der Vororte Berlins zur Wahrung gemeinsamer Interessen, 256n94

Verein für die Geschichte Berlins, 257n97

Verein für Sozialpolitik. See Association for Social Policy

Verein öffentlicher Gesundheitspflege, 257n95

Verein zur Förderung des mathematischen und naturwissenschaftlichen Unterrichts, 257n96

Vereinigung der Walderholungsstätten vom Roten Kreuz, 257n95

Versailles, 7

Vienna, 186; *Wald- und Wiesengürtel*, 102, 121, 129

Viersener Bruch (Rhineland), 20, 21

Vistula River, 134, 160

Vistula Delta, 138
völkisch nationalism. *See* radical nationalism
Volkserziehung, 113
Völkshagen (Duchy of Mecklenburg-Schwerin), 40
Volkspark plan. *See* Grunewald
Vosges Mountains, 274n23

Wagner, Adolph, 71–2, 75
Wald vs. *Forst*, 179, 240n10
Waldschutztag. *See* Forest Protection Conference
Waldsterben, 15, 24, 225
Wandervogel, 28–9
Wappes, Lorenz, 65, 68
Wartburg Castle (Thuringia), 30, 31, 207
Weber, Max, 71
Weindling, Paul, 273n6
Wermuth, Adolf, 127, 129–30
Werner, Anton von, 205
Wernicke, Erich, 160, 167, 168
Wesener, Hermann, 111–12, 113–14, 120, 121–2
West Prussia, 35, 132–3, 134, 161–4, 168
West Prussian Forest Ordinance (Westpreussische Forstordnung, 1805), 142
Westphalia, 20, 35, 40, 202, 266n55
Westphalian Natural Science Association (*Westfälischer Naturwissenschaftlicher Verein*), 35
Wetekamp, Karl, 117
Weyl, Hermann, 120–1

Wigonin/Wygonin (West Prussia), 146, 166
Wildungen/Błędno (West Prussia), 159
Wilhelm I, 16, 90, 203, 205
Wilhelm II, 16–17, 129, 130; *Hubertusjagd*, 90, 92–4, 96; *Volkspark*, 103–4, 119–20; negotiations with *Zweckverband*, 124–5, 126
Williams, John, 11, 223
Williams, Raymond, 10
Williams, Vaughan, 281n12
willow, 181
Wloch, Johann, 148, 158
Wloch, Katharina, 148
Wloch, Marianna, 148
Wolschke-Bulmahn, Joachim, 10
wood crisis, 23, 55
wood tariffs, 9, 58, 63–4, 247n95
wood theft, 5–9, 180, 241n21, 265n51. *See also* Tuchel Heath
Worms (Rhineland), 38–9
Woziwoda. *See* Schüttenwalde
Wreschen/Września school strike, 159
Wuppertal (Rhineland), 64
Württemberg (Kingdom), 17, 33

Zedlitz und Neukirch, Octavio von, 115
Zentralverband der Forst-, Land- und Weinbergsarbeiter, 245n76
Zweckverband Groß-Berlin. *See* Communal Association
Zwickau (Saxony), 55

GERMAN AND EUROPEAN STUDIES

General Editor: Rebecca Wittmann

1 Emanuel Adler, Beverly Crawford, Federica Bicchi, and Rafaella Del Sarto,
   The Convergence of Civilizations: Constructing a Mediterranean Region
2 James Retallack, *The German Right, 1860–1920: Political Limits of the
   Authoritarian Imagination*
3 Silvija Jestrovic, *Theatre of Estrangement: Theory, Practice, Ideology*
4 Susan Gross Solomon, ed., *Doing Medicine Together: Germany and Russia
   between the Wars*
5 Laurence McFalls, ed., *Max Weber's 'Objectivity' Revisited*
6 Robin Ostow, ed., *(Re)Visualizing National History: Museums and National
   Identities in Europe in the New Millennium*
7 David Blackbourn and James Retallack, eds., *Localism, Landscape, and the
   Ambiguities of Place: German-Speaking Central Europe, 1860–1930*
8 John Zilcosky, ed., *Writing Travel: The Poetics and Politics of the Modern Journey*
9 Angelica Fenner, *Race under Reconstruction in German Cinema: Robert Stemmle's
   Toxi*
10 Martina Kessel and Patrick Merziger, eds., *The Politics of Humour in the
   Twentieth Century: Inclusion, Exclusion, and Communities of Laughter*
11 Jeffrey K. Wilson, *The German Forest: Nature, Identity, and the Contestation of a
   National Symbol, 1871–1914*
12 David G. John, *Bennewitz, Goethe, Faust: German and Intercultural Stagings*
13 Jennifer Ruth Hosek, *Sun, Sex, and Socialism: Cuba in the German Imaginary*